SLOW
COOKER
DUMP
DESSERTS

SLOW COOKER DUMP DESSERTS

COZY SWEETS AND EASY TREATS TO MAKE AHEAD

JENNIFER PALMER

THE COUNTRYMAN PRESS

A DIVISION OF W. W. NORTON & COMPANY

INDEPENDENT PUBLISHERS SINCE 1923

For information about permission to reproduce selections from this book,
write to Permissions, The Countryman Press,
500 Fifth Avenue, New York, NY 10110

For information about special discounts for bulk purchases, please contact
W. W. Norton Special Sales at specialsales@wwnorton.com or 800-233-4830

The Countryman Press
www.countrymanpress.com

A division of W. W. Norton & Company
500 Fifth Avenue, New York, NY 10110
www.wwnorton.com

978-1-59157-453-1 (pbk.)

1 2 3 4 5 6 7 8 9 0

"LIFE IS UNCERTAIN. EAT DESSERT FIRST."

—ERNESTINE ULMER

SLOW COOKER DUMP DESSERTS
CONTENTS

Introduction

Slow cookers aren't just for dinner anymore! Sweet, sumptuous, and gooey desserts are as easy as 1-2-3 with this guide to the best slow cooker treats imaginable. Forget fancy ombré layer cakes and complicated icing creations that never look quite the same at home as when you saw them on Pinterest. *Slow Cooker Dump Desserts* features more than 50 straightforward, (mostly) five-ingredients-or-fewer desserts that you can make in a few hours. Whether it's a three-berry cobbler, some cinnamon buns, or a simple chocolate pudding cake, you'll be amazed at how easy it is to satisfy your sweet tooth with desserts cooked in your versatile slow cooker.

Stocking Your Pantry

Boxed pudding mix. If there is one secret ingredient to making slow cooker desserts moist and delicious, it is pudding mix!

Butter. Use unsalted butter.

Cake mix. Good ones to have on hand are white, yellow, and chocolate. Use them dry, adding only the ingredients specified in the recipes unless otherwise directed (that is, do not follow the preparation instructions on the box).

Canned fruit. Peaches and pineapple are the most common ingredients you'll need. But tropical fruit mixes with papaya or mango are great, too!

Canned pie filling. Apple pie filling will be your go-to.

Eggs. Use large eggs.

Frozen fruit. I recommend strawberries, raspberries, and blueberries. Mixed berry packages are also handy.

Vegetable oil.

Tips

The recipes in this book were made in a six-quart slow cooker. Cook times here reflect what worked best for me with my slow cooker. When making a recipe for the first time, I recommend checking on your dessert about half an hour before the recommended cooking time.

Dump desserts are meant to be moist and gooey—but you can always cook your dessert longer. The most common complaint I hear about baking in a slow cooker is that the resulting dessert is "too gooey." Slow cooker desserts *are* a bit moister than desserts baked in an oven, especially when the recipe calls for a fruit filling or pudding mix—but that doesn't mean the recipe has turned out wrong. If the dessert looks too moist, keep cooking on low and checking at half-hour intervals until it looks done or a toothpick inserted into the center comes out clean.

Use a slow cooker liner and nonstick cooking spray. For every recipe in this book, I recommend using a slow cooker liner and then spraying it with nonstick cooking spray. The liner makes cleanup easy and the spray keeps the desserts from sticking to the liner! If you don't want to spend the money on the liners, you can go ahead and spray the insert of the slow cooker directly. For the best-looking desserts though, you should try the liners at least once— you'll be glad when it comes to getting your Pineapple Upside-Down Cake out of the slow cooker intact!

Use a paper towel to combat condensation. The inside of the slow cooker lid can sometimes collect condensation that then drips back onto whatever is baking in your slow cooker. To prevent this, try placing a paper towel across the opening of the cooker and securing it with the lid. The paper towel will collect any extra moisture.

A Note about Presentation

Dump cakes aren't exactly the prettiest desserts in the world of baking. But that's what ice cream, whipped cream, and other garnishes are for! If you're concerned about the way the dessert looks when you're serving it (or if you just really love ice cream, as I do), add a heaping scoop of vanilla ice cream to your dessert before serving. Or some chocolate fudge topping. Or some cream cheese frosting. Well, you get the idea!

CHAPTER ONE

ALL CHOCOLATE

Molten Chocolate Hazelnut
Lava Cake

This isn't a cake in the traditional sense of a perfectly round dessert you can slice and serve. Nope! This is a gooey, messy, chocolaty dessert you can scoop into a bowl with your favorite ice cream and devour with a big spoon! It ain't pretty— but, man, does this cake taste good! If you're feeling fancy, you can add some freshly sliced strawberries or cocoa powder as a garnish

Yield: 8 servings   Cook time: 4 hours

Nonstick spray

One 15.25-ounce box devil's food cake mix

1 cup chocolate hazelnut spread

1 cup sour cream

1 cup milk

8 tablespoons (1 stick) butter

Line your slow cooker with a liner to make cleanup easier. Spray the liner (or just the insert, if you're not using one) with nonstick spray.

Mix all the ingredients together in a bowl and add to the slow cooker. Cook on low for 4 hours, or until the sides of the cake are cooked and the middle is soft. It's supposed to be a bit gooey in the middle—that's the molten lava!

Chocolate Peanut Butter Cup Cake

Chocolate peanut butter cups are one of my favorite desserts. So, I love making this cake that includes those delicious little treats with the bonus of even more chocolate and creamy peanut butter! For a delicious crunch, add ½ cup chopped peanuts to your batter.

Yield: 8 servings   Cook time: 2 hours

Nonstick spray

One 15.25-ounce box chocolate cake mix

1 cup hot water

3 large eggs

⅓ cup vegetable oil

½ cup creamy peanut butter

6 to 8 peanut butter cups, crumbled, plus more for garnish

Ice cream, for serving

Line your slow cooker with a liner to make cleanup easier. Spray the liner (or just the insert, if you're not using one) with nonstick spray.

Mix all the remaining ingredients, except the peanut butter cups, together in a bowl. Pour half of the batter into the slow cooker and top with about half of the crumbled peanut butter cups. Cover with the remaining batter and sprinkle with the remaining candy. Cook on high for 2 hours, or until a toothpick inserted in the center comes out clean.

Serve with ice cream and sprinkle with additional crumbled peanut butter cups.

Chocolate Chip Brownie Cookie Cake

A combination of brownies and cookies . . . sounds good, right? All you need now is ice cream!

Yield: 8 servings   Cook time: 2½ hours

Nonstick spray

One 18.3-ounce box fudge brownie mix

One 17.5-ounce package chocolate chip cookie mix

1¼ cups milk

8 tablespoons (1 stick) unsalted butter, melted

4 large eggs

1 tablespoon vegetable oil

Vanilla ice cream, for serving

Line your slow cooker with a liner to make cleanup easier. Spray the liner (or just the insert, if you're not using one) with nonstick spray.

Mix the remaining ingredients together in a bowl and blend well. Add to the slow cooker. Cook on low for 2½ hours.

Serve with vanilla ice cream.

"A balanced diet is a cookie in each hand."

—Anonymous

Classic From-Scratch Fudge Brownies

Simple and easy, these fudge brownies are guaranteed not to last long once you've had a taste!

Yield: 8 servings   Cook time: 2½ hours

Nonstick spray

12 tablespoons (1½ sticks) unsalted butter, melted

1½ cups granulated sugar

½ teaspoon salt

3 large eggs

1 cup unsweetened cocoa powder

1 cup all-purpose flour

Line your slow cooker with a liner to make cleanup easier. Spray the liner (or just the insert, if you're not using one) with nonstick spray.

Mix the butter, sugar, salt, and eggs together in a large bowl. Stir in the cocoa powder and flour until all the dry ingredients are incorporated. Add the batter to the slow cooker and spread evenly with a spatula. Cook on low for 2½ hours. Allow the brownies to cool before serving.

Tip: Instead of a standard slow cooker liner, try aluminum foil sprayed with cooking spray. The foil can help keep the edges of the brownies from overcooking.

Chocolate Salted Caramel Dump Cake

This sweet chocolate caramel cake with a hint of sea salt will satisfy all of your cravings at once.

Yield: 8 servings   Cook time: 2½ hours

Nonstick spray

One 15.25-ounce box devil's food cake mix

One 3.4-ounce box chocolate instant pudding mix

2 cups milk

4 tablespoons (½ stick) unsalted butter, melted

1 cup caramel topping

½ teaspoon sea salt

Ice cream, for serving

Chocolate syrup, for serving

Line your slow cooker with a liner to make cleanup easier. Spray the liner (or just the insert, if you're not using one) with nonstick spray.

Mix the cake mix, pudding mix, milk, and butter together in a large bowl. Spread evenly in the bottom of the slow cooker. Pour the caramel topping over the batter. Sprinkle the sea salt on top. Cook on low for 2 ½ hours.

Top with ice cream and drizzle with the chocolate syrup before serving.

German Chocolate Cake

German chocolate cake gets its name from American baker Samuel German. It's traditionally made with coconut and pecans. The cake is so popular it has its own US holiday: June 11 is National German Chocolate Cake Day!

Yield: 8 servings   Cook time: 3 hours

Nonstick spray

One 15.25-ounce box German chocolate cake mix

8 tablespoons (1 stick) unsalted butter, melted

1 cup water

3 large eggs

1 tablespoon vanilla extract

½ teaspoon salt

1 cup shredded sweetened coconut

1 cup milk chocolate chips

½ cup chopped pecans

Line your slow cooker with a liner to make cleanup easier. Spray the liner (or just the insert, if you're not using one) with nonstick spray.

Mix the cake mix, butter, water, eggs, vanilla, and salt together in a bowl. Add the batter to the slow cooker and sprinkle the coconut, chocolate chips, and pecans on top. Cook on high for 3 hours.

Black Forest Cake with Cherries

This cake originated in the Black Forest region of Germany but has become an American classic. This twist on a beloved recipe gets you the taste you love but with the ease of cooking in a slow cooker. Serve covered in whipped cream and garnish with fresh or maraschino cherries and chocolate shavings or sprinkles.

Yield: 8 servings   Cook time: 2½ to 3½ hours

8 tablespoons (1 stick) unsalted butter, cut into pieces

One 15.25-ounce box chocolate fudge cake mix

One 12-ounce can Cherry Coke

½ cup vegetable oil

3 large eggs

One 21-ounce can cherry pie filling

Whipped cream, for garnish

Fresh or maraschino cherries, for garnish

Chocolate shavings or sprinkles, for garnish

Line your slow cooker with a liner to make cleanup easier. Turn on the slow cooker and add the butter. It should melt while you're preparing the cake.

Mix the cake mix, Coke, oil, and eggs together in bowl and pour over the butter. Add the cherry pie filling over the cake batter. Cook on low for 2½ to 3½ hours.

Allow to cool and serve with whipped cream, cherries, and chocolate.

Chocolate Peanut Clusters

These chocolate treats travel well, so they make a great addition to birthday parties, picnics, and school lunches. Delicious peanuts and chocolate are an easy crowd-pleaser!

Yield: Makes 2 dozen clusters   Cook time: 1½ to 2 hours

Nonstick spray

One 12-ounce package semisweet chocolate chips

2 pounds salted peanuts

2½ pounds chocolate almond bark

Line your slow cooker with a liner to make cleanup easier. Spray the liner (or just the insert, if you're not using one) with nonstick spray.

Add the chocolate chips to the slow cooker. Cover with the peanuts. Top with the almond bark. Cook on low for 1½ to 2 hours.

Stir until smooth and drop the mixture by the spoonful into 24 paper cupcake liners. Allow the candy to harden before serving.

Tip: Burned peanuts are a real drag—be sure to check your slow cooker at 1½ hours to ensure nothing is overcooking.

Chocolate
Fondue Dip

What's more fun than dipping fresh fruit into warm, melted chocolate? Maybe a room full of kittens or puppies. This slow cooker chocolate dip is sure to be a hit at parties, backyard barbecues, or anytime you want a fun activity and dessert in one. Grab some fresh strawberries or marshmallows and get dipping!

Yield: 6 servings   Cook time: 2 hours

Nonstick spray

One 12-ounce package milk chocolate chips

One 10-ounce package marshmallows

½ cup heavy whipping cream

1 teaspoon vanilla extract

Fruit or additional marshmallows, for dipping

Line your slow cooker with a liner to make cleanup easier. Spray the liner (or just the insert, if you're not using one) with nonstick spray.

Add the chocolate chips, marshmallows, cream, and vanilla to the slow cooker and stir until mixed. Cook on low for 1 hour and stir, then cook for an additional hour.

Serve with fruit or additional marshmallows.

"There's no metaphysics on earth like chocolates."

—Fernando Pessoa

Slow Cooker
Hot Chocolate

Hot chocolate in your slow cooker? You must be having a party! This recipe is perfect for get-togethers—add a garnish bar so guests can have fun making an original treat. I suggest setting out a bowl of crushed candy canes, some marshmallows, a can of whipped cream, some caramel sauce, and shakers of cinnamon, nutmeg, or vanilla. Plus, the slow cooker will keep the hot chocolate warm for hours.

Yield: 6 servings   Cook time: 2 hours

6 cups milk

2 cups heavy whipping cream

1 cup milk chocolate chips

1 tablespoon unsweetened cocoa powder

1 teaspoon vanilla extract

Assorted garnishes, if desired

Place all the ingredients in the slow cooker and stir. Cook on low for 2 hours. Stir before serving—I like to use a ladle to serve the hot chocolate directly from the slow cooker.

Tip: You can store and refrigerate the leftover hot chocolate in mason jars or air-tight plastic containers. Just pour into a microwave-safe mug and reheat in the microwave before serving.

Chocolate Espresso Dump Cake

Cake with a kick! This double chocolate cake has the bonus taste of espresso. It makes the perfect grown-up treat.

Yield: 8 servings   Cook time: 3½ hours

Nonstick spray

One 15.25-ounce box chocolate cake mix

1¼ cups water

⅓ cup vegetable oil

3 large eggs

2 cups chocolate hazelnut spread

1 tablespoon espresso powder

3 tablespoons granulated sugar

Line your slow cooker with a liner to make cleanup easier. Spray the liner (or just the insert, if you're not using one) with nonstick spray.

Mix the cake mix, water, oil, eggs, 1 cup chocolate hazelnut spread, and the espresso together in a bowl until crumbly and add to the slow cooker. Spread the remaining cup of chocolate hazelnut spread evenly on top of the batter and add the sugar on top. Cook on low for 3½ hours.

CHAPTER TWO

FRUITY FLAVORS

Cherry Dump Cake

Sweet cherries are all you need to make this dump cake an easy winner.

Yield: 8 servings   Cook time: 3 hours

Nonstick spray

One 21-ounce can cherry pie filling

One 15.25-ounce box white cake mix

8 tablespoons (1 stick) unsalted butter, melted

Whipped cream, for serving

Line your slow cooker with a liner to make cleanup easier. Spray the liner (or just the insert, if you're not using one) with nonstick spray.

Add the cherry pie filling to the slow cooker. Mix the cake mix and butter together in a bowl until crumbly. Pour the cake mix on top of the cherry pie filling. Cook on low for 3 hours.

"I want to have a good body, but not as much as I want dessert."
—Jason Love

Peach Dump Cake

Sweet summer peaches make this dump cake a great summer treat.

Yield: 8 servings   Cook time: 3 hours

Nonstick spray

One 21-ounce can peaches, drained

One 15.25 box yellow cake mix

8 tablespoons (1 stick) unsalted butter, melted

Whipped cream, for serving

Line your slow cooker with a liner to make cleanup easier. Spray the liner (or just the insert, if you're not using one) with nonstick spray.

Add the peaches to the slow cooker. Mix the cake mix and butter together in a bowl until crumbly. Pour the cake mix on top of the peaches. Cook on low for 3 hours.

To serve, add a dollop of whipped cream to a bowl or a tall glass and top with peach cake and more whipped cream.

Strawberry Rhubarb Dump Cake

A sweet, jam-based dump cake inspired by my dad's favorite kind of pie—strawberry rhubarb. This recipe uses a white cake mix as a base, which lets the flavor of the fruit really shine through.

Yield: 8 servings   Cook time: 3½ hours

Nonstick spray

One 15.25-ounce box white cake mix

8 tablespoons (1 stick) unsalted butter, melted

2 cups strawberry rhubarb jam

3 tablespoons granulated sugar

Whipped cream, for serving

Line your slow cooker with a liner to make cleanup easier. Spray the liner (or just the insert, if you're not using one) with nonstick spray.

Mix the cake mix and butter together in a bowl until crumbly and add to the slow cooker. Dump the jam on top of the cake mix and add the sugar on top. Cook on low for 3½ hours.

Serve with whipped cream.

Blackberry Bramble Dump Cake

Blackberries are one of the most delicious—and healthiest—berries around. They're packed with fiber, vitamin C, and vitamin K. And lucky for us, they taste great!

Yield: 8 servings   Cook time: 3 hours

Nonstick spray

One 21-ounce can blackberry pie filling

One 15.25-ounce box white cake mix

8 tablespoons (1 stick) unsalted butter, melted

Line your slow cooker with a liner to make cleanup easier. Spray the liner (or just the insert, if you're not using one) with nonstick spray.

Add the blackberry pie filling to the slow cooker. Mix the cake mix and butter together in a bowl until crumbly. Pour the cake mix on top of blackberry pie filling. Cook on low for 3 hours.

Peach Gingerbread Cake

This is a delightful recipe using gingerbread cake mix—one of my favorites, as the mix comes packed with great flavor and spices. Peaches complement the spices nicely and make a light-tasting and fresh dessert that goes great with ice cream!

Yield: 8 servings   Cook time: 2½ to 3½ hours

8 tablespoons (1 stick) unsalted butter, melted

One 15.25-ounce box gingerbread cake mix

1¼ cups water

½ cup vegetable oil

3 large eggs

One 15.5-ounce can peaches, drained

Ice cream, for serving

Line your slow cooker with a liner to make cleanup easier.

Add the melted butter to the slow cooker. Mix the cake mix, water, oil, and eggs together in a bowl and pour into the slow cooker. Add the peaches over the cake batter. Cook on low for 2½ to 3½ hours.

Serve with ice cream.

"A party without cake is just a meeting."

—Julia Child

Triple Berry
Cobbler

Summer berries make this cobbler a bright, sweet, delicious treat perfect for after-noon tea, baby showers . . . or eating in front of the TV. My favorite berry mix is one with strawberries, blackberries, and raspberries—but any combination will do! Serve warm with vanilla ice cream.

Yield: 8 servings   Cook time: 3½ hours

Nonstick spray

3 cups mixed berries, fresh or frozen

One 15.25-ounce box vanilla cake mix

8 tablespoons (1 stick) unsalted butter, melted

3 tablespoons granulated sugar

Vanilla ice cream, for serving

Line your slow cooker with a liner to make cleanup easier. Spray the liner (or just the insert, if you're not using one) with nonstick spray.

Dump the berries in the slow cooker. Mix the cake mix and butter in a bowl until crumbly, add to the slow cooker on top of the berries, and add the sugar on top. Cook on low for 3½ hours, or until the berries are soft.

Serve with vanilla ice cream.

Blueberry Biscuit
Cobbler

For another easy and delicious cobbler variation, try using canned biscuits instead of cake mix. I love the sweet-tart taste of blueberries with this flaky crust, but you can use any berry filling you like.

Yield: 8 servings   Cook time: 3 hours

Nonstick spray

6 cups blueberries, fresh or frozen

¾ cup dark brown sugar

2 tablespoons cornstarch

2 teaspoons ground cinnamon

1 tablespoon lemon juice (optional)

One 16.3-ounce can refrigerated biscuits, quartered

Line your slow cooker with a liner to make cleanup easier. Spray the liner (or just the insert, if you're not using one) with nonstick spray.

Mix all the ingredients, except the biscuits, together in a bowl and add to the slow cooker. Place the quartered biscuits on top of the berry mixture. Cook on low for 3 hours, or until the biscuits are golden brown. If your slow cooker is gathering too much moisture, place a paper towel under the lid.

Slow Cooker Sweet Peach Cobbler

Oh, sweet baking angels and everything that's good in the world! Thanks for this peach cobbler recipe and the blessings it has bestowed on us! Namely, a satisfyingly sweet and easy recipe that takes nature's best fruit (or one of its best, anyway), cooked to perfection for us to enjoy.

Yield: 8 servings   Cook time: 3 hours

Nonstick spray

Two 15.5-ounce cans peaches, drained

¼ cup dark brown sugar

1 cup biscuit mix

½ cup granulated sugar

¾ cup milk

Line your slow cooker with a liner to make cleanup easier. Spray the liner (or just the insert, if you're not using one) with nonstick spray.

Add the drained peaches to the slow cooker. Whisk the brown sugar, biscuit mix, sugar, and the milk together in a bowl until blended. Pour the batter over the peaches. Cover and cook on low for 3 hours. Let stand until set, if needed.

Tip: For a sweet twist, try adding a pinch of cinnamon to the mixture before baking.

Raspberry White Chocolate Cake

White chocolate pairs perfectly with raspberries in this simple recipe. You can find frozen raspberries at any time of the year; make this extra special during summer months by garnishing with some fresh berries and a dusting of powdered sugar.

Yield: 8 servings   Cook time: 2 hours

Nonstick spray

One 15.25-ounce box white cake mix

1¼ cups milk

½ cup vegetable oil

3 large eggs

One 3.4-ounce box white chocolate instant pudding mix

½ cup white chocolate chips

1½ cups frozen raspberries

Line your slow cooker with a liner to make cleanup easier. Spray the liner (or just the insert, if you're not using one) with nonstick spray.

Mix the cake mix, milk, oil, eggs, and pudding mix together in a bowl in a bowl. Gently fold in the white chocolate chips and raspberries and dump into the slow cooker. Cook on high for 2 hours, or until the cake is set.

Strawberries & Cream Vanilla Cake

Fresh strawberries, whipped cream, and vanilla cake combine to create a delicious warm dessert that looks great, too. You can almost imagine you're at Wimbledon.

Yield: 8 servings   Cook time: 2½ to 3½ hours

8 tablespoons (1 stick) unsalted butter, melted

One 15.25-ounce box white cake mix

1¼ cups milk

½ cup vegetable oil

3 large eggs

2 cups fresh strawberries, sliced

1½ teaspoons vanilla extract

Whipped cream, for serving

Strawberries, for serving

Line your slow cooker with a liner to make cleanup easier.

Add the melted butter to the slow cooker. Mix together the cake mix, milk, oil, and eggs in a bowl. Pour the batter on top of the butter. Add the strawberries over the cake batter. Cook on low for 2 ½ to 3 ½ hours.

Allow to cool and serve with whipped cream and strawberries.

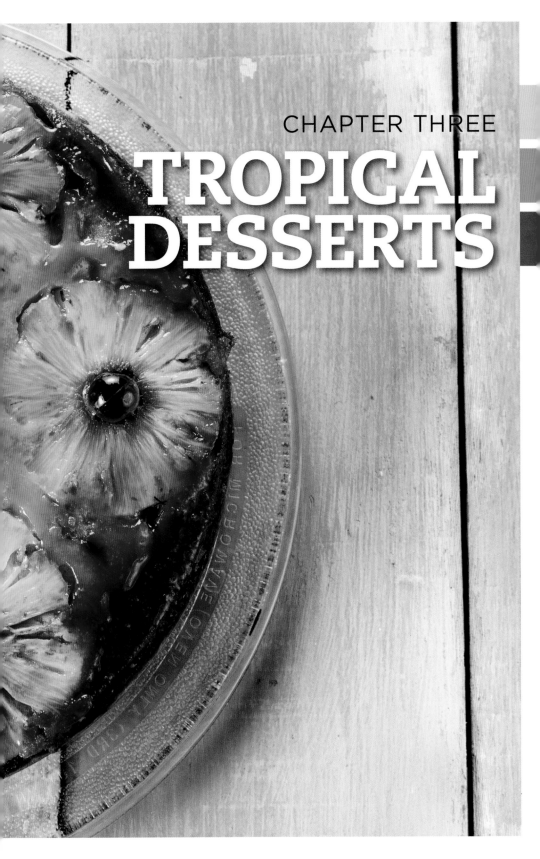

CHAPTER THREE

TROPICAL DESSERTS

Lemon Coconut
Cake

Lemon preserves take this recipe from "good" to "wow." The delicate flavor of the lemon is just irresistible!

Yield: 8 servings   Cook time: 3½ hours

Nonstick spray

One 15.25-ounce box lemon cake mix

8 tablespoons (1 stick) unsalted butter, melted

1 cup shredded sweetened coconut

One 12-ounce jar lemon preserves or lemon marmalade

3 tablespoons granulated sugar

Line your slow cooker with a liner to make cleanup easier. Spray the liner (or just the insert, if you're not using one) with nonstick spray.

Mix the cake mix and butter together in a bowl until crumbly and add to the slow cooker. Dump the coconut and lemon preserves on top of the cake mix and add the sugar on top. Cook on low for 3½ hours.

"Seize the moment. Remember all those women on the *Titanic* who waved off the dessert cart."

—Erma Bombeck

Pineapple Upside-Down Cake

Pineapple upside-down cakes are having a resurgence. This classic '70s recipe is updated and modernized for modern kitchens. Which means—dump the ingredients in your slow cooker and get ready to enjoy dessert!

Yield: 8 servings   Cook time: 3 hours

Nonstick spray

1 cup dark brown sugar

4 tablespoons (½ stick) unsalted butter, melted

One 20-ounce can pineapple slices, drained, juice reserved

12 stemless maraschino cherries, drained

One 15.25-ounce box yellow cake mix

½ cup vegetable oil

3 large eggs

Line your slow cooker with a liner to make cleanup easier. Spray the liner (or just the insert, if you're not using one) with nonstick spray.

Mix the brown sugar and butter together in a bowl and add to the bottom of the slow cooker. Add the pineapple slices in an even layer on top. Place a cherry in the center of each pineapple slice. Mix the cake mix, oil, 1 cup of the reserved pineapple juice, and eggs together in a medium bowl. Pour the cake batter into the slow cooker over the pineapple. Cook on high for 3 hours. Carefully turn out the cake upside down onto a cooling rack.

Banana Upside-Down Cake

There's nothing better than sweet bananas caramelized in brown sugar and rum. Can't you just taste it now? And it brings a heavenly scent to your kitchen! This upside-down cake will be a crowd favorite.

Yield: 8 servings   Cook time: 3 hours

Nonstick spray

1 cup dark brown sugar

4 tablespoons (½ stick) unsalted butter, melted

¼ cup dark rum

4 bananas, cut in half

One 15.25-ounce box yellow cake mix

1¼ cups water

½ cup vegetable oil

3 large eggs

1 teaspoon ground cinnamon

Whipped cream, for serving

Line your slow cooker with a liner to make cleanup easier. Spray the liner (or just the insert, if you're not using one) with nonstick spray.

Mix the brown sugar, butter, and rum together in a bowl and add to bottom of the slow cooker. Add the banana halves in an even layer on top. Mix the cake mix, water, oil, eggs, and cinnamon together in a separate bowl. Pour the cake batter over the bananas in the slow cooker. Cook on high for 3 hours. Carefully turn out the cake upside down onto a cooling rack.

Fruit Salad Slow Cooker Cake

Whether you go tropical—pineapple, papaya, and guava—or classic, canned fruit salad combines with yellow cake to create a dessert that will make you think you're on vacation. Grab a spoon and enjoy. Oh, and enjoying your dessert in a hammock hung between two palm trees helps, too.

Yield: 8 servings   Cook time: 3 hours

Nonstick spray

Two 15-ounce cans fruit salad (regular or tropical), drained

⅓ cup dark brown sugar

One 15.25-ounce box yellow cake mix

½ pound (2 sticks) unsalted butter

Line your slow cooker with a liner to make cleanup easier. Spray the liner (or just the insert, if you're not using one) with nonstick spray.

Add the fruit to the slow cooker. Sprinkle the brown sugar over the fruit, followed by the cake mix. Cut the butter into small pieces and lay over the cake mix. Cook on low for 3 hours.

Lemon Poppy Seed Lava Cake

My mom used to make this classic cake in her handy Bundt pan. This slow cooker version uses a secret ingredient: lemon pudding. Sift some powdered sugar over the top before serving.

Yield: 8 servings   Cook time: 3½ hours

Nonstick spray

One 15.25-ounce box yellow cake mix

1¼ cups water

½ cup vegetable oil

3 large eggs

One 3.4-ounce box lemon instant pudding mix

1 teaspoon vanilla extract

2 tablespoons poppy seeds

Powdered sugar, for garnish

Line your slow cooker with a liner to make cleanup easier. Spray the liner (or just the insert, if you're not using one) with nonstick spray.

Mix the cake mix, water, oil, eggs, pudding mix, and vanilla together in a bowl. Stir the poppy seeds into the batter. Dump the batter into the slow cooker. Cook on low for 3½ hours.

Garnish with powdered sugar.

Lemon Orange
Fairy Cake

In Victorian England, it was fashionable to believe in fairies. In fact, my English great-grandmother used to joke that her cakes were so light and airy the fairies loved them! (And light and airy cakes were a tough undertaking when you had no running water in the house.) Those ideas may not be fashionable now, but lemon and orange are always in style. This light citrus cake tastes so good it will have you believing in almost anything.

Yield: 8 servings   Cook time: 3½ hours

Nonstick spray

One 15.25-ounce box lemon cake mix

8 tablespoons (1 stick) unsalted butter, melted

3 cups canned mandarin orange pieces, drained

3 tablespoons granulated sugar

Whipped cream, for serving

Line your slow cooker with a liner to make cleanup easier. Spray the liner (or just the insert, if you're not using one) with nonstick spray.

Mix the cake mix and butter together in a bowl until crumbly and add to the slow cooker. Dump the oranges on top of the cake mix and add the sugar on top. Cook on low for 3½ hours.

Serve with whipped cream.

Vanilla Fig Cake

Figs and vanilla are a slightly unusual flavor combination but the taste is heavenly. A light flavor that's not too sweet makes this a sophisticated option for when you're feeling fancy—as sophisticated as a dump cake gets, anyway. Find fig preserves in the jam or jelly section of your local supermarket.

Yield: 8 servings   Cook time: 3½ hours

Nonstick spray

One 15.25-ounce box white cake mix

1 teaspoon vanilla extract

8 tablespoons (1 stick) unsalted butter, melted

1½ cups fig preserves

3 tablespoons granulated sugar

Line your slow cooker with a liner to make cleanup easier. Spray the liner (or just the insert, if you're not using one) with nonstick spray.

Mix the cake mix, vanilla, and butter together in a bowl until crumbly and add to the slow cooker. Dump the fig preserves on top of the cake mix and add the sugar on top. Cook on low for 3½ hours.

"One cannot think well, love well, sleep well, if one has not dined well."
—Virginia Woolf

Warmed Fruit Compote with Ginger

A warm bowl of sweet fruit kissed with a touch of ginger is a great comfort food (when you're not craving chocolate, that is). A mix of pear, apricot, and peaches makes this an easy dish for the whole family to love. Feel free to add other fruits according to your taste.

Yield: 8 servings   Cook time: 3 hours

Nonstick spray

Two 15.5-ounce cans pears, undrained

One 15.5-ounce can pineapple chunks, drained

One 15.5-ounce can peaches, drained

1 cup dried apricots, chopped

¼ cup dark brown sugar

½ teaspoon ground ginger

Vanilla ice cream, for serving

Shredded sweetened coconut, for garnish

Line your slow cooker with a liner to make cleanup easier. Spray the liner (or just the insert, if you're not using one) with nonstick spray.

Add the pears and pear juice, pineapple chunks, peaches, apricots, brown sugar, and ginger to the slow cooker. Stir until the fruits are mixed. Cook on low for 3 hours, or until the fruit is cooked through and the apricots are tender.

Serve in a bowl with vanilla ice cream, garnished with coconut.

CHAPTER FOUR

AMERICAN
CLASSICS

Fourth of July
Celebration Cake

This red, white, and blue dessert makes a festive, tasty addition to any back-yard barbecue or Fourth of July celebration. Garnish with fresh strawberries and blueberries.

Yield: 8 servings   Cook time: 2½ to 3½ hours

Nonstick spray

One 15.25-ounce box white cake mix

1¼ cups water

½ cup vegetable oil

3 large eggs

1 teaspoon vanilla extract

8 tablespoons (1 stick) unsalted butter, melted

1 cup sliced fresh strawberries

1 cup fresh blueberries

Whipped cream, for serving

Strawberries and blueberries, for garnish

Line your slow cooker with a liner to make cleanup easier. Spray the liner (or just the insert, if you're not using one) with nonstick spray.

Mix the cake mix, water, oil, eggs, and vanilla together in a bowl until well blended. Add the melted butter to the slow cooker and pour the batter on top. Add the strawberries and blueberries over the cake batter. Cook on low for 2½ to 3½ hours.

Allow to cool and cover with whipped cream. Garnish with additional strawberries and blueberries.

Apple Spice
Dump Cake

Spiced cake mix is packed with all those good spices that make apples taste so good—cinnamon, allspice, coriander, ginger, and nutmeg.

Yield: 8 servings   Cook time: 2½ hours

Nonstick spray

Two 20-ounce cans apple pie filling

One 15.25-ounce box spice cake mix

½ pound (2 sticks) unsalted butter, cut in cubes

Vanilla ice cream, for serving

Line your slow cooker with a liner to make cleanup easier. Spray the liner (or just the insert, if you're not using one) with nonstick spray.

Add the apple pie filling to the slow cooker. Mix the cake mix and butter together in a bowl until crumbly. Dump the mixture on top of the apple filling in the slow cooker. Cook on high for 2½ hours.

Serve with vanilla ice cream.

> "*Stressed* spelled backward is *desserts*. Coincidence? I think not!"
> —Anonymous

Warm Apple-Cranberry Dump Cake

Cranberries are a great taste for fall. Luckily, cranberries are also perfect for baking. In this recipe, the tartness of the cranberries is balanced by the sweetness of the apples. Dump all the ingredients together and wait for a warm, moist, flavorful cake to emerge!

Yield: 8 servings   Cook time: 2½ hours

Nonstick spray

4 cups peeled, cored, and sliced apples

1 cup cranberries, fresh or frozen

½ cup dark brown sugar

1 teaspoon ground cinnamon

1 teaspoon vanilla extract

One 15.25-ounce box spice-flavored or yellow cake mix

¼ cup applesauce

½ cup vegetable oil or melted butter

3 large eggs

Line your slow cooker with a liner to make cleanup easier. Spray the liner (or just the insert, if you're not using one) with nonstick spray.

Add the apples, cranberries, brown sugar, cinnamon, and vanilla to the slow cooker. Stir until mixed. Mix the cake mix, applesauce, oil, and eggs together in a bowl. Pour the batter on top of the fruit. Cook on low for 2½ hours, or until the cake is set.

Apple Pie
Coffee Cake

This cake is perfect for an indulgent breakfast, brunch, or a quick snack. Add a handful of chopped nuts to the top of the batter if you like. I like to garnish my coffee cake with a dusting of powdered sugar before serving.

Yield: 8 servings   Cook time: 3 hours

Nonstick spray

One 21-ounce can apple pie filling

¼ cup dark brown sugar

1 cup biscuit mix

½ teaspoon ground cinnamon

¾ cup milk

Line your slow cooker with a liner to make cleanup easier. Spray the liner (or just the insert, if you're not using one) with nonstick spray.

Add the apple pie filling to the slow cooker. Whisk the brown sugar, biscuit mix, cinnamon, and milk together in a bowl until blended. Pour over the apples. Cover and cook on low for 3 hours. Let stand until set, if needed.

Apple Cinnamon
Cobbler

Apples and cinnamon make the best baking partners. Not only do they taste great together, it smells intoxicating when you bake them! This apple cobbler with a hint of cinnamon is best served hot with a side of vanilla ice cream.

Yield: 6 servings   Cook time: 2½ hours

Nonstick spray

6 cups peeled, cored, and sliced apple

½ cup granulated sugar

1 teaspoon ground cinnamon

8 tablespoons (1 stick) unsalted butter, cut into cubes

One 15.25-ounce box yellow cake mix

Vanilla ice cream, for serving

Line your slow cooker with a liner to make cleanup easier. Spray the liner (or just the insert, if you're not using one) with nonstick spray.

Toss the apples, sugar, and ½ teaspoon of the cinnamon in a bowl and add to the slow cooker. Place the butter, remaining ½ teaspoon of cinnamon, and the cake mix together in a separate bowl and mix with a fork, until the butter is in small pieces. Dump on top of the apples. Cook on high for 2½ hours, or until the topping is lightly browned.

Serve with vanilla ice cream.

Classic Apple Crisp

For a quick and easy alternative to apple cobbler, try this classic apple crisp. Rolled oats and warm spices make this the ultimate comfort dessert.

Yield: 8 servings   Cook time: 2½ hours

Nonstick spray

6 medium apples, peeled, cored, and cut into wedges

¼ cup granulated sugar

¾ cup rolled oats

¾ cup all-purpose flour

¾ cup dark brown sugar

2 teaspoons ground cinnamon

¼ teaspoon ground nutmeg or allspice

8 tablespoons (1 stick) unsalted butter, cut into cubes

Line your slow cooker with a liner to make cleanup easier. Spray the liner (or just the insert, if you're not using one) with nonstick spray.

Toss the apples and granulated sugar in a bowl and add to the slow cooker. Place the oats, flour, brown sugar, cinnamon, nutmeg, and butter in a bowl and mix with a fork until the butter is in small pieces. Sprinkle the topping across the apples. Cook on high for 2½ hours, or until the topping is lightly browned. For a crispier topping, remove the lid of the slow cooker after 1½ hours and cook uncovered for the remaining hour.

Pumpkin Spice Cake with Cream Cheese Frosting

Pumpkin spice has somehow officially become the flavor of fall. Whether it's a pumpkin spice latte, a pumpkin spice muffin, or a pumpkin spice beer—there are lots of ways we can enjoy the taste. Here's one more. This pumpkin spice cake topped with cream cheese frosting is sure to be a hit.

Yield: 8 servings   Cook time: 3½ hours

Nonstick spray

One 15.25-ounce box spice cake mix

1 cup canned pure pumpkin

½ cup water

⅓ cup vegetable oil

4 large eggs

1 teaspoon ground allspice

One 16-ounce can cream cheese frosting

Line your slow cooker with a liner to make cleanup easier. Spray the liner (or just the insert, if you're not using one) with nonstick spray.

Mix the cake mix, pumpkin, water, oil, eggs, and allspice together in a bowl until well blended. Add the batter to the slow cooker. Cover and cook for 3½ hours.

Serve with a dollop of cream cheese frosting.

Classic Rice Pudding

Rice pudding is an excellent comfort food. And luckily, it's incredibly easy to make in a slow cooker. Add a few slivered almonds before serving for a bit of crunch.

Yield: 8 servings   Cook time: 2½ hours

Nonstick spray

4 cups cooked white rice

¾ cup granulated sugar

3 tablespoons unsalted butter, melted

1 teaspoon vanilla extract

Two 12-ounce cans evaporated milk

Slivered almonds, for garnish (optional)

Cinnamon, for garnish (optional)

Line your slow cooker with a liner to make cleanup easier. Spray the liner (or just the insert, if you're not using one) with nonstick spray.

Add all the ingredients to the slow cooker and stir. Cook on low for 2½ hours.

Stir and serve warm. Garnish with almonds and a dusting of cinnamon, if desired.

Classic Carrot Rum Pudding Cake

If you love carrot cake while it's still warm and gooey, try this adult variation. You can drizzle it with cream cheese frosting and sprinkle some shredded coconut or chopped walnuts on top of each serving when you're done. Why not both?

Yield: 8 servings   Cook time: 2 hours

Nonstick spray

One 15.25-ounce box carrot cake mix

One 3.4-ounce package vanilla pudding mix

½ cup applesauce

1 cup water

3 large eggs

¼ cup spiced rum

1 teaspoon ground cinnamon

One 16-ounce can cream cheese frosting

Shredded sweetened coconut and chopped nuts, for garnish

Line your slow cooker with a liner to make cleanup easier. Spray the liner (or just the insert, if you're not using one) with nonstick spray.

Mix the cake mix, pudding mix, applesauce, water, eggs, rum, and cinnamon together in a large bowl until blended. Pour the batter into the slow cooker. Cook on high for 2 hours, or until set in the middle.

Allow to cool and top with cream cheese frosting. Garnish with shredded coconut and chopped nuts.

Red Velvet
Pudding Cake

This red velvet cake is enriched with a chocolate pudding mix. The extra chocolate adds a bit of "oomph" to a regular old red velvet cake—plus the slow cooker ensures your cake is moist and flavorful (and easy to eat). Scoop into a bowl and serve with a dollop of cream cheese frosting.

Yield: 8 servings   Cook time: 3½ hours

Nonstick spray

One 15.25-ounce box red velvet cake mix

1¼ cups milk

½ cup vegetable oil

3 large eggs

One 3.4-ounce box chocolate pudding mix

One 16-ounce can cream cheese frosting

Line your slow cooker with a liner to make cleanup easier. Spray the liner (or just the insert, if you're not using one) with nonstick spray.

Mix the cake mix, milk, oil, eggs, and pudding together in a large bowl. Dump the batter into the slow cooker. Cook on low for 3½ hours.

Serve with a dollop of cream cheese frosting.

TAKING IT UP A NOTCH

Piña Colada
Scoop Pie

Okay, it's not a pie exactly. But by now you know that most of these desserts come out in a delicious gooey jumble. It's not the form that counts—it's how much pineapple goodness you can cram into one slow cooker! This scoop pie tastes just like a vacation. If you like piña coladas, this is the dessert for you!

Yield: 8 servings   Cook time: 3 to 4 hours

Nonstick spray

Two 16-ounce cans crushed pineapple, drained, juice reserved

1 teaspoon vanilla extract

1 cup all-purpose flour

1½ teaspoons baking powder

21 ounces coconut milk

1 cup shredded sweetened coconut

2 tablespoons vegetable oil

Vanilla or coconut ice cream or gelato, for serving

Line your slow cooker with a liner to make cleanup easier. Spray the liner (or just the insert, if you're not using one) with nonstick spray.

Add the drained pineapple to the slow cooker. Mix the vanilla, flour, baking powder, 7 ounces of the coconut milk, ⅔ cup of the reserved pineapple juice, ½ cup of the shredded coconut, and the oil together in a bowl. Pour the batter over the pineapple. Bring the remaining 14 ounces of coconut milk to a boil and pour slowly over the batter. Cover and cook on low for 3 to 4 hours.

Serve, garnished with the remaining ½ cup of shredded coconut and a scoop of ice cream or gelato.

Slow Cooker
Banana Split

Okay, so this is more like a banana split cake. But it's just as fun to eat as a good old-fashioned banana split. If you like, put a cherry on top—you've earned it!

Yield: 8 servings   Cook time: 2½ hours

Nonstick spray

One 15.25-ounce box yellow cake mix

1 cup water

½ cup vegetable oil

3 large eggs

One 3.4-ounce box banana cream instant pudding mix

½ cup pecan pieces or almond slivers, plus more for garnish

½ cup colored sprinkles, plus more for garnish

Vanilla ice cream or whipped cream, for serving

Hot fudge topping, heated, for serving

Maraschino cherries, for garnish (optional)

Line your slow cooker with a liner to make cleanup easier. Spray the liner (or just the insert, if you're not using one) with nonstick spray.

Mix the cake mix, water, oil, eggs, and pudding mix together in a large bowl until well blended. Add half of the pecans and half of the sprinkles to the batter and stir. Pour into the slow cooker. Cook on low for 2½ hours.

Scoop into bowls and serve with ice cream or whipped cream and hot fudge. Garnish with the remaining nuts and sprinkles and top each serving with a maraschino cherry, if using.

Tip: Remember, because of the pudding mix, this cake won't set in the traditional sense. It's gooey!

Salted Peanut
Chocolate
Pudding Cake

Salt, chocolate, nuts: What more could you want in a dessert? This one tastes amazing served warm with a scoop of vanilla ice cream, hot fudge, and more nuts.

Yield: 8 servings   Cook time: 2½ hours

Nonstick spray

One 18-ounce box fudge brownie mix

1¼ cups brewed coffee

½ cup vegetable oil

3 large eggs

½ cup salted peanuts (or pecans), plus more to serve

½ cup chocolate hazelnut spread

¾ cup granulated sugar

1½ cups boiling water

¾ cup unsweetened cocoa powder

Ice cream, for serving

Hot fudge topping, heated, for serving

Line your slow cooker with a liner to make cleanup easier. Spray the liner (or just the insert, if you're not using one) with nonstick spray. Mix the brownie mix, coffee, oil, and eggs together in a bowl. Add the peanuts or pecans to the batter and stir. Pour the batter into the slow cooker. Add the chocolate hazelnut spread on top of the batter and lightly spread it with a spatula so the batter is covered. Mix the sugar, boiling water, and cocoa powder together in a bowl. Pour over the batter. Cook on high for 2½ hours.

Remove from the slow cooker and let cool. Serve with ice cream, hot fudge, and nuts.

Lemon Blueberry
Pudding Cake

Lemon and blueberries come together to make this a colorful and delicious pudding cake.

Yield: 8 servings   Cook time: 2 hours

Nonstick spray

One 15.25-ounce box lemon cake mix

1¼ cups water

½ cup vegetable oil

4 large eggs

One 3.4-ounce box lemon instant pudding mix

1½ cups frozen blueberries

8 ounces cream cheese, softened

¼ cup granulated sugar

Line your slow cooker with a liner to make cleanup easier. Spray the liner (or just the insert, if you're not using one) with nonstick spray.

Using all but ¼ cup of the cake mix, mix the lemon cake mix, water, oil, and 3 of the eggs together in a bowl. Add the pudding mix to the batter and stir. Fold the blueberries into the batter. Pour into the slow cooker. Beat the cream cheese, sugar, remaining egg, and reserved ¼ cup of cake mix in a bowl. Fold the cream cheese mixture into the batter. Cook on high for 2 hours, or until the cake is set.

"Mousse: How pudding describes itself on its résumé!"

—John Oliver

Warmed Bread
Pudding

A classic comfort food that's so easy to make. The bread should be a bit dry (which is why day-old bread works best). Top with whipped cream and enjoy.

Yield: 8 servings   Cook time: 2½ hours

Nonstick spray

8 cups cubed day-old white bread (1-inch cubes)

½ cup raisins (optional)

2 cups milk

4 large eggs

1 cup granulated sugar

4 tablespoons (½ stick) unsalted butter, melted

1½ teaspoons allspice

⅛ teaspoon salt

Whipped cream, for serving

Line your slow cooker with a liner to make cleanup easier. Spray the liner (or just the insert, if you're not using one) with nonstick spray.

Add the bread and raisins, if using, to the slow cooker. Beat the milk, eggs, sugar, melted butter, allspice, and salt together in a bowl, using a whisk. Pour the mixture over the bread mixture. Stir so the bread is completely coated. Cook on low for 2½ hours.

Serve with whipped cream.

Classic
Cheesecake

To all of the cheesecake lovers out there—this recipe is for you. Add whatever toppings you like—strawberries, chocolate syrup, caramel sauce, and blueberry preserves all make for a tasty cheesecake.

Yield: 8 servings   Cook time: 2½ hours

Nonstick spray

8 tablespoons (1 stick) unsalted butter, melted

6 graham crackers, crushed

Three 8-ounce packages cream cheese, softened

¾ cup granulated sugar

3 large eggs

Line your slow cooker with a liner to make cleanup easier. Spray the liner (or just the insert, if you're not using one) with nonstick spray.

Mix the melted butter and crushed graham crackers together in a bowl. Add the mixture to the bottom of the slow cooker, making sure it is evenly distributed. Mix the cream cheese, sugar, and eggs in a separate bowl. Pour over the graham cracker mixture. Cook on high for 2½ hours. Let stand for 1 hour.

Refrigerate for 1 hour before serving with the topping of your choice.

Tip: Place the graham crackers in a resealable plastic bag and crush with a rolling pin.

Pumpkin Walnut Pudding

Spiced pumpkin seasoned with a walnut crunch. This is a fall classic in my household.

Yield: 8 servings   Cook time: 2½ hours

Nonstick spray

One 15-ounce can pumpkin puree

One 15-ounce can evaporated milk

⅓ cup granulated sugar

1 tablespoon pumpkin pie spice

One 15.25-ounce box spice cake mix

1 cup walnuts, chopped

4 tablespoons (½ stick) unsalted butter, melted

Whipped cream for serving

Line your slow cooker with a liner to make cleanup easier. Spray the liner (or just the insert, if you're not using one) with nonstick spray.

Add the pumpkin, evaporated milk, sugar, and pumpkin pie spice to the slow cooker. Stir until the sugar is dissolved and the ingredients are well combined. Add the cake mix and nuts on top of the pumpkin mixture. Pour the melted butter over the cake mix. Cover and cook on high for 2½ hours. Allow the pudding to stand for 30 minutes before serving. Spoon into bowls and top with whipped cream.

Cinnamon Rolls with Warm Maple Syrup

Cinnamon rolls are easy to make these days, thanks to those premade cans of dough you can get in the grocery store. This recipe requires no baking—just pop the dough in the slow cooker and relax. Plus, this recipe adds a bit of a twist as the butter and maple syrup make these extra rich and tasty.

Yield: 8 servings   Cook time: 2½ hours

4 tablespoons (½ stick) unsalted butter, melted

Two 12.4-ounce cans refrigerated cinnamon rolls with icing

6 large eggs

½ cup heavy whipping cream

1 teaspoon ground cinnamon

1 teaspoon vanilla extract

½ cup maple syrup

Add the melted butter to a lined slow cooker. Cut the cinnamon roll dough into 16 pieces per can (32 pieces total) and set the icing aside. Place the pieces into the bottom of the slow cooker. Beat together the eggs, cream, cinnamon, and vanilla together in a bowl. Pour the mixture over the rolls. Pour the syrup on top of the rolls. Cook on low for 2½ hours. Top with icing and serve warm.

Spiced Stuffed Apples

Spiced stuffed apples make for a fun dessert. The cooked apples look great when you serve them and they taste even better. Drizzle with a bit of maple syrup just before serving for an extra sweet flavor.

Yield: 4 servings   Cook time: 2½ hours

Nonstick spray

¼ cup apple juice

4 baking apples, cored

⅓ cup raisins

¼ cup dark brown sugar

½ teaspoon ground cinnamon

1 tablespoon unsalted butter, cut into 4 pieces

Maple syrup, for serving (optional)

Line your slow cooker with a liner to make cleanup easier. Spray the liner (or just the insert, if you're not using one) with nonstick spray.

Pour the apple juice into bottom of the slow cooker. Place the apples upright in the slow cooker. Mix the raisins, brown sugar, and cinnamon together in a bowl. Spoon the mixture into the center of each apple. Place pieces of butter on top of each apple. Cook on high for 2½ hours.

Drizzle with maple syrup, if desired.

Tip: For an alternative to raisins, try using chopped dried figs or apricots.

Caramelized Pears

Sweet, simple, and delicious. All this recipe takes is a few pears and a heaping helping of caramel sauce. What could be easier? I like these served in a bowl with vanilla ice cream.

Yield: 6 servings   Cook time: 2½ hours

Nonstick Spray

6 yellow pears, peeled and cut in half

1½ cups caramel topping

Ice cream, for serving

Line your slow cooker with a liner to make cleanup easier. Spray the liner (or just the insert, if you're not using one) with nonstick spray.

Add the pears to the bottom of the slow cooker. Cover with caramel topping. Cook on high for 2½ hours.

Serve in a bowl with ice cream.

"There is no love sincerer than the love of food."
—George Bernard Shaw

Chocolate Fudge

Fudge in a slow cooker? Oh yes we can! This is such a simple recipe you'll want to make it every day (it's that addictive). Top the fudge pieces with a sprinkle of sea salt if you're feeling decadent.

Yield: 8 servings   Cook time: 1 hour 15 minutes

Nonstick spray

2 cups milk chocolate chips

¼ cup heavy whipping cream

⅓ cup honey

½ cup white chocolate chips

1 teaspoon vanilla extract

Sea salt or powdered sugar, for garnish

Line your slow cooker with a liner to make cleanup easier. Spray the liner (or just the insert, if you're not using one) with nonstick spray. Line or grease an 8-inch square baking dish.

Add the milk chocolate chips, cream, and honey to the slow cooker. Cook on high for 1 hour. Add the white chocolate chips and vanilla and cook for another 15 minutes, stirring, until the white chocolate is fully melted.

Use a rubber spatula to pour the fudge into the baking dish. Refrigerate for about an hour, or until cooled, and cut into squares. Top with sea salt or powdered sugar.

Index

Photo Credits

Front cover: top right: © sarsmis/Shutterstock.com; top left: © robynmac/iStockphoto.com; center right: © DebbiSmirnoff/iStockphoto.com; center left: © Paul Binet/Shutterstock.com; bottom: © Segmed87ru/iStockphoto.com
Spine: © ZargonDesign/iStockphoto.com
Back cover, from top: © Segmed87ru/iStockphoto.com; © thefoodphotographer/Shutterstock.com

Page 2: © Roxiller/iStockphoto.com; page 8: © katerinabelaya/iStockphoto.com; page 11: © Grezova Olga/Shutterstock.com; pages 12–13: © Elena Veselova/Shuttersock.com; page 14: © naito8/iStockphoto.com; page 17: © Zoryanchik/iStockphoto.com; page 18: © Juanmonino/iStockphoto.com; page 21: © AnnaPustynnikova/iStockphoto.com; page 22: © Seeme/Shutterstock.com; pages 25, 60: © Trendy_Rowdy/iStockphoto.com; page 26: © Anna_Pustynnikova/Shutterstockom; page 29: © ginauf/iStockphoto.com; page 30: © rudisill/iStockphoto.com; page 33: © Liv friis-larsen/Shutterstock.com; page 34: © pixelliebe/iStockphoto.com; pages 36–37: © Sevda Stancheva/Shutterstock.com; page 38: © kcline/iStockphoto.com; page 41: © burwellphotography/iStockphoto.com; page 42: © msheldrake/iStockphoto.com; page 45: © AS Food Studio/Shutterstock.com; pages 46, 49: © Vezzani Photography/Shutterstock.com; page 50: © cobraphotography/Shutterstock.com; page 53: © StephanieFrey/iStockphoto.com; page 54: © iuliia_n/iStockphoto.com; page 57: © a_namenko/iStockphoto.com; pages 58–59: © p.studio66/Shutterstock.com; page 63: © Lessy/iStockphoto.com; page 64: © AnjelaGr/iStockphoto.com; page 67: © kourafas5/iStockphoto.com; page 68: © Elena Demyanko/Shutterstock.com; page 71: © Lanav/Shutterstock.com; page 72: © sf_foodphoto/iStockphoto.com; page 75: © a9photo/Shutterstock.com; pages 76–77, 82: © Saharosa40/iStockphoto.com; page 78: © jtyler/iStockphoto.com; pages 81, 100: © Paul Binet/Shutterstock.com; page 85: © fredredhat/Shutterstock.com; page 86: © DDiana/Shutterstock.com; page 89: © loooby/iStockphoto.com; page 90: © MShev/Shutterstock.com; page 93: © margouillatphotos/iStockphoto.com; page 94: © Nataliya Aramasova/Shutterstock.com; page 97: © Amawasri Pakdara/Shutterstock.com; pages 98–99: © Jarvna/Shutterstock.com; page 103: © giuseppepapa/iStockphoto.com; page 104: © viennetta/Shutterstock.com; page 107: © IndridHS/Shutterstock.com; page 108: © cobraphotography/Shuttestock.com; page 111: © Taylor Mathis/Shutterstock.com; page 112: © Yulia Davidovich/Shutterstock.com; page 115: © MSPhotographic/Shutterstock.com; page 116: © mama_mia/Shutterstock.com; page 119: © thefoodphotographer/Shutterstock.com; page 120: © Brent Hofacker/Shutterstock.com; page 122: © flyfloor/iStockphoto.com

INTEGRATING TECHNOLOGY IN NURSING EDUCATION

TOOLS FOR THE KNOWLEDGE ERA

Kathleen Garver Mastrian, PhD, RN
Associate Professor
Program Coordinator for Nursing
Penn State University, Shenango
Sharon, Pennsylvania

Dee McGonigle, PhD, RN, FACCE, FAAN
Associate Professor
Penn State University, New Kensington
Upper Burrell, Pennsylvania

Wendy L. Mahan, PhD
Instructional Designer
College of Health and Human Development
Penn State University
University Park, Pennsylvania

Brett Bixler, PhD
Lead Instructional Designer
Information Technology Services
Penn State University
University Park, Pennsylvania

JONES AND BARTLETT PUBLISHERS
Sudbury, Massachusetts
BOSTON   TORONTO   LONDON   SINGAPORE

World Headquarters

Jones and Bartlett Publishers	Jones and Bartlett Publishers	Jones and Bartlett Publishers
40 Tall Pine Drive	Canada	International
Sudbury, MA 01776	6339 Ormindale Way	Barb House, Barb Mews
978-443-5000	Mississauga, Ontario L5V 1J2	London W6 7PA
info@jbpub.com	Canada	United Kingdom
www.jbpub.com		

Jones and Bartlett's books and products are available through most bookstores and online booksellers. To contact Jones and Bartlett Publishers directly, call 800-832-0034, fax 978-443-8000, or visit our website, www.jbpub.com.

Substantial discounts on bulk quantities of Jones and Bartlett's publications are available to corporations, professional associations, and other qualified organizations. For details and specific discount information, contact the special sales department at Jones and Bartlett via the above contact information or send an email to specialsales@jbpub.com.

The authors, editor, and publisher have made every effort to provide accurate information. However, they are not responsible for errors, omissions, or for any outcomes related to the use of the contents of this book and take no responsibility for the use of the products and procedures described. Treatments and side effects described in this book may not be applicable to all people; likewise, some people may require a dose or experience a side effect that is not described herein. Drugs and medical devices are discussed that may have limited availability controlled by the Food and Drug Administration (FDA) for use only in a research study or clinical trial. Research, clinical practice, and government regulations often change the accepted standard in this field. When consideration is being given to use of any drug in the clinical setting, the health care provider or reader is responsible for determining FDA status of the drug, reading the package insert, and reviewing prescribing information for the most up-to-date recommendations on dose, precautions, and contraindications, and determining the appropriate usage for the product. This is especially important in the case of drugs that are new or seldom used.

Production Credits

Publisher: Kevin Sullivan
Aquisitions Editor: Amy Sibley
Associate Editor: Patricia Donnelly
Editorial Assistant: Rachel Shuster
Production Editor: Amanda Clerkin
Marketing Manager: Rebecca Wasley

V.P., Manufacturing and Inventory Control: Therese Connell
Composition: DSCS/Absolute Service, Inc.
Cover Design: Scott Moden
Cover Image: © Mark Bolton/ShutterStock, Inc.
Printing and Binding: Malloy, Inc.
Cover Printing: Malloy, Inc.

Library of Congress Cataloging-in-Publication Data

Integrating technology in nursing education : tools for the knowledge era / Kathleen G. Mastrian ... [et al.].
    p. ; cm.
  Includes bibliographical references and index.
  ISBN-13: 978-0-7637-6871-3 (alk. paper)
  ISBN-10: 0-7637-6871-5 (alk. paper)
  1. Nursing—Study and teaching. 2. Educational technology. I. Mastrian, Kathleen Garver.
  [DNLM: 1. Education, Nursing—trends. 2. Teaching Materials. 3. Educational Technology—
trends. 4. Nursing Informatics—trends. WY 18.2 I605 2011]
  RT73.5.I58 2011
  610.73071′1—dc22
                            2009038849

6048

Printed in the United States of America
15 14 13   10 9 8 7 6 5 4 3

*I dedicate this book to all who value and embrace knowledge.
You know who you are! And to my wonderful family and friends who
provide unremitting love, laughter, and support.—KM*

*I wish to acknowledge the love, support, and continued encouragement
of my best friend and husband, Craig. I would like to also acknowledge
the love, support, humor, and constant laughter from my son, Craig.
He is such an inspiring and charismatic gentleman that it makes me
extremely proud! I would also like to thank my family and friends
for their encouragement and support.—DM*

*I would like to dedicate this book to my husband, Mark, who is always patient
and supportive of my academic pursuits.—WLM*

*I would like to dedicate this to my family.
Without their support, I could not have completed my contributions
to this book.—BB*

Contents

Preface

Change, transform, innovate, adjust, and respond. These seemingly simple words may invoke anxiety attacks in nurse educators. It appears that everywhere we turn there are discussions of transforming healthcare delivery and the need to change the way healthcare workers are educated. Nurse educators are most comfortable covering well-defined portions of nursing content specifically designed to prepare nurses for licensing exams and safe clinical practice. Nursing education paradigms and curricula are clearly spelled out, steeped in rich traditions, and regularly reviewed by accrediting agencies. For the most part, nurse educators are contented with teacher-centered styles of education and the sense of expertise and educational control that these approaches engender.

In the current education environment, nurse educators may feel like jugglers, faced with a myriad of mandates that mimic the juggler's challenge of throwing and catching all of the balls successfully. In addition to satisfying the demands of our accrediting agencies and licensing boards, we are responsible for preparing a future generation of nurses to practice safely and in a high-quality manner in ever changing healthcare environments. How can we envision and articulate safe, high-quality practice in our curricula when the healthcare environments themselves are continuously transforming? What knowledge do our students need to acquire? What skills do they need to develop? What technologies do they need to master? We are responsible for preparing nurses for the knowledge era so that they are committed to the continuous acquisition and processing of information into knowledge and able to apply, generate, and disseminate that knowledge appropriately in practice. In the face of the daily and constant flood of new health information and knowledge, how do we decide what concepts and content to include and what strategies to use to challenge our students to learn? We are responsible for preparing nurses who can engage in critical thinking to solve problems and make appropriate care decisions. How can we effectively simulate practice skills in a laboratory or find appropriate real-time clinical situations to afford our students the opportunities to develop and hone their clinical practice skills? Nurse educators are also responsible for adapting to the changing environments of educational institutions who are promoting student-centered approaches to education and flexible and responsive learning environments, all within a budget! We, the authors, believe that using technology to design and deliver potent and compelling learning episodes may help nurse educators more successfully juggle the host of challenges they face in educating students in the knowledge era.

The idea for this book came about during the development of several online courses by the authors and the realization that there is no comprehensive teaching with technology text on the market. This text has four authors because we want to emphasize the need and illustrate the effectiveness of nursing faculty partnering with education experts and instructional designers to create potent learning episodes for students. In this text, we will:

- Examine the driving societal forces for technology integration in nursing education in the emerging knowledge era,
- Relate the changing educational and healthcare landscapes to the transformation of nursing education,
- Envision future technology needs for the global electronic era and the impacts on health care and the education of healthcare workers,
- Provide an overview of educational and instructional design theories as building blocks for technology integration in nursing education, and
- Demonstrate the use of evolving educational technologies to create potent and compelling learning episodes for students to prepare them for practice in ever-changing healthcare environments.

This book is designed as a resource for graduate level nurse educator courses and for practicing nurse educators who are interested in integrating technology in their teaching. It is intended to be a practical as well as thought-provoking treatise. Sections I and II are more theoretical in approach and are included to set the stage for the more prescriptive and illustrative sections (III–V) that follow. Each chapter contains a list of key words, reader-centered objectives, and learning activities that will challenge you to reflect on the theoretical and practical content presented, and apply what you have learned. We have deliberately taken a theory-based approach because we believe that nursing education is a practice specialty and that nurse educators need to engage in reflective and evidence-based practice to respond appropriately and successfully to the many forces driving the transformation of education. We hope you enjoy the book and find it useful for the successful integration of technology to transform your approaches to teaching and learning and for the development of potent and compelling learning episodes for your students.

Contributors

Nedra Farcus, MSN, RN
Instructor of Nursing
Penn State Altoona
Altoona, Pennsylvania

Nick Miehl, MSN, RN
Nursing Technology Lab and Simulation Center Coordinator
The Behrend College
Penn State Erie
Erie, Pennsylvania

Biographies

Kathleen Garver Mastrian, PhD, RN

Dr. Kathleen Mastrian is an Associate Professor and Program Coordinator for Nursing at Penn State University at Shenango. She earned as BS in nursing at Penn State, a master's in nursing from the University of Pittsburgh, and a PhD in medical sociology from Kent State University. She has been involved in the education of nontraditional aged students for 30 years in the RN to BS nursing program. She pioneered the use of Credit by Portfolio Assessment to award advanced standing nursing credit for registered nurses. She has also been active in the development of technology enhanced courses for registered nurses facilitating asynchronous participation and active and collaborative learning. She is one of the founding proposers to place the RN to BS program online for Penn State's World Campus, has developed two of the courses for that curriculum, and teaches at least one section per semester for the World Campus program. Recently, she has been asked to teach sociology for the World Campus and to facilitate the online teacher training course OL2000 for Penn State's World Campus. She has published over 30 nursing journal articles and recently coedited and published a textbook, *Nursing Informatics and the Foundation of Knowledge* (Jones and Bartlett, 2009), that has been marketed in the United States and abroad.

Dee McGonigle, PhD, RN, FACCE, FAAN

Dr. McGonigle received her BS degree in nursing from Penn State University, a master's degree in nursing from Indiana University of Pennsylvania, and her PhD in foundations of education from the University of Pittsburgh. She is an Associate Professor of Nursing, Information Sciences & Technology (IST) and Computational Science at Penn State University, a Fellow in the American Academy of Nursing, and the editor-in-chief of the *Online Journal of Nursing Informatics* (OJNI). She is actively involved in integrating active and collaborative learning strategies into traditional as well as online courses. Dr. McGonigle is interested in the educational impact of the human–technology interface. She conceptualized and was instrumental in the development and implementation of the Online RN to BS Nursing Degree program delivered through the World Campus. Dr. McGonigle has coauthored a textbook, *Nursing Informatics and the Foundation of Knowledge*, that was published by Jones and Bartlett (2009). She has over 100 publications, 30 funded grants, and 29 international and national presentations. She is a consultant to the Hartford Foundation grant at University Park, a faculty member of the Hartford Center for Geriatric Nursing Excellence at Penn State, has developed a doctoral level course on technological innovations in teaching and learning, led the development of the recruitment videos, and moderated the Hartford Center Radio Shows. Dr. McGonigle is committed to the insightful analysis of ethical dilemmas brought on by this volatile information age. She continues to search for a way to facilitate translation by helping those who know (researchers) and those who do (clinicians) communicate and share. Dr. McGonigle is also interested in the diffusion of innovative technologies, especially those impacting learning.

Wendy L. Mahan, PhD

Dr. Mahan received her PhD in instructional systems from the Penn State University. She has experience in the design, development, implementation, and assessment of online and blended learning courses. She has worked with faculty in a variety of content areas, with a focus on large enrollment, general education courses. Her current interests focus on integrating Web 2.0 technologies within a blended learning environment. Prior to entering the instructional design field, Wendy was a certified rehabilitation counselor.

Brett Bixler, PhD

Dr. Bixler has over 25 years of experience in the instructional design field. He is the Lead Instructional Designer with Education Technology Services, part of Information Technology Services (ITS), at Penn State. In his current position, Brett is working with the latest educational technologies and learning theories to produce learner-centered active and collaborative learning environments. Brett works with peers from across Penn State and other universities to discuss common issues and provide advice and guidance on a wide range of issues. He is responsible for a variety of other tasks, including instructional design, project coordination and management, faculty and staff development, curriculum development, educational technology training and assistance, formative and summative evaluation of projects, and Internet expertise.

Brett is actively investigating the use of games, simulations, and virtual worlds for educational purposes. He is in charge of the Educational Gaming Commons (see http://gaming.psu.edu) to support collaboration and initiatives in these areas throughout Penn State.

Driving Forces for Technology Integration in Nursing Education

The need to transform nursing education is becoming increasingly apparent. Healthcare information and knowledge are growing exponentially and nursing curricula that are rigid and laden with content may not be effectively preparing nurses for contemporary nursing practice. We need nurses who are able to apply knowledge appropriately in unique situations and who continue to build a knowledge base as knowledge evolves. We need nurses who embrace technology and use it appropriately. We need nurses who are innovators, collaborators, and critical thinkers. As Earl Koile, Professor Emeritus of Educational Psychology, University of Texas at Austin, once said, "Two professions most notably regarded as filled with 'nonlisteners' are medicine and education"(2004, para. 8). We can no longer afford to be "nonlisteners". We must listen to the societal forces that are pushing for transformation of nursing education and act accordingly.

In this section of the text we outline the driving societal forces for technology integration in the transformation of nursing education during this emerging knowledge era. Chapter 1 examines the calls for change in nursing education issued by key stakeholders. We emphasize that nurse educators need to commit to the implementation of evidence-based teaching practices and to developing the science of nursing education. In Chapter 2, we discuss the changing health-care landscape and examine the integration of technology as a force for trans-forming health care. We urge nurse educators to transform curricula to include wide exposure to healthcare technology and educational technologies to ensure that we are preparing nurses who are informatics, competent, and techno-savvy. Chapter 3 provides an overview of the unique characteristics of Net Generation students. We emphasize that these students think and process information differently than other generations, and urge educators to take steps to incorporate instructional strategies and technologies that address the needs and learning styles of the new generation. In Chapter 4, we discuss the diversity of nursing faculty and the challenges to and opportunities for education transformation engendered by evolving educational technologies. We urge nurse educators to embrace the characteristics of early adopters and envision ways to enhance social presence and the learning culture using technology. Finally, in Chapter 5 we take a broad look at some of the societal forces prompting the transformation of higher education institutions. The need for change in higher education is induced by the challenges associated with meeting the needs of a changing and diverse student population, maintaining quality education within lean budget parameters, as well as becoming more responsive to preparing graduates for workplace realities.

References

Koile, E. (2004). Quotations on teaching, learning, and education. Available at: http://www
.ntlf.com/html/lib/quotes.htm. Accessed July 22, 2009.

CHAPTER

1

Preparing Nurses for Contemporary Practice

Food For Thought

"It is not the strongest of the species that survives,
nor the most intelligent,
but the one most responsive to change."

Charles Darwin, 1809–1882

"Education is not filling a bucket, but lighting a fire."

William Butler Yeats, 1865–1939

Key Words

American Association of Colleges
  of Nursing (AACN)
Blog
Body of knowledge
Collaboration
Constructivism
Critical thinking
Curricular reforms
Evidence-based practice (EBP)
Informatics
Institute of Medicine (IOM)
National League for Nursing (NLN)

Patient-centered care
Pedagogic research
Problem solving
Quality and Safety Education
  for Nurses (QSEN)
Reflective practice
Science of education
Simulations
Technology Informatics Guiding
  Education Reform (TIGER)
Translational knowledge

Objectives

The educator will be able to describe the converging societal forces providing the impetus for curricular reform in nursing education.

The educator will be motivated to examine the current nursing curriculum for compliance with the inclusions suggested here.

The educator will be able to evaluate the need for modification of the current curriculum.

The educator will be able to advocate effectively for nursing curriculum restructuring.

Introduction

The scenario is a computer lab classroom with the nurse educator standing at the front and scrolling through a prepared presentation complete with screen captures to teach the nursing students how to set up and begin using the **blog** program provided by the university. The instructor is encouraging the students to use the blogs as an ePortfolio with opportunities to showcase best work and reflect on what they have learned in each class during their baccalaureate education. The presentation is going along nicely until one student raises her hand and says, "My screen does not look like the one you are showing us. I can't find the create blog button." The instructor pauses and points to the area on the screen capture where the create blog button is located. The students insist that the button is not there. The instructor logs in to the blog system and projects the live screen in the classroom and discovers that indeed the look of the dashboard has changed since she developed the presentation! Trying not to panic, the instructor takes a moment to locate the create blog command on the new dashboard. Before she is able to do so, a student calls out, "I found it, it is located...."

While most educators would be mortified at the above scenario, the truth is that when you are teaching with technology and about technology, you need to expect the unexpected. By calmly switching to the live view, taking a moment to explore the dashboard, and embracing the student's success in locating the create blog button, the instructor modeled **problem solving** behaviors and the benefits of **collaboration**. As we will note later in the chapter, problem solving and collaboration are essential components of nursing practice in the 21st century.

Let us also reflect for a moment on the instructor's preparation for teaching the class. Although the instructor was using technology for the presentation, the instructor was likely mimicking the way she had been taught. Opting for static presentation with screen captures imbedded in the presentation initially provided the instructor with a measure of control over content and, as it turns out, a false sense of security. The "glitch" in the technology actually provided a rich opportunity as a learning moment. The clear message to students is this, "I do not know all there is to know, I can learn from others, and we can all benefit by our willingness to take risks and solve problems through openness and teamwork."

Taking risks is not something that nurse educators routinely embrace because of our multiple responsibilities to accrediting agencies, State Boards of Nursing, and to healthcare agencies. We take our mission of preparing high-quality and safe practitioners very seriously. Our curricula tend to be closed, content laden, and rigid. We give lip service to student-centered education and active learning, but continue to disseminate information rather than challenging our students to construct their own knowledge bases. It is becoming increasingly clear that we must let go of the notion that we can cover all of the content that a nurse will need in practice and instead focus on teaching our students how to learn and how to find and apply new information when they need it. As Coonan (2008) suggests:

> risk is dangerous, as is the fear of the unknown; but without creativity, risk, and innovation, change will not occur. And without change there will be no growth and the system will remain stagnant while the environment changes around us and leaves us behind. (para. 3)

As nurse educators, we must respond to changes in healthcare environments, changes in the expectations of our patients, and help prepare our students to practice effectively in these ever evolving environments.

The Push for Change

Key healthcare stakeholders are calling for new paradigms in nursing education. Just as there is a gap in the translation of nursing research to practice, so too is there a gap in developing and translating **pedagogic research** to nursing education. Nurse educators need to commit to the implementation of evidence-based teaching practices and commit to developing the science of nursing education. We must transform our educational paradigms to respond to the calls for change issued in the reports of the **Institute of Medicine** (IOM, 2001, 2003), the **National League for Nursing** (NLN, 2003, 2005, 2008), the **American**

Association of Colleges of Nursing (AACN, 2008), the **Technology Informatics Guiding Education Reform** (TIGER) Initiative (2007), and the **Quality and Safety Education for Nurses** (Cronenwett *et al.*, 2007). Each of these key reports and their implications for nursing education will be discussed. We will conclude with a discussion of how the utilization of technology in the classroom may help us to meet the challenges of educating nurses for 21st-century practice. In addition, in subsequent chapters we will discuss the changing healthcare arena, the changing student, and the changing higher education environment and how these relate to the need to revise the paradigm of nursing education.

The IOM report of 2001, "Crossing the Quality Chasm: A New Health System for the 21st Century," clearly identifies the need for changes in the education of healthcare workers. The driving forces for change in the healthcare system discussed in the report will be presented in detail in Chapter 2. The increasing complexity of health care means that there is "more to know, more to do, more to manage, more to watch, and more people involved than ever before" (IOM, 2001, p. 1). Hence the preceding suggestion that nurse educators reject the notion that there is a finite **body of knowledge** for nursing practice that can be covered in an education program and instead focus on helping our students learn how to learn, learn how to build a body of knowledge for themselves, and learn how to find and apply appropriate knowledge to their practice. "Faced with such rapid changes, the nation's health care delivery system has fallen far short in its ability to translate knowledge into practice and to apply new technology safely and appropriately" (IOM, 2001, p. 1). The IOM report of 2003, "Health Professions Education: A Bridge to Quality," emphasizes the need for collaboration among health professionals, and also the appropriate application of technology and evidence-based practice. In addition, this 2003 report urges a shift to **patient-centered care** approaches and an emphasis on quality improvement and safety.

Building on the IOM reports, the NLN issued several reports also calling for changes in nursing education. In the 2003 position statement, the NLN emphasizes the need to form partnerships between students, teachers, clinicians, and researchers to reform nursing education and to develop the **science of education**.

> To accomplish this call for reform, nurse educators in partnership with nursing service must enact substantive innovation in schools, document the effects of the innovation being undertaken, and develop the science of nursing education upon which all practicing teachers can draw. The ultimate outcome of these efforts is evidence-based approaches to nursing education in which

students learn to provide skillful and compassionate nursing care in fluid and uncertain health care environments. (NLN, 2003, p. 3)

In the 2005 position statement, "Transforming Nursing Education," the NLN emphasizes the need for faculty to focus on student learning and to create appropriate educational environments. Some additional objectives for reforms suggested in this report include:

- Developing the science of nursing education to emphasize evidence-based education;
- Identifying nurse educators as specialty practitioners;
- Providing financial resources for faculty development and **curricular reforms**;
- Identifying and responding to changes in the complex practice environment; and
- Developing efficient and effective uses of educational resources. (NLN, 2005)

In 2008, the NLN released another position statement, "Preparing the Next Generation of Nurses to Practice in a Technology-Rich Environment: An Informatics Agenda." In this statement, the NLN indicates that nursing education must be reformed in order to prepare nurses who are "capable of practicing in a healthcare environment where technology continues to increase in amount and sophistication" (NLN, 2008, p. 2). There is a clear need for both students and faculty to achieve competency in **informatics** in order to practice in the ever evolving technology- and information-rich healthcare environment.

In 2008, the AACN released the "Essentials of Baccalaureate Education for Professional Nursing Practice." The nine essentials call for the integration and inclusion of liberal education in nursing curricula; knowledge and skills in leadership quality care and patient safety; knowledge and skills necessary to translate evidence into practice; mastery of information management and patient care technology skills; knowledge of content related to healthcare policy, and finance and regulation; skills in collaboration and communication across healthcare disciplines; considerations for disease prevention and the promotion of the health; development of professionalism and professional values including ethics of practice; and preparation to provide care across the lifespan and in multiple complex healthcare environments. The stated intent of the report is to "transform baccalaureate nursing education by providing the curricular elements and framework for building the baccalaureate nursing curriculum for the 21st century" (AACN, 2008, p. 3).

The TIGER initiative is the result of an invitation-only summit "to create a vision for the future of nursing that bridges the quality chasm with information technology, enabling nurses to use informatics in practice and education to provide safer, higher-quality patient care" (TIGER, 2007, p. 4). The summit was initiated in response to the IOM reports related to safety and quality, former President Bush's call for electronic health records implementation by 2014, and the recognition that information technology and informatics are central to nursing practice of the future. Indeed, the members of the TIGER summit called for "integrating informatics seamlessly into nursing, making IT the stethoscope of the 21st century" (p. 3). The pillars of the TIGER vision include:

1. Management & Leadership: Revolutionary leadership that drives, empowers and executes the transformation of health care.
2. Education: Collaborative learning communities that maximize the possibilities of technology toward knowledge development and dissemination.
3. Communication & Collaboration: Standardized, person-centered, technology-enabled processes to facilitate teamwork and relationships across the continuum of care.
4. Informatics Design: Evidence-based, interoperable intelligence systems that support education and practice to foster quality care and safety.
5. Information Technology: Smart, people-centered, affordable technologies that are universal, useable, useful and standards-based.
6. Policy: Consistent, incentives-based initiatives (organizational and governmental) that support advocacy and coalition-building, achieving . . . an ethical culture of safety.
7. Culture: A respectful, open system that leverages technology and informatics across multiple disciplines in an environment where all stakeholders trust each other to work together towards the goal of high quality and safety. (p. 4)

Cronenwett *et al.* (2007), as part of the Quality and Safety Education for Nurses (QSEN) initiative funded by the Robert Wood Johnson Foundation, defined each of the IOM (2003) core competencies for nursing education and developed statements of knowledge, skills, and attitudes necessary to meet these core competencies. The core competencies and definitions are:

- **Patient-centered care:** Recognize the patient or designee as the source of control and full partner in providing compassionate and coordinated care based on respect for the patient's preferences, values, and needs (p. 123).
- **Teamwork and collaboration:** Function effectively within nursing and inter-professional teams fostering open communication, mutual respect, and shared decision-making to achieve quality patient care (p. 125).
- **Evidence-based practice (EBP):** Integrate the best current evidence with clinical expertise and patient/family preferences and values for delivery of optimal health care (p. 126).
- **Quality improvement (QI):** Use data to monitor the outcomes and processes and use improvement methods to design and test changes to continuously improve the quality and safety of health care systems (p. 127).
- **Safety:** Minimize the risk of harm to patients and providers through both system effectiveness and individual performance (p. 128).
- **Informatics:** Use information and technology to communicate, manage knowledge, mitigate error, and support decision-making (p. 129).

In order to achieve these competencies and to implement them consistently in practice, nursing education must change. Cronenwett *et al.* (2007) suggest that clinical instructors will need to model interprofessional team engagement and communication skills, that clinical experiences and **simulations** need to be developed to include the skills associated with these competencies, and that clinical instructors use reflective papers and case studies to emphasize **critical thinking** skills in students.

Preparing Students for Contemporary Nursing Practice

What does contemporary nursing practice look and feel like? What do our students need to know, be, and do? These are questions that nurse educators struggle with every day. The one common theme that is prevalent in the discussions about contemporary practice is that there is no finite body of knowledge for nursing. Contemporary nurses must understand basic concepts related to the well-recognized paradigm of nursing: human beings, health, environment, and nursing (aspects of the profession and practice) and be prepared to apply them creatively in ever changing and fast-paced healthcare environments.

Peters (2000) argues that constructivist-learning approaches are well suited for nursing education. The active learning approach inherent in **constructivism** makes learning the responsibility of the learner, and empowers students with problem solving, critical thinking, and reflecting skills. These skills enable the learner to build and continuously refine a knowledge base by comparing existing knowledge with new situations and revising as necessary. The role of the educator in this process is that of mediator. "A constructivist teacher works as the interface between the curriculum and the student to bring the two together in a way that is meaningful to the learner" (Peters, 2000, p. 2).

Noveletsky (2007) articulates the constructivist approach in nursing education by advocating the use of **reflective practice** to build an individual knowledge base. Students can be taught to reflect while carrying out an action and/or reflect retrospectively. Reflection allows for identifying and critically examining the factors that impacted responses and actions in a clinical situation. This critical reflection helps a practitioner develop expertise in practice and build a knowledge base that can be applied in similar situations. We believe that in this ever changing healthcare environment, skill in and a commitment to reflective practice will help all nurses, from novices to experts, continuously refine and improve their professional practice by building a transformative and **translational knowledge** base.

Along these same lines, Brown and Doane (2007) emphasize that "the goal of nursing education is the development of nurses who consciously and intentionally develop, revise, adapt, expand, and alter nursing knowledge and practice to be responsive in particular relationships and clinical practice contexts" (p. 107). This is similar to a concept described by Redman (2008) as mindfulness. Brown and Doane developed a set of working assumptions to maintain what they see as a critical balance between the authority of content and methods, and the characteristics of students as learners and the self as a teacher:

- Nursing is responsive knowing-in-action.
- Objective/theoretic knowledge is a pragmatic tool.
- Nursing practice and education require creative capacity (Brown and Doane, 2007, p. 107).

Further, Brown and Doane (2007, p. 117) list tips for developing a student centered learning environment:

- Encourage students to foster the integral relationship between their personal and professional selves.
- Create the space for learners to see how who they are as a person shapes who they are as a nurse.
- Encourage the examination of particularities (i.e., what is unique, significant, similar, different).
- Pay attention to how you are taking up and expressing knowledge and how that is shaping you in particular moments of your teaching practice.

As we have emphasized previously in our discussion, nursing faculty must model knowledge building and commit to evidence-based teaching as well as evidence-based clinical practice.

Giddens *et al.* (2008) describe the development and implementation of a concept-based curriculum. In their discussion, they stress that by de-emphasizing content the focus turns to critical thinking in the application of concepts across multiple settings and in multiple age groups. Their approach includes two distinct lists of concepts, those related to health and illness, and those related to nursing as a profession. For example, health and illness concepts include but are not limited to skin integrity, infection, acid–base balance, family dynamics, coping, and developmental delay. The nursing professional concepts include such topics as accountability, caring, ethics, power, organizational structures, health policy, mentoring, and leadership. We believe that the concept approach to nursing education has the potential to transform nursing education and focus on developing professionals who know how to build and apply a knowledge base, thus preparing students for contemporary practice.

Role of Technology for Transforming Nursing Education

The need to change approaches to nursing education has been clearly established in the multiple calls for reform issued by key stakeholders and pioneers in nursing education reform discussed previously. We believe that the global integration of technology in nursing education can help technology use become seamless, painless, transparent, and ubiquitous. While we cannot expose our students to every possible type of technology they might encounter in future practice, we can help them to become proficient users of various technologies that currently support the delivery of quality, safe, and effective health care. For example, the following are just some of the technology-related outcomes suggested by the AACN report (2008) for baccalaureate nursing graduates:

1. Use telecommunication technologies to assist in effective communication in a variety of healthcare settings.
2. Apply safeguards and decision-making support tools embedded in patient care technologies and information systems to support a safe practice environment for both patients and healthcare workers.
3. Evaluate data from all relevant sources, including technology, to inform the delivery of care.
4. Recognize the role of information technology in improving patient care outcomes and creating a safe care environment.
5. Uphold ethical standards related to data security, regulatory requirements, confidentiality, and clients' right to privacy. (AACN, 2008, pp. 18–19).

The report suggests some of the following sample content for achieving these student outcomes:

- Use of patient care technologies (e.g., monitors, pumps, computer-assisted devices)
- Use of technology and information systems for clinical decision-making
- Computer skills that may include basic software, spreadsheet, and health-care databases
- Information management for patient safety
- Regulatory requirements through electronic data monitoring systems
- Ethical and legal issues related to the use of information technology, including copyright, privacy, and confidentiality issues
- Retrieval information systems, including access, evaluation of data, and application of relevant data to patient care
- Technological resources for evidence-based practice
- Technology and information systems safeguards (e.g., patient monitoring, equipment, patient identification systems, drug alerts and IV systems, and barcoding)

- Information literacy
- Electronic health record/physician order entry
- Decision support tools (AACN, 2008, pp. 19–20)

These very detailed examples of content provide clear direction for the use of technology in education. Please take the time to view the report for a complete list of outcomes and content suggestions. Nurse educators must use and embrace technology, demonstrate the effectiveness of technology, and role model seamless and ubiquitous use of technology for our students if we are to transform nursing education to meet the needs of contemporary nursing practice.

Learning Activities

1. Review the article by Noveletsky (2007) and identify areas in the curriculum where you can implement reflective practice techniques for your students.
2. Next, consider developing a process for reflective practice as an educator using a blog to document your successes and areas where you can improve.
3. Divide faculty into three groups. Assign Group A to read the 2008 AACN "Essentials of Baccalaureate Education for Professional Nursing Practice" and create a grid identifying where each of the essentials is covered in the curriculum. Assign Group B to review the 2007 TIGER initiative recommendations and create a similar grid. Finally, assign Group C to the QSEN initiative and to create a similar grid. Allow 3 weeks for this activity and reconvene the groups. What areas of improvement have you identified in the curriculum? How will you address these needed improvements?
4. Assign faculty to read Giddens *et al.* (2008) and consider the pros and cons of a concept-based curriculum.

References

American Association of Colleges of Nursing. (2008). *The essentials of baccalaureate education for professional nursing practice*. Available at: http://www.aacn.nche.edu/Education/pdf/BaccEssentials08.pdf. Accessed June 16, 2009.

Brown, H., & Doane, G. (2007). From filling a bucket to lighting a fire: Aligning nursing education and nursing practice. In L. E. Young & B. L. Paterson (Eds.), *Teaching nursing: Developing a student-centered learning environment* (pp. 97–118). Philadelphia, PA: Lippincott, Williams & Wilkins.

Coonan, P. (2008). Educational Innovation: Nursing's Leadership Challenge. *Nursing Economics*, 26(2), 117–121.

Cronenwett, L., Sherwood, G., Barnsteiner J., Disch, J., Johnson, J., Mitchell, P., et al. (2007). Quality and safety education for nurses. *Nursing Outlook*, 55(3), 122–131.

Giddens, J. Brady, D., Brown, P., Wright, M., Smith, D., & Harris, J. (2008). A new curriculum for a new era of nursing education. *Nursing Education Perspectives*, 29(4), 200–204.

Institute of Medicine. (2001). *Crossing the quality chasm: A new health system for the 21st century*. Available at: http://books.nap.edu/html/quality_chasm/reportbrief.pdf. Accessed January 27, 2009.

Institute of Medicine. (2003). *Health professions education: A bridge to quality*. Washington, DC: National Academies Press.

National League for Nursing. (2003). *Innovation in nursing education: A call to reform* (Position statement). Available at: http://www.nln.org/aboutnln/PositionStatements/innovation082203.pdf. Accessed October 20, 2009.

National League for Nursing. (2005). *Transforming nursing education* (Position statement). Available at: http://www.nln.org/aboutnln/PositionStatements/transforming052005.pdf. Accessed October 20, 2009.

National League for Nursing. (2008). *Preparing the next generation of nurses to practice in a technology rich environment: An informatics agenda* (Position statement). Available at: http://www.nln.org/aboutnln/PositionStatements/informatics_052808.pdf. Accessed October 20, 2009.

Noveletsky, H. (2007). Reflective practice. In M. J. Bradshaw & A. J. Lowenstein (Eds.), *Innovative teaching strategies in nursing and related health professions*. (4th ed., pp. 141–148). Sudbury, MA: Jones and Bartlett.

Peters, M. (2000). Does constructivist epistemology have a place in nurse education? *Journal of Nursing Education*, 39(4), 166–172.

Redman, R. (2008). High reliability organizations: Implications for nursing knowledge development. *Research and Theory for Nursing Practice*, 22(3), 165–167.

Technology Informatics Guiding Education Reform. (2007). *Evidence and informatics transforming nursing: 3-year action steps toward a 10-year vision*. Available at: http://www.aacn.nche.edu/Education/pdf/TIGER.pdf. Accessed February 3, 2009.

CHAPTER 2

The Changing Healthcare Arena

Food For Thought

*"To exist is to change,
to change is to mature,
to mature is to go on creating oneself endlessly."*
Henri Bergson, 1859–1941

"New insights fail to get put into practice because they conflict with deeply held internal images of how the world works . . . images that limit us to familiar ways of thinking and acting. That is why the discipline of managing mental models— surfacing, testing, and improving our internal pictures of how the world works— promises to be a major breakthrough for learning organizations."
Peter Senge, 1947–

*"Although the connections are not always obvious,
personal change is inseparable from social and political change."*
Harriet Lerner, 1944–

Key Words

Admission, discharge, and transfer (ADT)	Clinical blogs
Biosignals	Clinical guidelines
Biosurveillance	Computer literacy

Computerized tomography or computerized axial tomography (CT or CAT) scan	Interoperability
	Magnetic resonance imaging (MRI)
	MEDLINE
Data mining	Order entry management tools
Database	Patient-centered approach
Decision support tools	Population health
Diagnosis-related groups (DRGs)	Population registries
Electrocardiogram (ECG or EKG)	Regional health information organizations (RHIOs)
Electronic health record (EHR)	
Health information technology	Results management tools
Informatics competencies	Telehealth
Information literacy	Workflow

Objectives

The educator will be able to describe the forces and trends driving the transformation of health care.

The educator will be able to synthesize the implications of health technology integration for nursing education and advocate for curricular changes.

The educator will perform a self-assessment of personal learning needs related to informatics competencies.

The educator will develop a personal plan for acquiring informatics competencies that are integral to the transforming healthcare system.

Introduction

Carol is an RN who works in a small community based hospital on a very busy medical-surgical unit with 40 beds. Even though the hospital where she works is small, it is somewhat advanced in the world of technology. The hospital uses an electronic personal digital assistant (PDA) device for medication administration. This handheld device requires nurses to scan the barcodes on their employee badges to access the system to administer medications, and then to scan barcodes on the patient identification bands and the medication packages. This system is designed to eliminate medication errors in the hospital. Basically, without a badge a nurse cannot administer any medications. If a nurse forgets the badge or loses it, the human resources (HR) department can issue a new badge. Carol frequently forgets her badge and has had to go to HR two times in the past several months to have a new badge made. She was told that if she loses or forgets her badge again, her nurse manager would be notified and a disciplinary action would be initiated. Today, Carol was in a hurry to get to work and she once more leaves her badge at home. When she arrives at work, she discovers that she is assigned to be the medication nurse for the evening. Susan, Carol's best friend, also happens to be working the same shift, so Carol asks her if she can use her badge for the night so she does not get in trouble. Susan agrees and feels that it should not be a problem because her assigned duties for the shift do not include administering medications.

This scenario obviously has several important issues associated with it, and illustrates how technological changes designed to improve safety can still be subject to inappropriate uses and work-arounds. What happens if Carol makes an error, such as omitting a medication? In essence, Susan would be reported as having made the error. What if Carol has addiction problems and diverted medications from patients to herself? Again, the record of Susan's barcode scan would indicate that she had accessed the medications. There are also clear professional ethics and nursing practice law violations on the part of both Carol and Susan. It is also entirely possible that no patients were harmed and that the medications were administered without adverse incident and no one would be the wiser. The practice of borrowing a digital identity from another practitioner may be more common than we would like to believe. Sharing passwords, accessing records inappropriately, forgetting to log off of a system, and misplacing handheld devices containing sensitive patient information are all examples of issues associated with the integration of technology into the healthcare environment. On the other hand, technology integration is always evolving and has many potential benefits in improving quality, safety, and efficiency of healthcare delivery as we will discover in this chapter. Clearly, our students need to be prepared to use technology appropriately and to apply professional practice standards and ethics to this use.

Historical Overview

First, a stroll through healthcare history is necessary in order to understand how healthcare has changed and continues to evolve, and to identify the forces driving these changes. Ryan (1991) recalls that in the early 1950s, homes of patients were the most frequent site of healthcare delivery and only the sickest people or the dying were hospitalized. Most of the cost of health care was paid out of pocket. The Medicare and Medicaid programs established in 1966 provided a clear stream of income for hospitals as they were reimbursed for providing health care under these programs. Ryan (1991) suggests that these programs with their "open checkbooks" promoted the explosion of costs in the healthcare industry. In an effort to mandate cost containment (since voluntary efforts had failed miserably), **diagnosis-related groups** (DRGs) were established in 1984 to provide a payment threshold for reimbursement based on medical diagnosis. This program motivated hospitals to reduce stays and thus expenses: hospitals were reimbursed based on a fixed cost associated with the diagnosis, and early discharges resulted in lower expenditures and thus promoted profits. Diagnostic technologies also expanded exponentially and promoted fierce competition among hospitals to have the most and the best. As Ryan suggests, hospital workers did not always have clear directions for the appropriate use of these technologies, which further increased healthcare expenditures. Ryan concludes by noting that hospitals will need to focus more on community-based care and prevention as ways of delivering cost-effective health care.

Kilpatrick and Holsclaw (1996) suggest that the managed care policies enacted to curtail skyrocketing costs grew out of the efforts to make health care more businesslike. This in turn sparked competition among hospitals, the proliferation of hospitals, and the race to secure the best technology. Kilpatrick and Holsclaw also note that healthcare change was driven by increasing diversity and age of the population, increasing consumer responsibility and control over personal health, and new technology. Furthermore, they cite the increasing complexity of organizations, especially the trend toward mergers of healthcare providers and the shifting emphasis toward primary care and early intervention as important trends shaping healthcare transformation. The interesting paradox is that the proliferation of hospitals and the race to secure the best technologies for patient care resulted in not only increasing costs, but also poorer health outcomes for patients. Health care became fragmented as patients were shuffled from one specialist to another, services and tests were duplicated, and the quality of care declined because there was no efficient way to manage patient information and communication among various healthcare providers. As Clancy (2006, para. 5) posed, "How do we take a fractured system . . . keep up with scientific developments . . . and turn hundreds of millions of individual decisions into more value for the health care dollar?"

Transformation of Health Care

Health information technology has been advocated by many as the key to transforming health care (Brailer, 2005; Clancy, 2006; Eckman, Bennett, Kaufmann, & Tenner, 2007; Shortliffe, 2005). However, there has been some resistance to adopting these information management technologies. Part of the resistance stems from reluctance on the part of healthcare workers to change the way they work. Some view the information technologies as too disruptive, too time consuming, or too difficult to learn (Coye & Kell, 2006), while others view technology as dehumanizing and believe that it interferes with patient–provider relationships (Shortliffe, 2005). The challenge for healthcare providers is

> how to leverage the evolving technology and communications infrastructure in a way that is cost-effective; that supports health promotion, clinical care, and biomedical research; and that recognizes and encourages the development of standards and of the cultural change that will be required. (Shortliffe, 2005, para. 6).

Moehr and Grant (2000) suggest that there are several root technologies that can be identified as seminal to the development of current healthcare technologies. One of the first is in the computerized administrative functions of healthcare institutions. The development of systems to manage the business of hospitals and their accounting, payroll, and inventory functions eventually led to the development of the current business management and **admission, discharge, and transfer** (ADT) systems prevalent today. A second technology identified by Moehr and Grant was the development of **MEDLINE** out of the National Library of Medicine, thus improving the efficiency of medical literature distribution. This online access to scientific medical information led to the development of the current emphasis on evidence-based practice for all healthcare professionals. Early **population registries** designed to trace the incidence and prevalence of certain diseases (e.g., cancer or diabetes) have evolved into extensive **databases** central to the management of **population health** and are supportive of **data mining** and clinical research functions in modern health care. One of the first direct clinical uses of computer technology was for reporting laboratory results, followed closely by the development of computer-based diagnostic imaging functions such as **computerized tomography** (CT) scans and **magnetic**

resonance imaging (MRI). At about the same time, the computerization of **biosignals**, such as **electrocardiogram** (ECG or EKG) and brain waves (EEG), was becoming popular as intensive care units expanded in sophistication and monitoring equipment could acquire, interpret, and communicate complex biosignals (Moehr & Grant, 2000). While providers invested heavily in technology for clinical monitoring and diagnostic tools, many systems still managed information on paper, a largely inefficient and error-prone system (Eckman *et al.*, 2007). As Leichter, Gingrich, Linn, Butler, and Griggs (2006, p. 149) point out, "The current 20th century system on which we still rely is provider centered, price driven, knowledge disconnected and disease focused."

The next logical step in this evolution of healthcare technology was to link these technology systems together and shift from a fragmented diagnostic- and treatment-function focus to a **patient-centered approach**. Unfortunately the development of such integration was hampered by the fact that many of these early systems were incompatible with other systems; that is, they lacked **interoperability**. Systems had been adopted piecemeal without any consideration for how they might be used in the future. In addition, when hospitals merged there was little or no interoperability between systems, requiring some employees to learn a completely new system in order to do their jobs. Brailer (2005) emphasizes that substantial savings, perhaps as much as $77 billion annually, could be realized if patient information were able to be shared seamlessly across health care settings by using a standardized record along with hardware and software that support portability of information between and among health delivery sites.

Recognizing the need for improved patient safety, reduction in healthcare costs, and the need for seamless information exchange, in 2004 President Bush called for the development and implementation of the **electronic health record** (EHR) for all Americans by 2014. The US healthcare system is making progress on this goal. The Institute of Medicine (IOM, 2003) defined the eight essential components of an electronic health record as: (1) individual patient health information and data tools (information collected about a patient's health status), (2) **results management tools** (electronic collection of data and the integration of lab test results and biosignal monitoring), (3) **order entry management tools** (designed to reduce medication errors related to handwritten or misinterpreted orders), (4) **decision support tools** (computer reminders and alerts for intervention and direct links to **clinical guidelines** and evidence for practice), (5) electronic communication and connectivity tools (promoting collaboration and seamless communication of essential information among health team members and patients), (6) patient support tools (telemonitoring, education, and self-monitoring tools), (7) administrative processing tools (billing, scheduling, insurance validation, acuity functions), and (8) a reporting and population health management component (data collection and dissemination tools for incidence and prevalence of disease processes and **biosurveillance** and to provide databases with opportunities for data mining and clinical research).

A View of the Future

Leichter *et al.*, (2006) describe an intelligent health system for the 21st century with three essential components: the system must be individual centered where people have knowledge, incentives, and power to make choices; the system must have information technology that allows for secure sharing of data and provides access to expert systems that can analyze costs, quality, and outcomes of care; and the system must focus on prevention, wellness, self-management, and best practices.

Sachs (2005) predicts changes in health care that are likely to occur in the next 2 decades as health information is digitized. As he notes, interactions between industries and the consumer has changed in banking, commerce, and transportation as digitized devices and activities like ATMs, credit card use, online shopping, and Internet searches for airline tickets have become more commonplace. Sachs imagines similar shifts in consumer interaction will occur in health care. The use of EHRs and the increase in information exchange across **regional health information organizations** (RHIOs) will produce changes in quality, safety, benchmarking, and efficiency of healthcare delivery. Sachs also predicts that the large multiservice hospitals will give way to smaller specialty facilities organized to treat specific diseases. Decentralized care can be easily supported in a system where information flows freely among providers and the patient. Genetic testing will help to make treatment approaches more personalized and lead to better matching between disease and medical intervention. In addition, point-of-care technologies allow for rapid and appropriate intervention prior to transport to a health facility. Quality and safety issues previously associated with poor information access and exchange during patient transfers among facilities and hand-offs within facilities could be virtually eliminated in the new system.

> We are rapidly approaching an era where the size of a health system will be gauged not by the number of buildings on its campus but by its ability to move petabytes of data to the right people at the right time. (Sachs, 2005, p. 12)

Ela, Lang, and Lundeen (2006) describe the development of a partnership between nurse educators, nurse administrators, and an information technology company to develop a nursing knowledge system designed to support clinical decision making. "The initiative provides a model and venue for identifying, synthesizing, and embedding knowledge into intelligent information systems to enhance clinical decision making and improve nurse-sensitive outcomes for patients in all venues of care" (Ela *et al.*, 2006, p. 44). In addition to clinical decision support systems, various clinical information systems and electronic health records, nurses will increasingly use various interfaces including wearable technology and wireless handheld technologies in practice (Garrett & Klein, 2008; Hardwick, Pulido, & Adelson, 2007).

Implications for Nurse Educators

The previous discussion of the forces and trends driving the transformation of the healthcare system has clear implications for the education of nurses and other healthcare providers. Information technology as an integral part of clinical practice is here to stay, and the technologies will continue to evolve and impact clinical practice. While we cannot hope to train our students on every possible technology, we can help them develop transferable skills and appropriate attitudes toward technology that will serve them well for years to come.

Billings (2008, p. 51) suggests that using technology as a teaching/learning tool is essential to building transferable knowledge for clinical applications: "Thoughtfully designed real-world learning activities that use applied didactic content, require critical synthesis of information, and result in clinical decision making are needed." Billings (2008) also emphasizes the need to carefully select clinical facilities where students have full access to clinical information systems including databases, EHRs, and **telehealth** applications. In addition, curricula need to be evaluated and transformed to ensure that nursing students are meeting **informatics competencies**.

An obvious first step is basic **computer literacy** and keyboarding skills, although future advances in voice input devices may render keyboards essentially obsolete. We need to make certain that our students are well supported and understand change theory when learning new technologies so that they will develop enthusiasm, not resistance, to change. We may also want to encourage the use of handheld technology with easy access to clinical practice guidelines and medication databases. We need to shift the curricular emphasis from covering specific content and testing with multiple choice to access and application of appropriate knowledge to well designed and challenging clinical scenarios in simulation laboratories (see Chapter 14). In fact, we may need to push for reform in the licensing of nurses as the NCLEX licensing examination may not truly reflect the skills necessary for practice in a transformed healthcare system.

In addition to computer literacy, our students must understand **information literacy**, that is, how to secure and evaluate resources and how to apply knowledge to practice. Consumers and consequently our patients are increasingly empowered by the use of information technologies to research symptoms and diseases (Moehr & Grant, 2000) and nurses must be prepared to help patients find and evaluate appropriate resources. Patients are also participating in online support groups and **clinical blogs** related to their diagnoses. These activities help them develop a sense of control over healthcare choices as they expand their knowledge about their health and identify ways to manage their health issues.

We need to help our students see the big picture and help them appreciate how the new technologies change **workflow** and contribute to quality and safety in health care (Kirkley & Stein, 2004). In addition, we need to be certain that our students are well prepared in the ethical and legal aspects of healthcare technology use. They must understand the risks and threats to the security of private health information and they must commit to appropriate access and use of information, as described in the opening scenario of this chapter.

Practicing professionals and nursing faculty must also embrace and model acceptance of new and ever evolving technologies. While many states require continuing education for relicensure, there is little or no self-assessment of learning needs associated with these activities. We need to focus our continuing education experiences on those informatics competencies and skills that we are lacking so that we are also well prepared to practice in the transformed healthcare system.

Learning Activities

1. Access the nursing informatics competencies Web site (http://www.nursing-informatics.com/niassess/index.html) and perform a self-assessment of your competencies.

2. Develop a continuing education plan to acquire the skills and competencies you will need to teach students to practice in a transformed healthcare system.

3. In a group of faculty colleagues, identify the pros and cons of the multiple choice NCLEX test and brainstorm a new approach for licensing new graduates as registered nurses.

References

Billings, D. M. (2008). Quality care, patient safety, and the focus on technology. *Journal of Nursing Education, 47*(2), 51–52.

Brailer, D. (2005). Economic perspectives on health information technology. *Business Economics, 40*(3), 6–14.

Bush, G. W. Address before a joint session of the Congress on the state of the union, January 20, 2004. Available at: http://frwebgate.access.gpo.gov/cgi-bin/getdoc.cgi?dbname=2004_presidential_documents&docid=pd26ja04_txt-10. Accessed October 27, 2009.

Clancy, C. (2006, March 23). *Health information technology and health care transformation* (Remarks). eHealth Connecticut Inaugural Summit, Farmington, CT. Available at: http://www.ahrq.gov/news/sp032306.htm. Accessed October 27, 2009.

Coye, M. J., & Kell, J. (2006). How hospitals confront new technology. *Health Affairs, 25*(1), 163–173.

Eckman, B., Bennett, C., Kaufman, J., & Tenner, J. (2007). Varieties of interoperability in the transformation of the health-care information infrastructure. *IBM Systems Journal, 46*(1), 19–41.

Ela, S., Lang, N., & Lundeen, S. (2006). Time for a nursing legacy: ensuring excellence through actionable knowledge. *Nurse Leader, 4*(6), 42.

Garrett, B., & Klein, G. (2008). Value of wireless personal digital assistants for practice: Perceptions of advanced practice nurses. *Journal of Clinical Nursing, 17*(16), 2146.

Hardwick, M. E., Pulido, P. A., & Adelson, W. S. (2007). The use of handheld technology in nursing research and practice. *Orthopaedic Nursing, 26*(4), 251–255.

Institute of Medicine. (2003). *Key capabilities of an electronic health record system: Letter report.* Washington, DC: National Academies Press.

Kilpatrick, A., & Holsclaw, P. (1996). Health care in the new millennium: Implications for executives and managers. *Public Administration Quarterly, 20*(3), 365–380.

Kirkley, D., & Stein, M. (2004). Nurses and clinical technology: Sources of resistance and strategies for acceptance. *Nursing Economics, 22*(4), 195, 216–222.

Leichter, S., Gingrich, N., Linn, L., Butler, B., & Griggs, S. (2006). The Columbus program: Building a community model of a 21st century intelligent health system. *Clinical Diabetes, 24*(4), 149–152.

Moehr, J. R., & Grant, A. (2000). Medical informatics and medical education in Canada in the 21st century. *Clinical and Investigative Medicine, 23*(4), 275–280.

Ryan, J. (1991). The changing American hospital: back to the future. *Hospital Material Management Quarterly, 12*, 3.

Sachs, M. (2005). Transforming the health system from the inside out. *Frontiers of Health Services Management, 22*(2), 3–12.

Shortliffe, E. (2005). Strategic action in health information technology: Why the obvious has taken so long. *Health Affairs, 24*(5), 1222–1233.

CHAPTER 3

The Changing Student:
The Net Generation

Food For Thought

*"One mark of a great educator
is the ability to lead students out to new places
where even the educator has never been."*

Thomas Groome

Key Words

Brain plasticity	Kinetic learning	Net Generation
Digital divide	Millennials	Tweets
Generation Y	Neo-millennials	Twitter

Objectives

The educator will be able to distinguish the key differences between the Net
   Generation and previous generations.
The educator will be able to identify the characteristics of the Net Generation.
The educator will be able to explain the Net Generation's view of technology.
The educator will be able to describe the best instructional strategies to use with the
   Net Generation.

27

The educator will be able to define the digital divide, and explain how its meaning has changed over the last 10 years.
The educator will be able to describe the characteristics of the next generation, the Neo-millennials.

Introduction

Madison is an undergraduate nursing student. Over the holiday break, she is flying home to visit her family and friends. After the plane takes off, Madison reaches into her carry-on bag, and pulls out her notebook from her Nursing Theory course and a digital recorder, which she had used to record the instructor's lecture. She puts in her earplugs and goes through the notes she took in class, making corrections and filling in missing information in her notebook. After an hour, Madison puts the digital recorder and notebook away, and pulls out her iPod. She puts in her earbuds, shifts to a comfortable position in her seat, and nods off to sleep as she listens to music. Madison is awakened later on by the pilot's announcement to put all electronic devices away. She places her iPod in her bag and waits for the plane to land. Once permitted, Madison pulls out her phone from her purse, and calls her parents to make arrangements for them to pick her up outside the terminal. She then text messages her hometown friends to confirm meeting up with them later that evening. Finally, she text messages her boyfriend to let him know that she has arrived safely. While waiting for her baggage, Madison accesses **Twitter** from her phone to see what her friends back at school are doing. She **tweets** as well, indicating how excited she is to be back in her hometown.

Today, due to advances in technology, students are rarely on their own. They can contact their parents, friends, classmates, and instructors anytime and anywhere by using cell phones, texting, IMing, or e-mailing. They make friends through social networks like Facebook and MySpace. They let their friends know where they are and what they are doing using applications like Twitter or Loopt. They voice their opinions using the comment feature on blogs, message boards, and retail shopping sites. They can also access all kinds of information on the Internet using search engines like Google or specialized sites like Wikipedia and WebMD. In addition, they can stay home and access most journal articles online through their university's library system, or use a search engine like GoogleScholar.com or PubMed.gov.

This generation of students is known as the **Net Generation**. They are also referred to as **Generation Y** (because they followed Generation X) or **Millennials**. Technologies like the Internet and cell phone have been around since they were born (Oblinger & Oblinger, 2005), and they incorporate the technologies into their lives like those of us from older generations incorporated the radio or television.

In this chapter, we will look at the Net Generation's characteristics, their use of technology, how they learn, and what faculty can do to enhance the Net Generation's learning experience.

Net Generation Characteristics

The Net Generation has created a lot of buzz because they possess a number of unique characteristics that are the combined result of their upbringing and an easy access to technology. It might first be beneficial to compare the Net Generation to other generations, to get a sense of how different they are and why. It is important to note that each generation is shaped by world circumstances as well as how they and their families are personally affected by these events.

The oldest living generation, known as the Veterans, was born before 1946. Families in this generation experienced war and tough economic times, and were accustomed to making sacrifices. Their employers were typically bureaucratic organizations that had a distinct hierarchical structure. Employees were rewarded with promotions for hard work and dedication, and most people tended to stay with only one company their entire lives. As a result, this generation is patient, values hard work and loyalty, and has tremendous respect for authority. (Hart, 2008)

Members of the Baby Boomer generation were born between 1946 and 1964. This generation was wealthier than past generations, had strong family values, and a solid work ethic. Typically, the father was the breadwinner and the mother stayed at home to raise the children. Thus, the families who raised the Baby Boomer generation were stable, intact, and provided a supportive environment. The economy was strong during the time and one income provided a comfortable, middle-class lifestyle. As a result of these circumstances, members of this generation are responsible, optimistic, and tend to be workaholics (Oblinger & Oblinger, 2005).

Individuals in the next generation, Generation X, were born between 1965 and 1980. Generation X got its name from Douglas Coupland's book, *Generation*

X: Tales for an Accelerated Culture. They are products of divorced Baby Boomers. Since many mothers had to now work, Generation X children were known as latch-key kids, who came home from school to empty houses and minimal supervision (Hart, 2008). Instead of getting support from their families, they found it with their peers. They also experienced tough economic times; some were unable to find jobs following college graduation. This generation became known as slackers, unable to find their way in life. They took too long to grow up and become responsible adults. They are distrustful of their employer due to their experiences with downsizing and layoffs, so they value a balance between work and their personal life. Their characteristics include being independent, adaptable, and skeptical (Oblinger & Oblinger, 2005)

The Net Generation was born approximately between 1980 and 1995. They are the children of Baby Boomers who grew up in more prosperous times and had the financial means to raise a stable family, with some being born to older mothers or single mothers who used advanced fertility treatments (Howe & Strauss, 2000). Although divorce was still prevalent, it carried less of a stigma than it did in previous times, and parents were more likely to have joint custody and be actively involved in their children's day-to-day lives (Howe & Strauss, 2000). Unlike any previous generation, the Net Generation has been provided with numerous opportunities due to their family's support and financial stability, the availability of school and sports programs, and access to a multitude of technologies. Parents enroll their children in many activities, serve as coaches, manage their schedules, and provide support and encouragement.

Due to their parent's involvement, the Net Generation has many of the same characteristics as Baby Boomers, including having a positive view of life, being go-getters, and valuing family. Having a close, protective relationship with their parents has also resulted in some unique characteristics including being more sheltered, having a feeling of being special, setting high goals for themselves, and feeling pressured to study hard and do well (Howe & Strauss, 2000). The term "helicopter parents" has become popular in recent years due to the tendency of Baby Boomer parents to interfere in the lives of their children, in both school and job-related matters.

Parents, however, have not been the only influence over the Net Generation. This generation has grown up in a world where technology is an everyday part of their life, and has never known of a world where everyone is not connected. They routinely use computers, cell phones, and the Internet; technology is what they use to accomplish everyday tasks. These individuals, however, are not skilled in programming, troubleshooting, or fixing technology, just like members of earlier generations, generally cannot repair a television or program a VCR. To the Net Generation, technology is simply an ordinary means to communicate and socialize with others, get information, and complete school- or work-related assignments.

The unique childhood experience of the Net Generation has resulted in a number of traits that define this generation and impact their interactions with the world. These include being social and socially and politically aware, as well as having a preference for multitasking, visual/**kinetic learning**, and learning through trial and error.

Members of the Net Generation are highly social. Having been active in extracurricular activities from an early age, these individuals have learned to socialize with others and to be a member of a team. In addition, having access to multiple technologies, they have the opportunity to communicate with family and friends like none of the generations have in the past. They can contact those closest to them at any time and from anywhere. In addition, they are able to meet and make friends through other friends, interest groups, or networks, using social networks like Facebook or MySpace. This generation can also share their opinions through social rating sites like Digg, post their comments on blogs or online news articles, give feedback on videos posted to YouTube, and inform other consumers about the quality of items bought on retail sites like Amazon.

The Net Generation's friendships can be with people they know face-to-face or have met only virtually through social networking sites. Members of this generation have a tendency to share more intimate details with their virtual friends (and the public) that would make older generations cringe. For example, a popular blog by a nursing student included descriptions of her day-to-day duties in a nursing home interspersed with entries describing the horror she felt when her first patient died and doubts she was feeling about her fiancé and their upcoming nuptials.

Members of the Net Generation are also more socially conscious than generations past. Their involvement in extracurricular activities, easy access to information, and their ability to connect to people all over their world have made them socially and politically aware, as well as motivated about making a difference in the world. This is especially evident in the 2008 presidential election, where, according to The Center for Information and Research on Civic Learning and Engagement (CIRCLE) Web site, youth voter turnout rose to 23 million voters under the age of 30, up 3.4 million voters from the 2004 election ("Turnout by Education, Race and Gender and Other 2008 Youth Voting Statistics," 2008).

Due to using multiple technologies as they go about their day, the Net Generation has become experts at multitasking. They can go anywhere, let their friends know where they are, and instantly have conversations using a cell phone or text messaging. They are not big television watchers but tend instead to use it as background noise as they perform other tasks (Tapscott, 2008). Unfortunately, their tendency to multitask and keep themselves busy has led to short attention spans in the classroom and an aversion to reading. This often results in surface rather than in-depth learning and a lack of reflection on what they have been exposed to through lectures or reading (Tapscott, 2008). In addition, due to texting, using IM, Twitter (with a 140 character limit), and Facebook commenting features, this generation has developed a unique shorthand language, one that does not follow proper English usage, spelling, or grammar. Thus their literacy may be not as developed as compared to other generations (Oblinger & Oblinger, 2005).

Instead, the Net Generation has a preference for visual and kinetic learning. This means that they prefer to learn by looking at information in visual form such as graphics, videos, or animations. They also prefer hands-on learning where they are able to physically participate in an activity or act it out. The Net Generation has been exposed to video games with sophisticated and realistic graphics, enabling gamers to develop good visual-spatial abilities as they maneuver through virtual worlds. The use of sophisticated handheld controllers has allowed them to develop good hand-eye coordination and to experience such things as the jarring vibrations of a race car. The Wii, a gaming system produced by Nintendo in 2006, requires participants to physically move with the controllers, further enhancing the gaming experience, especially for kinetic learners.

In addition to gaming, the Net Generation is constantly being exposed to more intuitive technologies. The user-friendly and visually appealing features of the iPhone's touch screen is just one example. Learning through trial and error has never been easier. Thus, members of the Net Generation prefer to try things without reading instructions first, and they expect to receive immediate feedback to their actions.

The Net Generation and Educational Technology

The differences in the generations can also be observed by comparing educational technologies. Table 3-1 compares educational technologies by generation.

Note that the emerging technologies can be viewed on a continuum, from most passive (radio) to most engaged (simulations). The Veterans and the Baby Boomers experienced learning through passive listening and viewing, only interacting when called upon by the instructor. This supported the "sage on stage" role of the instructor which reflected views of respect for authority of those generations. The invention of the personal computer and CD-ROM in the 1980s led to more active learning, but generally in the form of "drill and practice" exercises (Reiser & Dempsey, 2002).

The incorporation of technologies into education has always been difficult. The instructional television movement of the 1950s had failed and the initial

Table 3-1   Instructional Technologies by Decade and Generation

Year	Instructional Technology	Veterans	Baby Boomers	Generation X	Net Generation
1930	Radio	X	X		
1940	Films and filmstrips, Overhead & slide projectors, Audio equipment	X	X	X	
1950	Instructional television	X	X	X	
1960	Public television		X	X	
1970	VCR		X	X	
1980	Personal computer, CD-ROM		X	X	X
1990	Internet, DVD, E-mail, Distance learning			X	X
2000	LMS, Web 2.0, Smart phone, PDA,GPS, Immersive environments				X

use of computers in schools was ineffective. Today, recent technologies are being used in higher education, but mainly by more innovative instructors and not always in a pedagogically sound way. As in the past, adopting technology for educational use has been slow and inefficient, with a tendency to attempt to fit the new technology into the old, traditional way of teaching, leading to blogs that act as message boards and videos of "talking heads." Although more students are being exposed to technology in the higher education environment, they are not using the Internet, personal devices, and Web 2.0 tools at the same level as they use them personally, with their peers.

It is this inability of educators to use technology in the same way as the Net Generation that has led to concerns about the effectiveness of education voiced in both the educational community and in the media. This gap between the generations may be leading to students feeling isolated and unchallenged in classrooms, from kindergarten through to the university.

The Net Generation and Instructional Strategies

Not only does the Net Generation use technology differently than previous generations, but their frequent use of technology, starting at a very early age, may also be changing how they learn due to a phenomenon called **brain plasticity**. Brain plasticity can be defined as the brain's capacity to reorganize its structure and function based on experiences over a lifetime (Kolb, Gibb, & Robinson, 2003). Unlike what was previously thought, the brain can continue to physically change as a result of stimuli received from outside experiences during adolescence and adulthood (Prensky, 2001b).

Unlike all other generations, members of the Net Generation are being exposed to and engaged with large amounts of information and virtual experiences through advances in technology, especially video games. This takes place especially during their teenage years, a time when the brain is undergoing restructuring and is particularly sensitive to outside experiences (Tapscott, 2008). As a result, it is believed that the Net Generation thinks and processes information differently from previous generations, and so traditional instructional methods may no longer be effective (Prensky, 2001a)

Educators therefore need to find new strategies to enhance learning for the Net Generation. No longer can the professor be the "sage on stage" who dominates the classroom with lectures that may range from 1 to 3 hours in length.

This method simply results in students losing interest and instead finding ways to connect: listen to their mp3 players, text message a friend, check e-mail, play games, or browse Facebook (Pardue & Morgan, 2008). As more campuses become wireless and students have access to laptops and mobile devices in the classroom, the struggle to gain students' attention and motivate them to learn in a traditional setting may become ever more difficult.

When developing instructional strategies, educators must consider the characteristics of the Net Generation. This generation is social, therefore, providing opportunities for collaboration is extremely important. Group activities and assignments in traditional and online courses can be enhanced using Web 2.0 technologies such as Google docs (which allows users to create, share, and edit documents), Gliffy (which allows users to create, share, and edit diagrams), and Ning (which allows users to communicate on an instructor-created social network). Web 2.0 tools will be covered more in depth in Chapter 12.

To capitalize on the Net Generation's ability to socialize equally well both in person and online, educators may also want to consider using a blended or hybrid course, where face-to-face and online components are combined. This format will give students more flexibility, greater opportunities for hands-on learning, and access to online resources. A benefit of a blended or hybrid course over an online course is the opportunity for the instructor to discuss the course format in detail with the students, emphasizing expectations for the students and the need for good time management skills (Martyn, 2003). Since most members of the generation grew up in an environment where adults planned and coordinated school and extracurricular activities, providing structure for them is extremely important (Pardue & Morgan, 2008). The blended format also allows faculty to address the needs of diverse learners; nontraditional students and students lacking technical skills will benefit from face-to-face guidance about the online technologies used in the blended course (Skiba & Barton, 2006).

Due to the Net Generation's aversion to reading and preference for visual information, instructors should be cognizant of text-heavy PowerPoint slides or online materials. Instead, graphs, diagrams, and flow charts should be used where appropriate, and text should be listed or bulleted to allow for easy reading. Related to this, careful attention should be given to developing online instructions for the course syllabus and activities (Wilson, 2004). Since this generation prefers to learn through trial and error rather than reading instructions, only the most pertinent information should be included in the syllabus in an uncomplicated layout. Instructions for activities should be brief, structured, and to the point, and be placed within the activity as opposed to in the syllabus or in the lesson overview.

To motivate students, instructors should use authentic learning tasks and assessments. Authentic learning tasks require individuals to do activities or create projects that are similar to what they would do if employed in the "real world." To address the kinetic learning preference of the Net Generation, instructors may want to design activities where students can physically participate in the learning experience (for instance, role plays or simulations). In assessing students, instructors may want to incorporate real-world projects that allow the students to use hands-on, technical skills such as creating a marketing video, developing a blog on a related topic, or creating a political interest group on a social networking site.

In addition to the above, instructors must remember that the Net Generation expects immediate feedback. So whatever instructional strategy is used, it is important to build in timely feedback to reduce frustration. The feedback should also provide some structure, including suggestions on how students can improve their performance.

The Digital Divide

While there is much talk about the connectedness of the Net Generation, those who are of lower socioeconomic status or minority groups may be overlooked. Not all members of the Net Generation own a new computer, have Internet access, or are technologically savvy.

The term **digital divide** addresses the separation between the "have" and "have nots" in terms of access to technology. This issue was first addressed in the 1990s, when the Federal government put some incentives into action to close the divide, including low-cost Internet connections for public facilities, funds to expand in-home access to computers for low-income families, and tax incentives to companies that donated computer and technical training (Marriott, 2006). These programs along with decreased pricing and the availability of refurbished computers have enabled more of the US population than ever before to own some type of computer (Hawkins & Oblinger, 2006). Even a low-income family making less than $25,000 a year can own a computer, if they see value in having one (Horrigan, 2008). In fact, since 1999, the increase in in-home Internet access has been highest among children and adolescents of minorities and of low socioeconomic levels than from any other group (Rideout, Roberts, & Foehr, 2005, p. 32).

In the past, the digital divide focused almost exclusively on computer ownership and Internet access, however, Hawkins and Oblinger (2006) indicate that examination of the digital divide should be extended to include the following five factors:

1. Machine vintage: The age of the computer, which impacts processing speed and memory;
2. Autonomy and freedom of access: The ability to access a computer 24/7 which may be impeded if the computer must be shared with family members or roommates, or is located in a public setting such as a library or university computer lab;
3. Connectivity: The speed in which the user can access the Internet, determined by the type of connection (dial up or broadband);
4. Online skills: The ability of an individual to effectively search, locate, and use online information; and
5. Computer-use support: The availability of a help desk or peer experts to assist individuals with questions about technology use, new technologies, and technical difficulties.

Thus, the digital divide no longer applies solely to computer ownership but to the quality of Internet access and the skills at using online resources (Marriott, 2006). Based on a survey of freshman at a midsized university, Cotton and Jelenewicz (2006) found that once college students began using the Internet for their assignments and other activities, factors such as race and prior Internet experience became insignificant, leading the authors to conclude that if access and support are provided in a university setting, the digital divide may be further decreased or eliminated.

This conclusion is supported by the results of the ECAR Study of Undergraduate Students and Information Technology (Caruso & Salaway, 2008), which surveyed 27,317 freshmen, seniors, and community college students at 98 universities and colleges in the United States. Results of the survey found that more than 80% of students own laptops, almost 54% own desktops, and 33% own both a laptop and a desktop. Of those who owned computers, 71% owned a laptop that was less than 1 year old, and almost 69% owned a computer that was 2 years old or less. Also of note, 66% owned an Internet-capable cell phone, almost 80% considered themselves able to use the Internet to efficiently search for information, and 40 to 59% agree that their college or university's IT services are always available for help.

Educators must be aware that some form of digital divide continues to exist despite all the advances in technology. The university, however, offers a resource-rich environment where incoming students, especially those who are from low-income families and certain minority groups, can have access to technology and support services, plus take advantage of programs that will allow them catch up with their peers' online skills.

It may be advantageous for faculty, especially those who teach at an undergraduate level, to survey their students at the beginning of the semester about their current skills and recommend appropriate training resources to those who need it.

Looking Ahead: Neo-Millennials

Although most educators are still struggling to adjust to the learning styles and preferences of the Net Generation, they must prepare themselves for a greater challenge. Students born after the year 1995 will soon be entering college classrooms. This generation is known as **Neo-millennials** (from the prefix neo, meaning "new", and the term "millennial", referring to the new millennium in which they will grow up) (Sankey, 2006).

Neo-millennials use immersive environments and augmented reality in addition to the world-to-desktop interface that the Net Generation uses (Dede, 2005, p. 1). This newest generation is no longer just an observer or user of technology, but rather a participant in technology. They create avatars of themselves to visit different online places and interact with people from all over the world. These unique and exciting environments permit the psychological sensation of sensory and physical immersion where it is possible to feel physically present rather than watching from the outside (Dede, 2005).

Thus, like their predecessors, the Neo-millennials will be social, but instead of interacting asynchronously with friends on Facebook, this generation will interact synchronously with other people's personalized avatars using a chat feature or talking into a headset. In online games like World of Warcraft or virtual environments like Second Life, individuals explore and play in realistic environments where they come into contact with other individuals, who may be team members, deadly enemies, potential friends, or just a stranger that they pass on the street.

Due to early exposure to these virtual, immersive environments, Neo-millennials are accustomed to exploring new environments based on what interests them or what catches their attention. As a result, they are global rather than sequential learners. Global learners learn when presented with pieces of information that they can absorb and then suddenly understand as a whole, whereas sequential learners learn through information that is presented in a logical, step-by-step fashion (Felder & Soloman, 1993). Unlike previous generations, Neo-millennials will not read instructional materials from top to bottom and left to right; instead, they will prefer to look at the content as a whole, and click on whatever they find most interesting (Willems, 2008).

In addition, Neo-millennials place value on knowing how to find information rather than actually knowing information because they are accustomed to having instant access to online resources, and they can freely interact with people, even experts, from all over the world (Aggerholm, 2006).

Keeping the characteristics of the Neo-millennials in mind, educators will need to make adjustments in the way they present instruction. Specifically, the content should incorporate various types of media, utilize conceptual graphics in place of large amounts of text, and be organized in a manner that allows the learner to choose a starting point and path of exploration (Willems, 2008; Dede, 2005). Educators who are more comfortable with gaming and technology may also want to create activities using free immersive environments like Second Life.

Summary

The Net Generation is the product of more highly educated and involved parents, strong financial stability, and advanced technologies. They have more opportunities than past generations, and as a result, have unique characteristics that are now challenging the traditional ways of teaching and learning. The ability to connect with others and access information from anywhere, along with exposure to videos, simulations, and games, has resulted in students who are extremely social, have shorter attention spans, prefer to multitask, have kinetic and visual learning styles, and who require immediate feedback.

Educators need to be aware that students think and process information differently from previous generations. Although it is not necessary to completely abandon traditional methods of teaching, educators can take steps to incorporate instructional strategies that address the needs of the new generation. In addition, educators must be aware that not all members of the Net Generation have access to the latest technologies or the skills needed to use them. Although the digital divide is narrowing, it still exists, and the higher education environment must continue to offer resources to assist students.

Learning Activities

Pick a simple topic in nursing, such as how to measure blood pressure. First, develop a traditional instructor-led lesson plan. Next, revise the lesson plan so that it is more suitable for a Net Generation audience. Finally, answer the following questions:

- What changes did you make in the traditional lesson plan to make it more suitable for the Net Generation?
- Would you do anything different for an audience of Neo-millennials?
- Is creating instruction for the new generation easier or more difficult? Why?

Get a group of students from your class together and join Twitter or Facebook. Add each other as friends. Provide updates to one another over a period of one week. Reflect on the following:

- Did you enjoy this experience? Why or why not?
- As a result of this experience, do you feel as though you know the members of your group better than others in your class?
- Why do you think microblogging services like Twitter and social networks like Facebook are so popular with newer generations?

References

Aggerholm, B. (2006, April 26). Educating the next wave: Today's techno-savvy students are a challenge, but universities have not seen anything yet. *The Record*. Available at: http://www.therecord.com/links/links_06042615593.html#. Accessed April 9, 2009.

Caruso, J. B., & Salaway, G. (2008). The ECAR Study of Undergraduate Students and Information Technology, 2008. *EDUCAUSE Center for Applied Research*. Available at: http://net.educause.edu/ir/library/pdf/ekf/EKF0808.pdf. Accessed March 23, 2009.

Cotton, S.R., & Jelenewicz, S.M. (2006). A disappearing digital divide among college students? Peeling away the layers of the digital divide. *Social Science Computer Review, 24*, 497–506.

Dede, C. (2005). Planning for neomillennial learning styles: Implications for investments in technology and faculty. *EDUCAUSE Quarterly, 28*(1), 7–12.

Felder, R. M., & Soloman, B. A. (1993). *Learning styles and strategies*. Available at: http://www4 .ncsu.edu/unity/lockers/users/f/felder/public/ILSdir/styles.htm. Accessed March 30, 2009.

Hart, J. (2008). Understanding today's learner. *The eLearning Guild's Learning Solutions e-Magazine*. Available at: http://www.elearningguild.com/articles/abstracts/index .cfm?id=282&action=viewonly. Accessed March 5, 2009.

Hawkins, B. L. & Oblinger, D. G. (2006). The myth about the digital divide. *EDUCAUSE Review, 44*(4), 12–13.

Horrigan, J. B. (2008). *Home broadband adoption 2008*. Pew Internet & American Life Project. Available at: http://www.pewinternet.org/~/media//Files/Reports/2008/PIP_Broadband_ 2008.pdf. Accessed March 23, 2009.

Howe, N., & Strauss, W. (2000). *Millennials rising: The next great generation*. New York: Vintage Books.

Kolb, B., Gibb, R., & Robinson, T. E. (2003). Brain plasticity and behavior. *Current Directions in Psychological Science, 12*(1), 1–5.

Marriott, M. (2006, March 31). Digital divide closing as blacks turn to Internet. *The New York Times*. Available at: http://www.nytimes.com/2006/03/31/us/31divide.html. Accessed April 9, 2009.

Martyn, M. (2003). The hybrid online model: Good practice. *EDUCAUSE Quarterly, 26*(1), 18–23. Available at: http://www.educause.edu/ir/library/pdf/EQM0313.pdf. Accessed March 5, 2009.

Oblinger, D. & Oblinger, J. (2005). Is it age or IT: First steps to understanding the net generation. In Oblinger & Oblinger's (eds) Educating the Net Generation. Available at: http://www.educause.edu/educatingthenetgen. Accessed March 5, 2009.

Pardue, K. T., & Morgan, P. (2008). Millennials considered: A new generation, new approaches, and implications for nursing education. *Nursing Education Perspectives, 29*(2), 74–79.

Prensky, M. (2001a). Digital natives, digital immigrants. *On the Horizon, 9*(5). Available at: http://www.marcprensky.com/writing/Prensky%20-%20Digital%20Natives,%20 Digital%20Immigrants%20-%20Part1.pdf. Accessed April 9, 2009.

Prensky, M. (2001b). Digital natives, digital immigrants, part II: Do they really think differently? *On the Horizon, 9*(6). Available at: http://www.marcprensky.com/writing/ Prensky%20-%20Digital%20Natives,%20Digital%20Immigrants%20-%20Part2.pdf. Accessed April 9, 2009.

Reiser, R. A., & Dempsey, J. V. (2002). *Trends and issues in instructional design and technology*. Upper Saddle River, NJ: Merrill Prentice Hall.

Rideout, V., Roberts, D. F., & Foehr, U. G. (2005). *Generation M: Media in the lives of 8–18 year olds*. A Kaiser Family Foundation Study. Available at: http://www.kff.org/entmedia/upload/ Generation-M-Media-in-the-Lives-of-8-18-Year-olds-Report.pdf. Accessed March 30, 2009.

Sankey, M. (2006). A neomillennial learning approach: Helping non-traditional learners studying at a distance. *International Journal of Education and Development using ICT, 2*(4). Available at: http://ijedict.dec.uwi.edu/viewarticle.php?id=224&layout=html. Accessed November 5, 2009.

Skiba, D. J., & Barton, A. J. (2006). Adapting your teaching to accommodate the net generation of learners. *OJIN: The Online Journal of Issues in Nursing, 11*(2). Available at: http://www.nursingworld.org/MainMenu/Categories/ANAMarketplace/ANAPeriodicals/OJIN/TableofContents/Volume112006/No2May06/tpc30_416076.aspx. Accessed November 5, 2009.

Tapscott, D. (2008). *Grown up digital: How the net generation is changing your world.* New York: McGraw Hill.

Turnout by Education, Race and Gender and Other 2008 Youth Voting Statistics. (2008, November). *The Center for Information & Research on Civic Learning and Engagement.* Available at: http://www.civicyouth.org/?p=324. Accessed November 5, 2009.

Willems, J. (2008). *From sequential to global: Exploring the landscapes of neomillennial learners* (Proceedings). Available at: http://www.ascilite.org.au/conferences/melbourne08/procs/willems.pdf. Accessed March 30, 2009.

Wilson, M. (2004). "Teaching, Learning and Millennial Students". *New Directions for Student Services: Serving the Millennial Generation,* Summer 2004, Issue 106, 59–71.

CHAPTER 4

Changing Faculty

Food For Thought

"If you always think like you've always thought,
you'll always get what you always got."

Anonymous

Key Words

Adobe Connect
Asynchronous
Blog
Critical thinking
Digital natives
Early adopters
Emoticons
Learning community

Learning culture
Personal digital assistants (PDAs)
Podcasts
Really simple syndication (RSS)
Social presence
Synchronously
Wiki

Objectives

The educator will be able to describe the characteristics of early adopters.
The educator will be able to identify ways to enhance the learning culture using
technology.

The educator will be able to describe social presence and ways to enhance it using technology.

The educator will be able to identify the best practice principles adapted for online education.

Introduction

Delve into the world of the educator. Once we were in lecture mode or the sage on the stage and then we moved to the guide on the side. Now we are the facilitator, mentor, and knowledge resource for our students. We should be striving to form a dyad with each learner to facilitate their learning experiences. Our educational skills must be broadened to include the technological tools necessary to enhance our art: The Art of Teaching. This integration must be thoughtful, decisive, and engaging. Take a brief walk through history with us and examine the challenges we face in this volatile *knowledge era* as you learn about early adopters' characteristics, learning culture/community, social presence, and best practices.

You have just entered a time warp and you are suddenly aware that you are living about 107,000 years ago. You are carrying a club for protection, wearing some garb, and just trying to survive in your environment. There are other people living with you and in order to stay alive, you must all work together. You have learned what you know from your peers and significant others. Sometimes it is gently learned, such as being taken by the hand and shown, and other times you are sure not to forget the lesson because you received a blow to the head by another's club. You are not sure that you like this place and enter the time warp to escape. You awake to Confucius teaching a nobleman about responsibility; it is around 560 BC and just as you are becoming absorbed in the lesson, you are zapped ahead in time over 100 years to meet Socrates. You are intrigued because he asks more questions than he gives information, only interjecting bits of wisdom selectively along the way. This approach is stimulating your own critical thinking and, just as you are about to enter into the dialogue, the time warp sends you to a one room school house in Kansas and it is 1882. Their school day started at 9 AM and you note that it is now 12 PM. Students scurry about erasing the blackboard, getting wood to stoke the fire, water for drinking from the outside well, and prepare to eat lunch. The students range in age from

5 to 13 years old and there is one teacher to convey all of the information for all of the subjects such as reading, writing, and arithmetic. Just as you are about to ask how this can work, you are catapulted to the 1920s in Boston. You are a student in a school that resembles what you know as high school with boys who are 12 years and older. There seems to be a set curriculum and you hear one boy yelling because he is being paddled, you see another boy cracked over his knuckles with a ruler for not knowing the answer to a question, and you are trying to determine how they are teaching. Just as you begin to muse about this type of educational practice you become aware that you are in an elementary grade in a public school in the circa 1950s. Students are learning cursive writing by tracing and then copying each letter of the alphabet in both upper and lower case. You are beginning to fall asleep watching the students write over and over again for more than 20 minutes. As you nod off into dreamland you wake with a start as a young child bumps into your desk. It is 1986 and these kindergartners are allowed to roam about the room to experience different things and interact. You blink and land in a graduate school class in 1990 where the students are seated listening to a professor drone on and on about—you cannot remember what and you begin to wonder—how interesting that the young kindergarten children were allowed to interact, explore, and experience their environment while the graduate students were sitting still and listening. The only interaction in the graduate class came from a student asking a question. Shouldn't education engage students and make them excited about learning and develop a passion for lifelong learning? Well, enough of those thoughts, it is now 2006 and you are listening to teachers struggling with the concept of integrating technology into education. Things have evolved to the point of sophisticated instructional systems and tools being available to educators of this era but there seems to be a reluctance to use these tools. You are on a college campus where the students have Internet-capable phones, personal digital assistants (PDAs), and/or MP3 players and are tuning into everything from lectures to music to sports information as they stroll around the campus; there is a disconnect between the educators and the students. Many of the educators are technologically challenged or lack the necessary skills or support to integrate technology into their courses. Some educators have used online tools providing 24/7 availability of course materials to their learners. The quality of these materials has often been questioned. Your next stop is 2090. People are wearing more technology than we have ever thought could exist. Everything is electronically enhanced. Education

as we know it has truly changed. Can you imagine what the educational arena looks like at this time?

This stumble through educational history has shown how educational theories, philosophies, strategies, and practices have come in and out of favor throughout our history. It evidences the diversity of educational methods but at no time in our history have educators faced more challenges than they do today in light of the unprecedented technological developments we are witnessing. You ask yourself, what makes a terrific educator in this technologically explosive era? Just as you get your question out, Socrates is before you and he asks you, "what have you learned on your educational journey through the time warp and how does it relate to your current practice?" Think about the following two quotes, then use your critical thinking skills and reflect on how you would respond to him . . .

Mankind's knowledge base is now doubling in a period of less than two years.

— Peter Cochrane

There has been more information produced in the last 30 years than during the previous 5,000.

— Price Pritchett

As faculty members, nursing educators must adapt and change. Think about this quote from Lily Tomlin, *"We're all in this alone."* We have all been students and, therefore, we have all experienced teachers, some were super, some good, and some bad. All of these experiences have helped to shape who we are and how we conceptualize education. Once we assume the role of the educator, it is our experience, education, and passion that shine through. Recall your first college courses, how were they taught? Think about the latest learning episode that you have created or participated in. Is it the same or different from those initial college courses you took? Reflect on your current practice and your use of technology to enhance the educational episodes that you deliver. Do you deliver face-to-face, blended, or online learning? How do you envision these delivery methods being the same and different?

We have all experienced how fast the world seems to be moving in this information age. Where it is going can only be imagined at this point. Experts believe that we as a society have never been more impacted by technology and information science; the resulting connectedness and information overload that we are seeing today leaves many of us stressed. The educational arena has been overwhelmed by these rapid changes. The institutions within which we teach and learn have been scrambling to keep up. Educators have tried to deal with the changing learner, educator, and landscape that we know as education.

One of the most significant changes has arisen from the evolution of Web 1.0 to Web 2.0 with its amazing tools and capabilities. Web 1.0 was mainly controlled by companies and users interacting through hyperlinks. You **synchronously** requested or shared information. Web 2.0 has changed who controls, and the way in which we interact with, the information available on the Internet. Web 2.0 is all about sharing and access. Users create and publish content. Searching has become quite transparent yet extremely more potent. You can still interact synchronously but there is an **asynchronous** transfer of data and information, too. You can set **really simple syndication (RSS)** feeds for example and information is sent to your designated machine as it is updated or launched. You can get this information on the go if you have an Internet-capable phone, Blackberry, PDA, or iPod for example or receive it when you return to your home machine. Content can be tagged by users, not just the owners of the content. According to Lemley and Burnham (2009), Web 2.0 tools are used in 53% of nursing curriculums compared to 45% usage in medical schools. Technology has created a significant change in the way we as educators interact, network, and deliver our course content since these powerful tools facilitate collaboration and shared learning.

As an educator, we know that our colleagues are diverse in their technological skills. Some do not read e-mail while others are developing virtual world simulations for their students. The educational paradigms will continue to morph as technology continues to propel our capabilities far beyond what we once thought possible. This chapter will focus on the changing educator.

Oldskies, Newskies, and Tweeners

A generation gap certainly exists in the area of technology. Some members of the population probably can remember their first TV and might even be able to remember when phones did not even have rotary dials on them. For this chapter, we will refer to this part of the population as the oldskies. They grew up with TV, but computers did not become personal until this generation was about 30 years of age. The tweeners are the generation who were on the fringe of personal computing. They were likely exposed to computers in high school and might even have had a college course or two but it was still not something that was commonly used. Now we come to the newskies who are also known as the digital immigrants or **digital natives**. Digital natives are those who have grown up with computers and sophisticated video games. Recent college graduates might have completed their graduate degree online or attended classes for their advanced degrees, or submitted an electronic version of their thesis or dissertation. They are comfortable with computers since they have used them from an early age—just as the oldskies were with TV. Often, children were helping their parents with the TV just as the tweeners and newskies were helping their parents with personal computers or handheld devices.

In academia, all three generations are working side by side. Keep in mind that "the average age of nurse educators holding PhDs is almost fifty-four" (LaRocco, 2006, para. 6). Having traveled across the United States, it is evident that many of these nurse educators are not comfortable with computers and the vast majority of these educators do not even fully understand what the term nursing informatics means. Some of these educators do not see the need to include a computer class in their nursing programs. How do we get them to be technologically savvy, potent nursing educators? The tweeners are more comfortable but may still be anxious to use computers in their work setting. The newskies are generally comfortable and use technology regularly including **personal digital assistants (PDAs)** that contain clinical databases and other resources. All of the educators in these three groups have basic philosophies of what nursing education should be, and have been ingrained to some degree with traditional lecture mode teaching styles. Even though they may have been bored and uninspired in some of their educational experiences, they continue the pattern of lecture: learners sit and listen. Faculty, including nursing educators, struggle with this changing technologically charged educational landscape. It is important that faculty feel supported by each other, their administrators, and their institutional practices in order to explore various instructional technologies and integrate them into their course work.

While we briefly addressed each group in generalities, keep in mind that individuals from either group can be technologically savvy, unenthusiastic about technology, or even phobic. Therefore, this grouping gives us an idea of some of the barriers various groups experience, it also stresses the fact that we all need to work together to engage learners and enhance learning outcomes. Educational institutions have realized the potential benefits of distance education for years and with the ability to make educational programming available world wide via the Internet, this has become a very competitive marketplace. However, as the old saying goes, "it is the weakest link that causes the chain to fail." In the case of online or distance learning, the faculty are often the weakest link in the success of these endeavors.

Early Adopter Characteristics

Rogers and Scott (1997) make a distinction between the first and last people in a system to adopt something new such as an innovation. They describe those who are first to adopt new technologies as **early adopters**, while those who are the last to adopt as the late majority or laggards. Early adopters represent the first 13% of the population to adopt new technologies, and have the most opinion control or leadership in their organization. Early adopters appear to emulate the average person in the organization, and as a result, people observe them as they adopt and seek them out for advice and perspective. According to Rogers and Scott, "The early adopter is respected by his or her peers, and is the embodiment of successful, discrete use of new ideas" (1997, para. 19). Therefore, we must engage the early adopters and encourage them to network with their peers to bring about institutional change. Ubiquity and the infiltration of technology into every aspect of one's life, such as the rise of portable technologies surpassing previous home and work setting use, have greatly impacted the characteristics of our present day early adopters. Refer to Box 4-1 for an overview of the Characteristics of Early Adopting Nursing Educators.

The UCLA Center states that, "Substantive changes require guidance and support from professionals with mastery level competence for creating a climate for change, facilitating change processes, and establishing an institutional culture where key stakeholders continue to learn and evolve" (n.d., p. 1). Early adopters are important in the case of learning new technologies because they are change agents. According to Miller, "Change agents are individuals who have the knowledge, skills and tools to help organizations create radical improvement. In short, the people who get tapped to make it happen" (2001, p. 1).

The impact of a diverse faculty pool challenges the faculty as well as the administrators trying to effect change. Each group has specific needs. According to the study conducted by Zayim, Yildirim, and Saka, "The early adopter faculty and the mainstream faculty in this study have different needs in training and support. It seems that formal training programs do not appeal to early adopter faculty members who have a level of expertise in technology use" (2006, p. 219). We must support the early adopters while we foster the development of the other faculty who may be lagging behind. As we strive to create vibrant learning communities for our learners, we must also strive to create stimulating and rewarding zones for faculty.

Box 4-1   Characteristics of Early Adopting Nursing Educators

The characteristics of early adopters are numerous and not all early adopters exhibit all of the characteristics listed. Early adopters tend to be:

Experimenters: They have a sense of adventure, are willing to explore and take risks.
Socially connected: They are respected and are opinion leaders who interact with their peers.
Grasp the bigger picture: They can envision the benefits of adoption.
Intrinsically motivated: Their motivation comes from within themselves not from others.
Self-taught: Their exploration and risk seeking behaviors causes them to learn as they go especially when they are adopting technologies where few people can assist them or they envision another use for a technology that no one else has conceptualized.
Confident: They are confident in their knowledge, skills, and abilities, and are not afraid to give honest feedback about products and services they are using (this makes them extremely valuable to developers).
Efficacious: They are efficient and successful for the most part and build on prior successes.
Embrace change: They are comfortable with change and take a positive attitude toward it.
Attracted to technology: They investigate, see the benefit of using technology, and have experienced the difficult learning curves with huge payouts.
Excellent teachers: They are clinically excellent, as well as didactically.
Think outside the box: They are not hung up on how things used to be done, but are always looking for better ways to engage students and enhance learning.
Careful in their adoption: They think critically about the integration and implementation of technologically-enhanced learning episodes.

Box 4-1   **Characteristics of Early Adopting Nursing Educators** (continued)

Visionaries: They see beyond today's challenges and have insights into the future; are ahead of the curve in adapting to current events while preparing for the future

Self-sufficient: They make things happen for themselves and affect change.

Favor revolutionary, radical, or innovative change: They look for sweeping changes in both thinking and behavior that is influential and far reaching, and understand that innovation is needed in education for it to survive the current economic and technology changes, as well as the impending challenges of an evolving global economy.

Think differently: They have been accused of thinking differently from the norm, but that is what allows them to be ahead of the curve,

(Determan, n.d.; Jacobson, 1998; Reagan, 2009; Rogers & Scott, 1997; Zayim, Yildirim, & Saka, 2006)

Online Communities

The purpose of online communities should be to establish a positive **learning culture** and **social presence** while building a sense of community. We believe online courses must develop a learning culture rich in social presence since social presence plays such a vital role in the learning process. This can only be accomplished by the developers of online courses deliberately creating powerful learning opportunities that generate a sense of community, open learning, and sharing of multiple and diverse perspectives, and demanding high-quality performance through active collaboration and peer review. In this positive learning culture, everyone learns from each other as well as from the teacher.

The Web 2.0 environment enhances learning by providing the capability to network learners' minds and develop a positive learning culture and online sense of community. It fosters collaboration and shared learning that stimulates reflective and **critical thinking**. This interaction or collaboration that facilitates the generation of knowledge can also bond the learners and the teacher. One of our ongoing challenges will be to maintain and sustain learning communities that foster collaborative learning.

According to Shen and Khalifa, "Social presence is considered to be a major design principle in computer-mediated communication and an important determinant of online community participation" (2008, p. 722). Social presence has been defined as "feeling that one has some level of access or insight into the other's intentional, cognitive, or affective states" (Biocca & Nowak, 2002, p. 409). Since social presence refers to the social or affective component of learning, it is grounded in a sense of shared interfacing and interaction where learners feel affectively connected. Educators can energize their learning episodes by behaving in an approachable manner for the learners and giving them positive cues such as smiling. The problem arising from the transitioning of our face-to-face persona to our online delivery persona begs the question: How do we develop a sense of community, rich in social presence, in online courses? A straightforward answer is simply transfer your behaviors to an online persona and easily replicate the characteristics by being available, interacting, using humor (some interject **emoticons** to show emotion), and providing support in your interactions with the learners. There are strategies and behaviors that will foster a sense of social presence in online communities. However, it is important to remember that our evolving and diverse learners will challenge us to adapt based on their specific needs as they navigate through their educational learning events.

Three basic tenets for the educator are:

1. As we move to online encounters with our learners, we must implement the potent tools available to us. Bottom line: Superb online teaching is superb online teaching!
2. Even classroom courses can be enhanced with technology such as Web 2.0 tools. Bottom line: Superb teaching is superb teaching!
3. We must use whatever works best for our learners since the ultimate focus is their education. Bottom line: Superb learning is superb learning!

Reflect on your teaching methods, students, and educational setting. Determine what kind of learning or educational community you want to develop. We should strive to build engaging learning communities for the learners as well as ourselves. It is easy to engage your community if you follow the Seven Principles for Good Practice that promote social presence:

1. Encourage contact between students and faculty.
2. Develop reciprocity and cooperation among students.
3. Encourage active learning.

4. Give prompt feedback.
5. Emphasize time on task.
6. Communicate high expectations.
7. Respect diverse talents and ways of learning (Chickering & Gamson, 1987, p. 1).

To increase social presence in an online environment, we must examine the seven principles and develop our materials so they encourage the feeling of social presence and community. In other words, we must establish learning episodes that:

- Recognize and respect the diversity of individual learners in how they learn and the skill sets they bring to the learning episode.
- Require high-quality performance, and provide clear objectives and time frames for assigned tasks.
- Demonstrate our social presence and commitment to each learner.
- Encourage learners to interact with each other in supportive, cooperative, and collaborative team building ways as well as with the teacher.
- Provide prompt feedback concerning performance, comments, or questions that arise.

It is important to note that feedback from the teacher is key, but it is just as important to have learner-to-teacher feedback. Web 2.0 tools give learners ways to communicate and provide feedback to the teacher in a nonthreatening way. This can easily be enacted to promote a vibrant learning culture and sense of community. According to Penn State University, this vibrant learning culture requires commitment from both the teacher as well as the learner:

> Imagine an atmosphere thick with the continual exchange of knowledge and ideas, teacher working with student, student working with student, researchers, graduate students, visitors, scholars of all types working together to learn and understand more, creating, clarifying what is unclear, learning to apply knowledge with technology, uncovering the unknown and assimilating the known. (2006, p. 5)

This is the type of vibrant learning we need in nursing to continue to promote our science. The technological tools available help to promote this culture and community. Educators are becoming more aware of the capabilities of online learning and are trying to develop online tools that bring their teaching persona out in cyberspace as well as in the classroom. Reflect on the Seven Principles for Good Practice (Chickering & Gamson, 1987) that foster social presence as you review the following list of online capabilities.

- Peer review: support for active, collaborative, cooperative learning; enhanced means for improving the learner's cognitive skills by observing student submissions through self- and peer-evaluation
- Instant access in a dynamic environment: enhanced opportunities for timely teacher–learner and learner–learner interaction in both synchronous and asynchronous formats (providing immediate information adding clarification to instruction while encouraging active learner participation in the learning process); a dynamic environment where changes can be made instantly (the syllabus, class events, and other course materials can be easily updated by the teacher as needed with the changes being available to the learners immediately); instant access to educational resources including required or supplemental online texts or Web-based companions to printed texts; ability to include activities that receive immediate feedback from prestructured feedback loops activated by the learner's response or action, time can be set for online interactive meetings between teacher-learner to receive bi-directional feedback
- Flexibility: a means to achieve the learning goals/objectives without having to meet at designated times in a physical classroom
- Self-pacing: the ability to progress at an individual's own pace through certain learning episodes since the learner can be immersed in the materials at any time
- Diverse Instructional Tools: a diverse set of instructional technology tools such as Web 2.0, embedded videos, text, links to the Internet, **podcasts**, simulations, gaming, and virtual worlds to support a variety of learning styles
- Professional opportunities: ePortfolio development opportunities for learners to showcase their work from a learning episode, course, or program of study

Implementing effective and engaging course work mediated by technology will enhance our opportunities to develop learning communities and advance nursing education. However, nursing educators are stressed over their workloads as well as their charge to prepare our future nurses. It is not easy to add a technological challenge to their teaching repertoire. Nursing educators must learn new ways of delivering their course content and engaging their learners. On one of my visits to a community college campus, I saw a young nursing faculty member struggling over clinical maps his students had submitted. We began to dialogue about teaching and his desire to move this "paper mess" to an electronic format where the learners could share and learn from each other. Just then, I saw a note he had hanging on the wall behind his desk. It said, "As I learn I teach and as I teach I learn." We discussed these potent words to remember since we are all in this together! As we try to build a community of learning, it is essential for the educator to remember that they too can enjoy the benefits of learning.

Conclusion

The nursing educator of today is beginning to experiment with online delivery and must be prudent in making decisions about course work. It is important to understand the concept of social presence in online courses in order to build learning communities that enhance learning and truly embrace a vibrant **learning community**. We recommend seeking the help of an instructional designer who will work with you to enact your content in an instructionally sound manner for the learner as well as for you, the teacher.

Learning Applications

Think about and reflect on each case study presented. Is this something you are doing already or is it something you would be willing to try? Educators must change and adapt to the profound transformations that accompany the explosion of technology in our field.

Case Studies

The recent invasion of Web 2.0 tools into the educational arena promotes active, experiential, and collaborative learning, and fosters publishing and research. It typically does this in a very engaging manner. As nurse educators prepare to teach our future nurses, they implement these tools. Here are several examples of how other faculty have changed their teaching methods and developed new learning episodes for the online environment or moved to a fully online delivery of the content. Each case study is intended to provide an example and cause you to reflect on your own teaching. Think about each case and how you could implement something similar in your setting.

CASE STUDY 1

A staff development coordinator in a large metropolitan hospital with three campuses and over 2,000 nurses changed a paper-based CE system they had in place to an online system that the nurses could access from anywhere. The learning episodes were placed on the Internet with an online quiz that provided instant feedback about their score and the correct answers with rationale. They had also set up a **blog** so nurses could share their thoughts on the CE offering. Nurses quickly responded with their thoughts about the offering and more. This blog quickly led to another blog being created for nurses to dialogue with each other over issues in their respective areas. Each department had their own blog site. The nurses felt connected to each other since they did not get to meet all of the nurses working in their areas at the other sites.

CASE STUDY 2

To facilitate doctoral students learning about Second Life and simulations, Dr. Bixler developed a Second Life simulation from Dr. McGonigle's content with the assistance of Dr. Mahan; one was a female patient with a fractured hip and the other one was a male with diabetes and dementia. Dr. Bixler explained his process for development and the time it took to create each scenario. These simulations could be adapted for use in a nursing program as well. It would provide nursing students with a brief overview of the patient and then ask them to develop a plan of care based on their findings. You will learn more about Second Life and simulations in Chapter 13. These simulations could be used prior to a nursing student attending their geriatric clinical rotation to help them prepare.

CASE STUDY 3

Community health nursing students would search the Internet accessing local, state, and national public health databases; observe the community and interview residents, government officials, and health department officials; analyze the data; and write a grant proposal. Faculty members collaborated to create very clear directions and a template, and set up an online discussion forum and chat room for the students. Their assignment was to write a grant proposal that identifies a plan to meet the needs of the community. Each school's students had a piece of the assignment and needed the other students' information in order to develop the proposal. As a team, all of the students were assigned roles and had to develop the proposal together. The faculty monitored the discussion forums and chat rooms and only judiciously provided feedback or direction. The students submitted their draft proposal to the discussion forum. The faculty reviewed the proposal, provided feedback and then the students had to finalize their proposal online.

CASE STUDY 4

While using **Adobe Connect** (formerly known as Breeze), a web conferencing tool, one faculty member uses the polling feature to make sure students are understanding the concepts. She also has the students using Adobe Connect for their team meetings and work sessions. They are able to work together in real time, synchronously, to develop and edit assigned course submissions. They can also record their session for later review. This is a potent social presence learning tool.

CASE STUDY 5

Using wikispaces.com, a faculty member created a **wiki** for each team in her course. She had the students developing the roles and responsibilities that nurses assume in a select area of practice. They worked on their wiki after each clinical day and by midsemester, had to share their wiki-generated lists with the entire class. Another faculty member took it one step further and created a wiki for the entire class and had each team link their wiki lists. One nursing faculty member who was a history buff had his students develop, maintain, and sustain a wiki about the history of men in nursing through the present day.

CASE STUDY 6

One senior faculty member stated that he believed in the "Socratic philosophy where my students inquire, question, explore and discover new information and knowledge. How can technology facilitate this for me?" When I asked this faculty member how he does this with each of his 30 students that he meets with face-to-face for 50 minutes, three times per week, he was quick to respond that he builds the complexity of his questioning as the classes progress. He begins with simple questions that everyone should be able to field and then he progresses to what he termed his "lullapahloser" (he gave me the spelling). The "lullapahloser" is a question that is very complex and designed to engage every student. It is a question that challenges their ability while raising other questions that tease out the ultimate answer.

We came up with the idea of a discussion board/chat format and split students into teams. The major question resided on the class discussion boards and the minor questions designed to help tease out the final answer were given to the teams in their private discussion boards. As each team came up with an "AHA," they added it to the "AHA" discussion board where the other class members could comment on it. We opened logged chat rooms for the students to dialogue about the question. When each team felt they had an answer to the question, they posted their answer on the major question class discussion board. The teacher was able to interact with all of the teams. Now, the delivery method was different but his underlying philosophy and skills came through and resonated in this new medium. He enjoyed his first venture into what he defined as "technology-mediated learning."

Reflect on an assignment or topical area in your teaching that you feel a technology tool could help the learner better grasp the concepts or material presented. Take the first steps. Change an in-class discussion to one that is done online. Set the time frame for the discussion and be very clear about what you would like to accomplish. Remember to allow them to discuss and try not to interject too much—just keep them on track. A learner's participation should be substantive and demonstrate a review of the material.

Thoughts To Ponder

Probable-Possible, my black hen,
She lays eggs in the Relative When.
She doesn't lay eggs in the Positive Now
Because she's unable to Postulate How.

--- Frederick Winsor (1956)

How does this saying relate to changing nursing faculty?

Recommendations

Be the early adopter and encourage networking so peers can share what they are doing. It is a terrific idea to create a repository of all of the best practices in teaching and learning for you and your colleagues including assessment tools and clear examples of implementation strategies. Since we act as part of an interdisciplinary team in the clinical setting, pull that through to the educational arena and team up with instructional designers, instructional technologists, and technology experts to foster your development.

The changing nurse educator is beginning to dabble in technology integration. One faculty member told me that it was something she could not avoid in her personal life and certainly not in her professional life now. We must all try and not be afraid to seek help or network to make the entry into uncharted waters less scary and more fruitful. Take a class or ask someone to mentor you. Nurse educators must learn as much as they can to help them grapple with the ever evolving, technology charged educational landscape.

It is a privilege and an honor to be able to teach future nurses or empower practicing nurses. Educators must change with the times since we are the role models for our learners; we must model the integration of technology into our learning episodes. Learners will be attracted to and engaged in our learning episodes if we energize them with collaborative technological tools focused on enhancing social presence and fostering shared learning.

Technology enabled education, a catalyst for Positive change.

— Jonathan Renaudon-Smith

References

Biocca, F., & Nowak, K. (2002). Plugging your body into the telecommunication system: Mediated embodiment, media interfaces, and social virtual environments. In D. Atkin & C. Lin (Eds.). *Communication technology and society* (pp. 409–447). Cresskill, NJ: Hampton Press.

Chickering, A., & Gamson, Z. (1987). Seven principles for good practice in undergraduate education. *Washington Center News*. Available at: http://learningcommons.evergreen .edu/pdf/fall1987.pdf. Accessed February 2, 2009.

Determan, M. (n.d.). *Marketing –Target market innovators, early adopters, influencers.* Available at: http://www.determan.net/Michele/mtarget.htm. Accessed January 27, 2009.

Jacobson, D. (1998). *Adoption patterns and characteristics of faculty who integrate computer technology for teaching and learning in higher education* (Doctoral dissertation). Available at: http://www.ucalgary.ca/~dmjacobs/phd/diss/. Accessed January 27, 2009.

LaRocco, S. (2006). Who will teach the nurses? *Academe Online*, 92(3). Available at: http://www
.aaup.org/AAUP/pubsres/academe/2006/MJ/feat/laro.htm. Accessed January 27, 2009.

Lemley, T., & Burnham, J. (2009). Web 2.0 tools in medical and nursing school curricula.
Journal of the Medical Library Association, 97(1), 50–52. doi: 10.3163/1536-5050.97.1.010

Miller, K. (2001). Becoming a change agent. In K. Miller, *The Change Agent's Guide to Radical
Improvement*. Available at: http://www.changeagents.info/2_0_about_us/2_4_pop_ups/2_
4_14_change_agents.pdf. Accessed March 12, 2009.

Penn State University. (2006). *The Pennsylvania State University assessment plan for student
learning*. Available at: http://www.psu.edu/vpaa/pdfs/assessment%20plan.pdf. Accessed
February 2, 2009.

Reagan, G. (2009). It's geek to you, but not to them: Meet the early adopters. *New York
Observer*. Available at: http://www.observer.com/2009/media/its-geek-you-not-them-
meet-early-adopters. Accessed January 27, 2009.

Rogers, E., & Scott, K. (1997). The diffusion of innovations model and outreach from the
National Network of Libraries of Medicine to Native American communities. *National
Network of Libraries of Medicine*. Available at: http://nnlm.gov/archive/pnr/eval/rogers
.html. Accessed January 19, 2009.

Shen, K., & Khalifa, M. (2008). Exploring multidimensional conceptualization of social presence in the context of online communities. *International Journal of Human-Computer
Interaction*, 24(7),722. Available at: ttp://ezaccess.libraries.psu.edu/login?url=http://
proquest.umi.com.ezaccess.libraries.psu.edu/pqdweb?did=1576329711&sid=3&Fmt=7
&clientId=9874&RQT=309&VName=PQD. Accessed February 2, 2009.

UCLA Center. (n.d.). Change agent mechanisms for school improvement: Infrastructure not
individuals (Information resource). Available at: http://smhp.psych.ucla.edu/pdfdocs/
systemic/change%20agents.pdf. Accessed March 12, 2009.

Zayim, N., Yildirim, S., & Saka, O. (2006). Technology adoption of medical faculty in teaching:
Differentiating factors in adopter categories. *Educational Technology & Society*, 9(2), 213–222.
Available at: http://www.ifets.info/journals/9_2/17.pdf. Accessed January 27, 2009.

CHAPTER 5

The Changing Higher Education Institution

Food For Thought

"In times of change, learners inherit the Earth,
while the learned find themselves beautifully equipped
to deal with a world
that no longer exists."

Eric Hoffer, 1902–1983

Key Words

Academy
Accessibility
Accountability
Accrediting agencies
Affordability
Analytics infrastructure
Benchmarking
Critical analysis
Critical thinking
Curricular framework
Data mining
Data warehouse
Diverse cultures
Enterprise Resource Planning (ERP)

Full-time equivalents (FTEs)
Globalization
Higher education
Hybrid
Information infrastructure
Information literacy
Innovation infrastructure
Integrative learning
Knowledge
Learning outcomes
Liberal Education and America's
    Promise (LEAP)
Online
Outcomes accountability

Philosophy	Strategic change
Problem solving	Teamwork
Quality	Technology infrastructure
Quantitative literacy	Workplace skills

Objectives

The educator will be able to describe the forces for change in higher education.

The educator will be able to discuss the impacts of increasing applications of technology in higher education.

The educator will be able to compare and contrast the forces for change in higher education with the forces for change in nursing education.

Introduction

Ed is excited to begin his new job as a mechanical engineer. He was very successful in his academic studies and graduated from a well-known public institution near the top of his class. He was offered a good job with a manufacturing company near his hometown. After about 2 weeks on the job, he is feeling less confident and is confused about what he is expected to do. He had anticipated being assigned to design projects and was looking forward to using the state-of-the-art computer design programs owned by the company. Instead, he finds himself writing and answering memos and e-mails and talking to potential customers on the phone. He struggles to write the memos and e-mails and he really dislikes talking on the phone. He does not always remember what questions to ask customers and he frequently has to call them back to get the necessary information. His days are also peppered with meetings; he is unsure of his expected role in the meetings and is nervous about asking questions or volunteering ideas. However, he has accumulated over $25,000 in student loan debt, so he is feeling a lot of pressure to do well on the job. Why does Ed feel so uncomfortable in this environment? Why does he feel unprepared to do the job he is being asked to do?

Unfortunately, new college graduates are experiencing scenarios just like this in many different environments. Most students attend college with the goal of finding a good job, yet many are disappointed to learn that they are ill-prepared to perform well in those jobs. It appears that there is a gap between the expectations of employers, the skills necessary to perform in the work environment, and the preparation of students in **higher education** institutions.

The Need for Change

The traditional **academy** has long held the belief that the primary mission is the pursuit of **knowledge**: to generate knowledge through research, to disseminate knowledge through teaching, and to apply knowledge through service to society. While the practical application of knowledge, **problem solving**, **critical thinking**, communication, and **teamwork** are skills expected in the workplace, the academy, to a certain extent, has resisted the development of programs that focus specifically on the application of knowledge and other **workplace skills**, dismissing this as training and not education. As college costs rise, there is a growing demand for **outcomes accountability** in the academy, a concept that may be somewhat foreign to those programs and majors that are not professionally accredited. Many curricula are structured to include a series of courses that students are required to take in the major, but there is no real organizing **philosophy** or **curricular framework**, nor are there well-defined student **learning outcomes**. Fortunately, in nursing education the **accrediting agencies** have long insisted on well-developed curricula that include learning outcomes. However, even in the nursing profession there exists a gap between what nursing is purported to be in the education arena and the reality of nursing practice on the job. This behavioral and informational gap between the educator and the clinician may cause a disconnect for the learner despite the exposure to clinical practice that is an integral part of nursing curricula.

Higher education institutions are feeling pressure to change in response to a growing number of forces. These pressures include meeting the needs of the changing and diverse student population, maintaining quality education within lean budget parameters, as well as becoming more responsive to preparing graduates for workplace realities. As Greenberg emphasizes:

> Congress, state legislatures, and public regulatory agencies are watching, more carefully than ever, the operating procedures of higher education institutions. They seek accountability for funds spent, students served, learning achieved, and research produced and they look for results in terms of students graduated, jobs secured, and public benefits earned. (2004, p. 12)

Interestingly, there is not wide agreement about the goals of a college education. Consider this statement from Greater Expectations, the national panel report from the American Association of Colleges and Universities (AACU, 2002):

> Many students and parents see college primarily as the springboard to employment; they want job-related courses. Policy makers view college as a spur to regional economic growth, and they urge highly targeted workforce development. Business leaders seek graduates who can think analytically, communicate effectively, and solve problems in collaboration with diverse colleagues, clients, or customers. Faculty members want students to develop sophisticated intellectual skills and also to learn about science, society, the arts, and human culture. For the higher education community as a whole, college is a time when faculty and students can explore important issues in ways that respect a variety of viewpoints and deepen understanding. (para. 13)

Consider also that nearly 75% of current high school students plan to attend college and that more adults are entering college in the hope of finding a better job (AACU, 2002). In what ways do higher education institutions need to change in order to meet these disparate expectations and prepare graduates for workplace challenges and life in an increasingly complex, diverse, and globalized society that is knowledge dependent?

The Greater Expectations panel (AACU, 2002) emphasizes the need for transformative changes in higher education to produce intentional learners who are empowered, informed, and responsible. Empowered learners possess intellectual and practical skills that include oral and written communication in a native and foreign language, the ability to analyze and solve problems using quantitative and qualitative approaches, to work effectively with and understand diverse groups, to interpret and evaluate information and transform it into knowledge that is appropriately applied, and to understand and manage change. Informed learners are those who possess a deep understanding of **diverse cultures**, society, and the natural world and thus apply this understanding to become contributing citizens. Responsible learners develop a sense of social responsibility and ethical judgment. The panel concludes that universities must dramatically reorganize to "promote the kind of learning students need to meet emerging challenges in the workplace, in a diverse democracy, and in an interconnected world" (AACU, 2002, para. 2).

A special commission organized in 2005 by then Secretary of Education, Margaret Spellings examined the status of higher education in the United States and identified the core goals that set clear expectations for all post-secondary educational institutions (US Department of Education, 2006):

- We want a world-class higher-education system that creates new knowledge, contributes to economic prosperity and global competitiveness, and empowers citizens;
- We want a system that is accessible to all Americans, throughout their lives;
- We want postsecondary institutions to provide high-quality instruction while improving their efficiency in order to be more affordable to the students, taxpayers, and donors who sustain them;
- We want a higher-education system that gives Americans the workplace skills they need to adapt to a rapidly changing economy;
- We want postsecondary institutions to adapt to a world altered by technology, changing demographics and **globalization**, in which the higher-education landscape includes new providers and new paradigms, from for-profit universities to distance learning. (p. xi)

The Spellings Commission report focuses on four key areas of change needed for higher education: **accessibility**, **affordability**, **quality**, and **accountability**. Access to postsecondary education is hindered by poor high school preparation, inadequate information, and guidance for preparing for and applying to college, and a clear gap related to college attendance for lower-income students. Issues of affordability are related to increasing tuition and additional fees, poor institutional cost management, and a complex and inefficient financial aid system. The quality of education is rated inadequate by the commission and the documentation of learning outcomes is lacking. Finally, there is a need for collecting and analyzing meaningful data to inform decision making and to support innovation (US Department of Education, 2006).

The Substance of Change

The National Leadership Council for **Liberal Education and America's Promise** (**LEAP**, 2008) report, College Learning for the New Global Century, extends the work of the Greater Expectations panel. This report delineates essential learning outcomes and core competencies for college graduates, includes employer survey results detailing employer expectations for college graduates, and identifies principles of excellence for higher education. According to the report, the 21st century realities of "scientific and technological innovations, global interdependence, cross-cultural encounters, and changes in the balance of economic and political power" (LEAP, p. 2) are driving the need to transform higher education. The essential learning outcomes for all college graduates emphasized in this report include:

- Knowledge of human cultures, and the physical and natural world gained through traditional studies of science, philosophy, arts, and humanities but focused by engagement in reasoned discussions of big questions;
- Development of intellectual and practical skills that include creative and critical thinking, **quantitative** and **information literacy**, **critical analysis** and problem solving, and teamwork;
- Development of personal and social responsibility by engaging with diverse communities; and
- Appreciation of **integrative learning** developed by application of knowledge and skills to new environments. (LEAP, 2008)

The report also emphasizes that the essential learning outcomes cannot be realized in general education courses alone, but must be interwoven throughout well-developed, cohesive, and informed curricula. Thus higher education must shift its focus "from accumulating course credits to building real-world capabilities" (2008, p. 7). These same sentiments are echoed in the Appendix of the LEAP National Leadership Council report (2008) that summarizes the results of employer surveys and focus groups. "Employers want college graduates to acquire versatile knowledge and skills. Employers also expressed a strong desire to see more emphasis on helping students put their knowledge and skills to practical use in 'real-world' settings" (2008, p. 10). In addition, employers emphasized that learning assessments need to test "communication skills and analytic reasoning and students' ability to apply what they are learning to complex problems" (2008, p. 10). Most employers also suggested that college transcripts are not useful for screening candidates.

Tagg also laments the inadequacies of college transcripts in providing information about what students know, "We have a vague feeling that students who get better grades are doing something better than students who get worse grades, but the transcript itself gives us no direct information about what they are doing in either case" (2008, p. 21). Tagg suggests the development of an outcomes transcript similar to the ePortfolios described in Chapter 16. Further, Tagg points out that that an overall outcomes accounting tool will also help students describe and understand their progress toward specific learning goals, and thus provide for students a sense of curricular coherency and the compass suggested following this paragraph. Meyer, Sedelmeyer, Carlson, and Modlin (2003) describe the use of the Essential Clinical Behavior System, a Web-based system designed to aid nursing student's self-report of clinical outcomes achievement as well as assisting faculty with making clinical assignments and evaluating student progress.

The LEAP National Leadership Council report further recommends that higher education institutions adopt seven principles of excellence regardless of the field of study in order to "prepare their graduates as fully as possible for the real-world demands of work, citizenship, and life in a complex and fast-changing society" (2008, p. 5). The principles of excellence are summarized here:

- **Aim High—and Make Excellence Inclusive**
- **Give Students a Compass**: Provide a focused plan of study based on specified learning outcomes.
- **Teach the Arts of Inquiry and Innovation**: Immerse students in analysis, discovery, problem solving, and communication.
- **Engage the Big Questions**: Teach through the curriculum to far-reaching issues such as science and society, cultures and values, global interdependence, the changing economy, and human dignity and freedom.
- **Connect Knowledge with Choices and Action**: Prepare students for citizenship and work through engaged and guided learning on real-world problems.
- **Foster Civic, Intercultural, and Ethical Learning**: Emphasize personal and social responsibility.
- **Assess Students' Ability to Apply Learning to Complex Problems**: Use assessment to deepen learning and to establish a culture of shared purpose and continuous improvement. (2008, p. 6)

Clearly, there is a need for a complete paradigm shift from a teaching institution that transmits discrete facts within isolated courses to a learning institution where students are challenged to be actively involved in the personal construction of their knowledge base within a well-designed and cohesive curriculum that contains specific learning outcomes. As Tagg (2008) summarizes,

"The task of colleges is to take students who come to them ill-prepared and equip them for careers that will increasingly demand not only a degree but also an array of cognitive and communication skills without which the degree will lose much of its value. In other words, learning and learning at a high level of cognitive functioning, is what the world of tomorrow will increasingly demand of college graduates—and of colleges" (p. 17).

Scott (2003) tackles the issues associated with making changes in complex organizations and offers eight key change lessons that will help to promote informed and **strategic change**.

1. There are far more options for improvement or innovation than there is time or resources to address them.
2. Change is not an event but is a complex and subjective learning/unlearning process for all concerned.
3. Enhancements in learning programs generate a need for improvements in the systems and infrastructure that underpin them.
4. The most successful changes are the result of a team effort in which the most appropriate and best positioned people are involved in a process of action learning.
5. The change process is cyclical, not linear.
6. Change does just not happen, it must be led.
7. Change is a mixture of external forces and individual action.
8. We must look outside as well as inside for viable change ideas and solutions. (p. 68–69)

Scott concludes that good ideas for change are not always easy to implement unless that change is strategically managed. "We have to get smarter at both the 'what' of change (identifying change ideas that will really make a difference for students) and the 'how' of change (making sure those ideas work in practice)" (2003, p. 65).

The Role of Technology in Transforming Higher Education

As higher education institutions respond to the forces challenging them to change, they will need to develop new and more efficient ways of doing business. In short, they will need to manage information more effectively and transform performance information into knowledge and apply that knowledge appropriately to develop a strategic vision, carry out their mission, serve their constituencies, and assess their performance. Technology can be effectively used to enhance teaching and learning and to manage services within the university. Green (2006) suggests that there is wide agreement in most higher education sectors that infrastructure, instruction, and management are the vital information technology functions in higher education.

The integration of technology to support teaching and learning appears to be much better developed than the IT processes for outcomes assessment and institutional effectiveness. As Nelson *et al.* (2006) describe, early education technology use began in the late 1960s with text-laden computer-assisted instruction programs that evolved into graphics enhanced instructional CDs and software programs designed to run on personal computers. Today, technology-based instruction includes complete programs or courses within programs offered **online**, courses offered in **hybrid** or blended formats that include both online and face-to-face components, and face-to-face courses that include technology or multimedia components to enhance student engagement. As technology-enhanced education evolves, many colleges and universities are using course management software such as Blackboard, Moodle, and Sakai to facilitate technology-enhanced course delivery. Nelson *et al.* (2006) suggest that course management systems have "the potential to bridge the gap between academic software focused on the learning process and **Enterprise Resource Planning** (**ERP**) systems focused on the management of the institution" (p. 251). Student data related to the recruitment and retention side of the system can be integrated with course performance data and utilized to assist in evaluation of curricula and program outcomes. Nelson *et al.* (2006), caution that the ethics of such collection and analysis of data need to be carefully weighed, and developed in such a way so as not to compromise student privacy.

Higher education institutions also are recognizing the need to integrate technology in the teaching and learning processes in order to meet the needs of the changing student populations as discussed in Chapter 3. In addition, as the economy shifts, more and more people will require continuing education or retraining, and technology-based education may be the most effective way to meet this need.

Technology-enhanced nursing education is evolving rapidly and is necessary in light of the explosion of health related information and technology use in health care. Nurses must be able to develop and effectively manage their knowledge as a foundation for evidence-based and reflective practice. In the chapters that follow, we will focus on these emerging technologies and demonstrate the use of these technologies to develop potent learning episodes based on education and instructional design theories.

In addition to technology focused on teaching and learning, higher education institutions can also use technology to manage their effectiveness. Graves (2005) outlines four critical stages of technology evolution to aid in the delivery of services, enhance institutional performance, and assess that performance. He suggests that developing and supporting a high-performance **technology infrastructure** is the necessary first step. This technology infrastructure should have a baseline network with security and disaster recovery functions linked to administrative and course management systems, ubiquitous access, hands-on technical support as well as 24/7 help desk functions. The **information infrastructure** can then evolve from this technology infrastructure providing a source for unified data and customizable Web portals, single log-on access and integrated systems. Investing in analytical software tools can then provide the transition to an **analytics infrastructure** that can drive decision making and help to prioritize performance initiatives. As strategic IT objectives and findings evolve, the institution can progress to an **innovation infrastructure** that is data driven and performance oriented.

> Academic leaders dedicated to using technology to improve institutional performance first must identity their performance indicators, establish the tracking and improvement of these indicators as an institutional priority, and support and oversee the management of a high-performance IT organization that is collaborating daily with other units in support of an innovation infrastructure and culture. (Graves, 2005, p. 90)

Many larger colleges and universities have adopted Enterprise Resource Planning (ERP) system software to integrate their administrative operations. ERP systems typically include financial, human resources, and student records systems, thus supporting functions such as financial management decision support, grants and research management, development activities, materials management, human resource management, and various student functions such as recruiting, registration, retention, academic progress tracking, and financial aid. Because these systems have fully integrated modules, changes in one part of the system result in automatic changes to appropriate records in other parts of the system (Nelson *et al.*, 2006).

Green (2006) supports the view that well designed information technology systems can be an integral part of institutional assessment by providing the data about performance and outcomes and supporting analytical tools such as **data warehouses** and **data mining**. However, he cautions, "Left unresolved is the methodology for the assessment. There is no consensual methodology—an effective *methodology*—for this work" (p. 43).

As a starting point, Graves (2005) identifies six key performance obligations of institutions as learning accountability, program accountability, expense accountability, affordability of access, convenience of access, and capacity for access. Learning accountability means **benchmarking** the quality of learning outcomes using such measures as retention, graduation rates, persistence rates, and the results of independent large-scale assessments such as the Collegiate Learning Assessment or the National Assessment of Student Engagement. Program accountability means responding to economic development or national workforce priorities by developing academic programs to meet these needs, and making these decisions based on quantitative data. Expense accountability means tracking direct and indirect costs of program development, instruction, and provision of services. Affordability of access is measured by comparing the annual change to the rate of tuition and fees to the annual Consumer Price Index, and tracking subsidies and grants to student **full-time equivalents** (**FTEs**) and direct expenses. Convenience of access is a measure of program flexibility for students as is the degree to which courses are delivered asynchronously or in blended or hybrid formats. Capacity for access is measured by projecting the demand for courses and programs based on total credit hours generated annually and examining the ratio of faculty FTEs to student FTEs. IT supported, data-driven outcomes assessments clearly have the potential to provide the quality information to support the effective transformation of higher education institutions.

In this chapter, we have outlined the need for change in higher education institutions. We have an obligation to help students like Ed from the opening scenario prepare effectively for the world he will face as he emerges from the protective folds of our institutions. We are making progress toward understanding what our students want, what employers expect, what society demands, and what we need to do to effect those changes.

Learning Activities

1. Compare the essential learning outcomes identified in the LEAP report to the AACN Essentials of Baccalaureate Education for Professional Nursing Practice discussed in Chapter 1.

2. Review Tagg's (2008) suggestions for developing an outcomes transcript and the work of Meyer *et al.* (2003) related to tracking nursing student clinical education outcomes. Develop a plan for tracking learning outcomes for your students utilizing the technology currently available in your institution. What are the strengths and weaknesses of your current system? In an ideal world, what type of system would you need to adequately track student learning outcomes?

References

American Association of Colleges and Universities. (2002). *Greater expectations* (National panel report). Available at: http://www.greaterexpectations.org/. Accessed May 11, 2009.

Graves, W. (2005). Improving institutional performance through IT-enabled innovation. *EDUCAUSE Review*, 40(6), 78–98.

Greenberg, M. (2004). A university is not a business (and other fantasies). *EDUCAUSE Review*, *39*(2), 10–16. Available at:http://www.educause.edu/EDUCAUSE+Review/EDUCAUSEReviewMagazineVolume39/AUniversityIsNotaBusinessandOt/157887. Accessed November 8, 2009.

Green, K. (2006). Bring Data: A new role for information technology after the spellings commission. *EDUCAUSE Review*, 41(6), 30–46.

Meyer, L., Sedelmeyer, R. Carlson, C., & Modlin, S. (2003). A web application for recording and analyzing the clinical experiences of nursing students. *CIN: Computers, Informatics, Nursing*, 21(4), 185–197.

National Leadership Council for Liberal Education and America's Promise (LEAP)/ (2008). College learning for the new global century. Available at the American Association of Colleges and Universities Web site: http://www.aacu.org/leap/documents/GlobalCentury_ExecSum_3.pdf. Accessed May 11, 2009.

Nelson, R., Meyers, L., Rizzolo, M. A., Rutar, P., Proto, M. B., & Newbold, S. (2006). The evolution of educational information systems and nurse faculty roles. *Nursing Education Perspectives*, 27(5), 247–253. doi: 1135542461

Scott, G. (2003). Effective change management in higher education. *EDUCAUSE Review*, *38*(6), 64–80. Available at: http://www.educause.edu/EDUCAUSE+Review/EDUCAUSEReviewMagazineVolume38/EffectiveChangeManagementinHig/157869. Accessed November 8, 2009.

Tagg, J. (2008). Changing minds in higher education: Students change, so why can't colleges? *Planning for Higher Education*, *37*(1), 15–22. doi: 1579372871.

US Department of Education. (2006). *A test of leadership: Charting the future of U.S. higher education*. Available at: http://www.ed.gov/about/bdscomm/list/hiedfuture/index/html. Accessed November 8, 2009.

Building Blocks for Developing Learning Episodes

It is imperative that nurse educators understand the foundations of educational theories and design as they develop learning episodes. This understanding must transcend a basic knowledge in order to clearly and effectively convey your educational messages. Consider the following example: Two children were playing school, Chuckie and Harriet. Harriet was the teacher and Chuckie was the pupil. As she tried to teach him arithmetic, he continuously drummed his fingers on the desk. She asked him to stop several times but he would only slow down the speed of the drumming. Harriet became frustrated and took a glass of water over to his desk. As she began pouring it on his head, she asked if he knew the difference between slowing down and stopping. Did he want her to continue to pour the water on his head slowly or stop pouring it altogether? This is a lesson Chuckie would not forget. Although Harriet's message was clear, this may not have been an appropriate way to teach or convey her message.

This section will provide you with the basic building blocks of learning theories, instructional design theories, and the instructional design process. You will be able to teach concepts like slowing down or stopping in an acceptable, effective, and efficient manner using appropriate learning theories and instructional design strategies. You will be able to craft learning episodes that provide powerful lessons for students to discover as they progress on their learning journey with you as their guide, mentor, facilitator, or coach.

In this section we will cover the building blocks and add some mortar to the mix to help you design, scaffold and build the instructional components of your learning episodes. In Chapter 6, you will be presented with an overview

73

of the learning theories. This chapter will outline two base theories that other theories overtly or covertly call upon in their descriptions: behaviorism and cognitivism. You will also be exposed to the learning theories and philosophies of humanism, constructivism, problem-based learning, and situated cognition. We will challenge you to think about different learning situations you have experienced while examining learning as a product and a process. You will stroll along the continuum of behaviorism, cognitivism, and constructivism. Chapter 7 provides guidance on how to design the instruction to enhance learning since the instructional design theories are the prescriptive, goal-oriented elements arising from the descriptive, learning theories. We will challenge you to select one of the instructional design theories and create a training session. Next, Chapter 8 explores the instructional design process. In Chapter 9, you will learn how to select media after you have defined the goal and objectives for your lesson, course, or curricula. This selection process will take place during the design process to ensure that the selected media elements are consistent with the learning objectives and the most appropriate media is used for the desired learning outcome. This section concludes with Chapter 10 describing and exploring copyright and fair use in education. It is so easy to use another's work today since we can generally capture it with one or two clicks of our mouse. Therefore, everyone must be cognizant of the importance of adhering to copyright, fair use, and the TEACH Act when developing educational programming.

CHAPTER 6

Overview of Learning Theories

Food For Thought

"Learning is not so much an additive process,
with new learning simply piling up on top of existing knowledge,
as it is an active, dynamic process in which
the connections are constantly changing
and the structure reformatted."

K. Patricia Cross, 1926–

Key Words

Behaviorism
Cognition
Cognitive apprenticeships
Cognitivism
Constructivism
Everyday cognition
Humanism

Problem-based learning (PBL)
Response
Scaffolding
Schema
Situated cognition
Stimulus

Objectives

The educator will be able to define the basic characteristics of behaviorism, cognitivism, humanism, constructivism, problem-based learning, and situated and everyday cognition.

The educator will be able to compare and contrast behaviorism, cognitivism, humanism, constructivism, problem-based learning, and situated and everyday cognition.

The educator will be able to identify the learning theories used to develop a lesson.

The nurse educator will be able to orally or textually justify choosing one or more learning theories as the best choice for development of instruction delivery by citing at least one relative strength and weakness of each chosen theory.

Introduction

The Theories into Practice (TIP) database (Kearsley, 2009) currently lists 57 theories of learning. Each theory, or lens, allows us different insights into the complex processes of human learning. We can also use these theories when we approach the design of an instructional situation, matching the instructional goals and objectives with a relevant theory, and contrasting them with discordant theories to discover weaknesses in our instructional approach.

This chapter will outline two main theories that other theories overtly or covertly call upon in their descriptions: **behaviorism** and **cognitivism**. This chapter will also touch upon other learning theories and philosophies: **humanism**, **constructivism**, **problem-based learning**, and **situated cognition**.

Learning as a Product: Behaviorism

Learning during the 1940s through the 1960s emphasized learning as something that produced a tangible outcome (Smith, 1999). If you learned something, others could observe that you learned it, for you interacted with your environment in an obvious way; you exhibited a particular behavior. Built upon the works of psychologists such as Thorndike, Pavlov, Watson, Guthrie, and Skinner (Bolles, 1975), the theory of behaviorism was widely adopted by educators and trainers.

Behaviorism is a theory of learning that implies the environment external to the learner is the only factor to consider in learning situations. The learner's mind is not considered. Thus, behaviorism focuses on external events and observable, quantifiable results (Ackerman, 1972).

You often hear the phrase stimulus-response used in discussions of behaviorism. Organisms receive a **stimulus**—an observable, outside force or event that causes a physical **response** in the organism. While there are many variations on this stimulus-response pairing, this is the most basic of definitions.

The behavioral instructional model focuses on what the learner should be able to do when the instruction is concluded, which makes the subsequent planning and implementation steps clear and effective. In addition, instruction is specifically targeted to the skills and knowledge to be taught and offers the appropriate conditions for the learning outcomes to occur.

Implications for Teaching and Learning

A criticism of behavioral instruction is that it lacks flexibility in meeting the varied needs of learners. This implies that the instruction built on behaviorism may be most appropriate when teaching procedural knowledge with an emphasis on the acquisition of basic skills.

If you examine a curriculum, course, or lesson, you will most likely find basic level facts and concepts that must be mastered by the students. It may be that behaviorist methods work best for students to acquire this information. Drill and practice exercises work extremely well in these situations.

The entire concept of learning goals and objectives comes from behaviorism. In fact, objectives used to be named behavioral objectives. Learning goals and objectives are critical in designing and delivering instruction. See Chapter 8 for more information on learning goals and objectives.

Learning as a Process: Cognitivism

Learning as a product ignores what goes on inside our heads, and learning that takes place "on the fly" such as parenting (Smith, 1999). When psychologists and learning theorists began looking at the mind, how it works, and how internal learning might take place, several learning theories and philosophies arose from these investigations.

Cognitive psychology originated as an extension to behavioral theory. Scientists could not use behaviorism to explain all aspects of the human condition, especially higher-order skills such as problem solving and creativity. The mind, it turned out, had to be examined to truly study human behavior. Learning has both internal and external components.

Cognitive psychology is the study of the mind and how it works. It focuses on mental processes that operate on stimuli presented to the perceptual and cognitive systems, and which usually contribute significantly to whether or not a response is made. These mental processes include insight, information processing, memory, and perception (Smith, 1999). **Cognition** is driven as much by what we know as by the information we take in.

The concept of **schema** is very important in theories of cognition. A schema is an organized structure consisting of linked concepts that coexist with many other schema. It is an abstraction and a generalization of our experiences, which change over time through exposure to new experiences. We either assimilate a new experience into an existing schema, or we accommodate a new experience by altering the schema so the new experience "fits" (Ausubel, 1968). Schema provide a context that affects how we interpret new experiences. It colors our anticipation of new information.

James Hartley (1998) writes "Learning results from inferences, expectations and making connections. Instead of acquiring habits, learners acquire plans and strategies, and prior knowledge is important" (p. 18).

He summarizes aspects of cognitive learning as follows:

- Prior knowledge needed for learning is important. The learner must be able to link older knowledge with new knowledge.
- Instruction should be well organized and clearly structured to facilitate learning, memory storage, and recall. Key ideas and concepts should be linked together.
- The ways tasks are structured in relationship to the environment they exist in is important. The key features of the tasks must be presented in a way that makes the learner attend to them.
- Learners are not all the same. The teaching methods used influence different learners differently.
- Cognitive feedback where knowledge of results is given is important. (Hartley, 1998)

The cognitivist instructional model emphasizes that the instruction must shift focus from the presentation of material and concern for overt behaviors to the creation of cognitive structures. In addition to teaching content instructors should design instruction, which can teach learners effective learning strategies. Moreover, the models should focus on the learner and the activities the learner can be engaged in to improve learning. The instructor's role is a strategy coach and facilitator who trains and encourages learners to use cognitive strategies and develop self-regulation skills. A criticism of cognitivism is that cognitivist techniques do not enable learners to initiate learning, thus learners depend on the instructor's cues for functioning.

Implications for Teaching and Learning

Cognitivism and schema theory has influenced education and educational technology in two ways:

- Activating prior knowledge and relevance of the new information. Advanced organizers, Gagne's third Event of Instruction (stimulating recall of prerequisite learning), and many other learning theories such as Reigeluth's elaboration theory all stress the importance of tying old instruction to new.
- Using mapping information, such as mental models, concept maps, outlines, and informational databases. These are all methods used to impose structure on what is learned, thus making it more memorable.

Humanism

Humanism is not a learning theory, but rather a school of thought that humans are unique in capability, and different from other animals (Edwords, 1989) since humans behave out of intentionality and values (Kurtz, 2000). Huitt (2001), in an analysis of Gage and Berliner (1991), describes five basic objectives of the humanistic view of education:

1. To promote positive self-direction and independence (development of the regulatory system);
2. To develop the ability to take responsibility for what is learned (regulatory and affective systems);

3. To develop creativity (divergent thinking aspect of cognition);
4. To develop curiosity (exploratory behavior, a function of imbalance, or dissonance in any of the systems); and
5. To develop interest in the arts (primarily to develop the affective/emotional system).

Huitt (2001) continues this analysis by writing that students will learn best what they want and need to know, that knowing how to learn is more important than acquiring a lot of knowledge, that self-evaluation is the only meaningful evaluation of a student's work, that feelings are as important as facts, and that students learn best in a nonthreatening environment.

Implications for Teaching and Learning

Huitt (2001) lists five implications of the humanistic view for designing learning environments:

1. Allow the student to have a choice in the selection of tasks and activities whenever possible.
2. Help students learn to set realistic goals.
3. Have students participate in group work, especially cooperative learning, in order to develop social and affective skills.
4. Act as a facilitator for group discussions when appropriate.
5. Be a role model for the attitudes, beliefs, and habits you wish to foster. Constantly work on becoming a better person and then share yourself with your students.

Constructivism

Constructivism is not a theory but rather a philosophy of education that states:

- Learning is an active process of constructing rather than acquiring knowledge (Perkins, 1991).
- Instruction is a process of supporting that construction rather than communicating knowledge (Mayer, 1999; Coleman, Perry, & Schwan, 1997).

In addition, constructivists view learning as activity in context. The situation as a whole must be examined during learning activities. Thus, constructivist learning requires the learner to actively select relevant information, organize it, and integrate it within existing knowledge structures (Mayer, 1999).

Jonassen (1999) states that the essential component in the constructivist learning environments (CLEs) includes a problem, question, or project as the focus of the environment, with various surrounding support structures. The problem must be interesting, relevant, and authentic. Three major components need to be included in the design of the problem:

- The context: A description of the problem surrounded by the physical, socio-cultural, and organizational climate in which the problem occurs.
- The representation or simulation: The problem must be interesting, appealing, and engaging. It must perturb or upset the learner cognitively. The problem needs to be authentic and relevant to the learner to promote engagement in the problem.
- The manipulation space: The learner must be provided opportunities to manipulate objects and interact with the environment, or at least generate hypotheses in order to provide rationales.

In CLEs, the learner also needs related cases, information resources, and cognitive tools. The related cases support learning by **scaffolding** student memory, providing different perspectives, themes, and interpretations, and should convey the complexity of the problem. CLEs should assist the learner in developing cognitive flexibility, a crisscrossing of a mental landscape (Spiro, Feltovich, Jacobson, & Coulson, 1991). CLEs have to provide prompt information resources to help the learner comprehend and solve the problem. Cognitive tools are computer tools that engage and assist in specific types of cognitive processing. There are five major types of tools differing in their functions:

- Problem/Task Representation Tools: Helps the learner to visualize and construct the mental model about how the objects behave and interact. Concept maps are one example of this.
- Static and Dynamic Knowledge Modeling Tools: Helps the learner to clarify an understanding of the problem. The questions "What do I know?" and "What does it mean?" are examples.
- Performance Support Tools: Helps the learner by sharing the cognitive load to perform routine tasks, such as calculation and memorization. Calculators are an example of this type of tool.

- Information Gathering Tools: Helps the learner to focus on problem solving and not be distracted by searching for information. Google is an example of this tool.
- Conversation and Collaborative Tools: Helps the learners by giving structured access to other learners and experts. Medical journals are an example of this tool.

In CLEs, learners are encouraged to engage in exploration, articulation, and reflection. Instructors are encouraged to provide instructional support in:

- Modeling, which focuses on the expert's performance (how to do it), including modeling the performance and the thinking processes (i.e., behavioral and cognitive modeling).
- Coaching, which focuses on the learner's performance (how am I doing) to provide motivational prompts, monitor and regulate the learner's performance, provoke reflection, and perturb learner's models.
- Scaffolding, which is a systemic approach to supporting the learners in different aspects of the learning environment (the tasks, the teacher, the learner, the materials, the tools), and is based on each learner's level of understanding and need (adjusting task difficulty, restructuring the task, or providing alternative assessments).

Reigeluth (1999) points out the major contribution of this model is that it provides a coherent instructional framework integrating much work in the constructivist arena.

Implications for Teaching and Learning

Because much of the constructivism process is internalized on the part of the learner, the implication is that only the learner can truly know what has been learned. Others can observe it and test it to the extent that it provides a viable, workable, or acceptable action relative to potential alternatives.

A second implication is that to communicate these constructions to one another, we must already exist in a community of some sort, a community that shares common experiences and has an agreement on a common set of values based on those experiences.

Designing constructivist learning situations should foster the selection, organization, and integration of relevant information. The selection and organization of relevant material can be accomplished by manipulating text with headings or boldface (Mayer, 1999). Adding textual summaries and key questions will also help. For other media objects, such as graphics, animations, and video, embedded arrows or other visual clues could be added to point out important areas. See Chapter 9 for more information on best uses of instructional text and media selection.

Teachers can also assist by:

- Modeling: Focus on the expert's performance, how to do it, and the thinking processes behind the doing.
- Coaching: Include feedback and corrections on performance, motivational prompts, and reflection activities.
- Scaffolding: A systemic approach to supporting the learner in different aspects of the learning environment (the tasks, the teacher, the learner, the materials, the tools), adjusting task difficulty and/or restructuring the task as needed when the learner encounters difficulty. (Jonassen, 1999)

Problem-Based Learning

Problem-based learning (PBL) is "the learning that results from the process of working toward the understanding or resolution of a problem. The problem is encountered first in the learning process" (Barrows & Tamblyn, 1980, p. 1). PBL uses realistic, complex tasks to challenge students to acquire the knowledge and skills they need to successfully complete the task, while giving them the opportunity to practice inquiry, critical thinking, problem solving, and teamwork (Duch, 1995). Well-designed tasks or problems will activate prior knowledge, provide detail-rich contexts, promote elaboration through discussion and decisions, and stimulate intrinsic motivation to learn.

Many variations on the PBL teaching approach exist. All start by giving the students a problem or set of problems to solve. Problems may be well structured and have a clear answer, or they may be ill structured, having many possible solutions.

One type of PBL that was initially common in medical education is the mini-case. A group of students is given several sentences of text that describes a medical situation. For example, a patient presents with yellow eyes. He complains of being tired, and had a recent operation. It is then up to the group to begin the following process after the presentation of the problem (Schmidt, 1983).

- Step 1: Clarify terms and concepts not readily comprehensible.
- Step 2: Define the problem.
- Step 3: Analyze the problem.
- Step 4: Draw a systematic inventory of the explanations inferred from step 3.
- Step 5: Formulate learning goals.
- Step 6: Collect additional information outside the group.
- Step 7: Synthesize and test the newly acquired information.

As students move through this process, more information is made available if requested. The end result is a solution to the problem.

Implications for Teaching and Learning

The faculty role in PBL is to guide, probe, and support student learning. Classes may be instructor-led, student-led, or a combination of both, depending on the student's abilities. Teamwork is critical for most PBL situations, so learning to work in teams is essential.

The main goal of PBL is to have students assume responsibility for their own learning. This in turn leads to higher levels of comprehension, improved social skills, and the ability to apply knowledge to novel situations (Rhem, 1998). Students should understand the following when in a PBL environment:

- Learners are responsible for their own learning. The instructor is a facilitator for the problem-solving process, not the fountain of knowledge.
- Learners are responsible for the decisions they make in the problem-solving process.
- Learning is collaborative.

Instructors should follow the following steps when developing PBL materials:

- Step 1: Analyze your course. Define the problem, the scope, and the complexity of the assignment. How much time will you allot?
- Step 2: Brainstorm common issues that might arise and plan for them.
- Step 3: Develop the framework for the problem. How will you present it to the students?
- Step 4: Identify the resources needed to solve the problem. Make these available if they are difficult for students to obtain or access.

Situated Cognition, Everyday Cognition, and Cognitive Apprenticeships

Situated cognition theory states that thinking, the contexts in which thinking occurs, and the resulting interactions are inextricably linked. Knowledge and meaning are a result of the interaction between the learner and an authentic situation, with meaning being generated "on the fly" (Young, 1993). Authentic situations thus coproduce knowledge through activity (Brown, Collins, & Duguid, 1989).

For a situation to be authentic, it must possess the following real-world problem solving attributes (Young, 1993):

- ill-structured, complex goals,
- an opportunity to detect relevant and irrelevant information,
- active generative engagement in finding, defining, and solving problems,
- involvement of the learner's beliefs and values, and
- an opportunity to engage in collaborative interpersonal activities.

Thus, situated cognition may be considered a form of problem-based learning.

In situated cognition, knowledge resides throughout the environment. For example, drivers use directional signs to gather information on where to proceed. Pea (1988) names this "distributed intelligence."

Researchers of **everyday cognition** are concerned with how people think and solve problems in non-formal situations (informal as opposed to formal thinking). Informal reasoning is different from formal reasoning. As Lave, Murtaugh, and de la Rocha (1990) state: "There is speculation that the circumstances that govern problem solving in situations which are not prefabricated and minimally negotiable differ from those that can be examined in experimental situations" (p. 67).

Informal reasoning is a process of situation modeling (Perkins, Farady, & Bushey, 1991), where "the reasoner builds a model of a situation as it is and might be, articulating the dimensions and factors involved in an issue" (p. 85). Common sense, casual, and intentional principles are invoked in the construction of these models.

Many plausible arguments exist for each issue in informal reasoning, making it impossible to chain issues together in a logical and infallible manner. Malleable elements (including environmental tools) bear heavily on possible arguments.

If one were to diagram an informal reasoning structure, it would probably resemble a bush with many short branches (Perkins *et al.*, 1991).

By comparison, formal reasoning stresses knowledge that is context-free and symbolic (Choi & Hannafin, 1995). This allows one to develop a strong argument for one side of an issue, so the other points of view can be discarded. The situation is less important. Issues can thus be chained together in a logical and infallible manner.

People using informal reasoning are involved in authentic (everyday) tasks, not tasks contrived (as in schools) to teach a specific point (Wilson, 1993). Authentic tasks are ordinary, meaningful tasks that take place within a culture's domain (Brown *et al.*, 1989).

It is the emphasis on the situation that brings situated cognition and everyday cognition together. Both state the importance of the situation to the process. Both are concerned with the ill-structured nature of these situations. Both argue for active, generative engagement in solving situationally-grounded problems.

The cognitive apprenticeship model (Collins, Brown, & Newman, 1989) is one methodology used to achieve a contextual learning environment. **Cognitive apprenticeships** use methods similar to those found in craft apprenticeships (Brown *et al.*, 1989), where learners have access to experts in a knowledge domain who guide their learning. Cognitive apprenticeship starts with modeled instruction, then proceeds to guided trials where the practitioners progressively assume more responsibility for their learning (Farmer, Buckmaster, & LeGrand, 1992). Learners also learn in the actual work environment, not in a classroom or other setting that is removed from the environment where the skills to be learned will be used.

Cognitive apprenticeships can utilize six teaching methods designed to help students.

1. Modeling: Occurs when an expert demonstrates a task to students so students can observe and build a conceptual model of the task processes (Collins *et al.*, 1989). For example, a nurse might take a student on rounds, showing the student what is done and how decisions are made for each patient.

2. Coaching: Occurs when a teacher observes a student performing a task, offering expert advice to guide the student to expert performance of the task (Collins *et al.*, 1989). The teacher may offer hints, scaffolding, feedback, modeling, and reminders while coaching the student.

3. Scaffolding: A teacher supports learners as they learn new skills, then takes the support away gradually (fading) until the student can perform the task autonomously (Guzdial, 1996). Bruner first used the term scaffolding in 1978, although other educators, such as Vygotsky, also discussed it conceptually (Roehler & Duffy, 1991). Scaffolding can take the form of suggestions, help, and/or physical supports such as cue cards (Collins *et al.*, 1989). The amount and type of scaffolding should match the student's capabilities that just enough information is provided to get the student through a difficult point in the task.

4. Articulation: Occurs when a student overtly states their knowledge, reasoning, and problem-solving processes in a domain (Collins *et al.*, 1987). This process provides insights into the student's thought processes and cognitive structure, enabling the expert to provide the necessary modeling, coaching, or scaffolding.

5. Reflection: Occurs when students compare their problem-solving processes with that of an expert, other students, and an internal cognitive model of expertise (Collins *et al.*, 1989). For tasks with covert components (like thinking), students can mentally recall their processes and state them, and hear about other's processes. For overt tasks (such as executing a physical skill), students can view videotapes of expert as well as their own performance. In any case, the purpose of reflection is to enable the students to see and correct mistakes on their own.

6. Exploration: Students are encouraged to problem solve on their own. When all the scaffolding of a task is removed via fading, the student is ready to explore. Exploration is needed so students can learn how to frame problems that are interesting and can be solved (Collins *et al.*, 1989). When students can do this, they are ready to explore a domain productively.

Sequencing allows students to build a conceptual map, so they can see how the part they are working on (current task) relates to the whole (the overall activity). There are three techniques that should be used to sequence instruction in a cognitive apprenticeship:

■ Increasing Complexity: Tasks should be sequenced and presented in such a way so that a student moves from needing very little expert skills and concepts to needing more and more of those skills and concepts (Collins *et al.*, 1989). This is akin to gradually entering a pool of water as opposed to jumping in all at once. This procedure is called progressive implementation (van Joolingen & de Jong, 1992). In progressive implementation, one starts with a simplified view of a domain and then moves through a series of steps to a view of the domain where all the important concepts are available.

- Increasing Diversity: Tasks should be sequenced in which a larger variety of skills and strategies are needed with each task the student attempts (Collins *et al.*, 1989). For example, if a student was learning how to land an airplane, the initial task might be for the student to operate the plane in only one dimension (forward). When the student responded correctly in that situation, the task would then allow the user to operate the plane in two dimensions (forward, side to side), then finally in three dimensions (forward, side to side, up and down). Each new task would introduce new, diverse skills.

- Global Before Local Skills: This is support (via scaffolding, modeling, or coaching) of the lower-level or composite skills needed to carry out a complex task (Collins *et al.*, 1989). This allows students to build a conceptual model of the relationship of the parts to the whole, and also allows them to concentrate on the higher-order thinking skills needed to solve the problem, without being bogged down by the lower-level skills.

- Sociology of Cognitive Apprenticeships: This is perhaps the clearest link between cognitive apprenticeships and situated learning. In cognitive apprenticeships, the student is immersed in the culture where the craft (and its required skill set) is to be perfected. The situation is more than critical for a successful apprenticeships, it cannot be separated from it. Skills are learned in the context of their application to realistic problems (Collins *et al.*, 1989). Experts are available for teaching those needed skills within the confines of the situation. The need to learn a skill is readily apparent within the confines of the situation. The rewards for learning a skill are intertwined and feed back into the situation.

Assessment within a situated learning environment must concentrate on the learner, the content, learning methods, instructional sequence, and sociological aspects. McLellan (1993) claims there are three kinds of evaluation one can use for a situated learning environment:

- Portfolios
- Summary Statistics
- Diagnosis

Portfolios are a gathering of a student's work and products into one place, so others can peruse the work and evaluate and comment upon it. In addition, portfolios show progress over time and can serve as a mechanism for self-reflection. As McLellan (1993) states:

> Using portfolios as a factor in evaluation allows students to thoughtfully choose and revise their work for presentation, trace the history of work development, and exhibit the range of their personal vision and style—all activities that are important parts of real-world performance. (p. 40)

Portfolios are difficult to assess thoroughly; they are not multiple-choice tests with right and wrong answers. Teachers and experts must devote a great deal of time to properly analyze a portfolio.

Summary statistics are information about what a student did, where a student went, and what paths were explored. Young, Kulikowich, and Barab (1997) discuss "dribble files," or continuous logs of user's actions, used for just this purpose. Summary statistics allow insight into the process a student takes when utilizing affordances within a situation, and also show what affectivities the student is aware of. For example, when students use a hypertext, the best path through that hypertext for that particular student can only be realized if current information about the student and the environment are both available (Young *et al.*, 1997).

Diagnosis is a combination of both portfolios and summary statistics, as well as the constant monitoring of student and learning activities in action (McLellan, 1993). The most simplistic diagnosis is, "Can the student perform adequately within the situation?" In this case, the situation is the test, as well as the learning environment. As Young *et al.* (1997) states, "Rather than standing apart assessing static knowledge, assessment should become part of the dynamic context" (p. 143).

Implications for Teaching and Learning

Four critical tasks should be considered when developing instruction for situated learning environments:

1. Select the situation or set of situations (generator set) that will afford the acquisition of knowledge. The generator set should afford students the best opportunities to detect the stable (unchanging between situations) elements of the subject domain.

2.   Provide scaffolding for novices to operate within the complex realistic context and still permit experts to work within the same situation. Students should be active generators of both problems and solutions, allowing each student to see problems from multiple perspectives.

3.   Provide supports that enable teachers to track progress, assess products, access distributed sources of knowledge, interact knowledgeably and collaboratively with individuals and groups, and provide for development of teachers through preparation and enhancement.

4.   Define the role and nature of assessment and what it means to assess situated learning.

Summary

Many learning theories exist. This chapter has touched on but a few. If learning theories are lenses through which we may observe learning, we can use these theories when we approach the design of an instructional situation, matching the instructional goals and objectives with a relevant theory or theories.

Ertmer and Newby (1993) propose a continuum that includes behaviorism, cognitivism, and constructivism. Behaviorism is used when learner's task knowledge is low, and the level of cognitive processing required is also low. Cognitive strategies work best when learner's task knowledge is in the middle range, and an intermediate level of cognitive processing is required. Constructivist strategies work best when task knowledge is relatively high, and the need for cognitive processing is also high. This is not to say that this is always the case. You may, for example, find that cognitive strategies work equally as well as behaviorist ones when task knowledge is high but cognitive processing is low. In many situations, learners may need to move fluidly between different forms of instruction based on different learning theories. Thinking about these learning theories as a continuum is an excellent way to match the learning situation with an appropriate learning theory.

References

Ackerman, J. M. (1972). *Operant conditioning techniques for the classroom teacher*. Glenview, IL: Scott, Foresman and Company.

Ausubel, D. P. (1968). *Educational psychology: A cognitive view*. New York, NY: Holt, Rinehart, and Winston.

Barrows, H. S., & Tamblyn, R. M. (1980). *Problem-based learning: An approach to medical education.* New York, NY: Springer Publishing Company.

Bolles, R. C. (1975). *Learning theory.* New York, NY: Holt, Rinehart, and Winston.

Brown, J. S., Collins, A., & Duguid, P. (1989). Situated cognition and the culture of learning. *Educational Researcher, 18 ,* 32–42.

Choi, J. I., & Hannafin, M. (1995). Situated cognition and learning environments: Roles, structures, and implications for design. *Educational Technology Research and Development, 43*(2), 53–69.

Coleman, S. D., Perry, J. D., & Schwan, T. M. (1997). Constructivist instructional development: Reflecting on practice from an alternative paradigm. In C. R. Dills & A. J. Romiszowski (Eds.), *Instructional development paradigms* (pp. 269–282). Englewood Cliffs, NJ: Educational Technology Publications.

Collins, A., Brown, J. S., & Newman, S. E. (1989). Cognitive apprenticeship: Teaching the crafts of reading, writing, and mathematics. In L. B. Resnick (Ed.), *Knowing, learning, and instruction: Essays in honor of Robert Glaser* (pp. 453–494). Mahwah, NJ: Lawrence Erlbaum Associates.

Duch, B. J. (1995, January). What is problem-based learning? [Newsletter] *Center for Teaching Effectiveness.* Available at: http://www.udel.edu/pbl/cte/jan95-what.html. Accessed July 1, 2009.

Edwords, F. (1989). *What is humanism?* American Humanist Association. Available at: http://www.jcn.com/humanism.html. Accessed June 4, 2009.

Ertmer, P. A., & Newby, T. J. (1993). Behaviorism, cognitivism, constructivism: Comparing critical features from an instructional design perspective. *Performance Improvement Quarterly, 6*(4), 50–72.

Farmer, J. A., Buckmaster, A., & LeGrand, B. (1992). Cognitive apprenticeship: Implications for continuing professional education. *New Directions for Adult and Continuing Education, 55,* 41–49.

Gage, N., & Berliner, D. (1991). *Educational psychology* (5th ed.). Boston, MA: Houghton-Mifflin.

Guzdial, M. (1997). *Components of software-realized scaffolding.* Available at: http://www.cc.gatech.edu/gvu/edtech/SRS.html. Accessed June 4, 2009.

Hartley, J. (1998). *Learning and studying. A research perspective.* London, England: Routledge.

Huitt, W. (2001). Humanism and open education. *Educational Psychology Interactive.* Available at: http://chiron.valdosta.edu/whuitt/col/affsys/humed.html. Accessed June 4, 2009.

Jonassen, D. H. (1999). Designing constructivist learning environments. In C. M. Reigeluth (Ed.), *Instructional design theories and models: A new paradigm of instructional theory* (Vol. 2, pp. 215–239). Mahwah, NJ: Lawrence Erlbaum Associates.

Kearsley, G. (2009). Explorations in learning & instruction: The theory into practice database [Web site]. Available at: http://tip.psychology.org/. Accessed May 6, 2009.

Kurtz, P. (2000). *Humanist manifesto 2000: A call for a new planetary humanism.* Amherst, NY: Prometheus Books.

Lave, J., Murtaugh, M., & de la Rocha, O. (1990). The dialectic of arithmetic in grocery shopping. In B. Rogoff & J. Lave (Eds.), *Everyday cognition: Its development in social context* (pp. 67–94). Cambridge, MA: Harvard University Press.

Mayer, R. E. (1999). Designing instruction for constructivist learning. In C. M. Reigeluth (Ed.), *Instructional-design theories and models: A new paradigm of instructional theory* (Vol. 2, pp. 143–159). Mahwah, NJ: Lawrence Erlbaum Associates.

McLellan, H. (1993). Evaluation in a situated learning environment. *Educational Technology, 33*(3), 39–45.

Pea, R. D. (1988, August). *Distributed intelligence in learning and reasoning processes.* Paper presented at the meeting of the Cognitive Science Society, Montreal, Canada.

Perkins, D. N. (1991). Technology meets constructivism: Do they make a marriage? *Educational Technology, 31*(5), 18–23.

Perkins, D., Farady, M., & Bushey, B. (1991). Everyday reasoning and the roots of intelligence. In J. Voss, D. Perkins & J. W. Segal (Eds.), *Informal reasoning and education* (pp. 83–105). Mahwah, NJ: Lawrence Erlbaum Associates.

Reigeluth, C. M. (1999). Introduction. In C. M. Reigeluth (Ed.), *A new paradigm of instructional theory* (Vol. 2, pp. 5–29). Mahwah, NJ: Lawrence Erlbaum Associates.

Rhem, J. (1998). Problem-based learning: An Introduction. *National Teaching and Learning Forum, 8*, 1–2.

Roehler, L. R., & Duffy, G. G. (1991). Teachers' instructional actions. In R. Barr, M. L. Kamil, P. B. Mosenthal, & P. D. Pearson (Eds.), *Handbook of Reading Research* (Vol. 2, pp. 861–884). Mahwah, NJ: Lawrence Erlbaum Associates.

Schmidt, H. G. (1983). Problem-based learning: Rationale and description. *Journal of Medical Education, 17*(1), 11–16.

Smith, M. K. (1999). Learning theory. In the encyclopaedia of informal education. Available at: http://www.infed.org/biblio/b-learn.htm. Accessed May 6, 2009.

Spiro, R. J., Feltovich, P. J., Jacobson, M. J., & Coulson, R. L. (1991). Knowledge representation, content specification, and the development of skill in situation-specific knowledge assembly; Some constructivist issues as they relate to cognitive flexibility theory and hypertext. *Educational Technology, 33*(9), 22–25.

van Joolingen, W. R., & de Jong, T. (1992). Modeling domain knowledge for intelligent simulation learning environments. *Computers Educator, 18*, 1–3, 29–37.

Wilson, A. L. (1993). The promise of situated cognition. *New Directions for Adult and Continuing Education, 57*, 71–79.

Young, M. F. (1993). Instructional design for situated learning. *Educational Technology Research and Development, 41*(1), 43–58.

Young, M. F., Kulikowich, J. M., & Barab, S. A. (1997). The unit of analysis for situated assessment. *Instructional Science, 25*, 133–150.

CHAPTER 7

Instructional Design Theories

Food For Thought

"Not perfection as a final goal,
but the ever-enduring process of perfecting,
maturing, refining is the aim of living."

John Dewey, 1859–1952

Key Words

Algo-heuristic theory
Anchored instruction
Assessment-centered environment
Bodily-kinesthetic intelligence
Community-centered environment
Conceptual elaboration sequence
Domain expertise
Elaboration theory
Expository teaching
4C/ID model
Flexibly adaptive instructional design
    (FAID) theory
Gagne's Nine Events of Instruction
Guided discovery

Interpersonal intelligence
Intrapersonal intelligence
Knowledge-centered environment
Landamatics
Learner-centered environment
Logical-mathematical intelligence
Methods of action
Methods of prescription
Multiple intelligence
Multiple intelligence teaching approach
    (MITA) model
Musical intelligence
Naturalistic intelligence
Nonrecurrent skills

Recurrent skills
Simplifying conditions method
Spiral sequencing
STAR (Software Technology for Action and Reflection) Legacy software

Task class
Task expertise
Theoretical elaboration sequence
Topical sequencing
Verbal-linguistic intelligence
Visual-spatial intelligence

Objectives

The educator will be able to define instructional design theory.
The educator will be able to explain the difference between learning theory and instructional design theory.
The educator will be able to explain the key elements of different instructional design theories.

Introduction

Diane has been working on her doctoral degree while serving as an instructor in the School of Nursing. She is currently taking a course on learning theory, and would like to apply what she has learned to develop a new online course for the nursing department. Unfortunately, Diane does not quite know how to do this. The learning theories provide a description of how people learn, but they don't give her specific methods or strategies. A colleague of Diane's recommends that she research the term instructional design theories to get the information she needs.

Instructional design theories are based on learning theories, and provide guidance on how to design or create the instruction to enhance learning. Instructional design theories are prescriptive, meaning they are goal-oriented and provide specific strategies for creating instruction. Learning theories, in comparison, are descriptive, meaning they describe a cause-and-effect relationship (Reigeluth, 1999).

Reigeluth and Carr-Chellman (2009, p. 8) indicate that instructional design theories pertain to six aspects of instruction, including:

- What instruction should be like.
- What the process for gathering information for making decisions about instruction should be like.

- What the process for creating instructional plans should be like.
- What the process of creating instructional resources should be like.
- What the process of preparing for implementation of the instruction should be like.
- What the process for evaluating the instruction should be like.

Although many instructional design theories exist, we will look at six in this chapter: elaboration theory, Gagne's nine events of instruction, flexibly adaptive instructional design, algo-heuristic theory, the 4C/ID model, and multiple intelligences.

Elaboration Theory

Elaboration theory was created by Charles Reigeluth. It is based in cognitive learning theory and addresses a holistic approach to selecting and sequencing information for instruction. Elaboration theory includes strategies that assist the learner in forming stable cognitive schema to which complex tasks can be assimilated and also builds cognitive scaffolding that makes subsequent, more complex knowledge easier to accommodate with existing knowledge (Reigeluth, 1999). Through these strategies, a learner has a better understanding, and retention and transfer are improved (Kearsley, 1994–2009).

In elaboration theory, topics and tasks are broken up into chunks of information as well as simplified into less-complicated, real-world versions that that the learner can understand. In order to use elaboration theory, two concepts must be understood: scope and sequence.

Scope

According to Reigeluth (1999), scope addresses what to teach or the nature of the content. It is how the content is separated into smaller chunks or groups, which are referred to as learning episodes. In using elaboration theory, scope should be considered simultaneously with sequence.

Sequence

Sequence involves placing the learning episodes into some type of logical order that assists the students in understanding and organizing the information.

According to Reigeluth (1999), sequencing makes the most impact on instruction under two circumstances. The first circumstance is when a strong relationship exists between the components within the learning episode. These relationships may be historical, procedural, or hierarchical. Historical is when the content is related through chronological sequence; procedural is when content is related through a step-by-step process; and hierarchical is when content is related through the attainment of specific learning prerequisites prior to the introduction of main topics or tasks. The second circumstance is when there is a large amount of instruction that takes more than a couple of hours to complete, as in a training module or unit of instruction or online course.

Reigeluth (1999) indicates that sequencing of content can be done in two ways, and these two ways exist on a continuum. **Topical sequencing** involves teaching a topic or task thoroughly before moving on to the next topic or task. **Spiral sequencing** involves first teaching just the basics of each topic or task, and then teaching them again at a greater depth, and then again at an even greater depth until all the goals are reached.

When making sequencing and scope decisions, one should consider the size of the learning episode, components within the learning episode, order of the components in the learning episode, and the order of the learning episodes within the instruction.

Types of Sequencing
Sequencing strategies should be selected based on the type of expertise trying to be established. The first type of expertise, **domain expertise**, is when the learner becomes an expert in a particular body of knowledge that is not tied to a specific skill, for example, biology (Morrison, Ross, & Kemp, 2004). When domain expertise is the goal, either **conceptual elaboration sequence** or **theoretical elaboration sequence** should be used. In conceptual elaboration sequence, the content starts with the broader, more inclusive concepts and gradually progresses to the narrower, more detailed concepts, which are then elaborated on (Reigeluth, 1999). In theoretical elaboration sequence, the content starts with the broader, more inclusive principles and gradually progress to the narrower, more detailed principles, which are then elaborated on (Reigeluth, 1999).

The second type of expertise, **task expertise**, is when the learner becomes an expert in a particular skill, such as taking a blood sample (Morrison, Ross, & Kemp, 2004). When task expertise is the goal, the **simplifying conditions**

method should be used. In the simplifying conditions method, the content starts with simplest real-world version of the task and gradually progresses to more complex versions of the task until mastery is reached at each of the lower levels (Reigeluth, 1999). This type of sequencing is used only with large and moderate to complex material where there is a degree of complexity among different versions of a task.

According to Reigeluth (1999), this theory is best used when instruction includes either cognitive tasks that are medium or complex in difficulty or psychomotor skills; when rapid prototyping is needed; when learner control is essential; or with content that is large and complex, but also has some type of relationship.

A good example of elaboration theory is in gaming, where players must demonstrate skills to overcome challenges that have increasing levels of complexity.

Summary of Elaboration Theory

Elaboration theory prompts course authors to carefully consider the organization of their information, and it provides them options for chunking, sequencing, and presenting the content in a text environment. This theory is broad and can be used with many different subject domains.

Although elaboration theory was designed for linear learning environments, it is still useful with today's students, even though they tend to be nonlinear learners, preferring to look at content in pieces in order of what is most interesting to them. In learning basic skills of increasing complexity, most learners can benefit from information organized in a sequential manner from less complex to more complex. As Willems (2008) points out, in gaming and virtual worlds such as Second Life, linear learning environments allow participants to acquire particular knowledge or skills before moving on to the next level of difficulty in the environment.

Gagne's Nine Events of Instruction

Robert Gagne developed the conditions of learning, a learning theory which consists of three different components: a taxonomy of learning outcomes, the identification of internal conditions of learning, and the identification of external conditions of learning (Gredler, 2001).

The third component of Gagne's learning theory, the external conditions of learning, includes a prescriptive set of nine sequential events of instruction that should be used to present instructional materials in a manner that supports learning. These events are based on the information processing learning theory.

Gagne's Nine Events of Instruction are outlined below:

1. Gaining attention: The initial presentation of the instruction should motivate or get the interest of the learner through a change in stimulus. This can be done through providing startling statistics, thought-provoking questions, poignant images, or some form of multimedia such as video or animation.

2. Informing the learner of the learning outcomes: The purpose of the instruction should be provided to learner. This can be accomplished by simply listing the objectives or asking questions that assist students in identifying the objectives.

3. Stimulating recall of prerequisites: The knowledge learners should posses to understand the instruction should be presented before the learner proceeds to the main content. This could include a listing of prerequisite knowledge or skills, a review of the main concepts, questions that help the learners recall prior knowledge, or a pretest.

4. Presenting materials: The presentation of materials should be considered carefully, with special attention paid to matching the content to the stated objectives, chunking information into manageable pieces, and sequencing the information. Multiple modalities should be considered to address the needs of diverse learners.

5. Providing learning guidance: Instructional strategies should be used to assist learners to learn the material. These could include strategies to categorize information, memorize important concepts, or connect new information to pre-existing knowledge.

6. Eliciting performance: Opportunities should be provided for learners to check their understanding through the use of questions or activities that are located throughout the content.

7. Providing feedback: Immediate and constructive feedback should be provided for all questions and activities.

8. Assessing performance: A formal way to assess learners' comprehension of the state learning objectives should be included and could be in the

form of criterion-referenced tests or more informal measures such as the learner demonstrating the skill.

9. Enhancing retention and transfer: Learners should be assisted in retaining information and applying it in the real world. Increase retention through summarizing or paraphrasing content or providing review questions. Increase transfer by relating content to everyday or work-related situations, or providing the learners with novel problems in which to use their new problem solving skills. (Gredler, 2001; Fenrich, 1997)

Note that initially, instructors will follow the nine events very carefully, but with increased familiarity of the model, the nine events can often be combined or rearranged.

Gagne's Nine Events focuses on the presentation of content to the learner rather than the engagement of the learners with the content. Smith and Ragan (1999) modified Gagne's Nine Events so that it can be used with problem-solving content, such as the content found in mathematics and science. Smith and Ragan's revised nine events include:

1. Deploy attention: Present a challenge or problem in a novel way.
2. Establish instructional purpose: State a problem that learners will learn to solve and point out that the problems will become increasingly complex throughout the lesson.
3. Recall prior knowledge: Explicitly review prior knowledge; suggest ways learners can reorganize knowledge in conducive forms; and identify similarities and differences with other problem-solving learning.
4. Present materials: Provide simplified, prototypical versions of the problem first, encourage students to think aloud as they solve problems, break problem into smaller goals, and isolate critical attributes of the problem.
5. Provide learner guidance: Generate analogies, ask guiding questions, provide hints, and present problem in alternative forms.
6. Elicit performance: Practice identifying goal states, breaking down the problem, evaluating the adequacy of a provided solution, and using well-defined problems first.
7. Provide feedback: Provide models of solutions, give hints or ask questions to assist learners in identifying the correct solution, and provide information on efficiency as well as effectiveness of solution.

8. Enhance retention and transfer: Summarize effective strategies, find similar problems outside the classroom, and explicitly state when strategies may transfer to other problem types.

9. Assess performance: Test ability to solve similar but novel problems, to justify solutions, and evaluate other solutions.

Summary of Gagne's Nine Events of Instruction

Gagne's Nine Events of Instruction is one of the most popular instructional design theories used in education because it is very easy to understand and implement in face-to-face and online environments.

Smith and Ragan's adaptation of Gagne's Nine Events of Instruction has made it more adaptable to the needs of today's learners. Using Smith and Ragan's modified list to design collaborative and authentic tasks, the instructor can provide opportunities for social interaction, hands-on activities and immediate feedback.

Flexibly Adaptive Instructional Design

The **Flexibly Adaptive Instructional Design (FAID) theory** was developed by Daniel Schwartz, Xiaodong Lin, Sean Brophy, and John Bransford of Vanderbilt University. This theory has its basis in constructivist learning theory, specifically, in situated cognition. FAID focuses on an instructional design that is based on basic principles of learning, but is flexible in that it can be customized based on the instructor's needs and the learner's needs (Schwartz, Lin, Brophy, & Bransford, 1999b). FAID was strongly influenced by **anchored instruction**, where learning and teaching activities are designed around an anchor, such as a case study or problem situation that encourages exploration by the learners (Kearsley, 1994–2009).

The primary goal of FAID is to teach a deep understanding of subject matter while also encouraging problem solving, collaboration, and communication (Schwartz *et al.*, 1999b). This is accomplished through the use of problem-based learning, followed by project-based learning.

STAR Legacy

To implement FAID, an instructional shell or template, called the **STAR (Software Technology for Action and Reflection) Legacy software**, was developed to create an environment that is learner-centered, knowledge-centered, assessment-centered, and community-centered (Schwartz, Lin, Brophy, & Bransford, 1999a). Brophy and Bransford (2001) describe each of these environments as follows:

- **Learner-centered environment**: Focuses on bridging the gap between what learners' currently know and what they need to know to meet the goals for instruction, through an organized structure of domain knowledge that can be used to solve problems
- **Knowledge-centered environment**: Focuses on helping the learners develop their own organization of the domain's concepts and apply them to new problems
- **Assessment-centered environment**: Emphasizes formative assessment and focuses on providing multiple opportunities for feedback
- **Community-centered environment**: Focuses on collaborative learning and a sense of community that facilitates instruction

The STAR Legacy shell consists of a seven-step inquiry cycle that is used to define critical phases in the exploration of a challenge or problem (Brophy & Bransford, 2001). The seven steps include look ahead and reflect back, the challenges, generate ideas, multiple perspectives, research and revise, test your mettle, and go public. When the STAR Legacy program is started, instructor and learners are presented with a graphic depicting the seven steps. Schwartz, Lin, Brophy, and Bransford (1999b) indicate that this graphic allows:

- Both the teacher and student to see where they are in the learning process.
- Both the teacher and student to skip around the steps of the cycle to modify the instruction according to their individual needs.
- The instruction to be flexible, so teachers are able to customize it to their needs.

The following is a description of each of the steps in the cycle:

1. *Look Ahead and Reflect Back*: This phase permits the students to understand the goals, challenges, and context that they will be facing as well as a measure of students' current knowledge and need for growth. This phase may be a pretest or an opportunity for students to attempt to answer questions before engaging in the lesson.

2. *The Challenges*: This phase involves presenting several challenges on the same topic to the students, each more complicated than the one before it. The challenges may take any form including designing a real-world project or answering sample items on a test. By going through each of the challenges and seeking a solution, the students can deepen their knowledge about the subject.

3. *Generate Ideas*: During this phase, students use the information they have gathered through video clips, Web-based instruction, audio notes, computations, or text during the initial challenge to help them to generate ideas with their classmates. The intended goal is to provide clarity to the students' thought processes and to encourage the exchange of ideas.

4. *Multiple Perspectives*: During this phase, students receive guidance on solving their challenges from expert sources that may include video clips of experts expressing their opinion, recorded interviews with specialists in a particular area, or research findings in a specific field. This phase is beneficial to the students because it brings together many different experts from varied fields who help to define issues and present multiple vantage points, which is something that could not be easily done in a traditional classroom setting. It also helps the students set realistic goals and encourages flexibility in their problem-solving skills.

5. *Research and Revise*: At this point, students are encouraged to explore and figure out a response to the initial challenge. Their research activities do not have to be technology-based; they can include lab experiments, Internet search, discussion and collaboration with other students, listening to lectures, looking at legacies of previous students, and completing skill-building exercises. After the students gather this information, they may revise their initial ideas for a solution to the challenge.

6. *Test Your Mettle*: This phase permits the instructor to review the overall progress and then to provide formative feedback on an individual level to see what each student has learned. Feedback can be obtained through a number of sources including multiple-choice tests, essays, and demonstrations. Note that students choose when they are ready to participate in this evaluation.

7. *Go Public*: In the final phase, the students evaluate each other's work, which gives them an opportunity to see different ways to approach the original challenge. The students may present their solutions through a

variety of methods, such as a Web site, multimedia presentation, or panel discussion. Due to the public nature of this phase, it serves to motivate students to make an effort to display what they have accomplished.

The STAR Legacy software is not necessary to incorporate FAID into the development of content. Instructors can simply use all or a selection of the seven steps represented in the STAR Legacy software to create effective instruction that is anchored in a realistic, real-world problem that promotes collaborative learning. (Schwartz, *et al.*, 1999b)

Summary of Flexibly Adaptive Instructional Design (FAID)

FAID focuses on problem and project-based instruction that is anchored in authentic contexts. The elements of FAID have been implemented using the STAR Legacy software shell. By working through a seven-step cycle for each of three increasingly difficult challenges, learners are able to construct knowledge that leads to a deep understanding of the subject matter.

FAID is based on situated cognition learning theory, which is one theory that is recommended for use with the Net Generation (see Chapter 3). Situated cognition includes the following principles: provision of authentic activities with real-world relevance, access to expert performances, provision of multiple perspectives, support for collaborative construction of knowledge, provision of opportunities for learners to reflect on their learning experience and compare their opinions to experts, articulation of arguments through a public presentation, provision of coaching and scaffolding, and assessment that is authentic and includes multiple indicators of learning (Herrington & Oliver, 2000).

To implement FAID, the Star Legacy software shell is not needed; one can use all or pieces of the seven-step inquiry cycle to create customized instruction that includes basic principles of learning.

Algo-Heuristic Theory (Landamatics)

Algo-heuristic theory was developed by Lev Landa, and was initially used to decrease the time it took to train employees to learn new skills in business and industry. Algo-heuristic theory provides a way to break down the complex mental operations of subject matter experts (SMEs) into simple step-by-step processes, where both the actions and underlying cognitive thoughts are described.

This information is used to create an algorithm or flowchart which includes key decision-making points. The flowchart is provided to novice learners who use it to learn the process and to internalize the underlying rules. Over time, the learners do not need to depend on the flowcharts and become real experts who are able to apply the principles in different situations.

Some key concepts of **Landamatics** include methods of action, methods of prescription, and general methods of thinking.

Methods of Action and Methods of Prescription

Landa (1999) states that there are two kinds of mental operations or methods:

1. **Methods of Action** (Ma's) are a system of actions that lead to solving problems or performing tasks.
2. **Methods of Prescription** (Mp's) are the underlying thought processes or instructions (prescriptions) that point out the action to be performed.

Normally when learners are trying to solve a new problem, they first discover methods of action and later convert them to methods of prescription. For example, when students are learning statistics, they will simply substitute numbers into equations based on examples that are provided in the textbook (methods of action). As they become more familiar with statistics and use them in research, they will come to understand the meaning of the equations (methods of prescription).

General Methods of Thinking

In conventional instruction, students who seem to grasp concepts in the classroom are often unable to apply the newly acquired knowledge outside the classroom. If an instructor does not show every variation in the classroom demonstration, the student will not be able to make appropriate generalizations when they are left to their own devices. Demonstrating the variation is not always feasible, however, and the more variations there are, the more room there is for inaccurate concept formation and application. According to Landa, the solution is teaching general methods of concept acquisition and application by purposely teaching methods of thinking (Ma's and Mp's) which lead to reliable generalizations. Landa indicated that methods of thinking can be taught through two teaching approaches, guided discovery and expository teaching, or a combination of the two. **Guided discovery** involves the learner performing a task or problem and then creating step-by-step instructions (method). Using these instructions, the learner repeatedly practices the task or problem-solving process until the instructions are no longer needed. The learner can then apply what has been learned to novel problems. **Expository teaching**, on the other hand, involves the instructor providing the learner with the task or problem and the instructions necessary to solve it. The learner then repeatedly practices the task or problem-solving process until the instructions are no longer needed. The learner can then apply what has been learned to novel problems.

Landamatics performance aids, such as manuals or computer software, can be developed to enable new personnel to function on the job immediately, without needing a formal training program (Landa, 1999). Although algo-heuristic theory has been used more for training in industry rather than in education, it has been used in areas of mathematics, science, and language.

Summary of Algo-Heuristic Theory

Algo-heuristic theory has been used successfully for implementing efficient training in business and industry. Complex procedures are broken down into a step-by-step process, and through repeated practice, trainees are able to automatize the procedures to the point that they become experts.

The goal of this theory is the creation of very linear instruction which conflicts with the nonlinear preference of today's learners. This theory, however, may be useful in the creation of smaller elements of instruction to assist the instructor in minimizing text and using more graphics. Specifically, instructions or explanations of complex processes can be replaced by flowcharts, diagrams, or decision trees.

4C/ID Model

The **4C/ID model** was developed by Jeroen J. G. van Merriënboer, and it addresses the learning of authentic, complex tasks as a whole rather than in parts.

Complex tasks are comprised of smaller constituent skills. In most instructional design theories (see elaboration theory and algo-heuristic theory), the constituent skills are isolated and presented sequentially to the learners in efforts to help them eventually learn the more complex task. In the 4C/ID model, complex tasks are not separated into their constituent skills, but rather learners are encouraged to coordinate and integrate the constituent skills as they learn the whole complex task (van Merriënboer, Clark, & de Croock, 2002).

Constituent skills can be classified as either nonrecurrent or recurrent (van Merriënboer *et al.*, 2002). **Nonrecurrent skills** are skills needed to solve novel problems and are guided by cognitive schemata. **Recurrent skills** are skills needed for routine problems and are guided by a set of rules.

According to the 4C/ID model, the learning environments of complex tasks can be described in terms of four interrelated components. These components serve as a blueprint for designing instruction:

1. Learning tasks: These are authentic, meaningful whole-task experiences that require the integrated use of knowledge, skills, and attitudes. Learning tasks are provided to the learners in order to promote schema construction for nonrecurrent constituent skills and rule atomization for recurrent constituent skills.

2. Supportive information: This is information that provides a bridge between the learner's prior knowledge and the performance of nonrecurrent constituent skills of the complex learning task. Supportive information focuses on the problem-solving and reasoning aspects of complex tasks and thus promotes schema construction.

3. Procedural information: This is step-by-step knowledge or rules that serve as the prerequisite to performing recurrent constituent skills of the complex learning task.

4. Part-task practice: If the learning tasks do not provide sufficient repetition then practice items are provided to learners to ensure automation of selected recurrent constituent skills. (van Merriënboer & Sluijsmans, 2009; Sarfo & Elen, 2007)

In the 4C/ID model, learners are presented with authentic, whole-task experiences rather than simplified pieces of a task presented in sequential fashion. These learning tasks are grouped into tasks classes, which range in difficulty from simple to complex. Initially, learners are given the easiest **task class**, along with embedded supportive and procedural information, and then progress through the more difficult task classes, with decreasing levels of support (Sarfo & Elen, 2007).

Janssen-Noordman, van Merriënboer, van der Vleuten, and Scherpbier (2006) provide the following example of a sequence of task classes for the complex, authentic task of a medical student encountering a patient with back pain (Table 7–1.)

Table 7-1   Example of Task Classes for Encountering a Patient with Back Pain

	Task Class 1	Task Class 2	Task Class 3
Presenting complaints	Clear, largely standard	Less clear	Vague
Availability of information	Readily available, easy	Less readily available, incomplete	Difficult to obtain
Patient's demands	Low	Realistic	High
Available times	No limit	Limited	Extremely limited

Within each task class, learners are given several different types of learning tasks, and although within each class these tasks are equivalent in difficulty, their features will vary, reflecting the differences of real-life scenarios (van Merriënboer & Sluijsmans, 2009).

Summary of 4C/ID Model

The 4C/ID model focuses on teaching complex tasks as a whole rather than simplifying the tasks into smaller pieces. The complex tasks are taught in varying levels of difficulty using different dimensions and levels of support, allowing the learner to confront the whole task, similar to a real-life situation.

Since this model focuses on the whole task rather than the smaller, linear steps, it may assist educators in transitioning their content to a format that is more suitable for neo-millennial students. As mentioned in Chapter 3, Neo-millennial students have a global learning preference where they must look at the "big picture" to understand its constituent parts (Willems, 2008).

Multiple Intelligences

Through his research, Howard Gardner concluded that human intelligence consisted of more than just the linguistic and logical abilities measured by intelligence, aptitude, and achievement tests (Gardner & Hatch, 1989). He proposed the theory of **multiple intelligence** in which he identifies and defines the criteria for eight autonomous human intelligences. The eight intelligences include:

1. Musical: The ability to produce and appreciate rhythms, timbre, pitch and patterns.
2. Bodily-kinesthetic: The ability to use body actions or handle objects skillfully.
3. Logical-mathematical: The ability to use numbers or logic to understand information.
4. Verbal-linguistic: The ability to use verbal and written language to understand information.
5. Visual-spatial: The ability to perceive and navigate the visual-spatial world accurately.
6. Interpersonal: The ability to read other people's moods, temperaments, motivations, and desires.
7. Intrapersonal: The ability to be introspective, and aware of own feelings and uses them to guide behavior.
8. Naturalistic: The ability to connect with nature. (Gardner & Hatch, 1989; Watrous-McCabe, 2005)

To create instruction that addresses the different intelligences that are possessed by individuals, Gardner (1999) recommends the following procedure:

- Select a few topics with powerful themes that can be taught in-depth.
- Use entry points to draw in the student including: telling stories, using statistics, stating the issue in terms of broader philosophical views, using works of arts, providing hands-on activities, or using role plays or collaborative groups.
- Provide examples, analogies, and metaphors to enhance understanding.
- Spend a significant amount of time on a topic and use multiple representations of the topic that address the different intelligences.

Gardner's model emphasizes an approach to understanding content rather than problem solving (Merrill, 2002). In 1991, however, Ellen Weber developed the **Multiple Intelligence Teaching Approach (MITA) model** for using Gardner's multiple intelligence theory with problem-based learning in educational environments. This model incorporates constructivist learning theory and consists of five phases designed to create challenging learning environments and to meet the needs of diverse learners (Weber, 2000). The five phases include:

1. Question possibilities: Questions are developed about a given issue or problem that address the students' interests, abilities, and expectations and provide opportunities for the students to get more involved in the content.
2. Target improvements: Targets are set to guide students past the problem to consider possible solutions.
3. Expect quality: Scoring criteria or rubrics are established to guide students through learning tasks.
4. Move resources: Authentic learning tasks and assessments are created that incorporate multiple intelligences.
5. Reflect on growth possibilities: Students reflect on the learning process. (Denny *et al.*, 2008)

Summary of Multiple Intelligences Theory

Multiple intelligences theory proposes that there are more than the two types of intelligences traditionally measured by ability, achievement, and IQ tests. This theory identifies eight autonomous intelligences along with a four-step procedure to address these intelligences when creating instruction.

Although this theory was developed over 20 years ago, three of the eight intelligences identified may be more evident in today's students due to their use of technology and interest in gaming, specifically the bodily-kinetic, visual-spatial, and interpersonal intelligences. As mentioned in Chapter 3, as the result of brain plasticity, the brains of the Net Generation are changing both in structure and in function. Students today think differently today than students of earlier generations. Using the multiple intelligences theory to design instruction that addresses a number of intelligences may improve learning and provide instructors with the opportunity to incorporate innovative technologies.

Learning Activity

Select one of the instructional design theories from this lesson and use it to create materials for a training session for the scenario that follows. You may either design a training presentation or instructional manual.

You are a trainer at a major energy drink company. Your company's researchers just discovered a tropical fruit grown by farmers on a remote island that provides an amazing amount of energy. They want to include the juice in a new energy drink product, however, they must figure out a way to purchase the fruit from the farmers of the island. They have found that all the island people are afraid of calculators and they prefer their own way of doing calculations. The company's president has asked you to go to the island, learn how the island people do the calculations, and then train the company's buyers. A few days later, you travel to the island and meet with the farmers. You find out the farmers do the calculations using a process of doubling and dividing the numbers. For example, if an island farmer has 10 bushels of fruit that he wants to sell for $12 each, he would go through the following procedure (Table 7–2):

- Create two columns: one for the cost, and another for the bushels of fruit.
- In the cost column, divide 12 in half until it is down to $1. (Note: The island people do not understand fractions, so they just ignore them.)
- In the bushel column, double the number of bushels down to where they meet the $1 in the cost column.
- Next, look at the number values in the cost column. Since dollar amounts that are even numbers are considered bad luck by all of the island people, they must be crossed out along with their corresponding numbers in the bushel column.
- Finally add up all the remaining numbers in the bushels column to find out that 10 bushels of fruit at $12 each will sell for $120.

Table 7-2

Cost	Bushels
$12̶	1̶0̶
$6̶	2̶0̶
$3	40
$1½	80
	120

References

Brophy, S., & Bransford, J. (2001). *Design methods for instructional modules in bioengineering.* Proceedings of the American Society for Engineering Education Annual Conference and Exposition, Nashville, TN.

Denny, M., Weber, E. F., Wells, J., Stokes, O. R., Lane, P., & Denieffe, S. (2008). Matching purpose with practice: Revolutionizing nurse education with MITA. *Nurse Education Today, 28,* 100–107.

Fenrich, P. (1997). *Practical guidelines for creating instructional multimedia applications.* Orlando, FL: Harcourt, Brace & Company.

Gardner, H. (1999). Multiple approaches to understanding. In C. M. Reigeluth (Ed.), *Instructional design theories and models: A new paradigm of instructional theory* (Volume 2, pp. 69–89). Mahwah, NJ: Lawrence Erlbaum Associates.

Gardner, H., & Hatch, T. (1989). Multiple intelligences go to school: Educational implications of the theory of multiple intelligences. *Educational Researcher, 18*(8), 4–10.

Gredler, M. E. (2001). *Learning and instruction: Theory into practice.* Upper Saddle River, NJ: Merrill Prentice Hall.

Herrington, J., & Oliver, R. (2000). An instructional design framework for authentic learning environments. *Educational Technology Research and Development, 48*(3), 23–48.

Janssen-Noordman, A. M., Merriënboer, J. J. G., van der Vleuten C. P., & Scherpbier, A. J. (2006). Design of integrated practices for learning professional competencies. *Medical Teacher, 28*(5), 447–452.

Kearsley, G. (1994–2009). Anchored instruction. *Theories into Practice Database.* Available at: http://tip.psychology.org/anchor.html. Accessed May 16, 2009.

Landa, L. (1999). Landamatics instructional-design theory for teaching general methods of thinking. In C. M. Reigeluth (Ed.), *Instructional design theories and models: A new paradigm of instructional theory* (Vol. 2, pp. 341–370). Mahwah, NJ: Lawrence Erlbaum Associates.

Merrill, M. D. (2002). First principles of instruction. *Educational Technology Research and Development, 50*(3), 43–59.

Morrison, G. R., Ross, S. M., & Kemp, J. E. (2004). *Designing effective instruction* (4th ed.). Hoboken, NJ: John Wiley & Sons.

Reigeluth, C. M. (1999). The elaboration theory: Guidance for scope and sequence decisions. In C. M. Reigeluth (Ed.), *Instructional design theories and models: A new paradigm of instructional theory* (Vol. 2, pp. 425–481). Mahwah, NJ: Lawrence Erlbaum Associates.

Reigeluth, C. M. & Carr-Chellman, A. A. (2009). Understanding Instructional Design Theory. In C. M. Reigeluth & A. A. Carr-Chellman (Eds.) *Instructional design theories and models: Building a Common Knowledge Base* (Vol. 1, pp. 3-26). New York: Routledge.

Sarfo, F. K., & Elen, J. (2007). Developing technical expertise in secondary technical schools: The effect of 4C/ID learning environments. *Learning Environment Resources, 10,* 207–221.

Schwartz, D. L., Lin, X., Brophy, S., & Bransford, J. D. (1999a). Software for managing complex learning: Examples from an educational psychology course. *Educational Technology, Research and Development, 47*(2), 39–59.

Schwartz, D. L., Lin, X., Brophy, S., & Bransford, J. D. (1999b). Toward the development of flexibly adaptive instructional designs. In C. M. Reigeluth (Ed.) *Instructional design theories and models: A new paradigm of instructional theory* (Vol. 2, pp. 183-213). Mahwah, NJ: Lawrence Erlbaum Associates.

Smith, P. L., & Ragan, T. J. (1999). *Instructional Design* (2nd ed.). New York, NY: John Wiley & Sons, Inc.

van Merriënboer, J. J. G., Clark, R. E., & de Croock, M. B. (2002). Blueprints for complex learning: The 4C/ID-model. *Educational Technology Research and Development, 50*(3), 39–64.

van Merriënboer, J. J. G., & Sluijsmans, D. M. (2009). Toward a synthesis of cognitive load theory, four-component instructional design, and self-directed learning. *Educational Psychology Review, 21*, 55–66.

Watrous-McCabe, J. (2005, July 25). Applying multiple intelligence theory to adult online instructional design. *The eLearning Developer's Journal*. Available at: www.elearningguild.com. Accessed June 2, 2009.

Weber, E. (2000, December). Five phases to PBL: MITA model for redesigned higher education courses. In P. Little, T. Seng, J. Conway, & H. Yin (Eds.), *Problem-based learning: Educational innovation across disciplines* (pp. 65–76). Available at: http://pbl.tp.edu.sg/Others/Articles%20on%20Others/Weber.doc. Accessed June 2, 2009.

Willems, J. (2008). *From sequential to global: Exploring the landscapes of neomillennial learners* (Proceedings). Available at: http://www.ascilite.org.au/conferences/melbourne08/procs/willems.pdf. Accessed March 30, 2009.

The Instructional Design Process

Food For Thought

*"It takes less time to do a thing right
than it does to explain why you did it wrong."*

Henry Wadsworth Longfellow, 1807–1882

Key Words

ADDIE
Chunking
Constructional design

Formative evaluation
Learning domains

Learning taxonomies
Summative evaluation

Objectives

The educator will be able to list and explain the five steps in the instructional design
  process (ADDIE).
The educator will be able to give two examples of instructional design models.
The educator will be able to explain how to conduct a goal analysis.
The educator will be able to explain how to conduct a learner analysis.
The educator will be able to explain how to conduct a task analysis.
The educator will be able to explain the purpose of learning objectives.
The educator will be able to explain how to write behavioral learning objectives.

The educator will be able to explain what occurs during the development phase.

The educator will be able to describe learning taxonomies.

The educator will be able to explain three different types of instructional strategies considered during the design phase.

The educator will be able to describe the difference between formative and summative evaluation.

Explain how and why the instructional design process needs to evolve.

Instructional Design Process

An instructional designer is an authority on how people learn and how best to create instruction and instructional materials to enhance learning. The instructional design process is a detailed, systematic process that takes into account the learner, the learning environment, the learning objectives, and the available resources. The process is typically completed by an instructional designer who works in conjunction with a subject matter expert (SME). A SME is an expert in their field and has a thorough knowledge of the content for the instruction being developed. In higher education, the SME is normally a faculty member.

Many models for the instructional design process exist. Gustafson and Branch (2002) identified 15 instructional models and classified them as either having a classroom, product, or systems orientation. Although instructional design models differ in their steps and purpose, all share a similar underlying framework, which includes the steps of analysis, design, development, implementation, and assessment. These five steps are known as **ADDIE** in the instructional design field. ADDIE is thought of as the basic or generic model for the instructional design process. The five steps of ADDIE are:

1. Analysis: Information about the instruction is gathered through a series of analyses, including goal analysis, learner analysis, and content analysis.
2. Design: The learning objectives are identified, assessment items are created, and strategies for creating and delivering the instruction are determined.
3. Development: The instruction is created, which includes activities such as writing text or scripts, creating images and multimedia, recording video or audio, and creating simulations.
4. Implementation: The instruction is delivered in the intended environment along with any needed support.

5. Evaluation: The effectiveness of the instruction and the instructional materials are determined through formative and summative evaluations.

Examples of specific models of the instructional design process include the Dick and Carey model and the Morrison, Ross, and Kemp model.

The Dick and Carey model is probably the best-known model and uses a very detailed, linear process that includes nine steps, typically represented as an algorithm. The nine steps include:

1. Begin with a needs assessment, and clear, measurable goals.
2. Conduct instructional analysis (hierarchical and cluster analysis), and analyze learners and contexts (knowledge, skills, attitudes, environment).
3. Write performance objectives in measurable terms.
4. Develop assessment instruments (criterion-referenced test items).
5. Develop instructional strategy (match learners to objectives).
6. Develop and select instructional materials.
7. Design and conduct formative evaluation of instruction.
8. Revise instruction by collecting, summarizing, and analyzing data collected during tryout sessions.
9. Design and conduct summative evaluation. (Dick & Carey, 1996)

The key characteristics of the Dick and Carey model include: It must start with a needs assessment, it is systematic rather than systemic, and it is based in military procedures and computer processing (Gustafson & Branch, 2002).

The Morrison, Ross, and Kemp model focuses on the perspective of the learner and is represented by an oval-shaped image composed of several layers, with nine key elements in the center. The nine elements include:

1. Identify the instructional problem and specify goals for designing the instruction.
2. Examine learner characteristics that will influence your instructional decisions.
3. Identify subject content, and analyze task components related to stated goals and purposes.
4. Specify the instructional objectives.
5. Sequence the content within each instructional unit for logical learning.
6. Design instructional strategies so that each learner can master the objectives.

7. Plan the instructional message and develop the instruction.
8. Develop evaluation instruments to assess objectives.
9. Select resources to support instruction and learning activities. (Morrison, Ross & Kemp, 2004)

The key characteristics of the Morrison, Ross, and Kemp model include: It is systemic rather than systematic, it has no distinct starting point and moves through the step-by-step process, not all nine elements need to be used, elements are interdependent upon each other (decisions made for one element will impact the decisions made about the other element), it is a more realistic model in terms of dealing with the instructional design process in real-world scenarios, and it is focused on the individual learner rather than on the content (Gustafson & Branch, 2002; Morrison, Ross, & Kemp, 2004).

Although the Dick and Carey model and Morrison, Ross, and Kemp model are different, both are built around the five steps of ADDIE. We will now look more in-depth at each step and what tasks are completed for each.

Analysis Phase

Several types of analyses are done at the start of the instructional design process. These include goal analysis, learner analysis, and task analysis.

Goal Analysis

A goal analysis involves examining the goal of the instruction and breaking it down into the sequential, step-by-step process that the learner must complete to obtain that goal. The format of a goal analysis is a visual depiction of the steps needed to obtain the identified goal. It is typically a numbered diagram, similar to a flowchart of a work process, which uses boxes for steps, diamonds for decision points, and arrows for direction (see Figure 8–1).

Figure 8-1 Goal analysis format.

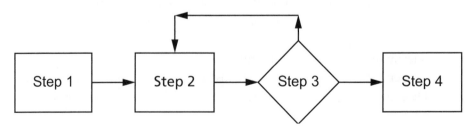

Conducting a goal analysis may initially seem relatively simple, but it is actually a very detailed and thoughtful process. Below is the six-step procedure recommended by Morrison, Ross, and Kemp (2004):

1. Identify the aim or intention(s) of the instruction (what is needed to solve the identified problem).
2. For each intention, establish the learning goals in terms of learners' behaviors.
3. Refine the goals, removing or combining duplicate information and clarifying vague information.
4. Rank the goals in order of importance or need.
5. Refine the goals again, examining the gaps between the instructional goals and the existing performance.
6. Finally, make a final ranking of the goals, considering how critical the goal is to performing the task and the overall effect of the goal.

Fenrich (1997) established the following guidelines to use with a goal analysis to determine if the length and depth of desired content is appropriate:

- A goal analysis generally identifies 5 to 15 steps; more steps indicate the goal is too big or the steps are too detailed.
- If the instruction includes the teaching of too many subordinate skills, it will bore students and impede learning.
- The instruction should match the targeted population; the goal analysis should identify the entry-level skills already acquired by this targeted population (not the exceptions).

The targeted population is identified using the next type of analysis, the learner analysis.

Learner Analysis

A learner analysis is conducted to ensure that the content matches the targeted audience. The learners must be considered when writing the learning objectives, selecting the methods of delivery, writing the content, creating examples, selecting instructional strategies, and determining appropriate assessment. When performing a learner analysis, some of the following characteristics may be considered:

- Demographics (age, gender, ethnicity)
- Prerequisite knowledge or skills
- Prior work experience or training

- Aptitudes and abilities
- Attitudes toward topic or instruction
- Maturity level/autonomy
- Geographic location
- Learning styles

In addition to these characteristics, individual learning differences must be addressed. These include individual learning styles or preferences, and disabilities.

There is no formalized way of conducting a learner analysis. In most cases, instructional designers in organizations and educational institutions are already familiar with their targeted audience, so they can complete this analysis rather quickly and informally. If this is not the case, Rothwell and Kazanas (1992) identified two approaches for conducting a learner analysis, neither of which requires a strict set of procedures:

- Derived Approach: simply brainstorming a list of relevant learning characteristics; and
- Contrived Approach: going through a general list of learner characteristics and determining whether each item is related to the instructional problem.

Although a learner analysis appears to be a very simple procedure, it has extremely important implications for the design of a course. Based on this analysis, specific instructional strategies are selected to ensure that the learners are able to meet the learning outcomes. Smith and Ragan (1999) list the following instructional strategies that can be determined using the results of a learner analysis:

- Pace of instruction
- Delivery of instruction
- Number of practice experiences
- Statements included to convince students of relevancy of the instruction
- Techniques for focusing attention
- Number and difficulty level of examples and practice items
- Context of examples and practice items
- Type of feedback given after practice items
- Amount of structure and organization (especially important in an online environment)
- Size of instructional chunks

- Level of learner control
- Reading level used in content
- Amount and type of reinforcement
- Time allowed for instruction

Examining the characteristics of the targeted audience is extremely important in designing instruction. Although not every individual need can be met, the instruction can be developed to accommodate different learning preferences, and remedial materials can be developed to assist those lacking in prerequisite skills or those with learning disabilities.

Task Analysis

Once the instructional problem has been identified and analyzed, and the needs of the targeted audience have been determined (via the learner analysis), the specific content to be included in a learning episode needs to be identified. Although this seems pretty straight forward at first, a subject matter expert or instructor may often find themselves struggling with issue. Questions often asked include: How much content is sufficient? How much is necessary versus how much is just interesting to an expert in the field? How much information will fit in an online lesson?

To determine what content to include in the instruction, a task analysis must be completed. Many different task analyses exist (see Jonassen, Tessmer, & Hannum, 1999, for a description of at least 26 types), and the one selected will be dependent on the learning context, the subject matter, and the desired objectives. Examples of task analyses include:

- Procedural analysis: for analyzing step-by-step procedures;
- Job task analysis: for analyzing job duties and requirements; and
- Critical incident analysis: for identifying best practices for ill-structured content.

A task analysis generally consists of the following steps (Jonassen *et al.*, 1999):

- Identify or create a list of all tasks that should be considered for the instruction.
- Sort and select the tasks that are most appropriate and feasible for the instruction, and eliminate those that are not necessary based on the learning objectives, context of the instruction, available resources, and prerequisite knowledge of the learners.

- Describe and elaborate the tasks identified in the initial inventory to ensure all instructional components are addressed.
- Sequence the tasks in the order that learning should occur, which may or may not be different than how the tasks are performed.
- Classify each task based on the level of performance and knowledge outcome required to ensure congruity between tasks and the assessment items, congruity between the tasks and the instructional methods, and also to ensure prerequisite sequencing.

A task analysis is useful in determining the content to be included in the instruction as well as the content that is not necessary and should be left out. Although it may seem time consuming, this initial planning will save time and energy during the course design phase.

Design Phase

The goal analysis, learner analysis, and task analysis comprise the analysis phase of the instructional design process. Next is the design phase, which includes identifying learning objectives, creating assessment questions, selecting instructional strategies, and deciding on a method of delivering the content.

Learning Objectives

Instructional designers and SMEs use learning objectives to guide them through all aspects of content creation including the activities, assignments, and assessment questions. Learning objectives are also important for the students. The objectives assist students in determining which information is most important, help them organize the new content into their existing schema, and serve as a means for students to monitor understanding of the material.

The process for creating learning objectives builds off the last step of the task analysis. Using the results of the task analysis:

- Identify and chunk similar items together, if needed.
- Based on the level of performance and knowledge outcome required, classify each task or task group based on either the cognitive, psychomotor, or affective **learning domains**.
- Locate a learning taxonomy for each of the domains identified. Learning taxonomies group learning in increasing levels of difficulty within a domain, along with an explanation of what each level entails.

■ Select the taxonomy level for the learning objective, and then write out the desired outcome. It is extremely important to use a verb that accurately reflects the level of learning expected.

Learning taxonomies provide guidelines for classifying learning outcomes. They consist of varying levels of complexity. There are many different learning taxonomies, and they focus either on the cognitive, psychomotor, or affective domains. An example of each type of taxonomy is given in Tables 8–1, 8–2, and 8–3. Note that different verbs are used to express the different levels of learning outcomes.

Writing Behavioral Learning Objectives

Behavioral learning objectives are most commonly used by teachers and instructors, and were first proposed by Robert Mager in the 1960s. This type of

Table 8-1   Example of a Cognitive Domain Taxonomy

Level	Description
Knowledge	Remembering information in the material through recognition or recall
	Example verbs: defines, lists, names, recalls, repeats, states
Comprehension	Understanding the meaning of the material and being able to demonstrate it or make use of it when asked to do so
	Example verbs: estimates, generalizes, interprets, summarizes, translates
Application	Understanding the meaning of the material and applying it in appropriate situations
	Example verbs: adapts, applies, employs, operates, relates
Analysis	Breaking down the material into its separate parts and identifying the relationships and organization of those parts
	Example verbs: analyzes, dissects, explores, infers, investigates, studies
Synthesis	Putting together elements or parts from different materials to form a unique whole
	Example verbs: designs, hypothesizes, integrates, plans, synthesizes
Evaluation	Making a value judgment of the material
	Example verbs: appraises, assesses, defends, evaluates, judges, values

Source: Bloom, B. S. (1956). *Taxonomy of educational objectives: Book I, cognitive domain.* New York: Longman Inc.

Table 8-2 **Example of a Psychomotor Domain Taxonomy**

Level	Description
Reflex movements	Actions done unconsciously and without reaction to a stimulus Example verbs: extends, flexes, grasps, hops, stretches
Basic-fundamental Movements	Action patterns are formed through combining reflex movements Example verbs: grasps, handles, jumps, pushes, pulls, runs, walks
Perceptual abilities	Actions are the result of stimuli in the environment; can be auditory, visual, kinesthetic, tactile, or coordinated movements Example verbs: dodges a ball, follows instructions, maintains balance
Physical abilities	Actions are the result of the development of highly skilled movements Examples: ballet exercises, distance running, typing, weight lifting
Skilled movements	Complex actions based on inherent movement patterns are performed with a degree of efficiency Examples: sports, recreation, dance, fine art activities
Nondiscursive communication	Communicating through bodily movements through a range of actions from facial expressions to choreography Examples: body postures, gestures, and facial expressions executed through dance movement and choreography

Source: Harrow, A. J. (1972). *A taxonomy of the psychomotor domain.* New York: David McKay Company, Inc.

objective states the specific, observable, measurable behavior that the student will exhibit to demonstrate that learning has occurred.

Behavioral learning objectives consist of three parts, easily remembered by ABC: audience, behavior, and condition. The definitions for each are as follows:

- Audience: The learner or targeted audience
- Behavior: What the learner should be able to do, stated in observable, measurable terms
- Condition/Criteria: The circumstances under which the learning will occur.

An additional part, degree, may also be added to the learning objectives, making the format ABCD. The degree is the level of accomplishment is expected and is either expressed as a percentage (80% of the time) or implied.

Examples of learning objectives include:

- When asked by the teacher (c), the student (a) will accurately list the 26 letters of the alphabet (b) 100% of the time (d) (cognitive domain).

Table 8-3 Example of an Affective Domain Taxonomy

Level	Description
Receiving	Awareness of the existence of certain phenomena and stimuli, and the willingness to focus on it and tolerate it Example verbs: favors, observes, prefers, realizes, recognizes
Responding	Actively attending to the phenomena or stimuli and achieving some sort of satisfaction from it Example verbs: contributes, engages, enjoys, performs, practices
Valuing	Accepting a value or belief and willing to be identified with it and committed to it Example verbs: devotes, influences, initiates, participates
Organization	Willing to organize values into a system, determine the relationships among them, and establish which are dominant and persuasive Example verbs: derives, evaluates, judges, relates, rejects
Characterization	Acting consistently with the values one has internalized at this level so that the person is characterized by the aspects of these values and has integrated them into a total philosophy or world view This level cannot be reached through formal education but rather over time through life experiences

Source: Krathwohl, D. R., Bloom, B. S., & Masia B. B. (1974). *Taxonomy of educational objectives: Book 2, affective domain.* New York: Longman Inc.

- When given the appropriate tools (c), the apprentice (a) will masterfully change a tire (b) on every type of automobile that comes to the garage with a flat tire (d) (psychomotor domain).
- The student (a) selects food brands that show zero trans fats (b) over brands with trans fats (c) when grocery shopping each week (d) (affective domain).

Writing Assessment Items
After writing the learning objectives, test items should be constructed immediately rather than waiting until after course content has been developed. Creating test items at this time ensures consistency between learning objectives and test items, and the test items, in turn, will guide the instructional strategies used in the content. When writing test items, use the specific behaviors identified in the learning objectives to do the following:

- Identify the response or performance required for each test item;
- Select the type of test item (multiple choice, matching, essay);

- Specify the conditions under which the performance is to occur including whether references, tools, or equipment is used; and
- Determine the environment in which the performance is to occur (speaking in front of an audience). (Dick & Carrey, 1996)

The relationship between the learning objectives, test items, and instructional strategies create the framework for the instruction, so great attention must be given to this process. It is especially important to consider each learning objective carefully, and to select the appropriate verb that reflects exactly what the students are required to do to demonstrate that learning has occurred.

Determining the Strategies to Use in the Design of the Instruction

Now that you have analyzed your goals, audience, and content, and established your learning objectives and assessment items, how do you go about selecting instructional strategies? Is there an established process? Are there specific techniques?

The design phase is probably the most difficult phase of the instructional design process due to the number of theories, models, strategies, and approaches from which one can select. Instructional strategies are based in educational and psychological research and prescribe the organization, sequence, and delivery method of instruction as well as the multimedia that is needed to achieve the instructional goal. In addition, a good instructional strategy guides the student's learning and prompts the student to actively make connections between existing knowledge and the new information presented in the lesson (Morrison, Ross, & Kemp, 2004). These strategies can be categorized in different ways, but for the purpose of this chapter, the categories will be delivery strategies, organizational strategies, and sequencing strategies.

Delivery Strategies

It is important to know from the start whether you are designing for a face-to-face, Web-enhanced, blended, or online environment. When selecting the delivery method, it is important to consider the following:

- The instructor's comfort level with technology. Instructors who are less comfortable with technology will prefer face-to-face or Web-enhanced environments. Once they become accustomed to a Web-enhanced environment, they may be more likely to try an online course. Interestingly, a blended environment requires the highest level of skill for an instructor, since he/she must have a good grasp on the advantages and disadvantages of the face-to-face and online environments, and know how to integrate the two effectively.

- The instructor's current workload and time commitment to the course. The workload for each type of environment varies. In face-to-face and Web-enhanced courses, preparation typically takes place at the same time that the course is offered. In online courses, the greatest amount of preparation occurs about a year before the course is even offered, when the course is being designed and developed. The blended learning environment requires both the initial preparation of the online course, and the ongoing preparation for the face-to-face meetings. Of all the environments, the online course will require more time to be spent on e-mail, since this is the only means of communicating with the instructor and clarifying information for students.

- The targeted audience's needs and preferences. Generally, traditional students prefer a mixture of face-to-face and technology, and nontraditional students prefer online courses. This is due to the fact that the younger students view college as a place to socialize and learn more about themselves. Older students, however, are typically juggling work, school, and family and like the convenience and flexibility that online courses provide.

- Resources available, including staff, time, and money. Online and blended courses typically require more staff, time, and money to develop due to the content that must be created, which may include text-based lessons, narrated PowerPoint presentations, custom images and animations, video clips, or simulations.

In higher education, course management systems have made delivering content for Web-enhanced, blended, and online learning environments extremely simple and secure. These systems also allow an instructor to develop interactive activities such as discussion forums, games, and quizzes with minimal technical knowledge. Course management systems and the different learning environments are discussed in greater detail in Chapter 11.

Organizational Strategies

Most lessons, whether they be face-to-face or online, consist of an introduction, body, and conclusion; what is included in each of the sections may enhance or deter learning. One of the most basic ways of organizing content is Gagne's

Events of Instruction, which was discussed in Chapter 7. Gagne provides nine sequential elements that should be included in a lesson to increase learning. These elements are based on information processing theory. Note that initially, instructors will follow the nine events very carefully, but with increased familiarity of the model, the nine events can often be combined.

Another example of a model that focuses on organizing content for problem solving is the STAR Legacy shell (also discussed in Chapter 7). The seven-phase cycle of the software shell is based on anchored instruction and provides an organizational structure for any lesson in any format. The phases include:

- Presenting the challenges
- Giving students the opportunity to generate ideas
- Providing multiple perspectives
- Giving students the opportunity to research and then revise their initial ideas
- Testing the students knowledge
- Having students present their ideas publicly
- Having the student reflect back on what they have learned

Although a number of different models exist for organizing content, a learning episode should always include several key aspects:

- Content that is motivating to the learner
- Learning objectives that are stated clearly at the beginning of the content
- Content that is connected to the learner's existing knowledge
- Strategies that help the learner focus on the important aspects of the content but does not overload the learner (such as **chunking** content or bulleting points).
- Examples of varying difficulty
- Opportunities for practice with immediate feedback
- A means of assessing the learner's performance
- Assistance to the learner to help transfer information to the real world

Sequencing Strategies
The order in which information is presented to the learner will influence their understanding and ability to organize the information with their preexisting knowledge. Sequencing is especially important in online learning, since the instructor is not physically present to address confusing material.

During the task analysis the sequencing of the content is addressed, but during the design phase it is important to review the content again, to ensure that the sequencing will work well with the delivery and organizational strategies. One must also consider the addition of practice problems, activities, assignments, and discussions.

Elaboration theory, which was covered in Chapter 7, can be used to sequence content. As you may recall, this theory proposes three types of sequencing:

- Conceptual Elaboration Sequence: Content starts with the broader more inclusive concepts and gradually progresses to the narrower, more detailed concepts, which are then elaborated on.
- Theoretical Elaboration Sequence: Content starts with the broader more inclusive principles and gradually progresses to the narrower, more detailed principles, which are then elaborated on.
- Simplifying Conditions Method: Content starts with the simplest real-world version of the task and gradually progresses to more complex versions of the task until mastery is reached. This type of sequencing is used only with large and moderate to complex material where there is a degree of complexity among different versions of a task.

Examples of other sequencing strategies include:

- Chronologic: Material is arranged according to when they occur in a time sequence.
- Difficulty: Easiest material is presented first, and then progresses to most difficult.
- Familiarity: Familiar information is presented prior to the unfamiliar information.
- Interest: Topics that are of most interest are presented first.
- Prerequisite: Prerequisite information is presented first.
- Procedural: Information is presented in order of a step-by-step procedure.
- Sophistication: The simplest, concrete topics are presented first and then progress to more difficult, abstract topics.

Decisions about the sequencing of the content will vary depending on the subject matter, and more than one strategy will probably be effective.

In addition to delivery, organizational, and sequential strategies, media selection strategies also need to be considered during this stage of the instructional design process. Media selection strategies will be discussed in detail in Chapter 9.

Development

The development phase of the Instructional Design Process involves the actual creation of the content and associated materials that will be included in the instruction. This phase is the lengthiest part of the instructional design process, due to the time needed to plan, create, review, and revise the materials.

Before beginning development, the instructor should do the following:

- Identify existing materials that can be used to reduce costs.
- Ensure that existing materials are clear from copyright restrictions.
- Determine the resources needed to create new content including personnel, time, and funding.

If new materials need to be created, the instructor should consider using the following:

- Course management tools like discussion forums, quizzes, and games.
- Images, maps or diagrams from public domain sites, like the Library of Congress.
- Images, maps or animations from learning repositories like MERLOT (Multimedia Educational Resource for Learning and Online Teaching).
- Lesson content and activities from open courseware sites, like MIT Open-CourseWare.
- Simple, inexpensive gadgets like a digital camera, USB camcorder or iPod, which allow an instructor to independently create and share content fairly quickly and easily.
- Web 2.0 tools like blogs, podcasts and Wikis. Many easy-to-use and free Web 2.0 tools are also available online which allow instructors to create narrated screen captures, comics, diagrams, etc.

In addition to creating content, Web 2.0 Tools are incredibly effective for creating engaging and collaborative activities for students. These include:

- Collaboratively creating documents, spreadsheets, diagrams.
- Sharing project-related websites and research articles using social bookmarking tools.

- Creating slideshows with narration and music.
- Recording a promotional message or advertisement as a podcast.
- Creating and sharing videos or a collection of photographs.
- Reflecting on internship or service-related experiences in a blog.

Although many instructors will need to develop their own content, some universities may have a centralized technology unit or instructional design unit that offers services or special initiatives for the creation of innovative courses. In these instances, the development of course materials will be completed with assistance of an instructional designer and a creative team that may include a graphic artist, multimedia developer, programmer and/or videographer.

Implementation

The implementation phase of the instructional design process involves trying out or piloting the instruction in the real world with the targeted audience.

Prior to actual implementation, especially when online environments and more sophisticated technologies are used, it is important to test the lesson's effectiveness with small groups of learners. Often, planned technologies can be tested with learners in an existing format of the course before they actually are offered in the redesigned course. At the very least, an instructor should enlist the help of a few colleagues to determine if the technologies integrated into the course are easy to use and effective for meeting the desired learning outcomes.

To prepare for the implementation phase, a guide should be created to let the instructor know what should be done for each lesson or each week, along with what the students should do as well. Usually the instructional guide is prepared by the instructional designer. The guide should contain the following:

- Lesson title
- Lesson goal
- Lesson objectives
- Lesson synopsis
- Equipment needed
- Materials needed
- Required time to complete

During the first offering of the course, it is extremely useful to collect student feedback about specific course elements and to note where any difficulties in understanding occur. This information can be used to revise the course for future offerings.

Evaluation

Evaluation is the final phase of the instructional design process. Evaluation is not to be confused with assessment. Evaluation addresses the effectiveness of the learning materials whereas assessment refers to whether the learners met the desired learning outcomes. There are two types of evaluation: formative and summative.

Formative evaluation measures how well the instruction supported the desired learning objectives. It is typically conducted by the instructional designer or instructor during the development phase, before the instruction has been fully implemented. The purpose of this evaluation is to determine the effectiveness of the instruction and pinpoint ways in which it can be improved. Morrison, Ross, and Kemp (2004, p. 243) recommend the following questions to be addressed during formative evaluation:

1. Given the objectives for the lesson, is the level of learning acceptable? What weaknesses are apparent?
2. Are learners able to use the knowledge or perform the skills at an acceptable level? Are any weaknesses indicated?
3. How much time did the instruction and learning require? Is this acceptable?
4. Did the activities seem appropriate and manageable to the instructor and learners?
5. Were the materials convenient, easy to locate, use, and file?
6. What were the learners' reactions to the method of study, activities, materials, and evaluation methods?
7. Do the unit tests and other outcome measures satisfactorily assess the instructional objectives?
8. What revisions in the program seem necessary (content, format)?
9. Is the instructional context appropriate?

Methods for collecting data for formative evaluations include:

- Providing the material to individuals on a one-on-one basis, and obtaining their feedback.
- Having small groups of students test out a technology or activity and give recommendations for revisions.

- Offering a pilot version of the course and observing/noting frequently asked questions or poor performance which may indicate problems with the content, instructions, activities, or assessment.

Summative evaluation, on the other hand, measures the degree in which the targeted learners obtained the desired outcomes of the instruction. It is conducted after the course has been implemented and is conducted by an outside source, rather than the instructional designer or instructor. The methods of data collection are similar to those of formative evaluation and may include observation, assessment, or surveys.

Results of a summative evaluation are used to determine if the instructional program will continue or be replaced by another form of instruction. Obviously, in an educational setting courses cannot be terminated, but summative evaluation will help the instructor identify inconsistencies between learning objectives and exam items, as well as the quality level of the instructional materials.

Although implementation and evaluation are the last two phases listed in the instructional design process (ADDIE), they are equally important to the other phases. In addition, both these phases should be kept in mind throughout the process.

Instructional Design Process and Today's Learner

The instructional design process is a systematic process that identifies specific pieces of information about the instruction including the goal, audience, tasks, learning objectives, test items, strategies, implementation, and evaluation. The process has been used for decades and has been effective in training and education with print, computer-based, and online materials.

The field of instructional design developed from behaviorism, so most of its theory base and procedures draw from the behaviorist tradition. In the past 20 years, however, there has been a paradigm shift away from behaviorism, first to cognitivism, and more recently to constructivism. Learning is no longer seen as a passive, teacher-centered process but rather as an active, learner-centered process, where knowledge is constructed by the student. Despite this shift, many aspects of instructional design process still remains tied to its behaviorist roots.

Jonassen (1999) recommended the following changes to the instructional design process based on constructivist learning theory:

- Learning objectives should not be provided by the instructor, but rather negotiated with the learner and used for the purposes of guiding instruction and self-assessment.
- The task analysis should not result in a single best sequence for learning but rather should identify multiple paths that a learner could take to reach the same goal.
- The goals of instructional design should not focus on measurable, observable learning outcomes but rather on how the knowledge can be used by the learner in authentic learning environments.
- Assessment should no longer be criterion referenced, in order to allow students to interpret information in their own manner.

Hannafin and Hill (2002) suggest a shift from instructional design to **constructional design**, which is based on the following constructivist principles:

- There are no absolute answer that student must provide but rather only the "best construction of current experience".
- Content is presented as a whole rather than being broken down into parts, and it is also presented in the appropriate context.
- There are no learning objectives but rather "layers of negotiation" among the teacher and learner, which allow for the learning environment to continually adapt to a learner's changing needs.
- The learning environments are collaborative, process-based, question-driven, and cyclical.
- The design of the instruction is learner-centered and follows four learning-by-design principles: Active learning, tangible learning products or artifacts that reflect their understanding, artifacts that are shared with others, and authentic learning contexts.

Hannafin and Hill indicate this shift from instructional design to constructional design would result in the following revisions in the instructional process or ADDIE:

- Analysis: The problem would be identified and described, and a vision of the new learning environment would be created that would allow a learner to explore and construct knowledge.

- Design: The learner would act as the designer by deciding on which learning goals to pursue, whether to participate in sequence of activities, and selecting their own preferred methods to solve problem.
- Development: Materials and resources would be created as needed by the instructor or instructional designer as well as the learner.
- Implementation: The instructor would act as guide or consultant while the learner manages his/her own learning.
- Evaluation: Learner will demonstrate understanding of an area through the creation of something (project, portfolio, etc) in response to the problem posed. (Hannafin & Hill, 2002)

As technology continues to evolve and student learning styles and preferences change, it is becoming rather apparent that the instructional design process must be reexamined, revised, or most likely, recreated. The process does not reflect the way in which today's students learn as a result of their constant interaction with ever-advancing technologies. As both students and technologies continue to change, the traditional instructional design process will become more obsolete, and the need to develop a more appropriate method for creating instruction will become more urgent.

Learning Activity

In groups, identify an instructional design problem, then working through the instructional design process (ADDIE), develop a lesson to address it. After completing the instruction, revisit it from a constructional design perspective. How would the process you used to develop the instruction change? How would the students' and instructor's roles change?

References

Bloom, B. S., Englehart, M. D., Furst, E. J., Hill, W. H., & Krathwohl, D. R. (1956). *Taxonomy of educational objectives: The classification of educational goals. Handbook I: Cognitive domain.* New York: Longman, Inc.

Dick, W., & Carey, L. (1996). *The systematic design of instruction* (4th ed.). New York, NY: Longman.

Fenrich, P. (1997). *Practical guidelines for creating instructional multimedia applications.* Fort Worth, TX: The Dryden Press.

Gustafson, K. L., & Branch, R. M. (2002). *Survey of instructional development models* (4th ed.). Syracuse, NY: Eric Clearinghouse on Information.

Hannafin, M. J., & Hill, J. R. (2002). Epistemology and the design of learning environments. In R. Reiser & J. V. Dempsey (Eds.), *Trends and issues in instructional design and technology*. Upper Saddle River, NJ: Merrill/Prentice Hall.

Harrow, A. J. (1972). *A taxonomy of the psychomotor domain*. New York: David McKay Company, Inc.

Jonassen, D. (1999). Designing constructivist learning environments. In C. Reigeluth (Ed.), *Instructional-design theories and models: A new paradigm of instructional theory* (Vol. 2). Mahwah, NJ: Lawrence Erlbaum Associates.

Jonassen, D. H., Tessmer, M., & Hannum, W. H. (1999). *Task analysis methods for instructional design*. Mahwah, NJ: Lawrence Erlbaum Associates, Inc.

Krathwohl, D. R., Bloom, B. S., & Masia, B. B. (1964). *Taxonomy of educational objectives: The classification of educational goals. Handbook II: Affective domain*. New York: David McKay Company, Inc.

Morrison, G. R., Ross, S. M., & Kemp, J. E. (2004). *Designing effective instruction* (4th ed.). Hoboken, NJ: John Wiley & Sons.

Rothwell, W. J., & Kazanas, H. C. (1992). *Mastering the instructional design process: A systematic approach*. San Francisco, CA: Jossey-Bass.

Smith, P. L., & Ragan, T. J. (1999). *Instructional design* (2nd ed.). New York, NY: John Wiley & Sons.

CHAPTER 9

Instructional Media Selection

Food For Thought

"What sculpture is to a block of marble, education is to a human soul."
Joseph Addison, 1672–1719

Key Words

Active voice
Advanced organizer
Analogical graphics
Animated GIF
Animation
Arbitrary graphics
Bandwidth

Font
Graphics Interchange Format (GIF)
Joint Photographic Experts group (JPEG)
Logico-mathematical graphics
Portable Network Graphics (PNG)
Representational graphics
Transformative graphics

Objectives

The educator will be able to name the five types of media examined in this chapter.
The educator will be able to justify uses of the five types of media examined in this chapter for a given situation.

Introduction

This chapter will introduce you to the types of media. You will receive some suggestions on proper use of each. Selection of media should occur after you have defined the goals and objectives for your lesson, course, or curricula. The selection process should take place during the design process.

All media can be divided in the follow components:

- Text
- Graphics
- Animation
- Audio
- Video

Instructional Text

Instructional text is text designed for learning situations. Text is often the primary way to present information in an online educational environment. If you follow a few basic rules for presenting text when you design information, students will understand it better. Following are some basic rules for structuring and presenting text. Many concepts presented here are from James Hartley's article: Eighty Ways of Improving Instructional Text (Hartley, 1981), and Winn's (1993) chapter on instructional message design.

Advance Organizers

A sentence or paragraph that explains what the student will do while interacting with text and other materials is called an **advance organizer** (Ausubel, 1968). Think of it as a guide students can read before they begin their interaction or reading to make the structure of the presentation apparent. An advance organizer may help your students focus their efforts in the direction you believe to be most beneficial. A sample advance organizer would be: "The following lesson is designed to introduce you to widgets. What are widgets? How do we use them? What are the potential dangers in using widgets?"

Titles

You may want to keep titles short and descriptive. For example, "Introduction to Kinetic Energy" is more effective than "An Introduction to One Form of Energy: Kinetic Energy."

Headings

Headings can break long passages of text into concept chunks. Examine your text and insert headings at appropriate places.

Questions in Text

Questions included in your text at the end of a section will allow students to reflect back on that section. This helps point out key concepts in a passage of text (Elen & Louw, 2006).

Readability Level

Ideally, you want the reading grade level of your text to match the level of your readers. On medium to long passages of text, it is possible to use readability formulas on the passage to roughly determine the reading grade level of the passage. These formulas are imperfect, considering only sentence length and word length while ignoring page layout, color, and other issues that could affect reading difficulty. Still, they can be useful at determining a general value. If possible, considering running several types of formulas on a passage to determine an average readability level. Here are two possibilities:

Flesch Reading Ease

You can determine the Flesch Reading Ease and the Flesch-Kincaid Grade Level to discover the readability and grade level of your text.

The Flesch Reading Ease formula is $RE = 206.835 - (1.015 \times ASL) - (84.6 \times ASW)$, where ASL is the average sentence length (i.e., the number of words divided by the number of sentences), and ASW is the average number of syllables per word (i.e., the number of syllables divided by the number of words) (My Byline Media, 2009). Higher numbers indicate easier to read text. Any score lower than 50 may be difficult to read.

Flesch-Kincaid Formula

The Flesch-Kincaid formula determines the US grade level of the text (Wikipedia, 2009). The formula is 0.39(total words/total sentences) + 11.8(total syllables/total words) − 15.59. For example, if you obtain a score of 6.8, the text in question is written at a US 6th grade reading level.

Other readability tests, such as The Simplified Measure of Gobbledygook (SMOG) test and the New Dale-Chall Formula (My Byline Media, 2009) may also be used to determine the readability of your text. It may be beneficial to run several of these tests on your text to gain a holistic understanding of the readability of your text.

Online tools are available to assist you in the use of these formulas. For example, if you search for "Flesch-Kincaid Readability Test" on the Web, there are links to several online and downloadable free tools you may use to determine the readability of your text.

Avoid Placing Many Acronyms Together

Do not use acronyms that the reader might not be familiar with. Keep language simple. For example, "Place the PDQ unit in the DSG ASAP." is hopelessly confusing!

Sentence Dos and Don'ts

Avoid multiple subordinate clauses. As a general rule, consider keeping sentences short. An example of multiple subordinate clauses would be "Answer four questions including at least one from at least two sections."

Use **active voice** whenever possible. Active voice is considered more appropriate for most reading situations. An example of active voice is "The rainfall affected the vegetation," as opposed to "The vegetation was affected by the rainfall."

Use positive terms whenever possible. An example of positive terms is "The patient's condition is unchanged," as opposed to "The patient is not declining."

Summaries

Summaries inform the learner that a lesson, unit, and passage is finished, and also organize and provide a synopsis of the material presented. Summaries often mirror an advance organizer, but are augmented with the key concepts covered by the material. A summary points out what was important in the text, and is a quick reference and refresher for students at a later time.

Text Presentation

The most basic form of text manipulation is to make certain words larger or bolder than the rest (Hartley, 1981). This gives emphasis to that type because it looks more important than surrounding text. In scanning a page, the emphasized elements stand out from the others; they take priority and will be read first.

In general, follow the same guidelines you would for a report, newspaper, or other print layout: Use the biggest **font** for headlines, a smaller font for sub-heads, and the smallest font for the main body of text.

There are two basic ways to manipulate text style: make the text bold and/ or italic. You can also underline text, but underlining has a special meaning on a Web page (indicating a hypertext link) so it is really not a good idea to use underlining for any other purpose or it will confuse the reader. When you make a font bolder than the rest, it gives emphasis to that type because it looks more important than its neighbors.

Italics are often used in printed matter to give emphasis to a word or two within a block of regular text. Italic type is generally harder to read than regular text and the reader has to slow down to read it. While italics work well on a printed page, they are best avoided on Web pages as they display horribly on a computer screen.

Text colors can be changed for effect and impact. You can also highlight important passages of text. In addition to changing the color of body text, you can also change the color of Web links, active links, and visited links. Be cautioned that many people are used to seeing the default blue, underlined text for an unused link, underlined red for an active link (in the process of being clicked), and underlined purple for a visited link. If you change these defaults, you may confuse the user.

If you want to set a specific background color for a Web page, make sure the text in the foreground is in contrast to the background. If the background is dark, use light-colored text, and vice versa. If your text color is too similar to the background color, it will be difficult to read.

Tables and Outlines

If you have a large amount of information that needs to be compared and contrasted, consider using a table or outline to organize the material for the learner. Learners are often unaware they should organize materials to compare and contrast them, to discover hierarchies, to list parts, or to investigate and think about cause and effect (Cook & Mayer, 1988).

Putting It All Together

If you were to structure your text presentations as suggested, here is an outline you would follow to do so:

- List objective(s).
- List **advanced organizer.**
- Use titles to divide major sections.
- Use headings to subdivide a major section.
- Text body should be divided into paragraphs with plenty of white space. Avoid small font sizes (below 12 point).
  - Use short sentences.
  - Emphasize key points or words in bold.
  - Use color for emphasis. Make sure there is a high degree of contrast between the foreground text and background colors.
- Use questions periodically to point readers to the key places in the text.
- Summarize the text, including all key points.

Writing Instructional Text: An Example

The following excerpt (see Figure 9-1) is from "The Stage In Action: An Introduction to Theater and Drama" by Helen Manfull (1989). The same text is used to show you how to break down text for an instruction. The example begins with an advanced organizer and lists the instructional objectives, then breaks down the print into a series of smaller chunks and bulleted lists, the most effective way to present instructional text, especially on the Web. Color and bolding are used where appropriate. The text is followed by several key questions and a summary.

Aristotle, then, conceived of tragedy as being the imitation of a major deed or action depicting through its enactment the striving of the human soul toward some goal with the intention of purging negative emotion while teaching oblique lessons of life. In examining the art form with his students, the Greek teacher concluded that tragedy contained six elements or components—plot, character, thought, diction, music and spectacle. Of the elements, three—plot, character and thought—were essentially the subject of plays; that is to say, plays are about stories and people and ideas. Two of the elements—diction and music—represent the tools or materials playwrights use to fashion their drama. Dramatists employ words, sound and symbols as well as verse and rhythm and music to create the play script. And the final element, spectacle, relates to the manner in which the art is presented to the consumer—in this case a staged production in a theatre.

Of all the elements, according to Aristotle, plot was the most important; he referred to it as "the first principle," "the soul of tragedy," "the first and most important part of Tragedy," and "the first level of all imitation," He was convinced, it would seem, that a play needed a strong storyline in order to accomplish its purpose. He probably reasoned that if you wished to write a play imitating a major action such as "to re-establish God's order in the realm," then the most expeditious and practical way to accomplish your aim was to find a story that could be used to demonstrate such a quest—just as Shakespeare did in Hamlet . "Plot," he said, "is the imitation of the action." By "action" in this instance he meant the one major profound deed that the play will depict; and plot now becomes the primary means of depicting or imitating that deed or action.

Figure 9-1   Example of noninstructional versus instructional text formatting.

Standard Paragraph Formation	Revised for Instructional Presentation
The Nature of Drama Aristotle, then, conceived of tragedy as being the imitation of a major deed or action depicting through its enactment the striving of the human soul toward some goal with the intention of purging negative emotion while teaching oblique lessons of life. In examining the art form with his students, the Greek teacher concluded that tragedy contained six elements or components—plot, character, thought, diction, music and spectacle. Of the elements, three—plot, character and thought—were essentially the subject of plays; that is to	The purpose of this reading is to introduce you to the key elements of a Greek tragedy according to Aristotle. When you complete this reading, you should be able to list without error the six elements of a Greek tragedy. You should be able to describe in writing Aristotle's conception of the plot, including all four of his descriptions. **The Nature of Drama** Aristotle, then, conceived of tragedy as being the imitation of a major deed or action depicting through its enactment the

(continues)

Figure 9-1 Example of noninstructional versus instructional text formatting. *(continued)*

say, plays are about stories and people and ideas. Two of the elements—diction and music—represent the tools or materials playwrights use to fashion their drama. Dramatists employ words, sound and symbols as well as verse and rhythm and music to create the play script. And the final element, spectacle, relates to the manner in which the art is presented to the consumer—in this case a staged production in a theatre.

Of all the elements, according to Aristotle, plot was the most important; he referred to it as "the first principle," "the soul of tragedy," "the first and most important part of Tragedy," and "the first level of all imitation," He was convinced, it would seem, that a play needed a strong storyline in order to accomplish its purpose. He probably reasoned that if you wished to write a play imitating a major action such as "to re-establish God's order in the realm," then the most expeditious and practical way to accomplish your aim was to find a story that could be used to demonstrate such a quest—just as Shakespeare did in Hamlet. "Plot," he said, "is the imitation of the action." By "action" in this instance he meant the one major profound deed that the play will depict; and plot now becomes the primary means of depicting or imitating that deed or action.

striving of the human soul toward some goal with the intention of purging negative emotion while teaching oblique lessons of life.

In examining the art form with his students, the Greek teacher concluded that tragedy contained six elements or components:

1. Plot
2. Character
3. Thought
4. Diction
5. Music
6. Spectacle

Of the elements, three—**plot, character and thought**—were essentially the subject of plays; that is to say, plays are about stories and people and ideas.

Two of the elements—**diction and music**—represent the tools or materials playwrights use to fashion their drama.

Dramatists employ **words, sound and symbols** as well as **verse and rhythm and music** to create the play script.

And the final element, **spectacle**, relates to the manner in which the art is presented to the consumer—in this case a staged production in a theatre.

Of all the elements, according to Aristotle, plot was the most important; he referred to it as

- "The first principle"
- "The soul of tragedy"
- "The first and most important part of Tragedy"
- "The first level of all imitation"

He was convinced, it would seem, that a play needed a strong storyline in order to

Figure 9-1 Example of noninstructional versus instructional text formatting. *(continued)*

accomplish its purpose. He probably reasoned that if you wished to write a play imitating a major action such as "to re-establish God's order in the realm," then the most expeditious and practical way to accomplish your aim was to find a story that could be used to demonstrate such a quest—just as Shakespeare did in Hamlet.

"Plot," he said, "is the imitation of the action." By "action" in this instance he meant the one major profound deed that the play will depict; and plot now becomes the primary means of depicting or imitating that deed or action.

Follow-up questions:

1. What are the six elements of a Greek tragedy?
2. How does Aristotle describe a plot? List all four ways.

Summary

Aristotle believed that a Greek tragedy contained the following elements:

1. Plot	4. Diction
2. Character	5. Music
3. Thought	6. Spectacle

Of these, he believed that plot was the most important. He referred to it as:

- "The first principle"
- "The soul of tragedy"
- "The first and most important part of Tragedy"
- "The first level of all imitation"

Instructional Graphics

The purpose of most instructional graphics is to help explain something to the viewer in a manner that hopefully increases retention of the subject matter (Duchastel & Waller, 1979).

Instructional graphics have seven possible functions:

1. Descriptive: To show what an object looks like
2. Expressive: To make an impact on the learner
3. Constructional: To show how the parts fit together into the whole
4. Functional: To show a process or the organization of a system in a simplified manner
5. **Logico-mathematical**: To display a mathematical concept such as a curve graph (some line graphs and charts with a scaled X and Y axis fall into this category)
6. Algorithmic: To show a holistic picture of the range of possibilities (flow charts fall into this category)
7. Data display: Illustrating textual data visually (bar charts, pie charts, and histograms fall into this category) (Duchastel, 1978)

Representational, Analogical, Arbitrary, and Transformative Graphics

Instructional graphics can be classified as representational, analogical, or arbitrary (Rieber, 1994). **Representational graphics** vary in detail from line drawings to photographs, but are alike in that they closely resemble the object(s) they depict (Winn, 1993). For example, in Figure 9-2, a stick figure can represent a person.

Figure 9-2   Example of a representational graphic.

Figure 9-3   Example of an analogical graphic.

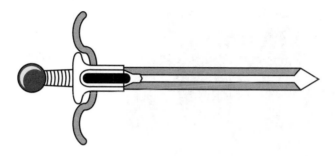

Analogical graphics show one thing and by analogy imply something else. For example, in Figure 9-3, a graphic of a sword might be shown to illustrate the concept of medieval warfare.

Arbitrary graphics include tables, charts, and cognitive maps (see Figure 9-4) that have no real-life counterpart that they are attempting to portray. These graphics are organizational in nature (Winn, 1993), and may also be interpretative in nature.

Figure 9-4   Example of an arbitrary graphic.

Annual Growth Chart

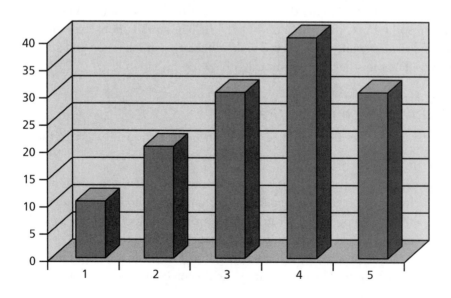

Figure 9-5 Example of a decorative graphic.

Flan is a variant of plain custard where some sugar syrup, cooked to caramel stage, is poured into the mold before adding the custard base.

Some graphics are simply intended to attract attention (see Figure 9-5). They serve merely as a stimulus or cue to the learner (Duchastel, 1978). The Web is flooded with these types of graphics, especially on commercial sites. These graphics are decorative in nature (Winn, 1993).

Graphics may also be **transformative** in nature, intended to facilitate or elicit cognitive processes, such as serving as a mnemonic learning aid for terms or concepts. For example, the caricature of Alfred Bandura (see Figure 9-6) is drawn so he looks like the "Bobo Doll." In Bandura's famous experiments on social learning, children observed violent behavior on television and afterwards behaved in a hostile manner towards a blow-up Bobo Doll.

Deciding When to Use Graphics

When one decides that graphics can enhance instructional materials, there are some factors to consider before proceeding:

- Resources available for course development: Is there enough time to locate or create the image? Is there someone who has the skills to draw the image or take a photograph? Is there equipment such as a digital camera or lighting to capture an image clearly?
- Restrictions around available images: Is the image in the public domain, or is it covered by copyright? Who do you contact to request permission

Figure 9-6 Example of a transformative graphic.

Source: The Pennsylvania State University. Used with Permission of PSU.

to use the image? Can using the image for educational purposes be considered fair use? Can the image be customized for your course?

■ Appropriate images: Are the planned images appropriate for the targeted audience? Do the learners have the prerequisite skills needed to interpret the images? Are images age appropriate? Will the images take too long to download for learners in rural areas who may have a dial-up connection?

■ Meeting learning objectives: If resources are tight, will the image assist students in meeting identified learning objectives, or would time be better spent on something else (including another image)?

What Graphics Should You Use?

The choice of what type of graphic to use for a specific purpose is often clear, but there are some instances where research particularly indicates what will be most effective (Duchastel, 1978; Rieber, 1994).

■ Use simple line drawings if the pace of the instruction is not under user control. This makes the accompanying text more meaningful and reduces the burden of details in the text (Dwyer, 1978).

- Use analogical graphics if the user has no prior knowledge of the presented concept (Rieber, 1994).
- Use arbitrary graphics to illustrate conceptual relationships that cannot be conveyed through representational or analogical means (Rieber, 1994).
- Be choosy. Make sure each graphic is essential, and limit what each graphic depicts, removing nonessential (and potentially distracting) elements (Baker & Bixler, 1990).
- Be consistent with the placement of graphics on the screen. Providing an explicit organization increases the memorability of new material (Bower, 1970).

Graphic design can also set the pace at which the user moves through the content. Sparse pages or screens with only one or two elements on them may establish a slower pace by placing emphasis on each element. In contrast, other designs can fill the page or screen with many elements and can imply a faster pace with less emphasis placed on individual elements. Content elements and screen designs can set up a rhythm for moving through material. This rhythm should reflect the purpose and meaning decided upon in the design phase of instructional materials.

Browser Considerations

Because it is impossible to determine in advance what browser will be used to receive the instruction, designers must either request graphics in a format that all browsers can adequately display, or specify which browsers must be used. The quality of graphics may be affected by this restraint. Color and density considerations for graphics and images dictate which format, such as GIF, JPEG, or PNG, is ideal.

The GIF Graphic Format

GIF (graphics interchange format) is the oldest and possibly most often used graphic format for delivery of graphics to the Web. All visual browsers know how to display GIF graphics. A GIF image can contain up to 256 colors, and the information about these colors is stored in the image itself. A GIF file can be anywhere from a 1-bit, black and white image to an 8-bit, 256-color image. Thus, for images that display well using only 256 colors or less, the GIF format

Figure 9-7   Graphic ideal for GIF format.

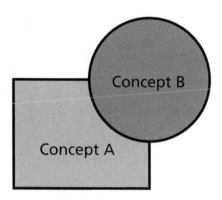

Concept A & B Intersection

is the format of choice. Graphics that fall into this category are usually those with lots of solid colors and those with little color variation, such as color cartoons and many technical illustrations. See Figure 9-7 for an example of a graphic ideal for the GIF format:

Notice it uses only a few solid colors. This graphic is only about 4 kilobytes (K) in size and will display quickly even on a computer using a slow modem to connect to the Internet.

The JPEG Graphic Format

The other most popular graphics format used to display graphics on Web browsers is the **JPEG (Joint Photographic Experts Group)** format. JPEGs contain 24-bit color information, as opposed to a GIF eight-bit scheme. This means JPEGs can contain millions of colors, as compared to a GIF 256-color maximum.

JPEGs are best used for images where 256 colors are just not enough, or color accuracy is very important. Photographs and color artwork are two examples where the JPEG format is often used. However, JPEGs do not offer the universal interlacing, transparency, or animation options that GIF images do. See Figure 9-8 for an example of a graphic saved as a GIF and as a JPEG format. Which looks better?

Figure 9-8   Comparison of GIF and JPEG graphics format.

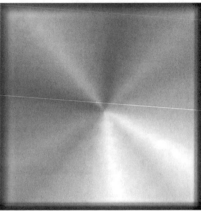

GIF Example   JPEG Example

The PNG Format

The **PNG (Portable Network Graphics)** format combines some of best features of GIF and JPEG. Like JPEG, PNG supports 16.7 million colors and compresses photographic images to smaller sizes than GIF does. PNG is a lossless compression method, meaning that no quality loss is incurred when it is applied to images.

Unlike GIF or JPEG, PNG can be stored at many different bit depths using different storage methods. GIF, for example, can be stored only in 8-bit or lower bit depths. JPEGs must be stored in 24-bit and no lower. PNG can be stored in either 8, 24, or 32 bits. PNG also has a multitude of different filtering methods. PNG was created to be a cross-platform file format and contains information about the characteristics of the authoring platform so that viewing software can automatically compensate and display the image correctly. What this means is that Macintosh computers and PCs, which utilize different display settings, can adjust properly for images created in the PNG file format.

PNG allows for transparent backgrounds and interlacing, and it even improves on those features by allowing for various degrees of transparency and two-dimensional interlacing, which transmits a rough overall view of the image faster than the one-dimensional scheme used by GIF. PNG supports a far more superior interlacing scheme than GIF. GIF interlacing gives a preview of the image after one-eighth of the image data has been recognized, whereas PNG gives a preview after only one-sixty-fourth of the image has loaded. While PNG has many excellent capabilities, this file format is not as popular as the GIF or JPEG format.

Bandwidth Considerations

Decisions must be made about what is most important on the screen and made most prominent. The emphasis could be on content such as text, animation, or video, but more likely it will be on headlines, navigation elements, or controls. One way to test prominence is by squinting at a screen until it is blurred. What catches the eye is the most prominent. The first, second, third, and fourth scan should reflect your decision on the hierarchy of the importance among content and screen elements.

Bandwidth basically refers to how much information can be transmitted at a given time. It is a good idea to utilize as little bandwidth as possible when using the Web, for bandwidth is at a premium.

Nearly all Web-based instruction is delivered as illustrated above. A remote server (it can be anywhere in the world) is connected to the Internet and thus to the Web. Your local computer is connected to the Web by either a direct connection or via a modem. Your local computer runs a browser that translates the electronic signals from the Web into text, graphics, sounds, movies, and so on.

Please note that a modem connection to the Web is much slower than a direct connection. A smaller pipe reflects this in the diagram. Just as more water can travel through a larger pipe in a set amount of time, so can more information pass through a direct connection then through a modem in a set amount of time.

This means you need to ensure your graphics are as small (in terms of storage space) as possible. Most graphics delivered via the Web are measured in kilobytes

Figure 9-9   Bandwidth illustration.

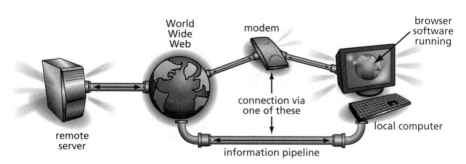

(K), or 1,000 bits. For example, a graphic may be 79K or 100K. Black and white (1-bit) images are generally the smallest, followed by grayscale images, then color images. Within color images, the range runs from 2-bit (four colors) through 8-bit (256 possible colors) to 24-bit (16.8 million possible colors) images. The more bits in a color image, the larger the file that contains the image.

Instructional Animation

Listed here are things to keep in mind when deciding if you need **animation**, and if you do, how to go about using it.

1. Look at your learning objectives. Are animations needed?
2. If animation is needed, examine different animation types for appropriate criteria.
3. Run your ideas by a graphics or animation expert.
4. Test out prototype animations with your target population of learners.
5. Test out prototype animations on the complete range of target delivery machines.
6. Keep in mind that complex animations may be better for learners already familiar with the basics in a given topic.
7. Animation may work best when combined with some sort of interaction or interactivity.
8. Use the same graphics and animations in testing situations as were used in the instruction.

Animation and Learning Objectives

Animations can be helpful in a learning environment if you need to teach a physical skill, or reproduce a lifelike movement. For simple animations, there is a special type of GIF file known as an **animated GIF** that may provide the animation you need.

Animated GIFs are formally called multiblock GIFs because multiple images can be stored as separate blocks within one single GIF document. This is very much the same as cel-based animation, where each frame in the animation is slightly different from the one preceding it. When the GIF file is viewed, the multiple images display, quickly and in succession, and produce a streaming animation.

Figure 9-10   Example of the frames of an animated GIF.

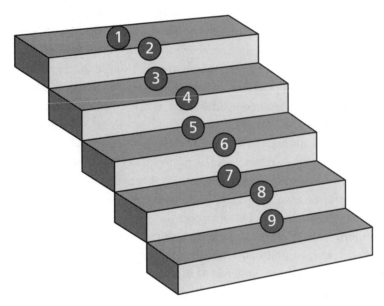

Just like other GIF files, the size of each frame affects the overall file size. For example, if you have a 100-frame animation with each frame totaling 5K, your animated GIF will be 500K. The beauty of animated GIFs is that they require no plug-ins, and the authoring tools to create them are often free and easy to learn. In this example, the ball appears to bounce down the steps by rapidly presenting a series of nine consecutive images where the ball is placed on a different part of the steps in every frame.

If you need sound in addition to motion, you cannot use an animated GIF by itself. Instead, you may want to consider other animation alternatives, such as Flash or video.

Instructional Audio

Why use sound in online instruction? Visuals may be enhanced by auditory cues. For example, you may have the auditory cue of a whistle that accompanies the visual of a steam locomotive. Audio can be used to build emotion and realism, especially in instruction involving action sequences or human drama. Imagine watching a movie clip without the audio!

According to Paivio (1986), the human cognitive system consists of two distinct channels for representing and manipulating knowledge: a visual-pictorial channel and an auditory-verbal channel (see also Baddeley, 1986, 1999). While some theorists believe active learning occurs when corresponding verbal and pictorial representations are in working memory at the same time (Mayer, 2002), others believe that cognitive overload is a possibility, where the learner can becomes overwhelmed with too much data to process at one time. Thus, it may be best to place audio under learner control, where the learner can activate and deactivate audio at will.

However, sounds and audio may increase user attention spans. Background music may be beneficial in some instances (Hallam, Price, & Katsarou, 2002), but other studies refute this. You must weigh the aesthetic benefits of the use of any music, perhaps placing it in areas not directly affecting instruction (such as in title screens).

Sound can be used for direct information, for example as a spoken narrative for providing information. Examples of direct information include speech in a section of text, speech in a video, and stand-alone narration. Speech is effective when communicating ideas that must be understood in a particular sequence (Winn, 1993).

Sounds can be used for direct playback, where the sound performs an encyclopedia function. For example, providing audio of the correct pronunciation of a medical term.

Sounds can be used for indirect information and feedback, as in a sound coupled with an event that informs the user something they did had an effect. For example, adding a "click" sound to an on-screen button when the user clicks on it.

Interrupts are sounds that tell the user something happened. A buzzer that goes off after a visual countdown is an example of this type of sound.

Sound can be used to draw attention to what is important at that particular moment. A ringing alarm signaling time to do something is an example of a sound that draws attention.

Finally, a sound can establish a relationship between two or more things. A buzzing sounds that accompanies a danger sign is an example of this.

Instructional Video

There are times when video is the most desired instructional delivery medium. It is helpful when you need to:

- Show realistic motion. For example, you may need to show how a pitcher throws a ball in slow motion.

- Provide an accurate recreation of something. For example, you may be training airplane pilots in a cockpit simulator or you may want to show sign language in action.
- Show human interaction. For example, you may want to show group dynamics in action.

Carefully consider the need for video before you include it in your designs. The use of video should be based on its effectiveness in a particular problem domain (Smith, Ruocco, & Jansen, 1999). Creating commercial-quality video is a costly, time-consuming process and a full discussion of it is beyond the scope of this chapter. However, home video is becoming quite popular, with many home instructional videos appearing on YouTube and the Web. If your audience will tolerate nonprofessionally produced video and you have a justifiable need for it, this may be a viable option.

Help with Media Selection

If possible, you should consult with an instructional designer on media selection for any instruction you develop. The instructional designer's role may include:

- Ensuring that the selected media elements are consistent with the learning objectives.
- Ensuring that the most appropriate media is used for the desired learning outcome (for example, if the goal is to teach a procedure, use a video to demonstrate it; if the goal is to learn a principle, use a simulation)
- Determining if the creation of multimedia elements realistically fit into the timeline for development and makes the best use of available resources.
- Writing instructions when needed.
- Ensuring that the appropriate learner controls are included.
- Sketching, storyboarding, or scripting the initial design of the graphic, animation, or video and working with the subject matter expert and multimedia developer to create the final product.

FINAL SELF-ASSESSMENT EXERCISE

Choose a passage of text related to nursing or nursing education from a book or article. The passage should be several paragraphs in length and should focus on only one or two main concepts. The passage should lend itself to the inclusion of at least one other media type, then perform the following:

1. Rewrite the text in an instructional format.

2. If appropriate, add graphics, animation, sound, and video to accompany the text. You need not create this media; just describe it.

3. Write a justification for how you rewrote the text and why you included or did not include media elements.

Use the following rubric to grade yourself (Table 9-1):

Table 9-1   Instructional Media Rubric

	Weak (1–10 points) Minimal references to information in the chapter content	Average (11–15 points) Adequate references to information in the chapter content	Superior (16–20 points) Fully referenced information in the chapter content	Score
Justification for text revision				
Justification for inclusion/exclusion of graphics				
Justification for inclusion/exclusion of animations				
Justification for inclusion/exclusion of sound				
Justification for inclusion/exclusion of video				
			Total (100 points possible)	

References

Ausubel, D. P. (1968). *Educational psychology: A cognitive view*. New York, NY: Holt, Rinehart, and Winston.

Baddeley, A. D. (1986). *Working memory*. New York, NY: Oxford University Press.

Baddeley, A. D. (1999). *Human memory*. Needham Heights, MA: Allyn & Bacon.

Baker, G., & Bixler, B. (1990). Computer-assisted design techniques for low-literate adults. *Computers in Adult Education and Training, 2*(1), 18–27.

Bixler, B. A. (2006, January 1). Writing educational goals and objectives. Available at: http://www.personal.psu.edu/bxb11/Objectives. Accessed May 19, 2009.

Bower, G. H. (1970). Organizational factors in memory. *Cognitive Psychology, 1*, 18–46.

Cook, L. K., & Mayer, R. E. (1988). Teaching readers about the structure of scientific text. *Journal of Educational Psychology, 80*(4), 448–456.

Duchastel, P. C. (1978). Illustrating instructional texts. *Educational Technology, 18*(11), 36–39.

Duchastel, P. C., & Waller, R. (1979). Pictorial illustration in instructional texts. *Educational Technology, 19*(11), 20–25.

Dwyer, F. M. (1978). *Strategies for improving visual learning*. State College, PA: Learning Services.

Elen, J., & Louw, L. P. (2006). The instructional functionality of multiple adjunct aids. *e-Journal of Instructional Science and Technology 9*, 1–17.

Hallam, S., Price, J., & Katsarou, G. (2002). The effects of background music on primary school pupils' task performance. *Educational Studies, 28*(2), 111–122.

Hartley, J. (1981). Eighty ways of improving instructional text. *IEEE Transactions on Professional Communication, 21*(1), 17–27.

Manfull, H., & Manfull, L. L. (1989). *The stage in action: An introduction to theater and drama*. Dubuque, IA: Kendall Hunt Publishing Company

Mayer, R. E. (2002). Cognitive theory and the design of multimedia instruction: An example of the two-way street between cognition and instruction. *New Directions for Teaching and Learning, 89*, 55–71.

My Byline Media. (2009). The Flesch reading ease readability formula. Available at: http://www.readabilityformulas.com/flesch-reading-ease-readability-formula.php. Accessed May 20, 2009.

Paivio, A. (1986). *Mental representations: A dual coding approach*. New York, NY: Oxford University Press.

Rieber, L. (1994). *Computer, graphics, and learning*. Madison, WI: Brown & Benchmark Publishers.

Smith, T., Ruocco, A., & Jansen, B. (1999). Digital video in education. *ACM SIGCSE Bulletin, 31*(1), 122–126.

Wikipedia. (2009, June 1). Flesch-Kincaid readability test. Available at: http://en.wikipedia .org/wiki/Flesch-Kincaid_Readability_Test. Accessed May 20, 2009.

Winn, W. (1993). Perception principles. In M. Fleming & W. H. Levie (Eds.), *Instructional message design: Principles from the behavioral and cognitive sciences* (2nd ed.). Englewood Cliffs, NJ: Educational Technology Publications, Inc.

CHAPTER 10

Copyright and Fair Use in Education

Food For Thought

*"The primary objective of copyright is not to reward the labor of authors,
but '[t]o promote the Progress of Science and useful Arts.'
To this end, copyright assures authors the right to their original expression,
but encourages others to build freely upon the ideas and information conveyed by a work.
This result is neither unfair nor unfortunate.
It is the means by which copyright advances the progress of science and art."*

**Justice Sandra Day O'Connor Feist Publications,
Inc. v. Rural Telephone Service Co., 499 US 340, 349 (1991)**

Key Words

Copyright
Fair use
MERLOT

Public domain
TEACH (Technology, Education, and
    Copyright Harmonization) Act

Objectives

The educator will be able to define copyright, fair use, and public domain.
The educator will be able to describe copyright and what it means for the author
    and user of a work.

The educator will be able to explain the importance of the TEACH Act.
The educator will be able to assess how fair use and the TEACH Act relate to one
another.
The educator will be able to locate a public domain image, animation, simulation, or
activity on MERLOT.

Introduction

The mere mention of the word "copyright" conjures up confusion, ambiguity, and of course, many questions. Is it okay to use an image in my online course? Since a course management system is in place at my institution, we can add whatever we want and it will let us know about copyright violations, right? YouTube allows me to imbed their videos, can I just use whatever I want? As long as I use less than 40 words from someone else, I do not have to cite it, right? What percent of someone's work do I need to use to have to seek permission? How many words do I have to change in an author's sentence to make it my own? Before you attempt to use another's work, you must fully understand both the author's rights as well as your own rights. Learning about copyright, fair use, public domain, and the TEACH Act will help you to avoid infringing on someone's copyright.

This text is not focused on copyright issues, but concepts like copyright, fair use, public domain, or the TEACH Act are very important for you to understand in order to properly use available online materials in your courses. A lack of understanding of these concepts can result in misuse of copyrighted materials or a fear of using online materials altogether.

Copyright

Copyright refers to "a form of protection provided by the laws of the United States" (title 17, US Code) to the authors of "original works of authorship, including literary, dramatic, musical . . . creations" (US Copyright Office, 2008b, para. 1). According to Wikipedia (2008), copyright is "symbolized "©" – is a legal concept, enacted by most governments, giving the creator of an original work exclusive rights to it, usually for a limited time (1).

Templeton (n.d.), chairman of the Board of the Electronic Frontier Foundation (EFF), states that:

> Copyright law secures for the creator of a creative effort the exclusive right to control who can make copies, or make works derived from the original work. There are a lot of subtleties and international variations but that's the gist of it. If you create something, and it fits the definition of a creative work, you get to control who can make copies of it and how they make copies. . . . (para. 3)

Fair Use

Fair use is typically judged on type of use, the amount of the work that is used, and the effect this use has on the actual copyrighted work. When in doubt get permission from the copyright owner.

Stanford University's (2008) Copyright and Fair Use Center has an abundance of information on copyright and fair use issues. The University of Texas (2001) offers an online course in copyright since this is such an important issue in a technological age that makes copying and using another's work as easy as a click or two.

Public Domain

According to Wikipedia (2008), **public domain** "is a range of abstract materials—commonly referred to as intellectual property—which are not owned or controlled by anyone. The term indicates that these materials are therefore 'public property,' and available for anyone to use for any purpose." Most materials created before 1923 are in the public domain. Lolly Gasaway (2003) created a matrix to help educators and others determine when US works pass into the public domain.

The works that are located in the public domain are growing and available for use in your learning episodes. Below is a list of sites to explore*:

- Comics: Digital Funnies Comics Preservation by Jonathan Barli is located at http://www.digitalfunnies.com/. (These comics are for sale in collections or as prints.)
- Movies and Documentaries: http://moviesfoundonline.com/public_domain.php

- Historical Images, Library of Congress Prints and Photographs Online Catalog: http://lcweb2.loc.gov/pp/pphome.html
- Medical Images, Centers for Disease Control and Prevention: http://phil.cdc.gov/phil/home.asp
- Agricultural Images, USDA Online Photography Center: http://phil.cdc.gov/phil/home.asp
- History, images of American Political History: http://bill.ballpaul.net/iaph/main.php
- Miscellaneous Images: http://pics4learning.com

In addition, learning repositories and open courseware initiatives are encouraging educators to share their educational materials with one another with minimal restrictions on use.*

- For an example of a learning repository,* see **MERLOT** at http://merlot.org/merlot/index.htm
- For an example of Open Courseware,* see the MIT Open Courseware site at http://ocw.mit.edu/OcwWeb/web/about/about/index.htm

*These sites were retrieved on March 15, 2009.

TEACH Act

The **TEACH (Technology, Education, and Copyright Harmonization) Act of 2002** was passed to revise and expand parts of the US copyright law governing the conditions under which accredited, nonprofit US educational institutions may use copyrighted materials without permission from the copyright owner and without payment of royalties. The focus of the TEACH Act is the use of copyright-protected materials for organized instructional activities in distance education rather than face-to-face traditional classroom settings.

Read more about the TEACH Act at one of the many available informational sites*:

- The Florida State University Center for Teaching & Learning: http://learningforlife.fsu.edu/ctl/explore/bestPractices/docs/TEACHAct.pdf
- The TEACH Toolkit at North Carolina State University: http://www.lib.ncsu.edu/publications/NLarchives/NL.vol.30/NL_30_7.pdf

- Penn State's Teaching with Technology TEACH Act site: http://tlt.its. psu.edu/dmd/teachact/

*These sites were retrieved on March 15, 2009.

Conclusion

Copyright, public domain, fair use, and the TEACH Act are important concepts that should guide your use of others' works and the dissemination of new work. We have briefly introduced these topics and encourage you to become familiar with them to avoid any potential problems.

Learning Applications

Read each of the following scenarios or case examples and reflect on the copyright, fair use, or public domain issues that are raised. Try to answer the questions before you read the response.

CASE 1

Dr. Jane Fair uses excerpts from 10 documentaries that she has taped from TV and compiles them into one video for her students to view. Has she violated copyright and fair use practice?

RESPONSE: Yes, since you cannot alter or combine off-air tapings.

CASE 2

Dr. Rob Fyles decides to record a radio broadcasted concert and plays this for his students in class. Is this okay?

RESPONSE: Yes, as long as it is relevant to the lesson and curriculum.

CASE 3

Kate Waterbee is a nursing clinical specialist in wound care for a large metropolitan hospital. She decides that she must have a photographic accounting of a specific patient's wounds that are not healing as anticipated in order to document treatment and reaction. She asks her patient to sign a Consent to Photography form provided by her employer.

1. Does this allow her to photograph the wound and share the photos with her graduate advanced practice nursing students? Kate decides that one of the patients, Pam, has interesting moles on other areas of her body including her face. Kate decides to take full body photos of Pam.
2. Did Kate have the right to do this?
3. Can Kate share these photos with her students?

RESPONSES:
1. Yes, as long as she maintains the patient's anonymity.
2. No. The moles are not part of the reason she is photographing the patient.
3. No. Refer to previous response. Face photos would also compromise the patient's anonymity.

CASE 4

Raymond Cosby decides that he would like to share an article with his class. It is 1500 words long.

1. Can he make one copy for each student in the class? Raymond really likes this author and finds two other articles from her and they are each under 1000 words.
2. Can he copy these articles for his students? Raymond is preparing for his next class that begins in 1 hour. He finds a superb article that he would like to share with his class but it exceeds the word limit. However, it would really maximize his teaching effectiveness and enhance the learning for the students. He decides to copy it for his students for them to use in this class.
3. Is this okay?

RESPONSES:

1. Yes. An article or essay less than 2500 words that includes copyright notice could be given to each student in one course. Raymond should always investigate if his university subscribes to a database that includes the article.

2. No. Only one article, poem, or essay, for example, may be copied from the same author during a semester.

3. Yes, since this would greatly enhance the learning episode and there is not time to seek permission, he could argue that it was a spontaneous decision on his part to use this article. When an article is used for educational purposes, it weighs in favor of fair use.

Reflect on the previous scenarios. How does fair use, copyright, and the TEACH Act impact your course content? Do you feel that the interpretation of fair use will continue to evolve in the educational arena? You should help your learners understand the importance of recognizing the need to respect other's work and not to use it as their own. Many learners are not trying to steal the work of someone else but get confused about this interconnected, sharing, editing, disseminating space we call the Internet.

We recommend that you view the Lawrence Lessig Keynote presentation (51 minutes) on digital media at the 2008 Symposium for Teaching and Learning with Technology at Penn State University. This is a great recap and synthesis for the idea of creativity, copyright, and culture in the 21st century. This is on YouTube at the following URL http://www.youtube.com/watch?v=bHBSNNYbyvg.

References

Feist Publications, Inc. v. Rural Telephone Service Co., 499 US 340, 349 (1991).

Gasaway, L. (2003). *When US works pass into the public domain.* Available at: http://www.unc.edu/~unclng/public-d.htm. Accessed March 15, 2009.

Hoon, P. (2002). *The TEACH toolkit: An online resource for understanding copyright and distance education.* Available at: http://www.lib.ncsu.edu/scc/legislative/teachkit/. Accessed April 23, 2009.

Newsome, C. (1997). *A teacher's guide to fair use and copyright.* Available at: http://home.earthlink.net/~cnew/research.htm. Accessed April 23, 2009.

Stanford University. (2008). *Copyright and fair use center.* Available at: http://fairuse .stanford.edu/. Accessed March 12, 2009.

Templeton, B. (n.d.). *A brief intro to copyright.* Available at: http://www.templetons.com/brad/ copyright.html. Accessed April 23, 2009.

United States Copyright Office. (2008b). *Circular 1: Copyright office basics.* Available at: http:// www.copyright.gov/circs/circ1a.html. Accessed April 23, 2009.

University of Texas. (2001). *Crash course in copyright.* Available at: http://www.utsystem.edu/ OGC/IntellectualProperty/cprtindx.htm. Accessed March 15, 2009.

Wikipedia. (2008). *Copyright.* Available at: http://en.wikipedia.org/wiki/Copyright/. Accessed April 23, 2009.

Wikipedia. (2008). *Public domain.* Available at: http://en.wikipedia.org/wiki/Public_domain/. Accessed April 29, 2009.

Evolving Educational Technologies

SECTION III

We believe that educational programming must evolve along with educational technologies. However, the need to use and integrate the latest technologies has a price; teachers and learners must constantly be learning new tools. We must strive for balance by remembering that the learning curve for using a new tool might very well stifle the learning and that too many tools can be hazardous to knowledge acquisition and dissemination. This section builds on the first two sections of the text and will help you to incorporate the right tools at the right time for the right educational benefit for the right learner.

Chapter 11 will explore the different learning environments in which we teach and learn. Various tools and application modalities will be described and explored, such as course management systems, student response systems, online, face-to-face, blended and clinical venues. In Chapter 12, we will look at the current evolution of Web tools and where this technology is going. The focus is on learning applications and how to add Web tools into a teaching repertoire. Chapter 13 will provide potent information on educational simulations, virtual worlds, and gaming. These interactive and highly social learning applications are extremely important for health care as we seek to develop communities of practice. Chapter 14 will help you to develop clinical practice simulations for your learners. Since health care is a practice-based arena, it is important for our learners to be exposed to real-world simulations prior to entering the actual clinical setting. Once healthcare professionals have been practicing, it is also necessary for the practitioners to hone their skills or learn new skills in non-threatening, authentic simulated situations. Chapter 15 will provide an overview of clinical practice tools. This is also where you will learn about informatics competencies for nurses. Chapter 16 will end this section with a discussion of technology tools for outcomes assessment. You will be introduced to assessment and teaching e-Portfolios. The portfolios will be examined in their relation to faculty and student assessment and development.

11

Variations in Learning Environments

Food For Thought

"Man is a tool-using animal"

Thomas Carlyle, 1795–1881

Key Words

Blended learning
Clickers
Hybrid courses
Open source systems

Stylus
3-C didactic model
Web-enhanced courses

Objectives

The educator will be able to describe the four types of learning environments.

The educator will be able to explain what a course management system (CMS) is and list its advantages and disadvantages.

The educator will be able to explain what an interactive whiteboard (IWB) is, how they are used, and list the advantages and disadvantages.

The educator will be able to explain what clickers are and list the advantages and disadvantages.

The educator will be able to define the basic characteristics and list the benefits of a standard tablet PC.

Introduction

Samantha sits down at her computer on a Tuesday night to complete some coursework. She logs on to the university's course management system and reviews PowerPoint slides of class notes for an Introduction to Psychology class. She also reads her weekly online lesson and completes several practice problems in preparation for her Accounting lab. Finally, she participates in a discussion forum for her online course on Art History.

Samantha's three courses differ in their learning environments. Her Introduction to Psychology meets face-to-face three times per week in a small auditorium. Her instructor asks questions to the class and collects their responses using clickers, which keeps them alert and engaged. The use of the clickers has also motivated Samantha to study her notes prior to each class, so she earns participation points by getting answers correct. Samantha's Accounting class, on the other hand, is a blended course. She is expected to learn the material by reading online materials and trying practice problems during the week, and then she attends a face-to-face lab meeting on Thursdays. In lab, she works collaboratively with other students on assigned problems for credit. Finally, Samantha's Art History course is completely online. It combines online lessons, online resources, textbook readings, and discussion forums. Samantha communicates with her instructor by e-mail only.

Types of Learning Environments

The use of technology in instruction can be viewed on a continuum, going from using technology within the face-to-face setting to having the entire course content online. The terms used to describe the various environments include face-to-face, web-enhanced, blended or hybrid, and online.

Face-to-face courses are the traditional environment where students meet regularly with the instructor at scheduled times. Today, instructors can take advantage of cutting-edge technologies that go beyond simple PowerPoint presentations. No longer do traditional courses need to be boring, with students sitting passively in their seats as spectators. Tools such as interactive white boards, tablet PCs, and **clickers** or polling devices can make learning active, engaging, and fun. These tools will be reviewed in more detail in the second part of this chapter.

Web-enhanced courses have traditional face-to-face meetings but include some online elements that students must access or complete on their own. For example, students attend class but are required to access homework problems and quizzes online. The introduction of course management systems in the late 1990s has led to an increase in Web-enhanced courses, particularly in higher education, due to the ease in which instructors can upload, track, and share materials.

Blended, or **hybrid courses** seamlessly integrate face-to-face and online components. There is no rule of thumb as to what percentage of content should be included in the face-to-face meetings versus the online environment, because it depends on the course being taught. The most important aspect of this type of course is that the face-to-face and online components build on one another and work together in a manner that makes sense and is beneficial to the students. If this does not occur, one of the components will lose its value, and students will focus on the component for which they are held most accountable.

Kerres and DeWitt (2003) created the **3-C didactic model** for **blended learning** that provides a step-by-step process for deciding how the content will be delivered. The steps include:

1. List learning objectives.
2. Classify each learning objective according to three components: Content includes facts or rules and simply requires memorization; communication includes concepts that must be discussed with the instructor or peers for greater clarification; and construction includes applied knowledge that must be practiced through individual or group activities.
3. Determine how much of the course will be devoted to each type of component (Rule of Thumb: content, 33%; communication, 33%; construction, 33%)
4. Determine delivery system based on aspects of that particular course.

The learning objectives that are classified as content are best presented in an online format, because students will be able to read and learn about them on their own, at their own pace. The objectives that are classified as either communication or construction must be examined more closely to determine if a face-to-face or online would be best. Specifically, the following questions should be addressed:

- Who is the audience?
- Is group work involved?
- What are the costs (time, travel, cognitive demands)

Many models of blended learning exist, but the basic underlying process in all include first identifying the content objectives and conducting some type of analysis before identifying the components for online and face-to-face delivery.

Finally, online courses have no face-to-face meetings, so students access all content from their computer. Online courses are ideal when the targeted students need flexibility in scheduling their courses or are at a distance. This type of delivery works especially well with adult students, since they are juggling their course work with employment and family life.

When designing for an online environment, the following should be considered:

- Targeted audience: What type of access do they have? What is their comfort level with online learning? What technical assistance will be provided?
- Class size: How many students will be enrolled, and will the creation of groups, peer assessments, and projects make the faculty workload more manageable?
- Lesson format: Will the format be text-based or use some technology such as video, narrated PowerPoints, Flash, Second Life, or Web 2.0? Is there enough time and available resources to create the desired format? Will the format be difficult for the targeted audience to access or understand?
- Synchronous versus asynchronous: Based on what you know about your targeted audience, will instruction be real-time or at the convenience of the learner? What are your obligations as an instructor?
- Interactivity: How will students interact with one another? How often will interaction occur? How will immediate feedback be provided by the instructor?
- Time management: How will students be kept informed about due dates and exams? What types of strategies will be used to keep them on track with reading and assignments?

- Expectations: How will the instructor convey expectations in an online environment in terms of the quality of the postings, written papers, and projects?
- Instructor's comfort level: Is the instructor savvy when it comes to technology? Is the instructor comfortable teaching in this type of environment? What type of support can be provided? Does the instructor understand the demands of an online course?
- Motivation: Will targeted audience be motivated to take and stay involved in the online course? How can the audience motivation be improved through the design of the course?

Technology Tools to Enhance Face-to-Face, Web-Enhanced, Blended, and Online Courses

Regardless of the learning environment, technology can support active learning, peer-to-peer collaboration, and instructor-student interactions. Although many tools exist, this section will examine course management systems, interactive whiteboards, clickers or polling devices, and tablet PCs.

Course Management Systems (CMS)

In higher education and industry, course management systems have made delivering content for Web-enhanced, blended, and online environments extremely simple and secure. Course management systems are online systems designed to support classroom learning in academic settings (Carliner, 2005). Using one of these systems, an instructor can easily upload files such as word documents, PowerPoint slides, or PDFs for student use and create interactive course elements such as discussion forums, games, and quizzes. Course management systems also include features that allow the instructor to track students' log-ons, activities, and grades. All this can be done with minimal technical knowledge. Examples of course management systems include Blackboard, Desire2Learn, and eCollege, which are commercially-available products, and Moodle and Sakai, both of which are open source systems. **Open source systems** mean that these content management systems are freely available and are supported by an online community.

Advantages of commercially available courseware management systems include ease of use, a low learning curve for the instructor, more opportunities for student interactivity, the ability to easily score and monitor student activity, and the standardization of the way courses are delivered at an educational institution. Disadvantages include the costs and the lack of flexibility in course layout.

Advantages of open source courseware management systems include no license fee, ability to customize, access to an online community for support, and continuous updates and improvements (Lakhan & Jhunjhunwala, 2008). Disadvantages include the hidden costs (server and storage space, training, support, and upgrades), problems integrating it with existing systems, and uncertainty about its availability over time (Brooks-Young, 2008; Martinez & Jagannathan, 2008).

Interactive Whiteboards

Interactive whiteboards (IWB) are used in face-to-face settings and are especially popular at the K through 12 level. An IWB is a large board mounted on a wall in front of the class that allows the instructor to share what is on a computer desktop with the class using a digital projector. The teacher can manipulate images displayed on the whiteboard by touching it or using a special pen. The whiteboard comes with its own software that is loaded onto the computer. This software allows the instructor to edit or annotate images on display and integrate online resources into the lesson, including informational sites, videos, graphics, and sound. Some IWBs also include ready-made lessons that can be used or altered by instructors. Although there are many different brands of IWBs, probably the one most commonly used is the Smartboard.

Like all technologies, IWBs take some time to learn and to use effectively. Letwin, Somekh, and Steadman (2008) indicate that it takes at least 2 years for instructors to become proficient with the IWB. Beauchamp and Parkinson (2005) also indicate that an instructor's mastery of the IWB takes time and is a progressive process where the instructors move from presenting the lesson in a linear format to a more discursive model where technology is used to explore ideas while keeping the main objectives of the lessons intact.

The instructor's ability to use the IWB tools and manipulate resources in response to students' questions and interests will invigorate the learning environment and keep the students engaged. When given control of the whiteboard along with some guidance, students will also have the opportunity to interact with the information on display, meeting the Net Generation's preference for visual/kinetic learning, as discussed in Chapter 3.

Instructors who use IWBs will experience many advantages over the traditional chalkboard, whiteboard, overhead projector, or PowerPoint presentation. These benefits include access to ready-made lessons and a wide variety of online resources; the ability to save, store, and print lessons; the capability to move seamlessly from an in-class presentation to online resources and teaching tools; the flexibility to use multiple methods and media to present content; the ability to address different learning styles and levels; and the opportunity to motivate students as a result of the interactive features and faster-paced lessons (Smith, Higgins, Wall, & Miller, 2005). Students will also benefit from the use of the IWB because they will be able to share and collaborate with peers to construct new knowledge; focus on the task at hand rather than taking notes (because everything done on the whiteboard can be saved and printed); take on an active role, rather than a passive role, in the classroom; and support their responses and ideas using a wide array of resources (Hennessy, Deaney, Ruthven, & Winterbottom, 2007).

Instructors may also encounter several drawbacks with the IWB. First, instructors need sufficient time and training to use the IWB and its software. Although initially new and exciting, the instructor's repeated use of the IWB may become routine, and the instructor may slip back into traditional methods of teaching. Similarly, upon initial use of the IWB, instructors may focus too much on the "bells and whistles" of the technology, and neglect to consider whether or not their approach to teaching with the whiteboard is pedagogically sound (Glover, Miller, Averis, & Door, 2007).

The use of the IWB itself cannot improve teaching skills; instructors must make an effort to use pedagogic techniques that are appropriate for the subject matter and students. Otherwise, they will use this technology in the same manner that they did with more traditional tools, resulting in their return to being the "sage on stage" (Zevenbergen & Lerman, 2007).

Clickers and Polling Devices

Student response systems such as clickers or polling devices can improve the in-class experience since professors can interact with their students electronically. These small remote devices can be used to easily take attendance, poll students, determine if key concepts are recognized and understood, or administer a quiz.

A student response system also encourages active learning and as discussed in Chapter 3, today's students prefer "hands-on" type activities.

Some instructors state that these technologies help increase interactivity in comparison to a non-clicker class, where only a handful of students are able to answer questions. Clicker technologies can actively engage the learners, determine their level of understanding of key concepts, and offer a means for the instructor to provide immediate feedback.

Using polling devices to conduct quick class polls about students' comprehension is extremely important and allows the instructor to restate or further explain those concepts the students are not grasping based on their responses. The anonymity of these polls can foster the expression of viewpoints that students may be reluctant to share openly in classroom. Although the collective student responses can be viewed on the public classroom screen, if a student answers a question wrong, the anonymity of the polling device takes away any awkwardness or public embarrassment. Since each device is numbered; however, the professor can download the class session's responses for review of each individual's performance after class.

A disadvantage of remote response systems is their cost, especially when they are packaged with expensive textbooks. As a result, some vendors now offer response cards with the purchase of their response systems. Depending on the purchase arrangement, these cards can be free for the students to use throughout the semester and then returned. In addition, as the technology continues to evolve, vendors are developing products that eliminate the need to obtain a remote response device, and instead use the students' personal cell phones, personal digital assistants (PDAs) or laptops with wireless capability.

Tablet PCs

Tablet PCs are similar to laptops, with one important exception. The screen is designed to be written and drawn upon. Most tablet PCs come equipped with a **stylus** for input. Some tablet PCs come with a detachable keyboard (called slates) that can be set aside. Other tablet PCs have a swivel screen that can be turned 180 degrees on the horizontal and then placed down on top of the keyboard, thus hiding the keyboard. Tablet PCs are meant to be held like a clipboard, freeing one hand to hold the stylus for writing and drawing. In addition, tablet PCs come equipped with specialized software that takes advantage of the screen. These applications accept stylus input, as well as the standard keyboard and mouse input. In all other respects, tablet PCs are physically just like most laptops.

Tablet PCs are often used as presentation devices in the classroom (Mock, 2004). They allow instructors to change and modify preplanned lectures and activities on the fly, providing for "extemporaneous adaptation of their presentations to match their audiences" (Anderson, Simon, Wolfman, VanDeGrift, & Yasuhara, 2004). For example, an instructor may begin drawing a formula, then easily alter it based on student questions. A variety of presentation tools also exist for tablet PCs, from modified PowerPoint presentations to applications specifically written for tablets. Examples include Classroom Presenter from the University of Washington and Dyknow Vision (Mock, 2004).

The tablet PC may also be viewed as an electronic blackboard (Mock, 2004). Instructors can display premade illustrations and photographs and then use multiple colors for line drawings, circles, and arrows that are superimposed on these images. Unlike a blackboard, information on the screen does not need to be erased and lost forever; it can be saved and later redisplayed. Similarly, instructors can use the tablet PC to mark up homework in a naturalistic way, circling areas, or crossing out passages (Mock, 2004).

In the hands of students, tablet PCs can increase interactions in the classroom (Tront, 2007). Students can use the tablet PC to learn collaboratively, test assumptions, sketch out ideas, or take notes. In addition to text, students can add arrows and other simple shapes to tie ideas together.

Summary

The advances in technology have lead to classroom tools that encourage active and collaborative learning in different learning environments. As with any technology, the instructor must take the time not only to learn how to use the tool, but also to understand the pedagogy behind it. When used appropriately, these current technologies can reinvigorate an instructor's lessons and motivate students to prepare for and participate in class.

Learning Activities

As an instructor, if given either an interactive white board, clicker system or your own tablet PC, how would you use it to transform the way you teach? What are the advantages of doing this? How would doing this change your presentation methods?

Now imagine all your students had their own tablet PC. What activities could you now ask them to do that were previously impossible?

References

Anderson, R., R., A., Simon, B., Wolfman, S. A., VanDeGrift, T., & Yasuhara, K. (2004). *Experiences with tablet PC based lecture presentation system in computer science courses.* Paper presented at the 35th SIGCSE Technical Symposium on Computer Science Education, Norfolk, VA.

Beauchamp, G., & Parkinson, J. (2005). Beyond the "wow" factor: Developing interactivity with the interactive whiteboard. *School of Science Review, 86*(316), 97–103.

Brooks-Young, S. (2008, April 11). Got Moodle? *THE Journal.* Available at: http://thejournal .com/articles/2008/04/01/got-moodle.aspx. Accessed July 24, 2009.

Carliner, S. (2005). Course management systems versus learning management systems. *Learning Circuits.* Available at: http://www.astd.org/LC/2005/1105_carliner.htm. Accessed July 24, 2009.

Glover, D., Miller, D., Averis, D., & Door, V. (2007). The evolution of an effective pedagogy for teachers using the interactive whiteboard in mathematics and modern languages: An empirical analysis from the secondary sector. *Learning, Media and Technology, 32*(1), 5–20.

Hennessy, S., Deaney, R., Ruthven, K., & Winterbottom, M. (2007). Pedagogical strategies for using the interactive whiteboard to foster learner participation in school science. *Learning, Media and Technology, 32*(3), 283–301.

Kerres, M. & DeWitt, C. (2003). A didactic framework for the design of blended learning arrangements. *Journal of Educational Media, 28,* 2–3.

Lakhan, S. E., & Jhunjhunwala, K. (2008). Open source software in education. *EDUCAUSE Quarterly, 31*(2). Available at: http://www.educause.edu/EDUCAUSE+Quarterly/ EDUCAUSEQuarterlyMagazineVolum/OpenSourceSoftwareinEducation/162873. Accessed July 24, 2009.

Letwin, C., Somekh, B., & Steadman, S. (2008). Embedding interactive whiteboards in teaching and learning: The process of change in pedagogical practice. *Education and Information Technologies, 13*(4), 291–303.

Martinez, M., & Jagannathan, S. (2008, November 10). Moodle: A low-cost solution for successful e-learning. *Learning Solutions Magazine.* Available at: http://www.elearningguild .com/articles/abstracts/index.cfm?id=289&action=viewonly. Accessed July 24, 2009.

Mock, K. (2004). *Teaching with tablet PCs.* University of Alaska, Anchorage, AK. Available at: http:// www.math.uaa.alaska.edu/~afkjm/papers/mock-ccsc2004.pdf. Accessed July 7, 2009.

Smith, H. J., Higgins, S., Wall, K., & Miller, J. (2005). Interactive whiteboards: Boon or bandwagon? A critical review of the literature. *Journal of Computer Assisted Learning, 21*(2), 91–101.

Tront, J. G. (2007). Facilitating pedagogical practices through a large-scale tablet PC deployment. *COMPUTER, 40*(9), 62–68.

Zevenbergen, R., & Lerman, S. (2007). Pedagogy and interactive whiteboards: Using an activity theory approach to understand tensions in practice. Proceedings of the 30th annual conference of the Mathematics Education Research Group of Australasia.

Web 1.0, 2.0, 3.0, 4.0 . . . and Beyond

Food For Thought

"My vision of school/classroom 2.0 is, more than anything else, about conversations. Traditional schools involved teachers and textbooks delivering information to students, and students reflecting that information back. To better serve their future, today's classrooms should facilitate teaching and learning as a conversation—two-way conversations between teachers and learners, conversations between learners and other learners, conversations among teachers, and new conversations between the classroom and the home and between the school and its community."

—David Warlick

"More than 90 percent of the technology that will affect our daily lives at the beginning of the 21st century has not been invented. This means that more innovations will be introduced in the next ten years than were produced throughout previous human history."

—Freeman Dyson, physicist and principal architect of the theory of quantum electrodynamics

Key Words

Social networking	Twitter
Social bookmarking	Web 2.0

Objectives

The educator will be able to define Web 2.0.

The educator will be able to describe Web 2.0 tools and begin to envision the next generation of tools and applications.

The educator will be able to identify at least three ways Web 2.0+ tools and applications could enhance learning.

Introduction

The World Wide Web, or the Web for short, bounded on the scene in 1990 and dazzled everyone with its ability to showcase large amounts of information for anyone to access. Web 1.0 was all about distribution, delivery, and consumption. From this simple beginning, **Web 2.0** evolved into an interactive environment with **social networking** and connectivity, where producing and sharing are key. Innovators are using Web 2.0 tools as facilitating platforms to develop excellent, accurate, and high-quality substance and services. This contributory environment requires us to be able to execute what we produce. Web 3.0 and even 4.0 looms as the change that will transform how we interact with each other and the world. It will change how we interact forever, being truly transparent and ubiquitous such as the new interactive surfaces. "Look ma, no hands!" is going to take on a totally new meaning shortly. This begs the question: How can we have such mundane, lack luster monikers associated with one of the most far reaching and metamorphosing change of our time, Web 2.0+? We could call them the "YOU Tools" or "Me Tools" or Read – write – draw – compose – think (capture) aloud – film – calculate – view – listen – share – WEB.

Well, you get the idea, there is so much more to come now that we have traversed into the 2s, 3s, and 4s of the next generation of computability! Understanding the movement from I seek to I do, from I consume to I produce and from I see it and can share it (kind of) to be able to shout look what I have done and instantly share with global communities of my choice—is paramount to be able to envision where we are going. Having said all of that, readin', writin', and 'rithmetic have taken on a whole new meaning with everything Web. The educational landscape has also changed with the times. Therefore, it is paramount that we appreciate and comprehend these changes and embrace them in our teaching repertoires to engage our learners!

The Web 2s, 3s, 4s, and beyond

The tools that are emerging on a daily basis have been radically changing individual as well as organizational capabilities. Teachers and learners can socially network, bookmark using del.icio.us, the Web 2.0 placard, and Wiki for free instantaneously. Computers and technology are evolving to the point where the semantic Web is a reality with machines reading, processing, and understanding cyberspacial data and generating information based on our complex queries. The Web is not just based in a semantic milieu, it is moving beyond words to spaces, images, and sounds. The technologies must keep up with the challenges and developments that are morphing the Internet. Tools must be able to locate media using other media without relying on a word-based search. Scanned photos could trigger searches for similar photos, paintings, or videos. According to Godin (2007), there will be so many things Web 4.0 can do and it is "about making connections, about serendipity and about the network taking initiative" (para. 1). Think about his scenarios:

> "I'm late for a dinner. My GPS phone knows this (because it has my calendar, my location, and the traffic status). So, it tells me, and then it alerts the people who are waiting for me" (para. 2).
>
> "My PDA knows I'm going to a convention. Based on my e-mail logs, it recommends who I ought to see while I'm there—because my friends have opted-in to our network and we're in sync" (para. 3).
>
> "I'm about to buy something from a vendor (in a store with a smart card or online). At the last minute, Web4 jumps in and asks if I want it cheaper, or if I want it from a vendor with a better reputation. Not based on some gamed system, but based on what a small trusted circle believes" (para. 4).

Let us think about these tools in relation to nursing education. What initiatives could be taken by our learners' PDAs or smart phones to help them complete assignments, meet with team members or with professors? What about for us as educators?

Consumer-Driven Web

The tools that we are referring to help us produce and generate. Web 2.0 (and we use this term loosely since there is a melding of tools and advances that challenges the static interpretation of its realm) is a status of wits in that we have tools available to us that can support and facilitate our work and play in ways we have not even conceived of as of yet. Our capacity to use and evolve these tools and their functionality is the core to this new Web movement and why static numbers do not reflect the strength, power, wisdom, and instinct of this new frontier of computational prowess.

The interconnected capabilities of the Web have made social networking a term that is dwarfed by the vastness of the sharing and interaction that occurs each minute in cyberspace. The Web has created an inclusive new culture that empowers each user to use and challenge the current tools. Just as we have moved to a learner-centered approach in our curriculums, the Web has become user-centric with the goal of harnessing the collective wisdom of many as in the case of Wikiversity (2009). They "invite teachers, students, and researchers to join . . . in creating open educational resources and collaborative learning communities" (para. 1). It is the individual and collective wisdom of the users and developers of the tools that continues to drive the Web movement.

E-Learning Web Tools

Imagine: John, a junior nursing student at Penn State University, is catching up with other nursing students at a local restaurant. They place their food order using the interactive surface on the table. Barbara has her PDA and John says that he is interested in reviewing the diagnostic exercise they began this morning in class. Barbara sets her PDA on the interactive surface and immediately the exercise images, text, and video are displayed. John and Barbara both begin manipulating the files. Kayla sees what they are doing and she is curious about their work since she is a sophomore in the nursing program. Soon three other nursing students join them in active discussions and the surface is alive with files being manipulated, shared, and stored on several different PDAs. John is still not sure that he fully understands why his initial nursing diagnosis was not correct. He opens an image of his professor on the surface and enlarges it. Soon the professor is conversing with the students through the surface. John begins to see how he missed critical assessment data that led to his misdiagnosis. The waitress brings their food orders and John places his credit card down on the surface. His credit card is charged and he places it back into his wallet.

This scenario is happening now. We need to enhance our understanding and capabilities to fully use what is currently available while stretching into the next level of capabilities. It is not an easy task to choose just a few tools to showcase in this text and we would like to encourage you to continue to investigate the available tools and network with global colleagues to find the best tools for your learning episodes. It is through active exploration that you will learn new ways to use the tools and discover new tools that are available.

The Web 2.0 tools have been classified in many ways. For our purposes, we will delineate five categories: social networking and communication, collaboration, social bookmarking, e-learning, and services.

Social Networking and Communicating

Social networking and communicating tools are designed for communication and staying connected to the ones you care about. This category includes Twitter, Jisko, MySpace, FaceBook, blogging, Wikis, YouTube, Kwippy, Jabbify, TeacherTube, RSS feeds, Feedster, people, hitch, and Daypop.

Twitter

Twitter is a free social networking service that allows users to send and receive information (tweets) about one another. Getting started requires that you sign up for Twitter at http://www.twitter.com and search for your friends to follow. This "friending" allows you to receive tweets from others and for others to see your tweets. Twitter is also known as microblogging, since you can only send a max of 140 characters per tweet.

Twitter keeps us informed about what people are doing or thinking about and these personal updates are known as tweets. The use of Twitter in the class is also called the back channel conversation. Its use to garner the intellectual capital has begun to increase. Students can tweet questions, provide answers to questions, and off-topic time can be spent discussing life outside of the educational setting.

To get started using Twitter, build your account and add a picture of yourself. Try to discover what has gotten attention and share whatever you may be thinking about at the moment. Once your students have become familiar with the technology, ask them questions to respond to. It is a great way to get other's opinions. Twitter is an excellent way to teach students to be succinct since Twitter allows tweets of only 140 characters. This helps them to be concise and makes it easy for the class to read and interact by commenting on each other's tweets; it is a great way to foster the development of a learning community by increasing social presence. Twitter can help to direct the learner's attention to important concepts.

As an educator, you must be cognizant of your time constraints. You do not have to read every non–class-related tweet. Use Twitter search capabilities and other tools such as Tweetdeck, TinyURL, or Twhirl to help use and manage Twitter.

An online doctoral course uses Twitter to help the learners keep in touch. The goal is to have the learners get to know one another, form friendships, and have some fun in the process. It is a great way to learn more about each other as well as about one of the most popular Web 2.0 tools. Twitter is free and a quick and efficient means of communicating with others. You do not have to limit your updates to what you are physically doing, but rather, indicate what you are thinking or what you are observing. You can also ask questions or just ramble. Remember, a sense of humor helps!

Collaboration Tools

The collaboration tools are developed from the force of shared thinking. Examples of these tools include Wetpaint, Skype, Adobe Connect, Knol, Jumptags, Kaltura, and Aviary. Wetpaint uses the best attributes of Wikis, blogs, forums, and social networks so you can construct a powerful online community. We use Wetpaint for our teams so they can create, collect, and organize their teamwork. It is as easy as using a Wiki to share and develop their ideas into a completed submission.

Social Bookmarking Tools

Social bookmarking tools enable users to centrally manage and share Web pages. The power comes from the ability to tag and save Web pages of interest, and then share them with selected users in your network. Some of the tools are Del.icio.us, Mobilicio.us, clipmarks, flagr, SocialMarker, SpeedTile, and Dropvine. Del.icio.us is used in one of our doctoral courses since learners can save bookmarks of their Web sites of interest to the Del.icio.us Web site. They tag them with keywords so they can be easily categorized and searched. Learners are encouraged to share their bookmarks with their team members and sometimes the entire class depending on the assignment. One class project is for the entire class to develop bookmarks related to evidence-based practice (EBP) and tag them according to a preestablished schema.

E-learning Tools

E-learning tools assist with online learning, organization, project management, course delivery, and the creation of study groups. Examples of e-learning tools are Notely, e-LEARNING community, Graspr, WePapers, Beanbag, Eduslide, Bojam, and MindBites. WePapers is free and designed for learners to expand their knowledge and share their wisdom. You can even create study groups at WePapers. One professor uses WePapers with his students who need assistance with their writing skills. This is an excellent way to direct them to quality papers that they can review; it helps them understand what he expects.

Web Services

Web services are those that are hosted to provide a suite of services or a central sharing location. These include Google Reader, Wikiversity, Flickr, Flick[IM], MuseStorm, ping.fm, and Napster. Google Reader constantly checks your favorite news sites and blogs for new content. Google Reader is used in one doctoral course to manage the course blogs. In this course, the learner creates and maintains a Teaching ePortfolio (TeP). Throughout the semester, the learner builds the TeP by adding reflections from the learning episodes and assignments. Team members are responsible for reviewing and providing thoughtful feedback to their teammates concerning TeP entries. The learner must refine entries based on this feedback as well as from reviewing their TePs (how they approached the assignment and crafted their TeP blog). Google Reader makes keeping up with the blogs a snap!

Summary

Web 2.0 fosters communication, collaboration, innovation, and imagination among teachers and learners. Teachers must take advantage of the benefits of these tools for learning and developing compelling learning episodes that engage students. Learning, like the tools, should be enabled 24/7. These tools are potent since they can be accessed anywhere, anytime, and by anyone. Teachers do not need to make sure that everyone has a specific program downloaded or the same computing capabilities; instead, learners only need high-speed access to the Web. Most schools provide such resources for students and so the great digital divide is being closed!

Issues of e-safety, individual/team, and assessment strategies need to be addressed as we implement these tools. Learners must be able to access and interact safely. Instructions must be clear and delineate those learning activities that require individual reflection and development and those that are team oriented. Assessment practices must also change to meet this new generation of educational tools to evaluate learning outcomes. According to Harrison:

> perhaps one key implication for practice, therefore, is for evangelists, innovators and visionaries (and policy-makers) to take careful account of just how much is being asked of teachers in encouraging the wider implementation of Web 2.0, and to recognize that relatively slow and cautious progress is inevitable. That progress may require inspiration sustained with resources that meet both the infrastructure and pedagogic challenges. But it may also require deeper consideration of the wider fabric of curricula, assessment, and established practices for designing sites of teaching and learning. (2008, p. 45)

Case Studies

CASE STUDY 1

A faculty member created a Wiki for the entire class. He had the students develop a document by brainstorming evidence-based practice (EBP) in the clinical setting. For the first 5 weeks, the students had to delineate the roles and responsibilities that nurses must assume to initiate and maintain EBP in their selected setting. They had to contribute at least one new thought or idea after each clinical day. During the next 7 weeks, each team had to formulate one clinical problem and refine it based on the EBP initiative established by the professor. In the last 2 weeks, they had to apply the STAR model for EBP to their clinical problem and share their completed project on the class Wiki.

CASE STUDY 2

The research course at one university adds guest speakers such as the authors of the text and other research experts by using Adobe Connect, a Web conferencing tool. The learners are able to discuss questions, issues, or make comments to the guest speakers in real time.

CASE STUDY 3

A staff development coordinator in a rural hospital developed a continuing education (CE) blog. Nurses were asked to describe any CE offerings they had participated in within the month and rate them using a specific scale. The staff development coordinator also announced upcoming CE offerings in a separate blog. This blog was active during the month the CE offering occurred and was maintained by the CE instructor. This provided the nurses an opportunity to apply what they had learned and then be able to blog about their experiences or dialogue with the instructor over concerns or questions.

Learning Application

1. For case study 1, how could you use a Wiki to enhance your course work?
2. In case study 2, the addition of online guest lecturers provides an interactive learning resource for the students. How could you incorporate an expert panel into your learning episode? Do you have interdisciplinary team members that could provide another insight into your content for your learners?
3. In case study 3, blogs are used for sharing information and experiences. How could you integrate blogging into your setting? Have you thought about using Facebook? What would be important for your learners to share?
4. Reflect on your practice area, how could the Web 2.0 tools enhance learning and promote a learning community?

Thought to Ponder

"The illiterate of the 21st century will not be those who cannot read and write, but those who cannot learn, unlearn, and relearn."

Alvin Toffler

What does this mean for traditional nursing education?

Recommendations

Incorporate the rich tools that this Web movement is creating into your learning episodes. Foster communication and collaboration while stimulating innovative and imaginative applications for your learners. Harness the benefits of these tools for learning to engage your students.

References

Godin, S. (2007, January 19). Seth Godin's vision of the Web [Web log message]. Available at: http://ubereye.wordpress.com/2007/01/19/seth-godins-vision-of-the-web/. Accessed May 5, 2009.

Harrison, C. (2008, November). *Web 2.0: Technologies for learning key stages 3 and 4*. Presentation conducted at Becta's Research Conference, Sheffield, England. Available at: http://events.becta.org.uk/display.cfm?resID=38826&CFID=5427928&CFTOKEN=fb03 65a4f3b1a4ca-DC2908BD-B5F5-7043-21BB3809DC3CCDCE. Accessed May 6, 2009.

Wikiversity. (2009, April 15). Wikiversity: Main page [Web site]. Available at: http://en.wikiversity .org/wiki/Wikiversity:Main_Page. Accessed May 6, 2009.

CHAPTER 13

Educational Games, Simulations, and Virtual Worlds

Food For Thought

"In our minds, the age of the rag doll is over.
Now we layer on top of the simulation this intelligence,
this awareness, this ability to respond, react,
get back up and grab onto things."

Chris Williams, Project Lead at LucasArts

Key Words

3-D
Avatar
Bloom's taxonomy
Bot
Constructivist
Feedback
Fidelity
Game
Massive multiplayer online role-playing
    game (MMORPG)

Microworld
MUD object-oriented (MOO)
Multiuser dungeon (MUD)
Multiuser shared hack, habitat,
    holodeck, or hallucination (MUSH)
Nonplayer character (NPC)
Serious game
Simulations
Simulator
Virtual world

Objectives

The educator will be able to identify a learning environment as a game, simulation, or virtual world.

The educator will be able to identify the different genres of games, simulations, and virtual worlds.

The educator will be able to compare and contrast games, simulations, and virtual worlds by listing the strengths and weaknesses of each type.

The educator will be able to use these strengths and weaknesses to justify choosing between a game, simulation, or virtual world as the best choice for instructional delivery in a given educational situation.

Introduction

Games. Simulations. Virtual worlds. You have no doubt heard all these terms before. What are they, and how are educators using them? The answer is a bit complicated, because the definitions of games, simulations, and virtual worlds are often muddied. People interchange them and define them differently. Adding to the confusion are simulations with gamelike characteristics, games embedded in virtual worlds, and virtual worlds being used as simulations. This chapter will introduce you to these three distinct yet overlapping technologies, by examining their definitions, strengths, and weaknesses. You will receive some suggestions on additional readings, along with some ideas on how to use these amazing tools in a college curriculum.

Educational Games

A **game** can be defined as a voluntary rule-based activity that motivates the player to achieve a goal state or quantifiable outcome via conflict with others or self. Players have a stake in the game's outcome. Games thus contain the following elements:

- Voluntary participation
- Rules (Used to verify the appropriateness of strategies)
- Goals (Used to limit usable strategies and to create a defined outcome)
- **Feedback** (Used to measure progress against goals)

- Interactions (These can be conflict: overt or covert; competition or opposition: with the game, with others, or with self)
- Representation (Game mechanics, graphics, rules, and goals all blend together to define what the game is about and to create an abstracted story of reality)
- Separation from reality (Safe environment: consequences are not externalized; may contain fantasy or impossible elements) (Bixler, 2008)

An educational game, one designed for learning, is a subset of both play and fun. It is a melding of educational content, learning principles, and computer games (Prensky, 2001). Digital game-based learning is organized to provide both education and pleasure. Play relaxes people, putting them in a receptive state for learning.

Another term used by researchers is serious games. A **serious game** is a type of computer game that is usually a partial simulation of real-world events or processes. (Wikipedia, 2005). Serious games use gamelike elements to provide education and training in a pleasurable experience. Most serious games simulate a world in which activity takes place. The learner may take on a first-person perspective and interact with other characters—both artificial and real (other real-life players). Serious games are usually composed of a main task or goal to accomplish, with one or more subtasks that lead towards accomplishment of this main task. In serious games, players also have the ability to manipulate the environment according to the rules of the games and affordances of the environments. Many serious games use **3-D** technologies to provide an immersive, real-world environment, as much as possible although this is not an essential element.

Educational games embrace the elements of traditional games, with several distinctions. Educational games work best when competition is minimized and emphasis is placed on the value of the experience (Hark, 1997; Nemerow, 1996). Control over the game flow may be stronger in educational games (Mungai, Jones, & Wong, 2002), and competency is stressed via feedback mechanisms. However, as Prensky (2001) insists, educational games should feel like a traditional computer game, from beginning to end.

Educational games create a continuous cycle of cognitive disequilibrium and resolution. The extent to which educational games cause cognitive disequilibrium without overwhelming the individual determines the quality of the engagement in the game (Van Eck, 2006).

Game Genres

Many different types of games exist today. Here are the main categories:

- Action: The emphasis is on combat and/or quick reflexes. In nursing education, action games could be used to fine tune motor skills and decrease response time in crisis situations.

- Adventure: The emphasis is on solving puzzles. In nursing education, adventure games could be used for any situation where there are unknowns to be discovered. One example is patient presentation, where you need to discover what ails patients by examining and questioning them.

- Construction/building/management: The emphasis here is on building something, then expanding and improving it by managing the operation. Nurse educators could use this type of game for any learning situation where they must build or synthesize something from component parts. This need not be a physical thing that is built; it could very well be a complex mental construct that can only be understood through knowledge of its constituent parts and how they interrelate.

- Role-playing games: Emphasis is on taking on the role of one or more characters and improving them as you progress through a storyline. Online versions of these are usually named **massive multiplayer online role-playing games (MMORPGs)**, more recently abbreviated to simply MMOs. Role-playing games would be an excellent way for nursing educators to guide students through any situation where students needed to learn about a particular job or skill that is sufficiently complex to require a sequenced step-by-step introduction to the parts of the job or skill.

- Strategy: Emphasis is on carefully planning your next moves, executing them, and adapting your strategies based on feedback. Strategy games are great for nursing education teaching moments where careful, up-front planning is critical, and on-the-fly adjustments to your plan may be needed to ensure its success.

- **Simulators**: The emphasis is on placing the player in a real-life competitive situation. Simulations are best used with a skill or set of related skills must be perfected. Operation simulations are the best example of this.

Strengths of Educational Games

- Games embody many motivational aspects.
- Games develop situated understanding (learning by doing).
- Games can foster the development of effective social practices.
- Games can flip-flop the traditional learning structure, where facts and concepts do not come first, they simple emerge as part of the game activity and are thus tied to the event in a natural way.
- Games build problem-solving skills

Weaknesses of Educational Games

- Some games take a long time to learn how to play. This is especially true for role-playing games and complex strategy games. It may take several hours over several weeks before students are familiar enough with the game mechanics that they can utilize the game for learning.
- There is a lack of educational game planning guides. Most games today are produced without any integrated learning theories. Game elements may enhance game play but distort learning by oversimplifying facts or complex processes.
- Educators are (mostly) not ready for them. Educators do not understand their value. Games are at odds with traditional curricula and are more **constructivist** in nature.
- Not all people like games. Not everyone enjoys the same type of game.

Books to Explore

For further information on educational games, consider reading: *Don't Bother Me Mom—I'm Learning!* by Mark Prensky, *A Theory of Fun for Game Design*, by Ralf Koster, *Learning by Doing*, by Clark Aldrich, and *What Video Games Have to Teach Us About Learning and Literacy*, by James Paul Gee.

Activities for Educational Games

Choose one of the following:

- Go to http://www1.umn.edu/ohr/teachlearn/tutorials/powerpoint/games/index.html and read about creating educational games with PowerPoint. Create an outline (not a working model) of a brief gaming episode in PowerPoint related to the lesson you are developing.
- Have you ever participated in an educational gaming activity? Write about it. Describe the game's purpose and what you learned from participating in the game?
- Locate an educational gaming activity relevant to your work. Explore it briefly. Write a short summary that includes what the goal is, the type of game it is, and your thoughts as to the effectiveness of the game.

Educational Simulations

A **simulation** is an attempt to recreate a real-life set of conditions or events with as much **fidelity** as possible (Alessi, 1988). They are carefully constructed to develop specific competencies (Aldrich, 2009). Airplane pilots, for example, are trained on aircraft simulators. They sit in a cockpit with instrumentation that closely mimics the real thing. They feel the plane shake as they pilot it. They receive visual feedback in the form of video screens in the windows. Traditional simulations usually do not adapt to the user's needs; the user is instead expected to adapt to the demands of the simulation. Simulations are often used when it is too costly or dangerous for the student to experience the real thing, at least initially. Unlike games, simulations are not designed to be fun.

Medical simulations have existed since models of clay and stone were used to represent conditions and diseases of humans. Today, we use realistic 3-D computer models of humans to investigate new medical possibilities and to test assumptions. We have simulations of drawing blood used to teach the process. We even have simulations of complex operations, designed to train surgeons on the latest surgical techniques.

Educational simulations add a teaching element to the simulation. They may initially simplify the environment so the learner can achieve early success, then gradually build up complexity until they reach a desired real-life state. Corrective feedback might occur as the user proceeds through the simulation, correcting user mistakes and ensuring success, then fades away when no longer needed. This process is called scaffolding (Guzdial, 1997; Jonassen, 1999). This feedback may be automated, but often is provided by a live coach or facilitator.

Simulations usually require the user to manipulate a set of variables or conditions to achieve an optimal outcome. Manipulation of these variables can be as overt as the turning of a dial, or as covert as choosing one overall procedural plan over another. This implies that there are multiple paths through the simulation, some leading to success, some to failure. The manipulated variables may change over time and the relationships between them must be verifiable. For example, if a student in a healthcare simulation is treating a patient, the patient's symptoms, health characteristics, and given treatment all interact in a logical, predictable way. Students must be able to see the result(s) of the choices they made.

Simulations may be experiential/task based, or symbolic/problem oriented (Weatherford, n.d.; Gredler, 1996). In experiential simulations, the learner takes on a serious role and executes a self-chosen series of decisions, manipulating the variables in the simulation toward a desired outcome. The learner is embedded in the simulation with a first-person perspective. As the learner makes changes, the simulation environment around the learner changes.

In symbolic/problem-oriented scenarios, the learner is one step removed from the given situation, and is usually directly manipulating variables and sees the results of changes immediately. Spreadsheets are often used for this type of simulation. Change a number on one column and you see the resulting changes in the rest of the spreadsheet. These types of simulations are good for discovering principles, misconceptions, relationships, and for fostering understanding, prediction, and solution development.

Microworlds

Related to educational simulations are **microworlds**. Computer-based microworlds are similar to traditional computer simulations, but differ in two key aspects. First, microworlds contain the most basic and appropriate elements of a domain as defined by an expert in that domain. Simulations, however, usually strive to completely recreate the environment they mimic and are judged on how well they do so. Second, a microworld allows the user to enter the microworld at a level appropriate to the user's cognitive level, thus matching the user's needs. Traditional simulations usually do not adapt to the user's needs; the user is instead expected to adapt to the demands of the simulation.

Strengths of Educational Simulations

Simulations are best used when you have a procedure or set of procedures that must be followed with complete accuracy. Failure to do so in the real world would result in injury or death, or damage of costly equipment. Simulations are usually hands-on. They are generally inspirational and motivating to participate in, for they provide a fail-safe environment for learning.

Simulations can increase the efficiency of an individual for a particular process. For example, operation medical simulations strive to impart not just accurate procedures, but also ones where the amount of time spent on the operation is reduced, thus potentially saving real lives.

Weaknesses of Educational Simulations

It takes a great deal of time and effort to create and test a simulation. It also costs a great deal if physical components must be included (think of the cockpit described earlier). Students may become frustrated in a simulation that does not contain adequate scaffolding. Depending on their nature, simulations may require frequent updates as real-world knowledge and statistics change. Thus, maintenance of simulations is a concern.

Summary of Educational Simulations

- A simulation is an attempt to recreate a set of conditions or events with as much fidelity to the real-life situation as possible.
- Simulations usually require the user to manipulate a set of variables or conditions to achieve an optimal outcome.
- Simulations may be experiential/task based, where the learner is immersed in a situation, or symbolic/problem oriented, where the learner is not immersed in the simulation.
- Simulations are best used when the learner must perform tasks with complete accuracy. They are also excellent for discovering principles, misconceptions, relationships, and for fostering understanding, prediction, and solution development.
- Simulations take a great deal of time and money to develop, and maintenance of the simulation may be a concern.

Books to Explore

For further information on simulations, consider reading: *Simulations and the Future of Learning*, by Clark Aldrich.

Activities for Educational Simulations

Choose one of the following:

- Go to http://scholar.google.com/ and search: "medical simulations in education". Pick an article that you are interested in and read it. Write a one-paragraph summary.
- Have you ever participated in a simulation? Write about it. What were the variables you manipulated? Was it experiential/task based, or symbolic/problem oriented? What did you learn from the simulation?
- Locate a simulation relevant to your work. Explore it briefly. Write a short summary that includes what the goal is, the type of simulation it is, and your thoughts as its effectiveness.

Virtual Worlds

Virtual worlds are constructed environments where the computer is used as a window to access the world. Wikipedia defines them as:

> A computer-simulated environment intended for its users to inhabit and interact via avatars. This habitation usually is represented in the form of two or three-dimensional graphical representations of humanoids (or other graphical or text-based avatars). Some, but not all, virtual worlds allow for multiple users. (2006, para. 1)

Most virtual worlds mimic a real-world environment to a large degree, although they also may include impossible abilities, such as breathing underwater without equipment. Most worlds today are 3-D, although text-based and 2-D ones exist and continue to be heavily used.

Most virtual worlds require you to create your in-world presence, or **avatar**. Your avatar interacts with both the environment and other avatars to form a rich exploratory and (in multiuser worlds) social experience.

Genres of Virtual Worlds

2-D Worlds

Multiuser dungeons (MUDs), MUD object-oriented (MOO), and **Multiuser shared hack, habitat, holodeck, or hallucinations (MUSHes)** are all online text-based ancestors of today's modern 3-D virtual worlds. The user starts in a virtual area that is described via text, and then types in commands ("go south" or "take the apple off the table") to manipulate the environment. As users can interact with other users, these environments are primarily used by educators for social collaboration.

Here is an example transcript of a MOO session:

> You are in the University Resource Center (URC). Doors out of the room
> are to your south and east. A receptionist sits behind a greeting desk to
> the north. One other person, Sally, is in the room at present.
> Talk to Sally.
> "Hi! If you are new here, first talk to the receptionist. I'm the math tutor,
> waiting for my student to show up. If you're here for math instruction,
> maybe you'll be assigned to me. For stopping by, here's a URC pen!"
> Take URC pen.
> You take the URC pen. It is blue and white with the URC logo on the
> side. You place the URC pen in your bookbag (inventory).
> Talk to receptionist.
> "Hello. Please type a verb followed by a noun. For example: Get help.
> Try it now."

As the example indicates, in this MOO the learner types in navigation commands and conversation lines, thus manipulating the environment and engaging in socialization. Sally was a real person, but the receptionist was a **bot** (short for robot), the equivalent of a **nonplayer character (NPC)**.

3-D Worlds

A variety of 3-D worlds exist as well. Online worlds include:

- ActiveWorlds (http://www.activeworlds.com/)
- Entropia (http://www.entropiauniverse.com/index.var)
- HipiHi (http://www.hipihi.com/en/)

- Kaneva (http://www.kaneva.com/)
- Moove (http://www.moove.com/)
- Outback Online (http://www.outbackonline.com/)
- Second Life (http://secondlife.com/)
- Sun's Virtual Workplace: MPK20 (http://research.sun.com/projects/mc/mpk20.html)
- Teleplace (http://www.teleplace.com)
- The Croquet Project (http://www.opencroquet.org/)
- There (http://www.there.com/)
- VSide (http://www.vside.com/faces/pages/help/help.xhtml)
- Virtual Worlds List (http://virtualworldsreview.com/info/categories.shtml)

Strengths of Using Virtual Worlds in Education

Virtual worlds provide many educational benefits. The two strongest benefits may be an immersive environment coupled with social interactions. Virtual worlds hold the promise of an immersive environment containing problems and contexts similar to the real world. In addition, multiuser virtual worlds allow users to meet, interact, and form social communities. In multiuser virtual worlds, the natural coupling of an immersive environment and social interactions provide for good learning experiences.

Other strengths include:

- The space is persistent. You can leave the world and come back to it. A corollary to this is that the space is ever changing. Areas you own may stay the same, but areas controlled by others will change, sometimes quickly and radically.
- Your physical presence in-world is always what you want. You can look how you want, whenever you want. No need to comb your hair—your avatar's hair is never mussed, unless you want it that way!
- Creed, color, body type, and sex are choices. Diversity is thus increased, and many of the negative real-world issues associated with lack of understanding of the importance of diversity are minimized. When you can appear as whatever you wish, you get to see past the surface of the individual.

- Real-world physical handicaps are minimized. People with physical handicaps can create a fully functional avatar capable of a complete range of interactions.
- The virtual space can be modeled to match your learning needs.
- Exploration and discovery are possible. When you have a large virtual space and can move about in that space quickly and easily, exploration is enabled.
- Dangerous, risky ideas can be explored. Virtual worlds are a safe area to try things, fail, and learn from those failures.
- Fantasy and imagination are enabled. When you can be whatever you want to be, and can create environments that defy the limitations of biology or physics, the gateways to imagination are unlocked.
- Activity can be recorded. This enables asynchronous sharing of synchronous activities. Learners can thus learn from each other across not only space, but time as well.

Weaknesses of Using Virtual Worlds in Education

Preparation to use a virtual world is the primary barrier to use. First, you have to become familiar with the world, and how to navigate and manipulate it. Likewise, your students will also need some time to enter the virtual world and familiarize themselves with navigation and manipulation options.

You also have to develop activities for your students with some degree of structure and a quantifiable, assessable outcome. In virtual worlds, this may mean simply identifying places to go, or it could be as complex as developing and programming objects for the students to interact with. Unlike with textbooks, there are few lessons out there one can take advantage of with virtual worlds.

The second barrier to use is availability of robust technology. Most virtual worlds require a fairly new computer with decent memory, a good graphics card, and a fast connection to the Internet. Running a virtual world program in public labs may be a concern. Many virtual worlds are in a constant state of change and improvement, leading to frequent updates of the program. In a public lab where write permissions are limited, it will be necessary to work with the Information Technology staff to devise a method to allow individuals, upon accessing the program, to download and install the updates. Unlike many lab applications where one program may be shared by multiple users at any given point in time, most virtual world programs require each individual to run his or her own program. Thus, methods must be devised and implemented to allow this to happen.

Books to Explore

For further information on virtual worlds, consider reading the following: *Synthetic Worlds: The Business and Culture of Online Games* by Edward Castronova and *Virtual Worlds: The Next Big Thing*, by Edita Kaye.

Activities for Virtual Worlds

Choose one of the following:

- Go to http://www.youtube.com/results?search_query=second+life+ education&search_type=&search=Search and watch three videos on education and Second Life, a virtual world. Write a one-page summary on the videos you watched.
- Have you ever participated in a virtual world? Write about it. What did you do in the world? What did you learn from it?
- Pick one of the virtual worlds listed here and register for membership. Explore it briefly. Write about it. What did you do in the world? What did you learn from it?

Game Type Versus Cognitive Level

Bloom's taxonomy of cognitive objectives, originated by Benjamin Bloom and collaborators in the 1950s, describes several categories of cognitive learning. Table 13-1 illustrates these.

It is useful to map these levels against the types of games to assist you in determining which type of game to use for a particular learning situation, as done in Table 13-2.

Table 13-1   Bloom's Levels of Cognitive Objectives

Category	Description
Knowledge	Ability to recall previously learned material
Comprehension	Ability to grasp meaning, explain, restate ideas
Application	Ability to use learned material in new situations
Analysis	Ability to separate material into component parts and show relationships between parts
Synthesis	Ability to put together the separate ideas to form a new whole and establish new relationships
Evaluation	Ability to judge the worth of material against stated criteria

So far we have examined the genres and game types, but have ignored one important element—the learners. There is some research and heuristics on learners you should use to assist you in determining which genre is appropriate for a particular learning situation.

Richard Bartle, a games theorist, has observed four types of gamers: achievers, explorers, socializers, and killers (Bartle, 1996). Achievers play games to build up their playing characters. Their goal is to be able to brag to others about their game status. Explorers are most interested in looking into the guts of the game—how it works or how to exploit its weaknesses. They want to interact with the game. Socializers play the game for the non-game interactive conversations that ensue during game play. The game is merely the place these conversations take place. Finally, killers are in the

Table 13-2   Bloom's Levels of Cognitive Objectives Versus Game Type

	Knowledge	Comprehension	Application	Analysis	Synthesis	Evaluation
Action	X	X	X			
Adventure		X	X	X	X	X
Construction			X	X	X	X
Role-play				X	X	X
Strategy			X	X	X	X
Simulation	X	X	X			

Figure 13–1 Bartle's player types and interests.

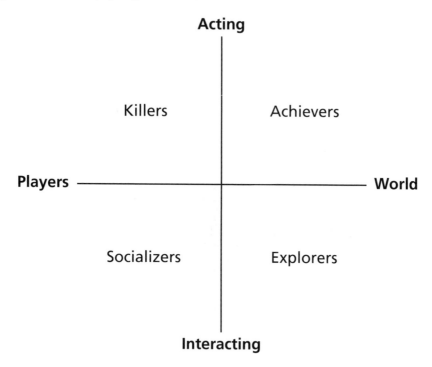

game to impose themselves on others—to cause the maximum amount of distress possible.

Figure 13-1 illustrates where the four player types fall between interest in acting versus interacting, and interest in other players versus interest in the game world.

It is not a stretch to map these player types onto simulations and virtual worlds as well (Figure 3-2).

What does this mean for you as an educational designer or user of educational games, simulations, and virtual worlds? We know that not all people like these environments, and maybe that is because the environments do not meet their needs as a player. Ideally, you should look for games, simulations, and virtual worlds that accommodate different player types. In reality, it will be difficult to find a single environment that will accommodate all types.

Figure 13-2   Virtual worlds and simulations mapped onto Bartle's player types.

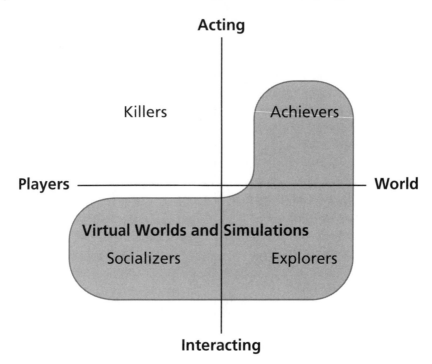

The Changing Role of Teacher

The traditional "sage on the stage" model of teaching will not work in virtual worlds. Consider the following observation:

> How would we react if students blipped in and out of existence during a class or were constantly talking over us as we delivered a lecture? While conducting courses in Second Life, a 3-D virtual environment, these kinds of behaviors are commonplace. Turn taking in discussions changes; student behavior changes; the environment we consider a classroom changes; thus, our pedagogy must change. The traditional model of instructor in front and students in seats simply does not work in an online environment such as Second Life. (Robbins, 2006)

Instead, a more constructivist approach may not only be desirable, but necessary. An in-depth discussion of constructivism is beyond the scope of this chapter, but the fundamental concept—where learning emerges from within an individual reacting to an environment—seems to naturally fit with virtual worlds.

Summary

By now you should see that while games, simulations, and virtual worlds each have distinct characteristics, there can be a great deal of similarity and overlap among the three genres.

Thus, you can have simulations in virtual worlds, simulations with gaming elements, virtual worlds used for simulations, and so on. The important thing is to know when to choose a simulation, virtual world, or game for a particular educational activity or series of activities.

Figure 13-3 illustrates where games, simulations, and virtual worlds sit on the intersection of goals and realism.

Figure 13-3   Intersection of games, simulations, and virtual worlds.

Simulations have specific goals and are usually as realistic as possible. Virtual worlds in and of themselves usually have no goals, and may be realistic or abstract. Most games have specific goals, but different game types have different levels of realism. Of course, this chart is an artificial attempt to impose order on an emerging and evolving set of interrelated genres, so it is not a perfect depiction. Still, this chart should help you when making decisions on which genre is the best fit for a given educational situation. Also, it is useful to match different game types to the cognitive learning for which they are best suited.

FINAL SELF-ASSESSMENT EXERCISE

Develop a mini-proposal for an educational game, simulation, or virtual world activity of your choice. Include the following:

1. Description of the educational game, simulation, or virtual world activity.

2. Rational for your choice of an educational game, simulation, or virtual world activity.

3. Strengths and weaknesses of your approach.

4. How you might compensate for the weaknesses.

Use the following rubric in Table 13-3 to grade yourself.

Table 13–3   Games, Simulations, and Virtual Worlds Design Rubric

Give yourself 1 point for minimal references to information in the chapter content (weak); 5 points for adequate references (average); and 10 points for information that is full referenced (superior).	
Description Rational Strengths Weaknesses Compensation for weaknesses **Total (50 points possible)**	

Thought To Ponder

The Gartner Group estimates that by 2011, 80% of people using the Web will have a virtual identity (Gartner Newsroom, 2007). What does this mean for nursing education and educational technology? We are entering an age where the vast majority of the younger population is not only conversant in these environments, but will also actively seek out virtual identities. Yet the creation and maintenance of these environments is costly in terms of time, money, and expertise. How can we bring games, simulations, and virtual worlds into educational environments without expending more time and energy?

References

Aldrich, C. (2009). Clark Aldrich's style guide for serious games and simulations. Available at: http://clarkaldrich.blogspot.com/. Accessed April 2, 2008.

Aldrich, C. (2009). Virtual worlds, simulations, and games for education: A unifying view. *Innovate*, *5*(5). Available at: http://www.innovateonline.info/index.php?view=article&id=727. Accessed July 2, 2009.

Alessi, S. M. (1988). Fidelity in the design of instructional simulations. *Journal of Computer-Based Instruction*, *15*(2), 40–47.

Bartle, R. (1996). Hearts, clubs, diamonds, spades: Players who suit MUDs. Available at: http://www.mud.co.uk/richard/hcds.htm. Accessed January 15, 2009.

Bixler, B. (2008). What is a game? Available at: http://gaming.psu.edu/node/315. Accessed July 6, 2009.

Gartner Newsroom. (2007, April 24). *Gartner says 80 percent of active Internet users will have a "second life" in the virtual world by the end of 2011* (Press release). Available at: http://www.gartner.com/it/page.jsp?id=503861. Accessed January 15, 2009.

Gredler, M. E. (1996). Educational games and simulations: A technology in search of a (research) paradigm. In D. H. Jonassen (Ed.), *Handbook of research for educational communications and technology*. New York, NY: Simon & Schuster Macmillan.

Guzdial, M. (1997). Components of software-realized scaffolding. Available at: http://www.cc.gatech.edu/gvu/edtech/SRS.html. Accessed June 4, 2009.

Hark, I. R. (1997). It's how you play the game. *Education*, *118*(1) 6–9.

Jonassen, D. H. (1999). Designing constructivist learning environments. In C. M. Reigeluth (Ed.), *Instructional design theories and models: A new paradigm of instructional theory* (Vol. 2, pp. 215–239). Mahwah, NJ: Lawrence Erlbaum Associates.

Mungai, D., Jones, D., & Wong, L. (2002). *Games to teach by*. Paper presented at the 18th Annual Conference on Distance Teaching and Learning.

Nemerow, L. G. (1996). Do classroom games improve motivation and learning? *Teaching and Change, 3*(4), 356–361.

Prensky, M. (2001). *Digital Game-based Learning* (1 ed.). Two Penn Plaza, New York, NY 10121: McGraw Hill.

Robbins, S. (2006, July 6). Another abstract for another conference. Available at: http://www.secondlife.intellagirl.com/2006/07/06/another-abstract-for-another-conference/. Accessed July 6, 2009.

Van Eck, R. (2006). Digital game-based learning: It's not just the digital natives who are restless. *Educause Review, 41*(2).

Weatherford, J. (n.d.). Instructional simulations: An overview. Available at: http://coe.sdsu.edu/eet/Articles/instrucsimu/start.htm. Accessed July 6, 2009.

Wikipedia. (2005). Definition of Serious Games. Retrieved November 16, 2005, from http://en.wikipedia.org

Wikipedia. (2006). Virtual world. Available at: http://en.wikipedia.org/wiki/Virtual_World. Accessed July 10, 2006.

CHAPTER 14

The 3 Ds of Clinical Practice Simulation: Development, Delivery, and Debriefing

Nick Miehl, MSN, RN

Food For Thought

"In virtually every sector of the healthcare workforce, there is a shortage of qualified people. Our state's network of simulation centers, working with medical colleges, nursing colleges, and technical colleges, will elevate the quality of education and also the capacity of current programs. Having more doctors, nurses, and technicians educated in this state-of-the-art manner will benefit the entire state of South Carolina."

Ray Greenberg, HSSC Chair and MUSC President

Key Words

Content experts
Debriefing
Environmental fidelity
Faculty facilitator
Equipment fidelity
Haptic devices
Human patient simulators

Intended learning outcomes (ILOs)
Partial task trainers
Physical fidelity
Psychologic fidelity
Screen-based systems
Simulation expert
Suspension of disbelief

Objectives

The educator will be able to summarize the process of simulation development, delivery, and debriefing using the simulation development model.

The educator will be able to compare and contrast the roles of content expert and simulation expert.

The educator will be able to evaluate the role of reflection in scenario debriefing.

Introduction

A student nurse enters a patient room and introduces him- or herself to their assigned patient. As the student begins to speak with the patient and begin to perform an initial assessment, the patient becomes unresponsive. The student calls for help and initiates the code blue system. A group of the student's peers enters the room and begins the ABCs of CPR. Next, advanced cardiac life support (ACLS) is initiated by the students. After a successful resuscitation, the simulation manikin awakens and the scenario is over. The **faculty facilitator** debriefs the students while the simulation technician resets for the next simulation scenario. On the outside, another successful simulation session has been run. Behind the scenes, what happened to allow for the simulation session to be successful? This chapter will examine the simulation scenario from start to finish: development, delivery, and debriefing.

Simulations

Broadly viewed, simulators can be described as tools that afford varying degrees of realism and functioning to serve a desired purpose. Simulators are designed to reproduce some aspect of the working environment ranging from replicating a simple task to replicating an entire environment such as a trauma resuscitation room (Gaba & DeAnda, 1998). A simulator is any device used to create a mock experience for nursing students to prepare them for clinical experiences with live patients. Simulation devices range in sophistication from computer-run high-fidelity manikins to mock-ups of body parts for practicing specific procedures. Simulation can be a powerful strategy for learning as realistic encounters or situations are emulated in an authentic and engaging manner. Simulations mimic the working environment and require the participant to demonstrate procedural techniques, decision making, and clinical judgment. Simulation offers an important context for nursing education, providing a safe, supportive, and structured environment to bridge the gap between the classroom and clinical (Bligh & Bleakley, 2006). Gaba (2004) describes the goal of simulation as "seamless immersion" in a simulated clinical practice environment, where the participants are convinced of the "reality" of the context. Furthermore, simulation impacts learning in unique and significant ways. The interactive nature of simulation alone motivates student learning (Gilley, 1990; Theall & Franklin, 1999). The learning that takes place is student centered and carefully constructed. This cooperative learning paradigm allows students with various life experiences to come together in an authentic setting and learn from one another (Hertel & Millis, 2002).

Central to simulation is the concept of fidelity. Four dimensions of fidelity are examined including environmental, equipment, physical, and psychologic (Beaubien & Baker, 2004; Jentsch & Bowers, 2001). **Environmental fidelity** is the match between the real and simulated environment with regard to sensory cues such as motion, sight, and sound. **Physical fidelity** is the degree to which the simulated environment, including the simulator, mimics the real environment. Are the participants using the same equipment that they would in the actual clinical environment? **Equipment fidelity** refers to the degree to which the equipment used is realistic to what would be found in a real clinical environment. Does the simulator emulate a realistic patient response? Finally, **psychologic fidelity** relates to the degree to which the participant perceives the simulation to be a realistic substitute for the real clinical environment.

The degree or level of fidelity employed in a given simulation is dependent on both the type of task and the level of the learner. An appropriate match between the task, the equipment, and the trainee will serve to maximize the psychologic fidelity and move the participant toward the **suspension of disbelief** while in the training scenario. Kantor and Waddington (2000) liken the suspension of disbelief to the conventions of the theater and the process by which the audience members are drawn into the action on the stage before them. Too little authenticity and the audience members lose interest and become critical of the performance. Too much and they are upset and potentially offended. This is true of simulation as well, if the scenario is too simplistic and lacks realism, the participants disengage from the learning and concentrate on the faults of the scenario, rather than focusing on the intended learning outcomes and purpose of the scenario. Scenarios that are overwritten and too complex frustrate the participants; they may develop a negative attitude toward simulation-based learning. Employing a standardized approach, or model, in the development and delivery of simulation-based learning scenarios can help to maximize the learning impact and overall quality of the simulation curriculum.

Simulation Development

Developing the simulation-based curriculum must be a cooperative effort between the **content experts** (course faculty) and the **simulation expert** (lab coordinator). The lead faculty for a given course is typically identified as the content expert and possesses a deep and insightful knowledge of both the content and objectives for the given course. The simulation expert is typically a faculty member who possesses technical expertise in the development of simulation scenarios, and has primary oversight over the development and integration of simulation-based curricula. Together, these experts cooperatively develop the simulation curriculum, starting with the simulation scenario (see Figure 14-1).

Review of Course and Clinical Content

Three key areas must be examined prior to developing a simulation-based learning curriculum, whether it is a single simulation scenario or the integration of simulation into an existing course curriculum. First, the course objectives or **intended learning outcomes (ILOs)** need to be identified as these will drive the development of the simulation scenarios. These ILOs must have a clear and direct relationship to the simulation curriculum. In the context of an existing course, these objectives will be identified in the existing syllabus. Second, the course content (didactic content) must be examined to ensure a direct link between theory and practice, or the classroom and simulation lab. Examining the course content will help the course faculty and lab coordinator identify content areas to further develop through simulation-based learning. Finally, the clinical component must be examined. Variations in the availability of population-based clinical experiences may directly influence how a simulation-based curriculum is developed. For example, if a school has difficulty in finding adequate pediatric clinical experiences, this may drive the development of a strong pediatrics simulation curriculum to augment the experiences that are difficult to obtain in the actual clinical environment. Once these areas have been carefully reviewed, the process of developing the simulation-based learning curriculum can begin.

Figure 14-1   Model for simulation development.

(A) Course Objectives (ILOs) → Course Content → Clinical Component

Course Content → Simulation-based Learning Content
Clinical Component → Simulation-based Learning Content

Simulation-based Learning Content → Simulation Development

(B) Simulation Domain → Establish Objectives → Task Analysis

Simulation Development → Input from content experts

Input from content experts → Simulation Domain

Input from content experts → (D) Establish objectives for students to meet prior to simulation

(C) Develop Scenario → Establish objectives for students to meet prior to simulation

Establish objectives for students to meet prior to simulation → Online Pre-Scenario Learning Module → Pre-test

Develop Scenario → Programming → Scripting → Staging → (E) Run Scenario

Task Analysis → Facilitation

Run Scenario ↔ Facilitation

Run Scenario → Debriefing → Post-test

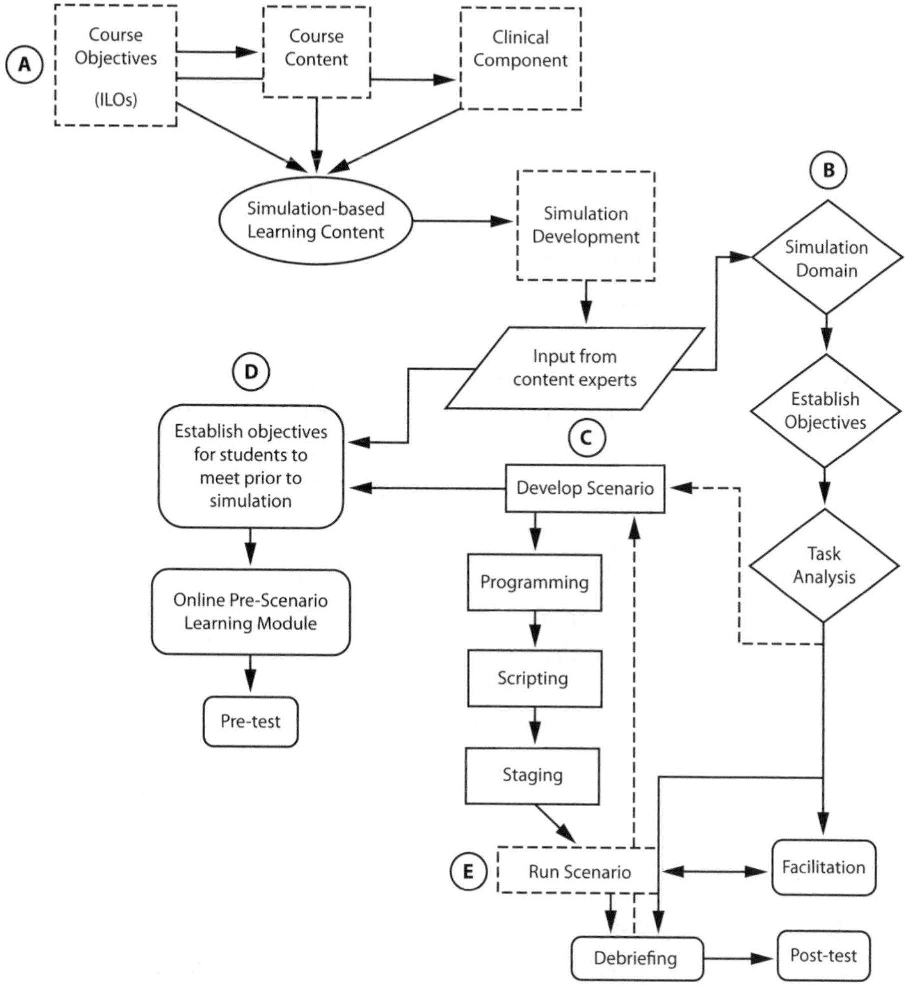

Source: Model was developed by Nick Miehl (2009) copyright

Establishing the Basics

First, the simulation domain is identified. This clarifies the central focus of the simulation scenario. Examples could include a medical–surgical scenario or a scenario focusing on communication and teamwork. This step establishes the foundation for developing the scenario. This beginning stage of scenario development is where the concept of fidelity plays a major role. This is where the stage is set for scenario development and each subsequent step must align with the previous step to keep the lens focused on a realistic simulation matched to the level of the learner.

Next, the scenario objectives are established. The objectives must reflect the intended outcome of the scenario, specify learner behaviors, and include enough detail to allow the participant to function effectively in the scenario (Jeffries & Rogers, 2007). Typically three to five objectives are identified. These objectives give the scenario structure and establish a baseline by which to evaluate the student. If there are too few objectives, the scenario will lack basic structure, too many objectives, and the scenario becomes restrictive and difficult for the students to successfully complete. In either case, the realism of the scenario (suspension of disbelief) will also suffer and can leave students with a negative view of the simulation experience. One must ask what the point of the scenario is, and what should the student take away from the experience. Questions such as these will help to guide the scenario development.

Simulation Task Analysis

Finally, a task analysis is developed to identify the tasks and identify in which order, if any, they must be performed. The analysis breaks down these essential tasks into subtasks by which the faculty member evaluating the participant can identify actual or potential errors in performance (Annett, 2003).

The task analysis can be based on protocols (such as ACLS), the nursing process (did the participant assess prior to implementing an intervention?) or procedural directions (insertion of a Foley catheter). Failure to complete these steps in the established order or fashion leads to a teachable moment with the students and the potential further group discussion during the debriefing period.

Development of the Simulation Scenario

Upon establishing the simulation domain, objectives, and task analysis, the content expert develops an outline of the simulation scenario, similar to a written case study. This case study is typically based on a real-life clinical experience, including laboratory and diagnostic data as well as anticipated interventions. Based on this outline, the simulation expert can begin to develop a realistic simulation scenario. This includes the selection of the appropriate simulator(s) to ensure optimum fidelity within the scenario. Selection of simulation equipment is largely based on the simulation objectives and may include a single manikin or a combination of manikins, task trainers, or other simulation equipment (see Table 14-1).

Table 14-1 Classification of Simulators (Maran & Glavin, 2003)

Partial task trainer	Designed to replicate part of the environment; typically resemble an anatomic area of the body; focus is on psychomotor skills
Screen-based systems	Used to model aspects of human physiology or pharmacology, simulated tasks, or environments; learners interact through the computer interface; focus is on decision making
Virtual reality and haptic devices	Used to present patients or environments in a realistic manner using a computer-based technology; often combined with partial task trainers or high-fidelity manikins to allow for physical interaction with the environment
Simulated patients (standardized patients)	Used for teaching communication and assessment skills; can be scripted to mimic physical conditions
Simulated environments	Used for recreation of an actual working environment; focus is on increasing psychologic fidelity
Integrated simulators (human patient simulators)	Used to allow clinicians to interact with the patient as they would in the real working environment; model-driven, or high-fidelity simulators combine lifelike manikins with complex computer programming to emulate an actual patient; include physiologic modeling and response to pharmacologic intervention; instructor-driven, or intermediate-fidelity simulators combine part- or full-body manikins with less complex computer programming, requiring the instructor to adjust physiologic parameters in response to interventions

Types of Simulation Equipment

Partial task trainers are typically used for psychomotor training, that is, learning the mechanics of a particular skill. These trainers typically resemble part of the human anatomy such as an arm for intravenous (IV) catheter insertion or a portion of the chest for central venous catheter insertion. Task trainers are often used in conjunction with **human patient simulators** to allow the participants to practice skills that are not possible to perform on the simulation manikin. Virtual reality and **haptic devices** utilize computer-based technology to present a realistic environment for the participant. Examples include virtual IV trainers and laparoscopic surgery trainers. While the participant is viewing a virtual patient on a computer screen, they are also manipulating some piece of equipment or haptic device, which gives realistic tactile feedback. Simulated patients (sometimes referred to as standardized patients) are often utilized to practice communication and interpersonal skills and can be used to simulate concepts that are otherwise difficult to realistically simulate with a simulation manikin, such as neurologic changes or mental health disorders. Integrated simulators, often referred to as human patient simulators or manikins, are full-body representations of a patient. Typically, these manikins will be referred to as high fidelity or intermediate fidelity. High fidelity refers to the incorporation of complex, technologically advanced computer programming and mechanics which allow the manikin to not only appear real, but also to act in a physiologically correct manner to various interventions and pharmacologic therapies, based on the programming or modeling of the simulator. Intermediate-fidelity manikins, while appearing similar to a high-fidelity manikin, are controlled primarily by an instructor. For example, if a particular therapy is delivered, the instructor must manually change the vital signs and other parameters and then the manikin will exhibit those changes.

Often these various pieces of simulation equipment will be combined to maximize the fidelity of a scenario. For example, in a cardiac arrest scenario, participants initiate ACLS protocol and begin treating the "patient," a high-fidelity simulator. A large-bore IV is needed for fluid resuscitation and medication administration, but the "patient" has poor veins and needs a central line. Until a line is placed, medications and fluids cannot be administered to the "patient." A central venous catheter insertion task trainer can then be used "at the bedside" to insert the central line. Perhaps the central line is difficult to insert on the task trainer and the "patient" (the high-fidelity simulator) develops a pneumothorax, and now a chest tube needs to be placed, all in the midst of caring for a patient in cardiac arrest. Virtual reality, haptic devices, and simulated patients can also be incorporated in a similar fashion to maximize the fidelity of the scenario and best meet the learning objectives. Another concept of great importance is the simulated environment. A simulated environment is a realistic recreation of the actual working environment. The more realistic the environment is (visual, auditory, olfactory, and tactile cues), the higher the psychologic fidelity will be. This also includes using the same equipment in simulation that is used in the actual working environment, which is discussed further in this chapter.

Once the simulation equipment has been selected, the programming and scripting for the scenario can begin. All of the elements for the simulation scenario are developed. The programming of the manikin takes place, and encompasses all of the physiologic responses that a real patient would exhibit, limited only by the fidelity of the simulation equipment. Scenarios can also be run without being preprogrammed and are run in real time by the simulation manikin operator. These must be used cautiously, as they can introduce a great deal of variability in how the simulation manikin responds, especially in simulation centers that have multiple personnel operating the simulation equipment. An important step in the development of the scenario is trial and error, that is, once the scenario is finished, it must put through a trial run to identify any programming or technologic issues that will need fixed prior to running students through the scenario.

A script of standardized responses is developed for the manikin operator including past medical and surgical history, psychosocial history, medication history, history of present illness, and responses to potential assessment questions or changes in patient condition. Prior to running the scenario, the simulation rooms are staged to replicate a realistic care environment. This includes not only the physical layout and appearance of the room, but placement of necessary equipment and supplies in the appropriate areas for participants to use during the scenario. Having a simulation center that is separate from a healthcare facility or organization can pose some unique challenges with regard to environmental and physical fidelity, most notably the space looks different and the equipment available is different from the actual care environment. While tailoring the space to look exactly like the care environment can be a difficult task, having groups of participants utilize their own equipment (such as a certain model of defibrillator or central line insertion tray) is often a very easy and easily received solution. This allows the participant to practice using the equipment that they would normally use in the care environment and greatly increases the physical and psychologic fidelity of the scenario.

Simulation Delivery

PreSimulation Activities

Allowing participants to prepare prior to the simulation scenario is key to success in simulation-based learning. The content expert develops materials for the participants to review prior to the simulation session. These materials serve to prepare the participants with the necessary information to successfully complete the scenario. For example, if the cardiac system is being reviewed for the week, the review for a simulation scenario of a patient experiencing a myocardial infarction might include acute coronary syndrome. This review focuses the participant's attention to a general concept, without revealing details of the scenario. As part of the preparation, a pretest activity is typically administered as part of assessing the participant's knowledge level. Completion of these presimulation activities by the participant helps to ensure successful participation in the simulation scenario.

Implementing the Simulation Scenario

When the time to run the simulation scenarios arrives, there are two main people responsible for keeping the sessions running smoothly. The faculty facilitator is responsible for guiding the students through the scenario and must be familiar with the simulation manikins and equipment, and how they react to various interventions, as well as how to circumnavigate some of the less realistic aspects that may be associated with the simulation equipment. Prior to starting the simulation scenario, the facilitator will deliver any remaining necessary scenario information including patient shift reports, student role assignments, and any other scenario-dependent information. The facilitator cannot make any assumptions about the participant's understanding of the simulation. Student prebriefing should be structured so as not to omit any important details about the session, environment, equipment, or simulator, and students should be instructed to engage in the scenario as themselves, not as a role-play (Alinier, Gordon, & Harwood, 2006). Once the scenario begins, the facilitator not only begins to evaluate the students, but also helps them navigate the scenario as needed by assuming the role of a healthcare practitioner giving orders or other roles as dictated by the scenario.

The simulation lab tech is responsible for any final preparations including equipment setup, adding makeup or special effects to the manikin to create a realistic physical appearance or injury, operation of the simulation manikin and audio/visual equipment, as well as resetting equipment between scenarios. The availability of such a support person allows the facilitator to solely focus on student performance within the scenario, while all of the technical aspects of running the various pieces of simulation and recording equipment is delegated to the simulation tech. These two roles draw a close parallel to that of the content expert and simulation expert who designed the simulation content, allowing each to focus on their specific area of expertise.

Who does what during the scenario? Jeffries (2008) suggests that a limited number of students should be directly involved in the simulation scenario. Typically, a scenario will involve two to four students each with a preassigned role including primary nurse, secondary nurse, charge nurse, or family member. Other roles can be created depending on the scenario. The remaining students act as observers, watching the simulation scenario remotely so as to not interfere with the live scenario. Students observing the sessions later become active participants in the debriefing. These observers benefit from analyzing the actions of their peers and actively participating in the debriefing process (Alinier *et al.*, 2006).

Simulation Debriefing and Evaluation

The **debriefing** is an integral part of the simulation session and should occur immediately after the conclusion of the scenario. If needed, the facilitator can also perform a short debriefing with the participants directly involved with the simulation prior to the larger group debriefing. The debriefing period must be a student-centered discussion with active participation by each member. The critical element in the process has been identified as reflection (Bremner, Aduddell, Bennett, & VanGeest, 2006). There are two elements to the reflection process as noted by Tanner (2006), reflection-in-action and reflection-on-action. Reflection-in-action references the participant's ability to read the patient, that is, to notice how the patient is responding to intervention in real time. This process takes place while immersed in the simulation scenario, and then is explored in greater detail during the group debriefing. Reflection-on-action reflects upon the scenario after it is finished, and includes looking at the overall impact of the interventions and actions performed. The facilitator should also help students to consider the affective domain, which can aid students in coping with the emotions felt during the scenario and help them to integrate the meaning of their experience (Lederman, 1992).

Tanner's clinical judgment model provides faculty with guidance to help students identify breakdowns, assess areas for growth, and consider learning experiences that focus on their growth. The process includes four main areas: (1) noticing, or the perceptual grasp of the situation at hand; (2) interpreting, or developing a sufficient understanding of the situation to be able to respond; (3) responding, or choosing a course of action deemed appropriate for the given situation; and (4) reflecting, or attending to the patient's responses to intervention while in the process of acting. The final step, not discussed above, is a review of the outcomes of the action focusing on the appropriateness of all the preceding aspects (Tanner, 2006). While Tanner's model looks at clinical judgment and clinical learning, Lasater's clinical judgment rubric (2007) builds upon Tanner's model to examine the development of clinical judgment in the simulated clinical environment. The simulation faculty facilitator can use the rubric to prompt students to reflect on and self-assess their performance in the simulation laboratory.

Conclusion

Simulation-based learning takes time and effort. It is a departure from the traditional lecture-based content delivery system. It is a paradigm of active, student-centered learning in an authentic environment. Incorporation of this learning strategy takes careful planning and a strategic approach for integration into the curriculum. Faculty acceptance is a crucial element. Two common reasons why simulation integration fails is when one member of the teaching faculty is responsible for all aspects of the lab, including scenario development and delivery in all content areas, or each member of the faculty is responsible for developing and delivering his or her own content. Either of the above creates a less than desirable situation for the faculty involved, and jeopardizes the effectiveness of simulation. It is my belief that one of the single most influential factors in achieving faculty acceptance is the adoption of a simulation expert, or simulation lab coordinator who works as a team member with faculty to develop realistic and effective scenarios. As demonstrated in the simulation development model, identifying and incorporating the distinct roles of content expert (faculty facilitator) and simulation expert (simulation tech) helps to capitalize on the strengths of each, whether clinical or technical expertise, in the development and delivery of the simulation scenario.

How do we know that simulation makes a positive impact on learning? Student evaluation is arguably one of the areas where further research is needed. It is vital for those who use simulation to seek out and review tools for evaluating student performance in simulation and to use (or create) tools that best meet their needs. Finally, those who use learning simulations need to share results about the impact of simulation and best practices within simulation-based learning to contribute to and expand the existing body of knowledge.

Learning Activities

1. Break the faculty up into groups by course, and establish one area of the curriculum into which a simulation could be incorporated. Based on the simulation development model, how would you approach the development and delivery of this content?

2. If your institution already utilizes simulation, how can the simulation development model help clarify roles and maximize the efforts of the faculty in developing and delivering simulation scenarios?

3. Consider the roles of the content expert and simulation expert (as well as the faculty facilitator and simulation tech). What are the pros and cons of adopting such roles? How could these roles enhance the development and delivery of simulation in your institution?

4. Review Lasater's article and discuss how this could be used in your evaluation of students as well as the student's self-reflection of their own performance.

References

Alinier, G., Gordon, R., & Harwood, C. (2006). Effectiveness of intermediate-fidelity simulation training technology in undergraduate nursing education. *Journal of Advanced Nursing, 54*(3), 359–369.

Annett, J. (2003). Hierarchical task analysis. In E. Hollnagel (Ed.), *Handbook of cognative task design (Human factors and ergonomics)* (pp. 17–35). Mahwah, NJ: Lawrence Erlbaum Associates.

Beaubien, J., & Baker, D. P. (2004). The use of simulation for training teamwork skills in healthcare: How low can you go? *Quality and Safety in Health Care, 13*, 151–156.

Bligh, J., & Bleakley, A. (2006). Distributing menus to hungry learners: Can learning by simulation become simulation of learning? *Medical Teacher, 28*(7), 606–613.

Bremner, M. N., Aduddell, K., Bennett, D. N., & VanGeest, J. B. (2006). The use of human patient simulators: Best practices with novice nursing students. *Nurse Educator, 31*, 170–174.

Gaba, D. (2004). The future vision of simulation in health care. *Quality and Safety in Healthcare, 13*(Suppl. 1), i2–i10.

Gaba, D., & DeAnda, A. A. (1998). A comprehensive anaesthesia simulation environment: recreating the operating room for research and training. *Anesthesiology, 69,* 387–393.

Gilley, J. W. (1990). Demonstration and simulation. In M. W. Galbraith (Ed.), *Adult learning methods: A guide for effective instruction* (pp. 261–281). Malabar, FL: Krieger.

Hertel, J. P., & Millis, B. J. (2002). *Using simulations to promote learning in higher education: An introduction.* Sterling, VA: Stylus.

Jeffries, P. (2008). Getting in S.T.E.P. with simulations: Simulations take educator preparation. *Nursing Education Perspectives, 29*(2), 70–73.

Jeffries, P. R., & Rogers, K. J. (2007). Theoretical framework for simulation design. In P. Jeffries (Ed.), *Simulation in nursing education: From conceptualization to evaluation* (pp. 21–33). New York, NY: National League for Nursing.

Jentsch, F., & Bowers, C. (2001). Use of commercial, off the shelf, simulations for team research. In E. Salas (Ed.), *Advances in human performance* (Vol. 1, pp. 293–317). Greenwich, CT: JAI Press.

Kantor, R. J., & Waddington, T. (2000). Fostering the suspension of disbelief: The role of authenticity in goal-based scenarios. *Interactive Learning Environments, 8*(3), 211–227.

Lasater, K. (2007). Clinical judgment development: Using simulation to create an assessment rubric. *Journal of Nursing Education, 46*(11), 496–503.

Lederman, L. C. (1992). Debriefing: Toward a systematic assessment of theory and practice. *Simulation and Gaming, 23,* 145–160.

Maran, N. J., & Glavin, R. J. (2003). Low to high-fidelity simulation—A continuum of medical education? *Medical Education, 37*(Suppl. 1), 22–28.

Tanner, C. A. (2006). Thinking like a nurse: A research-based model of clinical judgment in nursing. *Journal of Nursing Education, 45*(6), 204–211.

Theall, M., & Franklin, J. (1999). What have we learned? A synthesis and some guidelines for effective motivation in higher education. In M. Theall (Ed.), *Motivation from within: Approaches for encouraging faculty and students to excel: New directions for teaching and learning* (pp. 99–109). San Francisco, CA: Jossey-Bass.

CHAPTER 15

Informatics Competencies and Clinical Practice Tools

Food For Thought

"We think the PDA is the stethoscope of tomorrow.
Within five years, everyone is going to have one."

Chris Vincent, MD, Clinical Associate Professor of Family Medicine,
University of Washington and Swedish Family Medicine Residency

Key Words

Barcode Medication Administration
(BCMA)
Certification Commission for Healthcare
Information Technology (CCHIT)
Clinical decision support system (CDSS)
Clinical practice guidelines
Cochrane Collaboration
Computerized physician order entry
(CPOE)
Database
Data mining
Digital pen
Electronic health record (EHR)

Health Insurance Portability and
Accountability Act (HIPAA)
Informatics
Informatics competencies
Innovators
Interoperable
Joanna Briggs Institute
Modifiers
National Guidelines Clearinghouse
North American Nursing Diagnosis
Association-International (NANDA-I)
Nursing interventions classification (NIC)
Nursing outcomes classification (NOC)

Personal digital assistant (PDA)
Pretest for attitudes toward computers
   in healthcare (P.A.T.C.H.)

Radio frequency identification (RFID)
Universal serial bus (USB)
Users

Objectives

The educator will be able to describe the basic informatics competencies for professional nursing practice.

The educator will be able to assist students with the acquisition of informatics competencies.

The educator will be able to advocate for the inclusion of clinical technology tools in nursing curricula.

Introduction

Stephanie, a newly licensed registered nurse, is asked by her grandfather to call his physician about the report he received about the accidental discovery of a jugular vein thrombosis during a follow-up ultrasound of a carotid stent. Prior to calling the physician, Stephanie consults the medical information database that she has stored on her PDA and develops a list of questions that she wants to ask. Stephanie and the doctor are discussing whether the thrombosis is a new development and whether or not her grandfather should be admitted to the hospital to begin anticoagulant therapy. Stephanie points out that her grandfather is already taking Coumadin and they discuss whether it should be increased to effect a longer clotting time. During the course of the conversation, Stephanie asks whether the thrombosis could be related to an earlier radical neck dissection for a parotid tumor. The physician responds, "Oh, I forgot about that. I remember now, that's why we used a carotid stent rather than doing the endarterectomy." Stephanie also mentions that her grandfather had a CT scan with contrast 5 months ago that was ordered by his radiation oncologist as a follow-up to the cancer treatment. The doctor is able to access the CT scan photos and the final report from the hospital database and determines that there is no evidence of a jugular thrombosis on the previous scan. Together, they decide to consult the radiation oncologist to determine if another scan should be conducted and the primary care physician to determine if the Coumadin should be adjusted.

Since Stephanie was a nurse, was familiar with her grandfather's medical history, and had access to a reliable medical information database, she was able to ask the right questions and provide some direction for her grandfather's care. If Stephanie were a lay person, she might not have been able to make the potential connection between the previous surgery for the parotid tumor and the occurrence of the jugular vein thrombosis. This scenario illustrates the shortcomings associated with fragmented health information systems for persons with multiple medical problems for which they see a variety of specialists. If the health system had an **electronic health record (EHR)**, the medical history information for Stephanie's grandfather would likely be stored in a single record and would be readily accessible by all of the caregivers, providing a total picture of her grandfather's health status. The scenario also illustrates the value of ready access to medical and nursing information on a **personal digital assistant (PDA)**. As a new RN, Stephanie might not have been completely familiar with the causes and consequences of a jugular vein thrombosis, but she was able to get quickly informed and ask the right questions of her grandfather's physician. She was taught how to use the PDA as a clinical practice tool in her basic nursing program and now finds it invaluable in her clinical practice. In this chapter, we will discuss **informatics competencies** for nurses, examine various technology-based clinical practice tools, and advocate for the inclusion of informatics competencies and clinical technology tools in nursing education programs.

Informatics Competencies for Nurses

In 2008, the American Association of Colleges of Nursing (AACN) released The Essentials of Baccalaureate Education for Professional Nursing Practice report. The report emphasizes the need for developing competence in information management and the use of patient care technologies. The Essentials report suggests the following sample content to achieve information and patient care technology outcomes:

- Use of patient care technologies (e.g., monitors, pumps, computer-assisted devices)
- Use of technology and information systems for clinical decision making
- Computer skills that may include basic software, spreadsheet, and health-care **databases**
- Information management for patient safety

- Regulatory requirements through electronic data monitoring systems
- Ethical and legal issues related to the use of information technology, including copyright, privacy, and confidentiality issues
- Retrieval information systems, including access, evaluation of data, and application of relevant data to patient care
- Online literature searches
- Technologic resources for evidence-based practice
- Web-based learning and online literature searches for self and patient use
- Technology and information systems safeguards (patient monitoring, equipment, patient identification systems, drug alerts and IV systems, and barcoding)
- Interstate practice regulations (e.g., licensure, telehealth)
- Technology for virtual care delivery and monitoring
- Principles related to nursing workload measurement, resources, and information systems
- Information literacy
- Electronic health record/physician order entry
- Decision-support tools
- Role of the nurse informaticist in the context of health **informatics** and information systems (AACN, 2008, pp. 19–20)

In the faculty toolkit provided by the AACN to assist in the implementation of the Baccalaureate Essentials report, the following integrative learning strategies are suggested to help students meet the information and patient care technology essentials:

- Use information and patient care technology to communicate effectively with members of the healthcare team.
- Use clinical evidence and research to base and validate practice decisions related to information management and patient care technology.
- Participate in quality improvement activities and required regulatory reporting through information systems.
- Employ a range of technologies that support patient care, such as electronic health and medical records, patient monitoring systems, and medication administration systems.
- Use simulation and electronic medical records to access and analyze data relevant to the patient situation.

- Use information technology resources such as Wiki, Second Life simulation, or SkyScape.com to communicate with other healthcare professionals or students in other disciplines regarding a joint project.
- Develop a professional e-Portfolio. (AACN, 2009, p. 7)

As we discussed in Chapter 1, it is not possible to expose our students to all of the potential technologies they will encounter in practice, but we must expose them to enough technology to help them gain confidence in managing and effectively using it to support their professional practice. Similarly, nursing faculty must acquire technologic competence to design effective learning episodes for students and to model effective technology use in practice.

Kaminski (2008a) has a well-developed and frequently updated professional development Web site for nursing informatics competencies. She describes three distinct levels of expertise as **users**, **modifiers**, and **innovators** as well as three distinct levels of competencies: technical, utility, and leadership. Users are nurses who possess the basic informatics competencies that Kaminski suggests should be the minimum level for all nurses. At the user level of expertise, Kaminski (2008b) lists the following specific competencies.
Technical:

1. Uses word processing applications
2. Demonstrates keyboarding skills
3. Uses spreadsheet applications
4. Uses telecommunication devices to communicate with other systems
5. Uses e-mail systems to communicate with other healthcare professionals
6. Uses presentation applications to create slides, displays, overheads
7. Uses multimedia presentations
8. Uses Internet resources to locate client support groups and online resources
9. Uses sources of data that relate to nursing practice and care
10. Accesses, enters, and retrieves data related to client care via available hospital or nursing information systems
11. Uses database management programs to develop and access databases and tables
12. Uses database applications to enter and retrieve data and information
13. Conducts online and database literature searches
14. Uses decision support systems, expert systems, and other aids for clinical decision making and care planning

15. Uses computer applications to document client care
16. Uses computer applications to plan client care, including discharge planning
17. Uses computer applications to enter client data (demographic, vital signs, physiological data)
18. Uses information management systems for client education
19. Uses technology-based client monitoring systems
20. Operates peripheral devices (bedside and handheld)
21. Uses operating systems
22. Uses computer peripheral devices (CD ROMs, DVD, zip drives)
23. Uses computer technology safely
24. Navigates in Windows environment effectively
25. Demonstrates basic technology skills (load paper, change toner, use printer)

Utility:

1. Recognizes the relevance of nursing data for improving practice
2. Recognizes limitations of computer applications
3. Recognizes need for continual learning in informatics skills, applications, and knowledge
4. Recognizes the nature of computer–human interfaces and assesses impact on client care
5. Understands the basic process of using networks for electronic communication
6. Recognizes the basic components of computer systems

Leadership:

1. Uses computerized management systems to record administrative data (billing data, quality assurance data, workload data)
2. Uses applications for structured data entry (classification systems, acuity level)
3. Understands client rights related to computerized information
4. Recognizes the utility of nurse involvement in the planning, design, choice, and implementation of information systems in the practice environment
5. Incorporates a Code of Ethics in regards to client privacy and confidentiality (Kaminski, 2008b, para. 3–5)

Similarly, Kaminski (2008a) details competencies for modifiers who possess intermediate informatics skills and who use technology creatively in their practice, and competences for innovators who have expert skills and are involved in the application of informatics theory to practice as well as the design, development, and implementation of new technologies. The competencies for modifiers and innovators are beyond the scope of this discussion. However, if you are interested in reviewing them, please visit this Web site:

http://www.nursing-informatics.com/niassess/innovators.html

In addition to providing these very detailed lists of basic competencies, Kaminski (2008a) also provides a Web site with links to competency self-assessment tests, a **pretest for attitudes toward computers in health care (P.A.T.C.H.)** assessment, and a form for developing a personal informatics competency development plan. We have used these self-assessments and the personal development plans with our students in the basic nursing informatics course and urge you to do the same for yourself and your students. You can access these materials at the following Web sites:

- Self-assessment tests: http://www.nursing-informatics.com/niassess/tests.html
- P.A.T.C.H. test and personal development plan: http://www.nursing-informatics.com/niassess/plan.html

Clearly, there are important informatics and technology-related skills that our students must master for their professional practice. We have an obligation to ensure that our students have access to patient care technologies in the clinical practice facilities we utilize and in our clinical laboratories. If, for example, the clinical practice facility uses an EHR we must negotiate access for our students so that they can develop skill in utilizing this critical information management tool. Similarly, we must find ways to secure funding for purchase of these tools for our practice laboratories. The University of Maryland (Business Wire, 2006) reports on a partnership between their School of Nursing and Cerner Corporation to provide EHR software to their clinical simulation laboratory. Similarly, nursing faculty at the University of Kansas secured funding to purchase and modify an EHR software package for use in their clinical practice laboratory (Kennedy, Pallikkathayil, & Warren, 2009). If you are unable to secure funding for these demonstration technologies in your school of nursing, it is possible for your students to view some of these technology interfaces on the Internet, although many of the videos provided for open viewing on YouTube contain references to specific commercial products. Of course, partnering with a commercial provider will also result in proprietary preferences. In the sections that follow, we will discuss some of the essential clinical support technologies that we believe nursing students should experience and provide examples of how they can be effectively incorporated into baccalaureate education. Clinical simulation laboratory technologies and teaching strategies are presented separately in Chapter 14.

Electronic Health Records

EHRs are considered one of the solutions to the quality and safety crisis in health care. As we described in our opening scenario, a fully **interoperable** EHR would have provided the vascular physician with a comprehensive record of Stephanie's grandfather's medical history, and provided insights into the causes of his current situation. President Obama has emphasized the commitment to the comprehensive implementation of EHRs by committing millions of dollars to health information technology (Manos, 2009). While some functions of health care have been technology enabled for some time, it is imperative now that these functions be interoperable to allow for seamless data sharing among healthcare practitioners. To ensure that the goal of interoperability is met, the US Department of Health and Human Services recognized the **Certification Commission for Healthcare Information Technology (CCHIT)** in 2006 as the official certifying body for health IT products (CCHIT, 2008). The standardization of contents and functionality of EHRs among vendors is a bonus for nurse educators in that learning should be easily transferable as students transition from the academic environment to the practice environment.

The components of a certified in-patient EHR include:

- Basic demographic and clinical health information including a problem list and medication allergies;
- Clinical decision support providing clinician alerts on food and drug allergies, immunizations, drug interactions, orders for similar drugs, out-of range-dosages, drug side effects that are related to or may exacerbate the symptoms of current disease, duplicate orders, suggestions for follow-ups or related orders, dosage guidance based on age, weight, or lab

results; also included are nursing alerts for medication administration and allergy checks as well as support for **barcode medication administration (BCMA)** procedures;

- A **computerized physician order entry (CPOE)** system that supports electronic prescribing and allows for additions by nurses and other medical personnel; the system also supports predeveloped order sets and provides alerts if an order is contradicted based on the specific patient's criteria;
- A healthcare quality information component that allows for aggregate **data mining** and reporting functions;
- An electronic healthcare information exchange function that allows for the exchange of data between healthcare providers promoting safer hand-offs from one unit to another or one facility to another;
- Support for security and confidentiality of healthcare data by access control and authenticating procedures, records access auditing, secure data backup and recovery procedures, and encryption;
- Workflow support including late medication alerts, physician and nurse assignments, and physician directory and contact information. (CCHIT, 2009)

In an ideal world, students would have access to a practice version of an EHR so that they could gain skill in inputting assessment data, in developing patient care plans electronically, and in practicing, managing, and documenting care prior to entering the clinical practice site. You may want to check to see if the health center your program utilizes for clinical education has an EHR skills training lab that can be used to prepare students for clinical rotations.

In the absence of such practice tools, nurse faculty can still ensure that students are ready for practice by providing them with and requiring them to use standardized terminology tools for diagnosis (**North American Nursing Diagnosis Association-International,** or **NANDA-I**), nursing interventions (**nursing interventions classification,** or **NIC**) and nursing outcomes (**nursing outcomes classification,** or **NOC**) as they prepare their patient care plans. Many EHRs will have standardized nursing care plans or **clinical practice guidelines** based on common nursing approaches for specific medical diagnoses. However, students need the opportunity to gain confidence in modifying these plans for individual patient situations. In addition, care planning processes should be evidence based. Therefore, we need to require students to seek and utilize current practice research as they utilize the nursing process and develop patient care plans. If the EHR in the academic health system has a clinical resource database readily available, students need query and search skills in order to utilize the tool effectively. In addition, students should be exposed to the online evidence-based practice sites such as **National Guidelines Clearinghouse** (http://www.guidelines.gov/), the **Cochrane Collaboration** (http://www.cochrane.org/), or the **Joanna Briggs Institute** (http://www.joannabriggs.edu.au/about/home.php). Clinical faculty need to be fully versed in EHR components and use, and skilled at guiding students in technology learning and use.

PDAs and Other Mobile Technology

A PDA is a handheld computer that allows for mobile computing functions. PDAs are continuously evolving; some now function as smart phones in addition to having basic computer functions and Internet access. A smartphone with PDA is a handheld or palmtop computer that has gained appeal due to its small, portable size. The size is not reflective of the impressive performance capabilities that allow a user to store, access, and organize information such as calendar entries, documents, spreadsheets, databases, notes, and to-do lists. Your capabilities and access are limited by the processing speed and memory, and of course, the faster and more robust the memory capabilities are, the more the unit costs. As you consider purchasing a smartphone, it is important that you reflect on your current and future needs.

Most of today's smartphone operating systems are either Linux, PocketPC (Windows), or PalmOS (Palm). Since they can be used in networked environments including wireless configurations, they can theoretically give the clinician constant access to patient information, colleagues, and other necessary resources.

The applications available provide a wide range of functionality from simple to highly complex software tools. You can use dosage calculators, drug and specialty databases, educational applications, clinical forecasting tools, take dictation, or practice telenursing all from your smartphone. In addition, there are many add-ons available to enhance functionality, as well as ease of use.

Most smartphones come with office applications, sync software, Bluetooth, and cables. Office applications could include word processing, spreadsheets, database, and presentation software. The sync software is short for synchronize and functions to update information on both your computer and your smartphone. Bluetooth is a form of wireless connectivity that is commonly used in cell phones although it usually does not provide Internet access, it does facilitate file transfer between your smartphone and a computer. Cables are an inexpensive way to connect to a computer, essentially plugging the smartphone into your computer.

As smartphones continue to evolve, so do their capabilities and connectivity. Internet connectivity (Web browser and e-mail) provides the clinician with communication capabilities and constant access to real-time online data and information. Since the smartphone is portable, your connectivity must be ready whenever and wherever you need it. One way to establish connectivity is through the use of Wi-Fi. Wi-Fi compatibility provides for use at hotspots throughout the country such as cafes, coffee shops, hotels, restaurants, and universities. It can also use the existing wireless network in your agency or office. This feature can be added to a smartphone by purchasing a Wi-Fi adaptor.

Smartphones are particularly advantageous for community health nurses. They can be used to track patients, as point-of-care (POC) devices or calculators. The smartphone can take your dictation at the bedside or on the go as you travel between patients or appointments. As reference tools, they can provide ready access to clinical and drug databases; electronic textbooks, and reference materials; online journals such as MEDLINE, the Online Journal of Nursing Informatics (OJNI), and educational tools such as study guides; and care planning documents (Skyscape, n.d.; Dykes Library, 2009; PDA Cortex, n.d.). You can transfer information within your network even when you are in the field. Using your network, you can send a note to a case manager, update a physician on the status of a patient you visited in her home, or even send a prescription to the pharmacy. The PDA allows you to maintain your schedule or calendar and receive reminder alarms. You can even use your smartphone for professional development such as continuing education offerings or furthering your academic education online. Whether you are an avid smartphone user, beginning to use one, or just contemplating purchasing one, get involved and participate in the list that discusses smartphones and PDA functionality in nursing at PDA Cortex (http://www.rnpalm.com/nursing_pdas_listserv.htm).

The smartphone can enhance health care for our patients as well. We can monitor our patients and send surveys and questionnaires, and they can submit their responses to us as their healthcare provider or to a healthcare institution. The smartphone can enhance patient access to their clinicians especially if the patient is mobile; the smartphone can go where they go and they can keep in touch via e-mail, phone, fax, and instant or text messaging. They can maintain their appointment and medication schedule as well as receive patient education materials and access clinician recommended Web sites.

The educational arena has also embraced this technology. Nursing instructors are communicating and sharing information with their learners and clinical settings using smartphone technologies. Using wireless connectivity in class, instructors can receive instant feedback to determine if the key concepts are recognized and understood. Smartphones can even assist with discussions, provide study aids, interactive exercises, and quizzes. As a nursing student, the reference materials and podcasts available for course work could be stored on your smartphone for easy access. You could upload and download clinical documents and information with your instructor and clinical setting staff. In the clinical setting, the easy access to robust reference tools and materials such as dosage calculators help to reduce errors. The educational applications will continue to expand as more software and capabilities become available.

This is certainly not an exhaustive list of smartphone applications or equipment, and the truth of this information era is that the current will be the past by the time this is in print. As the future continues to unfold, so will our applications of smartphones in nursing.

In the clinical arena, PDAs provide real-time access to numerous clinical practice support modalities such as drug reference databases, medical diagnosis information references, and nursing care planning support that may have a positive effect on patient safety, and quality of care, and promote evidence-based practice (Farrell & Rose, 2008). Tilghman, Raley, and Conway (2006) discuss several cautions related to student PDA use at the POC in clinical settings. First, there must be clear guidelines and secure processes for accessing and storing private patient information on PDAs. Nursing faculty must ensure that all PDA use in the clinical setting is compliant with **Health Insurance Portability and Accountability Act (HIPAA)** rules and regulations for protecting patient privacy. Second, students must be made aware that the ready-access POC documentation does not replace critical thinking skills or other written references necessary for planning and implementing quality patient care.

PDA software is also continuously evolving and there are numerous packages available to support clinical nursing practice. If you are considering requiring your students to use PDAs, you will want to carefully consider functionality, pricing, ease of use, and durability. You should also carefully evaluate clinical support software for ease of use, price, readability, and reliability, as well as access to periodic updates. You can find a list of currently available clinical support software for PDAs by conducting an Internet search.

Small, lightweight tablet PCs are also being used more frequently in the clinical arena. These portable computers weigh about 3 pounds and can be carried to the patient's room or home, or mounted on a mobile docking station and wheeled to the POC. They are battery run, wireless, contain biometric or **radio frequency identification (RFID)** security authorizations, and are easily sanitized to prevent the spread of infection. These devices are designed to improve workflow efficiency by allowing nurses to access the EHR at the POC, update patient records as care is given (most employ writing surfaces, but some have voice recognition capability), access clinical diagnosis information, and support medication administration by providing barcode scanning technology.

Digital Pens

A **digital pen** is a unique way to capture and upload clinical information collected on paper in a setting where the EHR connections or mobile technologies are not readily available. These specialized pens contain a digital camera in the tip that records the position of the pen on the special paper and converts the dot matrices to readable data. When the clinician returns to the clinic, the pen is docked in a **universal serial bus (USB)** cradle and the data are uploaded to the clinic's system. Some of the newer digital pen software does not require special paper, but instead allows for regular printing of forms onto which the dot matrix grids are superimposed by the software as the form is printed. Note that you must keep in mind the memory limitations; the memory will generally hold around 40 pages of captured digital paper. Some of these new marvels are using Bluetooth wireless technology that can send your captures directly to your computer. The file formats vary by manufacturer but are typically GIF or JPEG, making them easily shared and supported, and the text that is written can be converted through optical character recognition to use in word processing (Digital Pen Systems, 2007). Consider this example from Sweden:

> The Anoto digital pens will primarily be used to facilitate documentation and information transfer, in order to improve the quality of elderly homecare in the city. The technology has already been deployed successfully in . . . two towns north of Stockholm, where homecare nurses use the digital pen to register their arrival and departure times on each visit and tick off the services delivered to each patient, on a digital form. (Wireless News, 2007, para. 4–5)

Students might also consider using digital pens for note taking in classes to facilitate the exchange of information with each other. Think of the educational applications for being able to capture 40 pages of material and upload it to your computer to share and exchange.

Clinical Decision Support Systems

A **clinical decision support system (CDSS)** is a database software program that matches data provided by patients and gathered from clinician assessments to a knowledge base constructed from what is known about a health condition or issue to help clinicians make better informed clinical diagnoses and treatment decisions. The effectiveness of the CDSS is limited by what is known or understood about a disease or condition, the currency of the information stored in the database, as well as the quality of the data provided by the patient or the clinician assessment. In addition to the knowledge base, the CDSS also has an inference mechanism that processes the inputted data (e.g., signs and symptoms reported by patient and entered into the database) systematically searching and relating the data to the knowledge base via computer algorithms. While CDSSs are not yet widely used by physicians to arrive at a diagnosis, they are being increasingly used as part of an EHR for the generation of clinical practice guidelines once a diagnosis has been established. They are also useful in case management support by providing alerts and reminders for clinical intervention and follow-up in the management of chronic illnesses (Kong, Xu, & Yang, 2008). Since one can readily predict that the use of CDSSs will increase in the future, nurse educators should ensure that database searching and data mining skills are included in nursing curricula. While each program will have individual procedures, general database searching skills that can be learned in a tutorial are likely to be readily transferable. To view an example of a CDSS, please visit the following Web site: http://dxplain.org/demo2/frame.htm/.

Clinical Databases and Data Mining

Databases are collections of data that are structured or organized in a consistent manner to allow for sorting and organization of such data to generate information and knowledge. Many clinical IT systems rely on database technology to collect, sort, and store clinical information, and to provide ready access to clinicians. Data mining is best described as a process of analyzing stored or captured data for trends, and generating new ideas or knowledge about a phenomenon. For example, data mining techniques were used by Google to provide information about an apparent flu outbreak by aggregating information from public search queries related to flu symptoms. You can see the results of the aggregate data at the FluTrends Web site: http://www.google.org/about/flutrends/how.html. Similarly, Sabhnani, Neill, and Moore (2005) describe using a system that tracks over-the-counter (OTC) retail pharmacy sales trends to predict disease outbreaks. Their database tracks and records sales data of over 9,000 OTC healthcare remedies, and compares the current sales rate to a previously identified baseline for 10,000 stores identified by zip code. Incorporating examples such as these into nursing curricula help students appreciate the power of databases and data mining techniques for knowledge building.

Data mining techniques also support the reporting requirements functions of clinical entities since administrators can generate aggregate data reports related to clinical care outcomes such as medication errors or the incidence of pressure ulcers. Clinical research is also supported by data mining in that researchers can search the clinical database to uncover the relationships between discrete factors and generate testable hypotheses for additional research. Chen, Fuller, Freidmen, and Hersh (2006) emphasize the need to protect the identity of patients when using data mining techniques on medical records and the need for careful interpretation of knowledge discovered by data mining.

> Knowledge and patterns discovered by computers need to be experimentally or clinically validated in order to be considered rigorous, just like any knowledge generated by human. Errors and incorrect associations could propagate quickly through electronic media, especially when large databases and powerful computational techniques are involved. (Chen et al., 2006, p. 23)

Ideas for learning episodes to help students appreciate the effectiveness and potential pitfalls of data mining might include:

- A search of the HIPAA (http://www.hhs.gov/ocr/privacy/index.html) Web site for specific provisions and rules related to the use of patient data for research.
- An online library search for a nursing research study that uses data mining of a clinical database as a source of data for the research study.

We hope that this overview of informatics competencies and clinical practice tools has provided a spark for curricular revisions in your school of nursing. We urge you to examine your own level of informatics competency and find ways to increase your level of competency so that you can model informatics competency for your students. We also urge you to incorporate exposure to technology-based clinical practice tools in your curricula, and to be vigilant in following the literature for new practice tools as they emerge.

Learning Activities

1. Conduct an audit of your current nursing curriculum to identify what nursing informatics competencies are currently included, and where or how additional competencies can be developed.
2. Explore the current uses of clinical technology tools in your clinical practice sites and develop strategies for helping students acquire skill in their use.
3. If you have not yet completed a personal informatics competency development plan (as suggested in Chapter 2 activities), access this Web site and complete a plan: http://www.nursing-informatics.com/niassess/plan.html

References

American Association of Colleges of Nursing. (2008, October 20). *The essentials of baccalaureate education for professional nursing practice*. Available at: http://www.aacn.nche.edu/Education/pdf/BaccEssentials08.pdf. Accessed June 16, 2009.

American Association of Colleges of Nursing. (2009, February 19). *Nurse faculty tool kit for the Implementation of the baccalaureate essentials*. Available at: http://www.aacn.nche.edu/Education/pdf/BacEssToolkit.pdf. Accessed June 16, 2009.

Business Wire (2006, April 24). University of Maryland School of Nursing, Cerner Team to bring healthcare information technology to nursing students; Partnership will bolster students' skills, offer innovation for nursing education. doi: 1026345201

Certification Commission for Healthcare Information Technology. (2008). *CCHIT governance, funding and organizational structure.* Available at: http://www.cchit.org/about/organization/index.asp. Accessed June 17, 2009.

Certification Commission for Healthcare Information Technology. (2009). *Concise guide to CCHIT certification criteria.* Available at: http://www.cchit.org/files/certification/09/guide/Concise-GuideToCCHIT_CertificationCriteria_May_29_2009.pdf. Accessed June 17, 2009.

Chen, H., Fuller, S., Freidmen, C., & Hersh, W. (2006) Knowledge management, data mining, and text mining in medical informatics. In H. Chen, S. Fuller, C. Freidman, & W. Hersh (Eds.) *Medical informatics: Knowledge management and data mining in biomedicine* (pp. 3–33). New York, NY: Springer.

Digital Pen Systems. (2007). Technology. Available at: http://www.digitalpensystems.com/technology.html. Accessed June 17, 2009.

Dykes Library. (2009). Clinical reference. Available at: http://library.kumc.edu/m. Accessed June 29, 2009.

Farrell, M., & Rose, L. (2008). Use of mobile handheld computers in clinical nursing education. *Journal of Nursing Education, 47*(1), 13–19.

Kaminski, J. (2008a). *Competencies.* Available at: http://www.nursing-informatics.com/niassess/competencies.html. Accessed June 16, 2009.

Kaminski, J. (2008b). *User level competencies.* Available at: http://www.nursing-informatics.com/niassess/users.html. Accessed June 16, 2009.

Kennedy, D., Pallikkathayil, L., & Warren, J. (2009). Using a modified electronic health record to develop nursing process skills. *Journal of Nursing Education, 48*(2), 96–100.

Kong, G., Xu, D., & Yang, J. (2008). Clinical decision support systems: a review of knowledge representation and inference under uncertainties. *International Journal of Computational Intelligence Systems, 1*(2), 159–167.

Manos, D. (2009, January 8). Obama: EHRs for Americans by 2014. *Healthcare IT News,* Available at: http://www.healthcareitnews.com/news/obama-ehrs-americans-2014. Accessed June 15, 2009.

PDA Cortex. (n.d.). The Journal of Mobile Informatics and PDA Resources for Healthcare Professionals. Available at: http://www.pdacortex.com/. Accessed June 29, 2009.

Sabhnani, M., Neill, D., & Moore, A. (2005). Detecting anomalous patterns in pharmacy retail data (p.58–61). Available at: http://www.dmargineantu.net/AD-KDD05/DMMAD-2005.WorkshopNotes.pdf#page=60. Accessed June 16, 2009.

Skyscape. (n.d.). Nursing. Available at: http://www.skyscape.com/estore/store.aspx?category=36. Accessed June 29, 2009.

Tilghman, J., Raley, D., & Conway, J. (2006). Family nurse practitioner students utilization of personal digital assistants (PDAs): Implications for practice. *ABNF Journal 17*(3), 115–117.

Wireless News. (2007, September 27). City of Stockholm to Use Anoto's Digital Pen to Improve Elderly Care Services. doi: 1343068491

CHAPTER 16

Technology Tools for Outcomes Assessment

Food For Thought

"Institutional assessment efforts should not be concerned about valuing what can be measured but, instead, about measuring that which is valued."

Banta, Lund, Black, & Oblander, 1996

"All assessment is a perpetual work in progress."

Suskie, 2005

"Description of a grade: An inadequate report of an inaccurate judgment by a biased and variable judge of the extent to which a student has attained an undefined level of mastery of an unknown proportion of an indefinite material."

Dressel, 1983

"Teachers assess to test; educators assess to assist learning."

Carter, 2002

Key Words

Assessment	Evidence
Authentic assessment	Formative assessment
Blog	Reflective commentary
e-Portfolios	Summative assessment
Evaluation	Teaching e-Portfolio (TeP)

Objectives

The educator will be able to describe an e-Portfolio, specifically a teaching e-Portfolio (TeP), and list at least three ways it can be used in the assessment of an educator.

The educator will be able to examine the e-Portfolio process and describe how he or she can develop his or her own TeP.

The educator will be able to identify at least two ways to enhance the quality of assessment and discuss how this could be captured in a TeP.

Introduction

Portfolio assessment programs are being implemented on both the teacher and student levels. They signify a philosophical shift in attitudes concerning the role of assessment in education. We no longer conduct assessments of learning but instead conduct assessments for learning. This paradigm shift is a step toward enhancing the teaching learning process through mutual participation requiring active feedback and self-reflection on the part of both the teacher and the learner.

e-Portfolios

Electronic portfolios or **e-Portfolios** are electronic presentations of one's knowledge, skills, education, and examples of work or career achievements. It is a personalized collection of evidence and reflective commentary that can be shared with others electronically. The e-Portfolio allows users to include narrative comments that focus on why specific evidence is important, the ways in which the user values what has been learned or why it is important for his profession. This narrative reflection of the evidence describing one's experiences within the e-Portfolio is known as **reflective commentary**. The **evidence** refers to the artifacts, productions, attestations, or other examples that demonstrate an individual's knowledge, skills, or valued attributes. According to Johnson (2009), e-Portfolios are "Web-based collections that include evidence of knowledge and skills" (p. 386).

Assessment

Many people confuse assessment and evaluation. **Assessment** means collecting information for the purpose of making educational decisions; **evaluation** is the process of making judgments about the worth of a student's products or performance. Evaluation may be based on assessment, but not always. For example, if you were a student in a course, the various projects and assignments that you complete would serve as a means of assessing your performance. These assessments would determine your grade in the course, an evaluation. Class performance on these assessments would also aid the instructor in evaluating the strengths and weaknesses of the course materials. For instance, if a large percentage of the class does not perform well on a certain assignment, this may indicate that additional information should be included or expanded in a particular lesson.

This brings us to the next question: When should teachers construct assessments? The assessment of a learning episode (or module) should be based on the stated learning objectives. In some instructional design models, such as the Dick and Carey (1996) model, construction of assessment items is done immediately after the creation of the learning objectives in the design phase. This ensures that there is consistency between the objectives and assessment items, and allows the instructor to work on the assessment at a less hectic time in the instructional design process.

In the Morrison, Ross, and Kemp (2004) model, however, learning objectives are created and revised throughout the instructional design process, so assessment items are best created at the end of the development phase, when all the objectives are finalized. Many instructors prefer to create their assessment items at this point because they have a clear picture of what they want from their students. Regardless of the timing, the important thing to remember is that the requirements of the assessment must match the learning objectives, both in terms of content and the expected level of performance (such as classification on a taxonomy).

There are many types of assessment methods, with objective tests being the most common because they are the more traditional way of testing. Objective tests are also the easiest and quickest items to grade. In addition, instructors who use objective tests greatly reduce their workload because these tests can be scanned and scored by computers ("bubble sheets") or automatically scored and recorded by a course management system such as ANGEL or BlackBoard.

Types of assessment include:

- Objective: These tests use multiple choice, true/false, and matching items. Students must select the correct answer from those provided. Appropriate for low-level cognitive objectives.

- Constructed response: These include fill-in-the-blank and essay questions. Students plan and construct their own answer to questions. Typically used for the cognitive domain or affective domain.
- Performance tests: These use observation and judgment to assess either a process or product completed by the student. These may include papers, projects, and presentations. May be objectives in the affective, cognitive, or psychomotor domains. Specific types of performance tests include portfolios and authentic assessment.
  - Portfolios: Systematic collections of student work over time, which include reflections, self-assessments, and examples of work.
  - **Authentic assessment:** Assessments that emphasize what students can do rather than what they know. These assessments represent how the knowledge will be applied in a real-world context and are beneficial for aiding transfer.

Validity and reliability are important factors to remember when we construct assessments. Validity means that an assessment measures what it is suppose to measure. To ensure validity, base assessment items on the learning objectives, ensuring that they reflect both the content of the course or learning episode and learner's expected level of performance.

Reliability means that an assessment consistently measures what it is supposed to measure. A common way of assessing reliability is test-retest outcomes.

The assessment continuum consists of formative and summative assessments. **Formative assessment** helps us to see learning in progress. **Summative assessment** measures what was done or accomplished at the end. Therefore, during formative assessment, you could discuss and assess a student's progress while they are developing their e-Portfolio. If you assessed the e-Portfolio when it was complete and assessed if they met the learning objective or outcome, this would be a summative assessment.

Now that we have reviewed common assessment methods, let us move to the present and future of assessment. In the past, we assessed to assign a grade and typically the student did something for us to assess. The assessment typically took place without the student being actively involved in the process. That is, if the student submitted a paper or took a test, these materials were assessed without the student participating or contributing. There was not a conversation that occurred during the assessment and sometimes, the student was not even able to discuss the assessment after it was completed as in the case of papers submitted at the end of the semester.

Assessment has changed and for the better! We no longer conduct assessments of learning but instead conduct assessments for learning. The students are actively involved in the process. The assessment should provide a road map for the teacher and the learner, and help them both decide what to do next. Assessments are more focused on the individual's performance based on his or her own individual ability and achievement. All of this is done with the eye on the goal: to meet the learning objectives. The student or stakeholder must be involved in order to know where he has been and where he is going. It is now up to the student to take control and reach the goal. Without their buy-in or engagement, how can students possibly reach a goal?

Education has changed over the years with more emphasis being placed on real-world application. Assessment strategies must also evolve to evaluate this approach. Authentic assessment is intended to evaluate the learner's abilities in real-world situations. The learner's critical thinking, creativity, written and oral skills, and ability to apply what has been learned to new situations is assessed. Rote memorization and restating of facts are not appropriate illustrations that the student has integrated the material. The key to student success lies in the ability to demonstrate skills and conceptual understanding by applying what has been learned to solve real-world problems. What is valued is the learning process and the learning outcome.

It is becoming easier for instructors to move away from traditional types of assessment and more toward authentic assessment. Instructors can now create activities and assessments where students can work collaboratively in teams to solve realistic, real-world problems using a variety of Web 2.0 technologies. One of the major tools that can be useful in developing such authentic learning is the e-Portfolio where a student collects evidence of learning and engages in reflection about that learning.

Teaching e-Portfolios (TeP)

A teaching portfolio is a collection of work compiled over time that describes and demonstrates various characteristics of an educator's teaching ability. The **teaching e-Portfolio (TeP)** is a digitized compilation of our teaching that we develop and share in an electronic format. It can be used by the individual for reflection and improvement as well as for purposes of formally assessing performance or progress, including promotion and tenure. The TeP is constructed by a teacher to provide ongoing evidence of developments, achievements, and accomplishments. Therefore, it must be updated as works in progress, as we continually grow and enhance our skills and knowledge. During the development of the TeP, the individual should take time to reflect on teaching by thinking through his or her own philosophy, approach, and outcomes while collecting, selecting, and adding evidence to provide work examples.

It is very important that we, as teachers, understand e-Portfolios as they relate to the teaching and learning journey. The TeP should describe what we do in an organized and digitized format in order to enhance our own development and demonstrate our ability. The examples of our work that we choose should highlight how we approach teaching and learning. Schools across the country are looking to improve the quality of teaching. What better way to showcase our experience and expertise than through a reflective, thorough TeP?

The TeP is a record of how you value teaching and the format varies by setting and discipline. For the purpose of this text, we have developed a template that you could follow. Your TeP should be concise but thorough. It should not be painful to develop or overwhelming to review. We have chosen a **blog** format to build our TeP and Dr. McGonigle has provided her TeP as an example (see Box 16-1). The advantage of using a blog for a TeP is that you can create entries as you go, and locate and organize them later using tags. Thus, it is very important that you tag all of your entries. Tagging is simply a way to make your TeP searchable by keywords. You can use multiple keywords for each entry. Your TeP will be continually updated as you seek feedback, and enhance your teaching repertoire and skills. See Box 16-2 for TeP tips.

A TeP is a collection of work compiled over time that describes and demonstrates various characteristics of one's teaching ability. The TeP is a digitized compilation of one's teaching that is developed and shared in an electronic format. It can be used by the individual for reflection and improvement as well as for purposes of formally assessing performance or progress, including promotion and tenure.

TePs and Faculty Assessment

As faculty, we must engage in e-Portfolio and authentic assessment as well. Faculty members must develop a TeP to demonstrate how they help students learn and how they refine their teaching. Teaching is an art and, as such, must be honed, explored, and sculpted. As teachers, we should listen to our learners

Box 16-1   Dr. Dee McGonigle's TeP

A. Goals

By Dr. Dee McGonigle on March 24, 2008 6:29 PM

1. Teaching Philosophy

Learning

A learner-centered approach is a must since it is my belief that I must form a learning dyad with each learner in order to meet her/his needs and enhance her/his educational experience. Learners have varying learning abilities and capacities. Their own reality and unique aptitudes provide varying levels for progression within structured learning frameworks. Each course that a learner enters must provide life-long learning potential by motivating and stimulating the learner's ability to think critically, grow and develop. As clinical nurses, the learners are faced with the necessity to make fast-paced decisions in an ambiguous clinical environment. It is imperative that I help them employ evidence-based practice (EBP) strategies in their clinical practice. EBP requires that practitioners employ the best evidence possible, moderated by their clinical judgment, patient situation and preferences, to provide the highest quality of care for their patients. The ability to implement EBP is paramount in our rapidly evolving clinical environments and demonstrates our ability to harness the healthcare information explosion to improve patient care. Merging education, experience, practice and research will enhance Empowering learners to creatively think and be excited about learning in their professional and personal lives without structured educational episodes.

Teaching

Teaching is an art that requires life-long learning to gain mastery. As teachers, we must synthesize our experience, education, research and practice in order to engage our learners. The engagement of the learner truly involves them in the process of learning and they actively participate in their own learning venues. The crafting of educational episodes that engage learners is truly an art to be mastered. This interactive, collaborative learning environment transforms the educational process as well as the participants; the learners are no longer passive vessels being filled by a lecturer but instead they are active participants. To help them advance based on their unique aptitude in learning. Providing useful information and skills for their future while providing critical thinking abilities. The skills instilled should facilitate their decision-making ability and EBP capabilities in their professional and daily life.

As a constructivist, I believe that we each construct or exist in our own reality and extract meaning from our current knowledge structures; the learner constructs knowledge

(continues)

Box 16-1   Dr. Dee McGonigle's TeP (continued)

from their own experiences. This philosophy requires me to facilitate and support learning initiated and directed by the learner through active or discovery learning. It is truly a learner-centered approach. I continue to learn from my own experiences, the literature and the learners that I have had the pleasure of interacting with about the dynamics of teaching and nursing so I can improve my effectiveness and continue on my path to mastery. Each learner in every course provides an experience from which I can learn and grow.

Technology facilitates the connectedness of learners to me and each other. The tools help provide them with 24/7 access to course materials, including gaming, Podcasts, Vodcasts, and webcasts, as well as to me and other students through discussion forums, chats, instant messaging, telephone, Adobe Connect, and email. The use of technology can enhance our work but it also requires that we stay abreast of upgrades and latest developments while we choose the most suitable technologies to support our specific educational needs.

2. Primary Goal

My primary goal is to instill a thirst for education and have a beneficial effect on the learner's current and future professional practice to ultimately enhance patient care and the nursing profession. Challenging learners to critically think through their experience and educational perceptions while searching for the best evidence for the patient given their situation and preferences. To encourage students to seek autonomy in the face of collective thought and to break free of cookie-cutter practice strategies in favor of individualized, evidence based clinical judgments to improve patient care.

B. Responsibilities

By Dr. Dee McGonigle on March 24, 2008 6:25 PM | Permalink | Comments (0) | TrackBacks (0)

1. Courses taught

Specifically, in the last six semesters, I have taught the following courses:

Course	Description	Enrollment
NURS 200 W	Introduction to Nursing Research	14
NURS 457	Introduction to Nursing Informatics	55
NURS 417	Community and family Health Nursing	14
NURS 418	Capstone Experience	14
NURS 390	Transition	30

All of these courses are technologically enhanced with NURS 390 totally delivered online and NURS 457 being able to be completed totally online if the learner so chooses. NURS 417 requires the learners to think through community health advancing their practice from individual patient to family, group and population based aggregates. NURS 418 requires the students to interact electronically as a team to develop the ideal healthcare delivery system based on a simulation I adapted.

Over the years, I have received funding to develop and enhance my course work. These innovations have been well thought out applications of technologies that enhance content delivery and access. Every creative innovation has been assessed for its educational impact in relation to how learners think and learn. Some of the enhancements have included hot seats, fish bowls, podcasts, vodcasts, cyberspacial quests, gaming strategies such as crossword puzzles and Jeopardy as well as educational strategies requiring students to interact electronically with the authors of the course's text or internationally known ethicists.

Course Web Spaces: ANGEL and iTunes U

ANGEL is the course management system used by Penn State where my courses reside. Crossword puzzles in NURS 457 are added to help learners review prior to taking a quiz. Jeopardy-type games developed for NURS 200W are designed to facilitate learning the differences between qualitative and quantitative research. Learners won prizes.

iTunes U is Penn State's access to select course materials, lectures, seminars, athletic updates, and other valuable information related to the university.

Podcasting and Vodcasting on iTunesU for NURS 200W and NURS 457.

2. Advising

Currently, I advise 7 students. The majority of students seek advice concerning graduate programs since they have plans of study provided to them upon entrance into our nursing program. To date, 50 of my advisees have become advanced practice nurses in a range of specialties including informatics which was a direct result of having taken NURS 457.

3. Instructional Innovations

Initiated online nursing courses such as NURS 458 Ethics, added case studies, critical thinking, simulations and cyberspacial quests to courses. Instrumental in the development of the online RN to BS Nursing Program.

4. Extraordinary Efforts for Under-Represented Groups

I have encouraged several men to pursue their baccalaureate degree in nursing at Penn State.

5. Use of Disciplinary Research

When possible, NURS 200W learners have assisted in my research such as knowledge structuring. I incorporate my research into my teaching when appropriate based on the course and learners.

6. Evaluation Activities

Participated in the beta testing of online course evaluations at Penn State.

(continues)

Box 16-1 Dr. Dee McGonigle's TeP (continued)

7. Instructional Service

Have participated on instructional committees related to course review and sharing of intercampus teaching strategies. These efforts have been very time-consuming, up to 10 hours per week, but immensely rewarding to share perspectives and philosophies.

8. Learning About Teaching

Have attended and presented at numerous national and international conferences and have done extensive reading on thinking, knowledge structuring, learning theories, teaching strategies, instructional technologies and nursing informatics.

9. Extramural funding

Received over $800,000.00 in funding to promote NP training and instructional resources.

C. Teaching Evaluations

1. Student evaluations

The SRTE scores have been extremely positive in all of my courses. My Instructor Quality rating ranges from 6.0 to 6.93 on a scale form 0–7.

2. Peer Evaluation Summary

All peer teaching evaluations that I have received have been very favorable and commended my ability as an educator.

3. Colleague Teaching Letters

4. Teaching Awards Received

5. Self-Evaluation of Teaching Deficiencies

One of my major issues is in the amount of material that I try to cover. At times, it can be overwhelming especially since I teach technology-enhanced courses. I work very hard to create instructionally sound learning episodes and not overwhelm the learners.

D. Evaluations

In general, student evaluations of my courses have been extremely positive. Some of the written comments have stated "really met my needs", "treated me as a professional", "knows her stuff", "extremely knowledgeable", passionate about teaching", "loved this course", "learned a great deal", and "makes learning fun". My peer reviews have also been very complimentary especially in the integration of technologies.

E. Teaching Products

1. Student Successes

Many of my students/advisees have obtained their graduate degrees. Some students have advanced within their own facilities after enhancing their computer skills and informatics knowledge in the NURS 457 course I teach.

2. Teaching Materials

Available online in ANGEL.

F. Results

It would be difficult to exactly measure how much I contribute to the professional development of the nursing students who earn a baccalaureate in our School. Generally speaking, they do very well in their professional and academic careers.

G. Publications

I have one book on nursing informatics in progress and another one on teaching with technology under contract. Several book chapters, two workbooks and over 80 articles and proceedings. Also developed 20 Computer Assisted Instructional (CAI) Units. Some examples are below.

Books:

Mastrian, K., McGonigle, D., Mahan, W. & Bixler, B. (In Progress). Technological Innovations in Teaching and Learning (working title)

McGonigle, D. & Mastrian, K. (2009). Nursing Informatics and the foundation of knowledge. Sudbury, MA: Jones and Bartlett.

Workbooks:

McGonigle, D. (2006). Obstetric Emergencies (Part I). Brockton, MA: Western Schools.

McGonigle, D. (2006). Gynecologic Emergencies (Part II). Brockton, MA: Western Schools.

Book Chapters/Sections:

McGonigle, D. (2009). Personal Digital Assistants. In Handbook of Informatics for nurses and healthcare professionals (4th ed.), (Hebda, T. & Czar, P., Eds), Upper saddle river, NJ: Pearson, pp. 417–419.

McGonigle, D. & Mastrian, K. (2008). Information systems in case management. In Powell, S & Tahan, H. (Eds), CMSA Core Curriculum for Case Managers (2nd ed.), 292–323.

McGonigle, D., Mastrian, K. & Pyke, R. (2008). Telehealth and telenursing in case management. In Powell, S & Tahan, H. (Eds), CMSA Core Curriculum for Case Managers (2nd ed.), 324–346.

McGonigle, D., Mastrian, K., & Farcus, N. (2004). Usability Testing for Online Nursing Education: Thinking Aloud and Heuristic Evaluation. In Annual Review of Nursing Education, Volume 2 (Oermann, M. & Heinrich, K., Eds), NY: Springer, pp. 125–136.

Articles:

Mastrian, K. & McGonigle, D. (2008). Cognitive Informatics: An essential component of nursing technology design. Nursing Outlook, 56 (6), 332–333.

(continues)

Box 16-1 Dr. Dee McGonigle's TeP (continued)

Loeb, S, Penrod, J., Kolanowski, A., Hupcey, J., Haidet, K., Fick, D., McGonigle, D. & Yu, F. (2008). Creating Cross-disciplinary Research Alliances to Advance Nursing Science. Journal of Nursing Scholarship, 20 (2), 195–202.

Mastrian, K., McGonigle, D., & Pavlekovsky, K. (2007). Information Systems Case Management Practice Series: Part 3: Case Management IS Implementation Processes, Additional Technology Tools and Future Directions. Lippincott's Professional Case Management: The Leader in Evidence-Based Practice, *12*(5), 297–299.

McGonigle, D., Mastrian, K., & Pavlekovsky, K. (2007). Information Systems Case Management Practice Series: Part 2: Case Management IS Goals, Benefits, System Selection or Development. Lippincott's Professional Case Management: The Leader in Evidence-Based Practice, *12*(4), 239–241.

McGonigle, D., Mastrian, K., & Pavlekovsky, K. (2007). Ethical Realism Revisited. Lippincott's Inside Case Management, *12*(3), 183–187.

Mastrian, K., McGonigle, D., & Pavlekovsky, K. (2007). Information Systems Case Management Practice Series: Part 1: Introduction to Information Systems (IS) and Case Management IS. Lippincott's Professional Case Management: The Leader in Evidence-Based Practice, *12*(3), 181–183.

Mastrian, K., McGonigle, D., & Farcus, N. (2004). Webliography: Resources for case managers of the developmentally disabled. Lippincott's Case Management, 9 (6), 305–307.

Farcus, N., McGonigle, D., & Mastrian, K. (2004). Webliography: Interdisciplinary resources for geriatric case managers. Lippincott's Case Management, 9 (5), 244–245.

McGonigle, D. (1999). The WWW: Health-care information gold mine at your finger-tips. Journal of Care Management.

Mastrian, K. & McGonigle, D. (1999). Innovative Strategies to Promote Critical Thinking. Nurse Educator, 24 (1), 45–47.

McGonigle, D. & Wedge, K. (1998). Tips, tools, and techniques: Surfing the Internet. Nursing Case management, 3 (6), 240–246.

McGonigle, D. & Mastrian, K. (1998). Learning along the way: Cyberspacial quests. Nursing Outlook, 46 (2), 81–86.

Bio-Sketch

Dr. Dee McGonigle received her baccalaureate degree in nursing from Penn State University, a master's degree in nursing from Indiana University of Pennsylvania, and her doctorate in Foundations of Education from the University of Pittsburgh. She is the Editor-in-Chief of the Online Journal of Nursing Informatics and a tenured, Associate Professor of Nursing and Information Sciences & Technology at Penn State University. She is actively involved in integrating active and collaborative learning strategies into traditional as well as on-line courses. Dr. McGonigle is interested in the educational impact of the human-technology interface. She is committed to the insightful analysis of ethical dilemmas brought about by this volatile information age. Dr. McGonigle's current areas of interest are in knowledge structuring, the ethical implementation of the care management process and healthcare informatics as well as the effect of the human-technology interface on job performance and information management.

Note: This is a template based on the requirements for a professional faculty teaching portfolio.

Visit Penn State University's e-portfolio support Web site at http://portfolio.psu.edu to access information a bout e-portfolio development and use.

and determine what they need and want from the learning episodes we create. Teaching and learning go hand in hand. As a teacher, Dr. McGonigle believes in a learner-centered approach, meaning that the instructor serves as the facilitator of student learning rather than presenter of information. Our distinctive teaching identity must come through loud and clear as one reads our TeP.

Box 16-2   TeP Tips

- Add to your TeP often based on your own personal needs.
- Remember that the TeP should reflect your work, skills, and knowledge; each addition should showcase your abilities.
- Keep your entries concise.
- Proofread your entries (this includes spelling and grammar checks) before you post them. When you connect for feedback, your reviewers should just be concerned with the content and you should not expect them to proofread for you.
- Review the thoughtful feedback you receive and incorporate as needed to create a potent TeP that truly reflects your individual talent.
- Refine your TeP based on the thoughtful feedback as soon as you review the comments. Do not wait since you might lose things that occurred to you in the moment if you return later. Once you enter the changes, reread and edit your refined entry.
- Do not hesitate to refine previous entries based on new knowledge or changes that have taken place subsequently; this should be a work in progress.

For more information, read the article: Overview of e-Portfolios at http://www.educause.edu/ir/library/pdf/ELI3001.pdf (Accessed June 29, 2009).

The TeP reflects our assessment and improvement processes. It evidences how we view teaching and learning, while planning for, monitoring, and sharing evidence related to teaching, learning, and performance. Developing our TeP requires that we collect, select, reflect, and connect. In the TeP environment that we create, we must collect our work or evidence in digital form, organize it, and select from our own unique pool of evidence what we choose to feature. It is through our reflection or reflective commentary that we describe why we feel this evidence is important, taking our TeP to the next level. Finally, we connect or network by sharing our TeP to receive feedback to further enhance our portfolio.

TePs for Faculty and Student Assessment

Assessment strategies for using e-Portfolios will continue to evolve with the technology. Two examples of e-Portfolio systems that facilitate the collection, presentation, and dissemination or sharing of e-Portfolio materials are ANGEL e-Portfolio and iWebfolio. As Johnson (2009) points out:

> Portfolios can be particularly helpful in areas where higher-level thinking and analysis are essential. For instance, being a good doctor is more than being able to get high scores on exams. Doctors need to be able to collect information, analyze the information presented, relate it to past experience, apply related knowledge, evaluate various options and from this present a diagnosis and a plan of action. In short, doctors need to be able to think critically and make informed decisions. In learning to become a doctor, portfolios can be used to capture, support and improve this type of thinking as it develops. Like the artist, the medical student can connect, share and present cases and findings and include with this evidence the reflective commentary that serves to unveil how they arrived at their decision, what information or experiences were vital, and how their action plan evolved. (pp. 386–387).

An additional use of an e-Portfolio is illustrated by the allocation of e-Portfolio space by the State of Minnesota to each of its citizens to, "reach their career and education goals" (eFolio Minnesota, n.d.). "In the context of a knowledge society, where being information literate is critical, the portfolio can provide an opportunity to demonstrate one's ability to collect, organi[z]e, interpret and reflect on documents and sources of information." (European Institute for E-Learning, n.d., para. 1)

Web-based technologies will continue to evolve and develop better ways to support an individual's ability to articulate personalized representations of who they are and what they are doing. The assessment questions themselves have not changed, but the ability to support the reflective thinking process and the sharing of results with others through electronic portfolios have greatly enhanced the assessment process. TePs are truly the best mechanism to reflect how educators and learners are performing. Educators clarify and evaluate educational objectives, plan for instruction, devise assignments or tasks, motivate and engage our students, provide guidance and feedback based on our assessment strategies for learning, and measure their progress. Learners assimilate the content, participate in the learning process, and assess their own learning as individuals and in the context of their learning peers. As TePs extend into all facets of education, assessment techniques and reporting structures will need to be revised to fully utilize this robust assessment tool.

Conclusion

TePs are a potent way to assess the teacher's progress, achievement, and development; they can reflect the teaching persona from the classroom through the attainment of career goals. They provide an easy, portable format for viewing a teacher's work that is not restricted to the linear paper-based evaluative materials of the past. The mobile digital format truly supports lifelong learning and professional growth and development along with responsibility, accountability, and assessment.

The rationale for using portfolios as assessment tools for both teachers and learners is evident. Students can showcase their learning in a portfolio and we can use the portfolio as evidence of learning and program outcomes. Just as we assess our learners, we too must assess our own skills while our students and administrators also assess us. We were once the keepers of the assessment and now we are only a component. The TeP is a self assessment exercise that is grounded when we connect and receive feedback from our students, colleagues, peers, administrators, and friends and family.

Learning Application

1. What are the top five pieces of evidence that you would select to be featured in your own TeP? Why would you select these pieces of evidence? What was it about them that made you think they would represent who you are?
2. Take the first steps toward improving your teaching game! Begin to develop your TeP and remember that even small advances move us toward our goals.

References

Banta, T. W., Lund, J. P., Black, K. E., & Oblander, F. W. (1996). *Assessment in practice: Putting principles to work on college campuses.* San Francisco: Jossey-Bass.

Carter, D. (2002, June). Quotes on Assessment. Available at: http://wku.edu/teaching/db/quotes/byassess.php. Accessed December 18, 2009.

Dick, W., & Carey, L. (1996). *The systematic design of instruction* (4th ed.). New York, NY: Longman.

Dressel, P. (1983). *Grades: One more tilt at the windmill.* In A. W. Chickering (Ed.), Bulletin (p. 12). Memphis: Memphis State University Center for the Study of Higher Education.

eFolio Minnesota (n.d.). Welcome page. Available at: http://www.efoliominnesota.com/. Accessed August 29, 2007.

European Institute for E-Learning (EIfEL). (n.d.). Why do we need an ePortfolio? Available at: http://www.eife-l.org/publications/eportfolio/. Accessed August 29, 2007.

Johnson, G. (2009). E-Portfolios: Processing and disseminating of professional accomplishments. In D. McGonigle & K. Mastrian (Eds.), *Nursing Informatics and the foundation of knowledge* (pp. 385–393). Sudbury, MA: Jones and Bartlett.

Morrison, G. R., Ross, S. M., & Kemp, J. E. (2004). *Designing effective instruction* (4th ed.). Hoboken, NJ: John Wiley & Sons.

Suskie, L. (2005). Quotes on assessment. Available at: http://wku.edu/teaching/db/quotes/byassess.php. Accessed December 18, 2009.

On the Horizon

SECTION

IV

The two chapters in this section are designed to get you to imagine future transformations in education as technology tools evolve, knowledge expands, and students change. In Chapter 17, you will learn more about the knowledge era and how it may transform education through the emphasis on collaboration, knowledge discovery, and knowledge sharing. You will learn about the importance of developing learning communities for your students to collaborate and to build and share knowledge. Communities of practice are also discussed in Chapter 17 as means of connecting practitioners with others in their specific fields of practice.

Chapter 18 is focused on possible future technology that may be useful for engaging the students of the future who will surely differ from our current students. Characteristics of future students are predicted and special emphasis is given to a discussion of personal learning environments that allow for diagnosis of learning types and the prescription of individualized learning modules designed by a learner's needs. While the endless potentials of future education technologies are fascinating and exciting to imagine, we urge you to use the learning and instructional design theories presented in the book as you embrace these new technologies to design potent and compelling learning episodes.

CHAPTER 17

Knowledge Era Communities of Practice and Learning

Food For Thought

"It is probably true quite generally that in the history of human thinking the most fruitful developments frequently take place at those points where two different lines of thought meet. These lines may have their roots in quite different parts of human culture, in different times or different cultural environments or different religious traditions: hence if they actually meet, that is, if they are at least so much related to each other that a real interaction can take place, then one may hope that new and interesting developments may follow."

Werner Heisenberg, 1901–1976

Key Words

Avatars	Knowledge management (KM)
Cohort	Learning communities
Community of practice (CoP)	Navigationism
Knowledge era	Team

Objectives

The educator will be able to describe the characteristics of the knowledge era.
The educator will be able to describe learning and practice communities.
The educator will be able to relate knowledge era skills to learning and practice communities.
The educator will explore selected strategies for creating, building, and sustaining online learning communities.
Presented with a virtual course scenario, the educator will be able to identify at least two ways to build and sustain a learning community.
The educator will seek a community of practice (CoP).

Introduction

The connectedness afforded by information technology has dramatically changed the ways in which people acquire, process, generate, and disseminate knowledge to develop their personal knowledge foundation. In addition, information and knowledge are expanding at exponential rates. Marsick (1998) suggests old ideas and frames of reference learned in formal education may not be appropriate for application in the knowledge era. Today's citizens often find themselves challenged to learn continuously and are increasingly turning to **learning communities** and communities of practice as ways to generate, process, and share knowledge and ideas appropriate to their education, work, and lives. In this chapter, we will discuss two main types of communities, learning communities and communities of practice, differentiated on the basis of when and where these are used. For the purposes of this discussion, learning communities are those that are largely organized around a formal educational experience and communities of practice are those connections that are formally organized or that develop more informally to meet occupational, global, or personal knowledge-building needs.

Knowledge Era

Knowledge-related references abound in the scholarly and popular literature. Before we can talk effectively about learning communities and communities of practice, we need to first explore the important concepts related to knowledge and the **knowledge era.** Bertels and Savage (1999) propose that our society is evolving from the industrial era and moving toward a knowledge-based economy that will value knowledge and intellectual capital recognizing knowledge workers for both what they can do and what they know. This is in stark contrast to the narrowly defined work tasks and hierarchical organizations prevalent in the industrial era. Atkin (1999) agrees,

> Work requiring unskilled [labor] is disappearing, work that was once considered to be semi-skilled is now highly skilled in terms of design, materials and technology use, teamwork and range of skills required. All human work has a much higher knowledge component, is at a much higher level of intellectual skill and learning skill. (p. 9)

In a report from the New Zealand Council for Educational Research (NZCER, 2009) titled The Knowledge Age, the shifting organization identifies agrarian and preindustrial knowledge as "know-how," industrial age knowledge as "know-what," and knowledge for the knowledge era as "know what" knowledge, used as a resource to do things differently and better, and is the basis for creating new knowledge. This report further explains and defines knowledge era knowledge:

> Knowledge is no longer being thought of as 'stuff' that is developed (and stored) in the minds of experts, represented in books, and classified into disciplines. Instead, it is now thought of as being like a form of *energy*, as a system of networks and flows—something that *does* things, or makes things happen. Knowledge Age knowledge is defined—and valued—not for what it *is*, but for what it can *do*. It is produced, not by individual experts, but by 'collectivi[z]ing intelligence'—that is, groups of people with complementary expertise who collaborate for specific purposes. (para. 3).

As we have emphasized repeatedly in this text, critical thinking, teamwork, and collaboration skills will be important to the knowledge workers of the future.

Clearly, there are important implications for the transformation of education in the knowledge era. Scardamalia and Bereiter (in press) believe that educating for the knowledge age can be thought of as a developmental trajectory spanning "the natural inquisitiveness of the young child to the disciplined creativity of the mature knowledge producer" (para. 2). They advocate specific knowledge-building education techniques that recognize knowledge as a social construction.

That is, formal education activities must incorporate project-based learning assignments that incorporate and help students to hone collaboration, knowledge sharing, and knowledge discovery skills. They define knowledge building as "as the production and continual improvement of ideas of value to a community, through means that increase the likelihood that what the community accomplishes will be greater than the sum of individual contributions and part of broader cultural efforts" (para. 4).

The literature related to **knowledge management (KM)** for organizations also emphasizes collaboration as an important performance-enhancing strategy. Gorelick and Tantawy-Monsou (2005) discuss ways to improve performance in organizations by utilizing a KM approach that integrates people, processes, and technology. They suggest that organizations who are effective users of KM are "learning organizations" and that the use of KM "promotes a collaborative environment for capturing and sharing existing knowledge, creates opportunities to generate new knowledge, and provides the tools and approaches needed to apply what the organization knows in its efforts to meet its strategic goals" (p. 128).

While Brown (2006) also embraces the idea of social construction of knowledge, he argues that **navigationism** (ability to navigate through complex information spaces and make sense of the knowledge uncovered) is an important skill for the future. He further advocates participation in a **community of practice (CoP)** to enable learners and knowledge workers to co-construct new meanings and develop consensual knowledge through collaboration. Brown outlines important skills and competencies for learners in the future in a navigational paradigm:

- The ability (know-how and know-where) to find relevant and up-to-date information, as well as the skills required to contribute meaningfully to the knowledge production process. This includes the mastery of networking skills and skills required to be part of and contribute meaningfully to communities of practice and communities of learning. This implies that the basic communication, negotiation, and social skills should be in place.
- The ability to identify, analyze, synthesize, and evaluate connections and patterns.
- The ability to contextualize and integrate information across different forms of information.
- The ability to reconfigure, re-present, and communicate information.

- The ability to manage information (identify, analyze, organize, classify, assess, and evaluate).
- The ability to distinguish between meaningful and irrelevant information for the specific task at hand or problem to be solved.
- The ability to distinguish between valid alternate views and fundamentally flawed information.
- The ability to make sense of things and to have chaos management skills (p. 116).

Brown urges educational institutions to ensure that learners develop skills to be effective collaborators and networkers in order to survive in the knowledge era.

Communities of Practice

Developing and sustaining CoP in work environments are beyond the main scope of this chapter. However, educators need to understand how the effective collaboration skills that learners acquire in learning communities during their formal education may promote the development of CoPs in their future professional lives. We will confine our remarks here to a brief overview of this important and emerging trend for work in the knowledge era. Wenger (2006) defines a CoP: "Communities of practice are groups of people who share a concern or a passion for something they do and learn how to do it better as they interact regularly" (para. 1). He suggests that CoPs have three important characteristics: the domain, the community, and the practice. Wenger defines a domain as a shared interest about which people are passionate and possess some competence related to the domain. The community aspect relates to the joint activities that are undertaken by the group to build relationships and build knowledge about the domain. The practice denotes that the members of the community are practitioners of something and through the CoP develop and share resources, knowledge, and solutions to problems. The recent improvement of Internet-based communications technologies has the potential to promote the global expansion of CoPs.

Nursing is a profession that is particularly suited to the development of CoPs, especially in light of new knowledge generated and disseminated every day. The many nursing LISTSERVs are evidence of the growing practice of sharing knowledge in a CoP. Caring, a nursing informatics organization, has a very active LISTSERV where members post questions to other members and request information and experiences related to informatics. For example, a member of the list might ask others about their experiences related to a specific issue in implementing a barcode medication administration system, or about training procedures for implementing an electronic medical record. One of the difficulties with a LISTSERV as a CoP is that the discussion is not moderated; so many threads on the same topic could be running simultaneously. An example of a well-organized and global CoP is the Cochrane Collaboration (http://www.cochrane.org/) an international organization that promotes and supports collaboration among healthcare professionals to develop evidence-based practice recommendations for healthcare interventions. A nursing practice council within a healthcare organization is also an example of a CoP. In the future, we hope that the use of CoPs in nursing will grow beyond knowledge sharing and promote more knowledge discovery and sense making.

Learning Communities

This text is designed to teach you how to integrate technologic innovations into your teaching repertoire. As we increasingly move to blended and online teaching environments, it is important to consider how the learner is connected to the course, the professor, and students. Consider that as we have learners working together in our face-to-face courses, it becomes apparent that the presence issue enhances the cohesion of the class. In the online or virtual educational arena, presence is often an abstraction and the majority of learners may not actively interact. In other settings, learners interact by texting, using audio and video modalities, or in some learning episodes, learners may virtually engage in activities as **avatars**, which are online representations of human forms. We encourage you to explore the concept of learning communities and to implement strategies designed to create, build, and sustain them. Building and nurturing learning communities is not a new concept but must now be reconsidered in light of online learning environments that tend to isolate learners if the learning episodes are not constructed appropriately. As we discover more and more about how people think and learn, it becomes imperative that we develop learning communities that promote those activities and behaviors that enhance learning and performance through collaboration.

An online learning community garners mutual support for the common goals of learning and performing. It is the educator's challenge to foster, enhance, and nurture the learner's experience and learning in a learning community. Educators have been discussing the idea of learning communities for quite some time.

One barrier is that learners may not understand the importance of building a learning community, and thus they may resist the online collaborations with other learners. Many colleagues say that building a learning community is only possible when you have a **cohort** (same group) in a program of study online rather than individuals who take online courses with different classmates over time. We would argue that it is extremely important to build learning communities in every learning episode we design—everyone committed to the learning should be part of the community. We must create learning communities that support and nurture the members to facilitate a sense of belonging and learner engagement in the learning process. In each learning episode that you create, you should carefully consider the community culture that is reflected within the learning environment. In a community, the members expect to work together for the mutual betterment of the community as a whole. In a course setting, the learning community's members expect to work collectively to learn together and enhance their performance. Just as in a **team** (together everyone achieves more), the learning community setting and roles assumed by the learners show that they are prepared to take on and engage in activities that support the common goal of mutual learning. According to Wikipedia (2008),

> An online learning community is a common place on the Internet that addresses the learning needs of its members through proactive and collaborative partnerships. Through social networking and computer-mediated communication, people work as a community to achieve a shared learning objective. Learning objectives may be proposed by an instructor or may arise out of discussions between participants that reflect personal interests. In an online community, people communicate via textual discussion (synchronous or asynchronous), audio, video, or other Internet-supported devices. Blogs blend personal journaling with social networking to create [environments] rich with opportunities for reflection.

Wikipedia itself is written and organized by an online community rather than just random individuals.

The concepts of learning communities and interactivity are enhanced when there is also a relationship for supporting, nurturing, and sustaining formed as the learner connects with the educator. Therefore, as we venture into new educational territories prompted and evolved by the technologies that serve them, we must remain cognizant of the need for learners to feel connected and have a sense of community. The emerging technologies are changing learning communities and we must adapt our learning episodes to engage the learner and enhance the learning experience. According to The Washington Center (n.d.), "Students involved in learning communities become more intellectually mature and responsible for their own learning and develop the capacity to care about the learning of their peers" (para. 9). This is so important because we expect our learners to carry this community kinship through to their work settings in the form of CoPs.

Creating, Building, and Sustaining Online Learning Communities

There are various strategies that educators can implement to create, build, and sustain learning communities. Two specific strategies are student-to-student interaction and team activities. Guidelines for developing each of these strategies that can be used to promote online learning communities follow.

Establishing Guidelines for Student-to-Student Interaction

Blogs and threaded discussions are two ways to easily promote student-to-student interaction. Whether blogs or threaded discussions are used, students should be provided with guidelines for proper etiquette, or netiquette, as is it known in the online environment.

Sample guidelines include:

- Treat everyone with respect; everyone's opinion is important.
- Remember to provide rationale for your comments and responses.
- Never criticize another person, but instead, state your position.
- Always add to the discussion with thoughtful contributions. Contributions such as, "I agree" are not acceptable to be considered as input into the threaded discussion.

- Tune in frequently. You should enter the discussion at least every other day and preferably every day to enhance the dialogue and exchange of ideas and knowledge.
- Always proofread your entries before you post them. This is best done by compiling (saving often) your responses in a word processing document so you can use the spell-checker feature, and then copying and pasting them into the discussion forum.
- Your subject line should indicate your post's main theme or idea.
- Always remember that the people you are dialoguing with are just reading text so be careful not to include anything that could be considered offensive by another member of your team. Since there are no facial expressions, gestures, or other nonverbal communication to judge, your meaning must come through only in text format.
- To stay on topic in a threaded discussion, reply in the same thread so you keep the discussion going.

Establishing Guidelines for Teams

In your role of instructor, if you are going to have learning teams, it is extremely important to provide information about teaming—not only the expectations you have for the team, but also the expectations members should have of other team members.

For example, when creating student teams, have them do the following:

- Assign specific readings about teams and team membership responsibilities.
- Complete a peer team assessment form developed to have each learner evaluate each team member's performance, including his or her own.
- Choose a team representative who is responsible for interfacing between the instructor and the team throughout the educational episode. This is similar to the committee chairperson who would be responsible for interacting with the executive team in a work setting.
- Initiate divorce proceedings if team members are having an issue with one of their members.

Refer to Appendix A for an example of guidelines that could be provided to student teams. In addition to providing these guidelines, it is also important for the educator to meet with each team in a live and synchronous format to help them begin their team activities. Our challenge as educators is to bring the richness of community to our learning episodes. We must engage our learners and fuel their fire to learn through communicating, collaborating, supporting, and nurturing one another throughout the learning process.

Global Learning Communities

Global CoPs are developing on many fronts. Corporations and professional groups are recognizing the advantages of interacting globally to exchange ideas and develop knowledge and cross-cultural understanding that will serve the evolving global economies in the knowledge era. Consider the richness of experiences that could be afforded your students by developing a global learning community in a course. One way to accomplish this is to contact a nursing instructor in another country and brainstorm learning assignments that feature online collaboration between your students. For example, you could jointly develop a family case study that each of the student groups would analyze separately and develop a nursing intervention plan. Students could then examine the plans comparing approaches and discuss similarities and differences in approaches and how these relate to their respective cultures (particularly family roles and responsibilities) and the opportunities or constraints in each of the healthcare systems. The potential for learning in this example is vast, and some aspects may be quite serendipitous.

Putting It All Together

Learning communities develop and grow based on the commitment of their members. As an educator, you must understand the individual learner's needs and learning style. The learner must be open and involved in this process. Your personality, teaching skills, and repertoire will also have a direct effect on the strategies and methods you choose to build, nurture, and sustain your learning communities. Building and sustaining learning communities require an investment and commitment from both you as the teacher and also from the learners who must become active participants in the development and nurturing of their own learning community.

Mahan and McGonigle (authors of this text) advocated the use of these six Rs: reflect, reveal, reassess, responsibility, requisite, and rubric in a graduate education course. Reflect on what you would like to accomplish in the learning episode. Reveal your learning goals. Reassess each goal and formulate every step necessary to meet each learning goal. Delineate responsibility for achieving the learning goals. Establish a requisite timetable for meeting the goals. Finally, determine rubric criteria for each of the learning goals and use these to evaluate achievement.

Conclusion

In summary, we hope that we have convinced you of the importance of attending to community as you construct your learning episodes. In order to engage learners fully in the educational experience and promote sharing, collaboration, and learning, consider ways to promote interaction in the learning community. As learners experience the positive effects of a learning community, perhaps they will recognize the potential benefits of joining practice communities in their respective fields. We believe that once learners connect to enhance their skills, knowledge, and wisdom, they will continue to seek these important connections as they develop in their professional lives. Please read more about the important concepts of CoPs and learning communities. We also urge you, the educator, to seek out and join a community of practice to enhance knowledge sharing and development in your professional life.

Learning Activity

Reflect on the technologies that you have learned about in this book and employed in your teaching. How have these technologies impacted your level of interactivity and connectedness, or enhanced your sense of team membership and community? Think about ways in which you could incorporate technologies into your learning episodes as a strategy for building a learning community that will extend beyond your educational episodes and ignite CoPs as your students enter the professional world.

References

Atkin, J. (1999). *Reconceptualising the curriculum for the knowledge era part 1: the challenge.* Available at: http://www.learning-by-design.com/papers/challenge_recon.pdf. Accessed December 18, 2009.

Bertels, T., & Savage, C. (1999). A research agenda for the knowledge era: The tough questions. *Knowledge and Process Management, 6*(4), 205–212.

Brown, T. (2006). Beyond constructivism: Navigationism in the knowledge era. *On the Horizon, 14*(3), 108–120.

Gorelick, C., & Tantawy-Monsou, B. (2005). For performance through learning, knowledge management is the critical practice. *The Learning Organization, 12*(2), 125–139.

Marsick, V. (1998). Transformative learning from experience in the knowledge era. *Daedalus, 127*(4), 119–136.

New Zealand Council for Educational Research (NZCER). (2009). The knowledge age. Available at: http://www.shiftingthinking.org/?page_id=58. Accessed July 28, 2009.

Scardamalia, M., & Bereiter, C. (in press). Knowledge Building. In *Encyclopedia of Education, Second Edition*. New York, NY: Macmillan Reference Library. Available at: http://www.ikit.org/fulltext/inpressKB.pdf. Accessed July 21, 2009.

The Washington Center (n.d.). *What are learning communities?* Available at: http://www.evergreen.edu/washcenter/lcfaq.htm#21. Accessed March 12, 2009.

Wenger, E. (2006, June). *Communities of practice a brief introduction*. Available at: http://www.ewenger.com/theory/index.htm. Accessed July 29, 2009.

Wikipedia. (2008). Online learning community. Available at: http://en.wikipedia.org/wiki/Online_learning_community. Accessed April 25, 2008.

Food For Thought

*"For tomorrow belongs to the people
who prepare for it today."*

African Proverb

Key Words

Blogs
Cloud computing
Course management systems (CMS)
Expert systems
Folksonomies
Learning management system (LMS)
Mashups

Open source
Personalized learning environment (PLE)
Semantic-aware applications
Smart objects
T3 connection
Web 2.0
Wikis

Objectives

The educator will be able to identify key trends that will most likely affect the use of
education technology in the future.

The educator will be able to list the technologies and concepts that relate to those
key trends.

The educator will be able to list how students are changing.
The educator will be able to identify ways in which educators can address the needs of current and future students.

Introduction

Nell walks up the steps of the Diamond building on State Campus. It's a nice day, and Nell quickly uses her Cyber-vision contacts, or "Cyves," to check the weather. Appearing before her in midair is a map of the local area, with weather data on her visual periphery. Even though the map looks all clear, she flicks her eyes toward the data, causing it to move into her center of vision. Sure enough, there is a 20% chance of rain in the evening. Bummer. Nell dismisses her private heads-up display with another flick of her eyes and proceeds into the building.

Nell steps into the classroom for the first time. She's early—only a few other students have preceded her. Sitting down, she again calls up her Cyves and checks her social networks. One friend is at the beach and broadcasting live a view of the tide coming in. Another is at work, lamenting the slow, archaic **T3 connection** he has to the Internet.

More students file in. Nell fires a quick note to her friend. "Archaic! You should see this classroom! Probably the same chairs my grandmother sat in!"

Hey!" her friend replies. "I read all about the Diamond building. It may look old, but it's outfitted with the latest stuff. Wait until you get one class in—you'll see!"

Nell takes a moment to scan the results of a smart scan she started last night on the upcoming gardening season. Correlated for her are a set of recommendations for her gardening efforts this year. It looks like it will be a dry season, so the tomato variety she grew 4 years ago will probably do well, although the report notes she only rated them a three out of five on her personal taste scale. The smart scan also lists a number of new tomato varieties she might want to use, inferred from her personal taste scale she's added to over the years.

Just then an older woman enters the room. She is dressed casually, but has an air of authority about her. "Must be the prof," thinks Nell. A quick scan with her Cyves confirms that she is the professor. Around the woman springs virtual data, visible only to Nell:

Name: Dr. Janice Stephenson
Occupation: Professor of Sociology, State University
Hobbies: Golfing, reading

The rest of the data is scrambled. Only those Dr. Stephenson has given rights to can view it. "Probably pictures of her cats," snorts Nell.

While Nell is sizing her professor up, the professor is doing the same to the entire class. A quick stare and a brief smile as she glances at Nell leaves her a bit disconcerted. "What did she read?" What DIDN'T she read? Oh boy."

"Welcome class!" begins Dr. Stephenson. As she speaks, a large video screen behind her springs to life, and an avatar of her uses sign language to also greet the class. The text of her voice is also visible. Nell realizes that everything is being recorded for all to view whenever they want. She wonders if a summary personalized to her learning styles will also be available.

"This class is an introduction to State U, but it's really more about how to make the most of your experiences here. Many of you probably think this classroom is old-fashioned, and until recently, you'd be correct! But take a closer look. Embedded in each chair is a full connection to the Internet. Just push the green button on the side—go ahead, it's OK," she prompts.

Nell pushes her button and sees her classmates doing the same. Sure enough, a virtual monitor and keyboard appear in the air before her. The chair must have read her public info, for it is displaying information just as she views it from her home computer.

"Now," Dr. Stephenson continues, "Most of you have Cyves, so you probably don't need this. But it's here for those that do. You might also notice that the chairs are highly mobile, automatically adjust to your contours, and can be configured in several ways. So breaking up into groups is easy. We can also pull up screens from the floor to partition the room off if need be. Lighting is controllable via several quadrants, making the room very flexible. Imagine what it was like for your parents in college. Can you believe some classrooms had no technology, the chairs were fixed to the floors, and people were actually *uncomfortable* as they learned! Amazing! Even the classrooms that had technology were limited. Usually only the professor had access to the video projectors and the Internet. In fact, some professors liked it that way! They actually discouraged students from bringing technology to class. I can't imagine how anyone could really learn without the constant access to information we now have."

"But I digress. Sure, we all know that learning happens many ways. Hopefully, you'll even find me useful as part of your learning experience! You also have access to sources of information that continue to astound me. Most important, you have access to each other. Remember that."

A man three seats to Nell's right raises his hand. "Yes, uh, Joe?" responds Dr. Stephenson.

"Meaning no disrespect, professor, but why do we need classrooms at all? We could all just meet virtually, couldn't we?"

"An excellent question, Joe! You're right—we could just meet virtually. We could use Cyves or our mobile devices. Yet despite all the wonderful technology we possess, people are still social creatures. We need to be with others, not all the time, but enough so that classrooms are still needed. For this class, we'll meet once a week here. The other two classes will be virtual. Other questions? Ah, I see Mary has posed a question on the backchannel for the class. For those of you new to all this, we use the technology to create another channel of information, a backchannel, as the class proceeds. It's a great way to strike while the fire is hot. In this case, our backchannel is simply text on a Web page we can easily display. Let's call it up now."

Dr. Stephenson proceeds to display the backchannel page on the video screen. It reads:

Mary: I know this is supposed to be an introduction to life as a student, but I'm a transfer student. Do I really need all this?

Dr. Stephenson smiles. "Thirty years ago, you would have been forced to sit through classes where I, the fount of all knowledge and goodness, would have imparted redundant knowledge into your head. Today, we have ways to avoid that! Remember the battery of tests and quizzes you took as part of your entrance process? They're not just busywork. We've used them to put information about you into our Learning Management System, Aether. The LMS will prescribe things to you here at State U. Things you might be interested in, things you definitely need, and for things you already know, you'll be given the chance to opt out of them. You will also receive instruction in the forms you like. For example if you like games and there is a game with a Creative Commons License attached to it so State U can use it legally, *and* it covers the content you need you'll be playing a game. So I believe for you, Mary, there will be some specialized assignments you'll receive—subject to my approval, of course. Maybe I'll even ask you to contribute your information and insights for future classes! Yes, this class and its information is more than just me. It's you! And you, and you, and you! You are all part of the process, so be prepared to be active participants in your learning, not just passive recipients."

Key Technologies That Will Affect Education

The above story was a tiny slice on the many possibilities the future holds. It does not begin to touch on the possibilities nanotechnology, cheap fusion power, or what embedded communication devices might bring to education. Instead, it concentrated on the more tangible possibilities that are logical extensions of what we can do today. The following key elements are alluded to in the story:

- Next-generation classrooms
- Web 2.0 technologies, social networking, collective intelligence, and user-created content
- Cloud computing
- Semantic-aware applications
- Smart objects
- Open source technologies
- Learning Management Systems (LMSs) and Personal Learning Environments (PLEs)
- Specialized educational modules delivered just in time
- Mobile devices
- Educational gaming, simulations, and virtual worlds

Each will be briefly discussed in the following paragraphs. First, let us examine some givens for the near future.

The growth of information will continue. It is now estimated that human knowledge doubles every 1 or 2 years (Biech, 2007). In part, this is due to our ability to share data that is now inexpensive and easy to obtain like never before.

Computers continue to increase in power while dropping in cost. Moore's Law states that computing power in a given chip doubles every 2 years (Wikipedia, 2009a). This points to an ever increasing level of ability for computation.

Bandwidth continues to increase, allowing faster access to information, and thus access to larger amounts of information in a given period of time. The number of connections between computers and systems continues to increase. Metcalfe's law implies that as the number of connections in a system increases, the value of the system increases due to the increased communication possibilities (Wikipedia, 2009b).

Both increased computing and bandwidth power facilitate access to learning materials anytime or anyplace. While this is not universally true yet as many countries lack the infrastructure and wealth to make this a reality, movement towards this ideal is slowly happening.

Technology will become more and more transparent to the user (Murray & Erdley, 2009). The upcoming generation of digital natives will use many electronic tools without the learning curve from which digital immigrants suffer. In addition, we are developing better user interfaces for electronic technologies that allow us to concentrate on using it rather than on learning how to use it. Finally, we are developing **smart objects** that provide us with data for decision-making purposes. Some new cars can e-mail you when they need servicing. We have motion sensors that turn on lights when we enter a room. There are running shoes that track our heart rate and other vital signs.

While all of this is both wonderful and fascinating, we must always strive to remember that it is not the technology, but the pedagogy and our use of them that should drive the use of technology in education. Engagement of the individual or group is the key for successful uses of educational technologies.

Next-Generation Classrooms

Next-generation classrooms will be more versatile physically and electronically. Physically, they will be far more versatile than the typical classroom of today. Instructors and students will be able to reconfigure room arrangements on the fly, from lecture styles to group work.

Electronically, the instructor and students will have the power of the world at their fingertips and will be able to use that power without fiddling with cables or projector. As Mr. Arbogast, a consultant that redesigned classrooms for Central Michigan University stated, "The goal is that no matter where you are in the space, you should have access to high-quality material, and it should be as easy as picking hot or cold on a faucet" (Carlson, 2004).

Web 2.0 Technologies, Social Networking, Collective Intelligence, and User-created Content

Web 2.0 is defined by Wikipedia as the second generation of Web development and Web design that facilitates information sharing and collaboration on the World Wide Web. The advent of Web 2.0 led to the development and evolution of Web-based communities, hosted services, and Web applications. Examples include social-networking sites, video-sharing sites, **wikis, blogs, mashups** and **folksonomies**. (Wikipedia, 2009c)

Web 2.0 technologies allow for rich interactions between faculty and students, and between students and other students. They enrich classroom discussions and activities via the backchannel, and they extend conversations beyond the classroom. They allow for personal expression and thus may introduce affective learning into otherwise purely cognitive learning situations.

Web 2.0 technologies also make it far easier to publish your knowledge for all to see. This enables faculty to keep courses current, make changes on the fly, and even invite their students to contribute to an ever growing base of knowledge centered on relevant course topics. In short, Web 2.0 technologies allow all to contribute to the learning experience.

Cloud Computing

Instead of storing everything on a local machine and then sending pieces of information to others or to the Web, all of your e-mail, bookmarks, and files are stored on robust servers connected to the Internet. That is one loose definition of **cloud computing**. It also refers to using data and resources external to you to perform computations locally.

Today we have access to tools such as Google Docs and Gliffy, programs that are Web-based so there is nothing to install. These tools also store your files on remote servers so you can access them from any Internet and Web-enabled device. While this does allow easy sharing of data, it also frees you from tying your data to one machine. In turn, this facilitates technologic transparency, assisting you in reducing the how questions so you can concentrate on what you wish to accomplish.

Semantic-Aware Applications

What if your applications could help you discover connections between ideas that might not be readily apparent? That is the idea behind **semantic-aware**

applications (Johnson, Levine, & Smith, 2009). These smart applications can also help you answer questions by pulling in data from a variety of resources and consolidating it, saving you time and effort. For example, if you do a Web search on "nursing innovations in the 1990s" you probably will receive links to a number of Web sites. It is up to you to examine each site, pull out the information you want, and then put it all together. The ideal semantically-aware application could do all that for you, freeing your time to think deeply about the subject. With so much data out there, and more being added each day, we will all need tools like this!

Smart Objects

Imagine you are on a spur-of-the-moment blind date. You know nothing about the person you are just now shaking hands with. Now imagine you had some way of pulling up information about that person right then and there. You could discover you are both avid gardeners and thus have a great topic to discuss over dinner. Conversely, you might discover your date is really into the vascular systems of slugs, and it is time to fake that emergency phone call!

Now imagine you are walking down the street in a strange city. As you look at the buildings to either side, you are able to pull up information about each one. There on the corner is a shabby-looking restaurant, but the average rating is 4.5 out of 5 stars, so you decide to try it.

Smart objects contain data about themselves, where and how they were made, what they are for, where they should be, and something about their environment (Johnson *et al.*, 2009). They can also share this data with other smart objects, including people.

In the near future, we may be fortunate enough to have a rich overlay of data on our perceptions that we can easily access. This, in turn, will facilitate better-informed decisions and save us time.

Open-Source and Open-Content Technologies

The Open Source Initiative (2009) defines **open-source** and open-content technologies as "a development method for software that harnesses the power of distributed peer review and transparency of process." While this defines a software development process, the open source concept is now being used to develop learning materials and objects released as open content, meaning you can use and possibly modify them for your teaching and learning purposes. So it is now possible to pull an excellent lesson off the Web and use it in your class, providing you follow the rules of use associated with that lesson or learning object. If you know of a great lesson or learning object, use it!

Creative Commons (http://creativecommons.org/) is an organization striving to assist those who wish to release their lessons and learning objects in the open. This organization has created several varieties of licenses you can attach to your works that protect your intellectual property according to your needs. At one extreme, you can release your works for others to use, change, or even make a profit on. At the other, you can allow others to download your work and share them with others as long as they mention you and link back to you; however, they cannot change them in any way or use them commercially.

Learning Management Systems (LMS) and Personal Learning Environments (PLE)

You may be familiar with **course management systems (CMSs)** such as Blackboard, WebCT, or ANGEL. These systems include informational tools, such as a syllabus and roster, social tools like discussion forums, quizzes and tests, and management tools such as grade books. In the future, CMSs will have all that, but will also include diagnosis and prescription capabilities to ensure a **personalized learning environment (PLE)**. Such environments are named **Learning management systems (LMSs)**, as they manage not only courses, but learning as well. While many systems today call themselves LMSs, they do not yet have the diagnosis and prescription systems.

Diagnosis may be accomplished via **expert systems** that monitor an individual's actions (time on task or quiz scores) to build a learner profile that is accessed to determine optimal learning sequences, adjust learning paths on the fly, and prescribe next steps for the learner. Diagnosis may also happen by asking individuals to determine their best learning styles. For example, via assessment and monitoring, the system may determine that a student is a visual learner with shown preferences for social interactions while learning. In that case, perhaps a virtual learning environment would be prescribed for some learning situations.

The end result of this behind-the-scenes observation of the individual is a personalized learning environment that meets the needs of the individual to result in an optimal learning experience.

Learners may also be actively involved in personalizing their own learning environment. Today it is possible to easily set up customized interfaces, sometimes called portals that give you access to the information you want. You can pull in data via Really Simple Syndication (RSS) feeds from many places. RSS is just a way to subscribe to a data flow, like a blog or news reports, so it shows up for you when and where you want it, as opposed to going to a site each day to browse for information. RSS readers, programs that allow you to pull in RSS feeds from multiple sources in one place, abound. Some of these readers now have primitive semantic awareness in that they will suggest to you other RSS feeds you may be interested in based on your current feeds. In the future, we will see more and more of this.

Specialized Educational Modules Delivered Just In Time

Tied to the concept of LMSs and PLEs is learning that happens when the learner wants it. It is commonly accepted that the learner better receives learning that is relevant to the learner's needs. By leveraging the diagnosis and prescription abilities of future LMSs, combining that with the delivery capabilities of PLEs and open source educational materials, it will be possible to cobble to together customized learning experiences on the fly, delivered when and where you need it.

Mobile Devices

The power of mobile devices such as cell phones continues to grow. Today, you can browse the Internet on these devices nearly as easily as you can on a desktop computer. Social networking tools are also available on them. Some LMSs are taking advantage of this. There can be little doubt that this trend will continue to grow. As The 2009 Horizon Report (Johnson *et al.*) states,

> New interfaces, the ability to run third-party applications, and location-awareness have all come to the mobile device in the past year, making it an ever more versatile tool that can be easily adapted to a host of tasks for learning, productivity, and social networking. (p. 4)

Educational Games, Simulations, and Virtual Worlds

The use of educational games, simulations, and virtual worlds for education continues to grow. A great deal of research effort and monies is being directed towards the discoveries of their best uses. As we discover best practices here, the power of technology increases to allow more powerful experiences, and learners come prepared to utilize these environments, we'll see more and more of them used for educational purposes (The New Media Consortium, 2007).

The Future Student

Although it is impossible to predict exactly what students will be like in the future, we do know that technology will play a huge role. We already have seen the impact of technologies like the Internet, video games, social networking sites; Web 2.0 tools; instant messenger; and gadgets, like mp3 players and smartphones.

Today's students, unlike any other generation, have access to technology early in life and during their formative years of growth and development. As a result, current college students, the Net Generation, have the following characteristics:

- Social
- Multitaskers
- Prefer visual information over text
- Learn through trial and error
- Short attention span

There is even evidence that suggests the structure and function of their brains are different from other generations. Studies have shown that game players can process visual information better, and have better perceptual vision and hand-eye coordination than those who do not play games (Tapscott, 2009).

Students entering college starting in 2012, the neo-millennials, are going to be more advanced due to the constant development of sophisticated technologies and their availability to the average middle-class American family. In addition to using a world-to-desktop interface like the Net Generation, this generation will also use multiuser virtual environments and mobile, virtual resources, which are psychologically immersive (Dede, 2005). They no longer see technology as an improvement to everyday life, it is now a seamless part of their everyday life. The neo-millennials:

- Are holistic learners instead of sequential learners, in that they prefer to look at the big picture rather than having information presented in pieces, in a sequential fashion;
- Are accustomed to personalizing their online environment;
- Have excellent visual-spatial abilities;
- Prefer learning in authentic contexts;
- Place importance in doing rather than in knowing, because an abundance of information is online, at their fingertips;
- Are fluent in many types of media.

As technology continues to progress and is easily available to the masses, students will continue to evolve and develop unique characteristics unlike we have seen in generations past. Thus, it is extremely important for educators to take steps now to examine their technology skills and teaching strategies. Specifically, educators should ask themselves the following questions:

- Am I aware of the newest technologies, specifically the ones that can influence learning?
- Do I provide opportunities for learners to choose their own path to reach desired learning objectives?
- Am I allowing learners to assist in selecting the learning objectives?
- Do I incorporate opportunities for collaborative learning?
- Do I use various forms of media and activities to accommodate different learning preferences?
- Am I using visual information where appropriate to replace text?
- Am I providing authentic activities and assignments?
- Do I provide guidance about how to filter information available online?

The traditional ways of teaching, which are based in behaviorist and cognitivist theories, are no longer effective. Their emphasis on sequential, step-by-step learning and reliance on teacher-created, measurable objectives do not meet the needs of today's learner. Thus, it can easily be foreseen that these traditional methods will only weaken and become obsolete as technologies advance and students continue to evolve. Teaching methods for current students and the neo-millennials should be rooted in constructivist theory, specifically situated cognition, which was covered in Chapter 6. Of course, as time progresses, yet unknown learning theories will replace even the constructivist theories.

Conclusion

We are living in an exciting time with all the advances in technology, but we must acknowledge that the presence of this technology early in students' lives will have huge consequences on their brain development, learning preferences, and classroom needs. We want to emphasize a point we made earlier, effective educators must always strive to remember that it is not the technologies; it is the pedagogies and our use of them that should drive technology use in education. Engagement of the individual or group is the key for successful uses of educational technologies.

Learning Activities

1. Envision a single learning activity for an individual or group in the year 2020. What are the technologies that might be used, and how would they be best used pedagogically? Write a short informal story that describes your vision.
2. Using an existing lesson, revise it so that it meets the needs of incoming students in 2012. Indicate what specifically you changed about the lesson and why you did it.

References

Biech, E. (2007). 10 tips, tools, and tactics for successful change management. Available at: http://astd2007.astd.org/PDFs/Handouts%20for%20Web/SU402.pdf. Accessed August 8, 2009.

Carlson, S. (2004, February 27). The next-generation classroom. *The Chronicle of Higher Education*, p. 26.

Dede, C. (2005). Planning for neomillennial learning styles: Implications for investments in technology and faculty. *EDUCAUSE Quarterly*, *28*(1), 7–12.

Johnson, L., Levine, A., & Smith, R. (2009). *The 2009 Horizon Report* (Chapter 10). Available at: http://wp.nmc.org/horizon2009/chapters/semantic-aware-apps/. Accessed August 11, 2009.

Murray, P., & Erdley, S. (2009). Emerging technologies and the generation of knowledge. In D. McGonigal & K. Mastrian (Eds.), *Nursing informatics and the foundation of knowledge* (pp. 397–420). Sudbury, MA: Jones and Barlett.

New Media Consortium (2007). Massively multiplayer educational gaming. In *The Horizon Report 2007 Edition*. Available at: http://wp.nmc.org/horizonproject/2007/massively-multiplayer-educational-gaming. Accessed August 11, 2009.

Open Source Initiative. (2009). Home page. Available at: http://www.opensource.org/. Accessed August 11, 2009.

Tapscott, D. (2009). *Grown up digital.* New York, NY: McGraw Hill.

Wikipedia (2009a). Moore's law. Available at: http://en.wikipedia.org/wiki/Moore%27s_law. Accessed August 6, 2009.

Wikipedia (2009b). Metcalfe's law. Available at: http://en.wikipedia.org/wiki/Metcalfe%27s_Law. Accessed August 6, 2009.

Wikipedia (2009c). Web 2.0. Available at: http://en.wikipedia.org/wiki/Web_2.0. Accessed August 6, 2009.

Exemplars for Integrating Technology in Nursing Education

SECTION

V

In this final section of the book, we will demonstrate the use of evolving educational technologies to create potent and compelling learning episodes for students to prepare them for practice in ever changing healthcare environments. Instead of separate chapters, this section is presented as a series of learning episode exemplars that are numbered sequentially. We hope that by sharing some of our favorite learning episodes, you will be inspired to use them as prototypes to create similar episodes that fit your particular curriculum. Within each of the exemplars we have provided a brief discussion linking the learning episode to The Essentials of Baccalaureate Education for Professional Nursing Practice (American Association of Colleges of Nursing, 2008).

Tying a specific learning theory to any of these exemplars is difficult. In real life, several theories may be inferred in these situations. In general, these exemplars exhibit constructivist processes, although situated cognition is necessarily a part of any case-based scenario, where the learner is drawn into an authentic situation and must define the problem. In some exemplars, flash cards are used, an indication of a behaviorist approach.

As you read through the exemplars, look for the following:

- From behaviorism:
  - Drill and practice activities
  - Activities that are situated "outside" the learner that produce a tangible, observable, and objective outcome
- From cognitivism:
  - Linking to prior knowledge

- Organized materials
- Feedback
- From humanism:
  - Promotion of self-direction and independence
  - Development of creativity and curiosity
  - Group work
- From constructivism:
  - Learning tools, such as performance support and information gathering tools
  - Modeling, coaching, and scaffolding
- From problem-based learning:
  - Guides, probes, and supports for student learning
  - Having students assume responsibility for learning
- From situated cognition, everyday cognition, and cognitive apprenticeships:
  - Modeling, coaching, and scaffolding
  - Promotion of metacognitive skills, such as reflection
  - Supports that enable teachers to track progress, assess products, access distributed sources of knowledge, and interact knowledgeably and collaboratively with individuals and groups

There are several key skill elements that we emphasize in the exemplars. First, we want our students to develop skill in critical thinking, that is, to get in the habit of paying close attention to their thinking and try to improve it by analyzing and evaluating it. As Paul and Elder (2006, p. xviii) suggest, "Critical thinking is the disciplined art of ensuring that you use the best thinking you are capable of in any set of circumstances." Huckabay (2009) demonstrates the relationship between the key elements of critical thinking and the nursing process, and urges faculty to consider explicitly how critical thinking skills are developed in their curricula. You will note that the learning episodes presented here require creative and critical thinking, and application of theories and principles from previous learning.

In addition to developing critical thinking habits, we also want our students to engage in reflective practice striving toward excellence. "Thinking about practice in the context of theoretical learning helps narrow the gap between theory and practice and puts learners in a continual learning cycle" (Horton-Deutsch & Sherwood, 2008, p. 947). We hope that by requiring students to write reflective journal entries, they will come to realize the value of reflective practice as a tool for professional development. "Reflection is about learning from experience, a critical aspect of knowledge development and a skill essential to leadership development" (Horton-Deutsch & Sherwood, 2008, p. 947). Tanner's (2006) clinical judgment model also emphasizes reflection by identifying two distinct types: reflection-in-action that occurs during engagement in an assignment, and reflection-on-action that occurs after the fact. In these exemplars, we emphasize the reflection-on-action element and agree that "Reflection-on-action and subsequent clinical learning completes the cycle; showing what nurses gain from their experience contributes to their ongoing clinical knowledge development and their capacity for clinical judgment in future situations" (Tanner, 2006, p. 209). We hope to demonstrate to our students the value of reflection and encourage them to engage in reflective thinking and practice.

We frequently ask our students to share and comment on each other's work, creating an atmosphere of collaboration rather than competition among students. It has been our experience that these teaming (refer to Appendix A for Teaming Guidelines) and collaboration elements of learning episodes essentially raise the bar for all students as students who struggle witness and ultimately benefit from the work of students who excel. Another aspect that students learn during team assignments is that everyone has something useful to contribute and that collaboration among professionals results in a far superior product than any one person can achieve alone. We hope that these lessons learned will carry over into professional practice.

Some of the exemplars presented here challenge students to analyze critical aspects of case-based scenarios. As Tanner (2009, p. 300) emphasizes,

> Case-based teaching holds great promise for helping learners develop habits of thought that the nursing profession has identified as central to practice—EBP [evidence-based practice], critical thinking, and clinical judgment—learning to draw on these skills in the context of realistic clinical situations. (p. 300)

We strive to make our cases as realistic as possible but also complex and challenging. Case analyses require critical thinking and application of theories and knowledge, challenging our students to make connections between theory and practice in a safe environment. We have found these case-based approaches to be quite effective in engaging our learners. We hope that you agree!

References

American Association of Colleges of Nursing, (2008, October 20). *The essentials of baccalaureate education for professional nursing practice.* Available at: http://www.aacn.nche.edu/Education/pdf/BaccEssentials08.pdf. Accessed June 16, 2009.

Huckabay, L. (2009). Clinical reasoned judgment and the nursing process. *Nursing Forum, 44*(2), 72–78.

Horton-Deutsch, S., & Sherwood, G. (2008, November). Reflection: An educational strategy to develop emotionally-competent nurse leaders. *Journal of Nursing Management, 16*(8), 946–954.

Paul, R., & Elder, L. (2006). *Critical thinking tools for taking charge of your learning and your life.* Upper Saddle River, NJ: Pearson Prentice Hall.

Tanner, C. (2006). Thinking like a nurse: A research-based model of clinical judgment in nursing. *Journal of Nursing Education, 45*(6), 204–211.

Tanner, C. (2009) The case for cases: A pedagogy for developing habits of thought. *Journal of Nursing Education, 48* (6), 299–300.

EXEMPLAR

I

Communication

What is therapeutic communication? Can we talk about it effectively or is it something that we recognize when we perform or observe it? This exemplar is designed to help students focus on therapeutic communication with an eye toward improving their long-term performance. As you will see in the long-term assignment associated with this lesson, we expect our students to blog about professional communication at least once every week during clinical rotations. The communications thread is one that should be ongoing throughout the education program, with the goal of reflecting each week on communication and striving to improve personal performance in this area. The blogs are part of the student's e-Portfolio and will provide a clear picture of student progress in this critical outcome area. We also want our students to be aware of bullying in the clinical arena and to be prepared to respond confidently and appropriately to these inappropriate behaviors. Part 2 of this exemplar includes an exercise related to bullying. Aspects of American Association for Colleges of Nursing's Essential VI: Interprofessional Communication and Collaboration for Improving Patient Health Outcomes is the focus of this lesson. Students are required to apply foundational knowledge, integrate concepts, and generate new knowledge about therapeutic communication. The reflective practice assignments help them understand that they must learn how to learn, and continuously apply new learning to their practice.

Objectives

■ Identify examples of positive and negative communication performed or observed in the clinical arena.

■ Analyze the examples thoroughly, identifying specific aspects of therapeutic communication such as active listening, reflection, open-ended questioning, recognition, encouragement, and offering of self.

■ Develop strategies for self-improvement related to communication skills in clinical practice.

Activities

Short-Term Assignment

1. Access the library's journal database and search for two scholarly articles related to therapeutic communication. Then, search on the Internet for at least two credible Web sites related to therapeutic communication. Prepare a short overview of the elements of therapeutic communication that you have identified from your sources.

2. View the short video of an actual nurse–patient interaction posted on the course management system.

3. Apply the concepts on therapeutic communication that you discovered in your searches to the video that you viewed. Prepare a summary of all of the therapeutic communication techniques you observed in the video.

4. Post your summary to the discussion forum in the course management system.

5. Review the posts of others and compare and contrast your responses to those of others.

Note to the reader: The power of this assignment is that the video is available for the students to view as needed as they are reflecting on what they saw and developing their individual response. It is also fine for the demo video to be less than perfect and even better if the students identify something that does not conform to what they have read or learned about therapeutic communication. The key is that we want the students to pay attention to therapeutic communication and apply principles to practice. By reading the responses of others and comparing them to their own, students may gain additional insights into therapeutic communication.

Long-Term Assignment

1. Keep an ongoing record of positive examples of therapeutic communication you have initiated or observed in the clinical setting in the blog section of your e-Portfolio. Describe examples of negative communication and how the situation or behaviors could have been changed to a positive therapeutic interaction. You must blog about at least one positive and one negative example during each clinical week for the remainder of your nursing education program. It is important for you to get in the habit of reflecting critically on your clinical practice performance.

2. During the last 2 weeks of the semester, develop a podcast with your team demonstrating one positive therapeutic communication episode from each team member based on real scenarios from the reflective practice blogs. Describe the scenario for each episode and why it was positive. Post your podcasts in the space provided.

3. Subscribe and listen to the other teams' podcasts.

Bullying in the Clinical Arena

1. View the short video on bullying posted in the course management system that depicts an incident of bullying by a doctor toward a nurse.

2. In your assigned team, find and build information on bullying to share with each other using Delicious (http://delicious.com/) a social bookmarking Web site.

3. Next, establish a team Wiki on Wet Paint (http://www.wetpaint.com/wiki) to develop a team script and the rationale for scenes you will use relating to collaboration among health teams.

4. Develop a bullying scenario in a 2-minute team video and launch it to the course management system with a description of the scenario and team-generated remedies for the bullying depicted.

5. View the other teams' videos and suggested remedies. Reflect on the other scenarios presented by your peers. Do you agree with their suggested remediation? Provide rationale for your perspective based on the information your team uncovered about bullying.

EXEMPLAR

II

Leadership and Quality Care

The leadership and quality care assignments relate to American Association of Colleges of Nursing's Essential II: Basic Organizational and Systems Leadership for Quality Care and Patient Safety. We want to prepare nurses who can think critically about the profession and identify strategies to enhance the nursing profession and positively impact patient care. The ultimate goal is to provide the best care possible for our patients. In these assignments, the learners must reflect on their own practice, opinions, and biases. The sharing of their work helps to promote a learning community and it enhances their reflective practice and critical thinking skills. We have also included the scoring rubrics for these assignments to illustrate the use of them as a way to direct student work.

Objectives

- Reflect on your own nursing practice and conduct a self-assessment of your practice.
- Assess others' practice reflections and identify common knowledge issues and themes that emerge from the collective summaries.
- Determine if variability in nursing education preparation for entry into practice is or is not a barrier to full professional status for nursing; provide rationale and documented support for your perspective.
- Determine if telenursing will enhance or negatively impact the nurse–patient relationship and the nursing profession and provide rationale and documented support for your perspective.

- Investigate the history of the nursing profession and the history of nursing education through cyberspace quests or scavenger hunts.
- Assess the state of nursing science, leadership, and patient care through cyberspace quests or scavenger hunts.
- Reflect on your experience as a nurse and a nursing leader to identify and analyze an issue that is likely to impact the nursing profession in the future.

Activities

Assignment 1: Summary of a Clinical Nursing Situation

1. Perform a self-assessment of your nursing practice and submit a summary of a clinical practice situation in which you were unhappy with your nursing practice. Describe the situation, specify the area of your discomfort, and suggest what you would do differently if confronted with a similar situation. Limit your discussion to 250 words.

2. Post your completed essay to the Critical Thinking I: Summary of a Clinical Nursing Situation discussion forum in the course management system. Posting your essay here will allow all members of the class to review postings and participate in meaningful discussion in the upcoming weeks.

3. Your submission will be graded according to the following scoring rubric: Exemplar Table 2-1.

Rubric: (20 possible points)

Exemplar Table 2-1

Criteria	0	2.5	5
Situation description	Does not describe the situation	Adequately describes the situation	Thoroughly describes the situation
Area of discomfort	Does not describe area of discomfort	Adequately describes area of discomfort	Thoroughly describes area of discomfort
Behavior now if confronted by similar situation	Does not describe what would be done differently if confronted with a similar situation	Adequately describes what would be done differently if confronted with a similar situation	Thoroughly describes what would be done differently if confronted with a similar situation
250-word parameter	Less than 50 words	Less than 100 words	Does not exceed 250-word parameter

Part 2

1. Access the discussion forum and read the submissions of your classmates.
2. Analyze the collective posts, answering the question: "What common clinical knowledge issues and themes emerge from the situations?" Summarize your findings, limiting your individual analysis to 250 words. Submit your completed essay to the Critical Thinking I: Individual Analysis Discussion Forum in the course management system.
3. Your submission will be graded according to the following scoring rubic: Exemplar Table 2-2.

Rubric: (20 possible points)

Exemplar Table 2-2

Criteria	0	5	10
Common clinical knowledge issues and themes emerge from the situations	Does not discuss and analyze cases submitted and/or does not answer the question: What common clinical knowledge issues and themes emerge from the situations?	Adequately discusses and analyzes cases submitted and answers the question: What common clinical knowledge issues and themes emerge from the situations?	Thoroughly discusses and analyzes cases submitted and answers the question: What common clinical knowledge issues and themes emerge from the situations?
250-word parameter	Less than 50 words	Less than 100 words	Does not exceed 250-word parameter

Assignment 2: Variability in Nursing Education

1. Choose one of the following viewpoints to defend:

   - Variability in education preparation for entry into practice is a barrier to full professional status for nursing.
   - Variability in educational preparation for entry into practice is not a barrier to full professional status for nursing.

2. Research information supporting the viewpoint you have chosen. From the literature (articles, books, online resources, interview, news stories, in-house newsletters) you review, create a response (no more than 250 words) that supports your viewpoint.

3. Post your response in the Critical Thinking II: Discussion Forum for the viewpoint that you have chosen.
4. Your submission will be graded according to the following scoring rubric: Exemplar Table 2-3.

Rubric: (30 possible points)

Exemplar Table 2-3

Criteria	0	5	10
Writes a two-sentence introduction explaining the viewpoint	Does not write the two-sentence explanation	The two sentences adequately explain why the viewpoint was chosen	The two sentences thoroughly explain why the viewpoint was chosen
Post information from the literature and other resources under the correct discussion forum using APA format by the due date	Does not post information from the literature, does not use APA formatting, or was not submitted by the due date	Does post but provides minimal information from the literature and other resources using APA format	Does post and provides high-quality information from the literature and other resources using APA format
250-word parameter (does not include two-sentence introduction)	Less than 50 words	Less than 100 words	Does not exceed 250-word parameter

Assignment 3

1. Choose one of the following viewpoints to investigate and defend:

   ■ Telenursing will negatively impact the nurse–patient relationship and the nursing profession.
   ■ Telenursing will enhance the nurse–patient relationship and the nursing profession.

2. Research information supporting your viewpoint. Analyze and synthesize the literature (articles, books, online resources, interview, news stories, in-house newsletters) you found to create a response (no more than 250 words) that supports your viewpoint.

3. Post your response to the Critical Thinking III: Discussion Forum for the viewpoint that you have chosen.

4. Your submission will be graded according to the following scoring rubic: Exemplar Table 2-4.

Rubric: (30 possible points)

Exemplar Table 2-4

Criteria	0	5	10
Convincing argument to support position and 250-word parameter submitted by the due date	Does not provide a convincing argument to support position, contains less than 50 words, or is not submitted by the due date	Adequately develops a convincing argument to support position, or contains less than 100 words	Thoroughly develops a convincing argument to support position, does not exceed 250-word parameter, and posted on time
Grammar and spelling	Improper use of grammar, or one or more words are misspelled	Improper use of grammar without any misspellings	Proper use of grammar without any misspellings
APA formatting	Does not use appropriate APA formatting	Has two or less errors in APA formatting	Has no APA formatting errors

Assignments 4: Cyberspace Quests

A cyberspace quest is like a scavenger hunt for information on the World Wide Web. You are required to find sites as described in each quest below. For each Web site found, provide the complete URL and a brief description of the information found there. Once a site has been posted, it may not be used by another student. The idea is to explore and share information related to nursing from many different sites on the Web.

- You will work alone. No one may assist you since the cyber patrol will frown [: ( ] on such behavior. It could cause you to be thrown into a cyber cell and never heard from again!
- For each item you scavenge, you must follow the example of how to submit a Web site.
- You must also follow any additional instructions for each specific quest.

By sharing your work with your classmates, you will end up with an annotated reference list for each topical area covered by the cyberspace quest missions.

Cyberspace Quest: Mission I

1. Find two sites related to the history of nursing as a profession.
2. Find two sites related to the history of nursing education.
3. Post your findings to the discussion forum provided in the course management system.
4. Your submission will be graded according to the following scoring rubic: Exemplar Table 2-5.

Exemplar Table 2-5

Criteria	0	5	10
Two nursing history Web sites and two history of nursing education Web sites	Does not submit any nursing Web sites, or the Web sites do not relate to the assigned topics	The Web sites relate to the assigned topics, but less than four Web sites are submitted	All of the Web sites are submitted and they relate to the assigned topics
Example for Web site submission	Does not follow the example provided for Web site submission	Follows the example provided for Web site submission but omits one or more of the required elements	Thoroughly follows the example provided for Web site submission

You may choose to submit all four sites in one posting, submit two postings (one for history of nursing as a profession and one for history of nursing education), or four separate postings. Be sure to include meaningful subject lines for each posting.

Rubric: (20 possible points)

Cyberspace Quest: Mission II

1. Find a site related to nursing theory.
2. Find a site related to cultural aspects of nursing practice.
3. Find a site related to healthcare reform and the impact on nursing.
4. Find a patient education site for a disease of your choice. Evaluate the accuracy of the information presented.
5. Post your responses to the discussion forum in the course management system.
6. Your submission will be graded according to the following scoring rubric: Exemplar Table 2-6.

Rubric: (20 possible points)

Exemplar Table 2-6

Criteria	0	5	10
Web site related to nursing theory, cultural aspects of nursing practice, healthcare reform and the impact on nursing, and a patient education site for a disease of your choice	Does not submit any nursing Web sites or the Web sites do not relate to the assigned topics	The Web sites relate to the assigned topics, but less than four Web sites were submitted, or does not accurately evaluate the information presented on the patient education Web site	All of the Web sites are submitted, they relate to the assigned topics, and the information presented on the patient education Web site is accurately evaluated
Example for Web site submission	Does not follow the example provided for Web site submission	Follows the example provided for Web site submission but omits one or more of the required elements	Thoroughly follows the example provided for Web site submission

Cyberspace Quest: Mission III

1. Identify and analyze an issue that is likely to impact the nursing profession in the future. Thoroughly explain the dynamics of the issue and why you think it will be an issue in the future.
2. Find three credible Web sites related to this issue and summarize how each Web site relates to the issue.
3. Your submission will be graded according to the following scoring rubic: Exemplar Table 2-7.

Rubric: (30 possible points)

Exemplar Table 2-7

Criteria	0	5	10
Future nursing issue	Does not develop a nursing issue for the future	Adequately develops a nursing issue for the future	Thoroughly develops a nursing issue for the future
Three nursing Web sites related to the future issue described	Does not submit any nursing Web sites or the Web sites do not relate to the future nursing issue	The Web sites relate to the future nursing issue but submits less than the three required Web sites	All of the Web sites are submitted and they relate to the future nursing issue
Example for Web site submission	Does not follow the example provided for Web site submission	Follows the example provided for Web site submission but omits one or more of the required elements	Thoroughly follows the example provided for Web site submission

EXEMPLAR III

Evidence-Based Practice (EBP)

Typically, evidence-based practice (EBP) is introduced in the research course or a nursing curriculum and embraced as an important outcome of nursing research. While EBP may be discussed in other courses, we need to remember that we model more than we say. EBP should be given the same weight as other concepts that thread through the curriculum if we want our students to grasp its importance. We must make sure that each nursing course addresses EBP so learners become comfortable assuming an EBP in their professional lives. This exemplar relates to American Association of Colleges of Nursing's Essential III: Scholarship for Evidence-Based Practice. There are two assignments included in this exemplar, the first is course-based and the second, contributed by Nedra Farcas, illustrates how EBP can be threaded through a curriculum with cross-course assignments.

Activities

Assignment 1: Course-Based EBP Assignment

The following scenario begins the EBP learning episode.

Last evening I assumed care for three ICU patients. One of the patients had been scheduled for a thoracentesis; however, the previous nurse had not written down the verbal orders nor had she informed me.

The physician came to the unit expecting the patient and equipment to be ready, but it wasn't. The patient was extremely upset with me; she did not want to hear that

I did not know the procedure was to be performed or that as a result of the lack of communication, new medication orders had not been enacted. The patient complained to the physician that the other nurse had known the procedure was to occur. I felt terrible.

Lesson Overview

This brief case study is a good example of the change of shift problems (handoffs) arising from our current method of reporting off to one another. This lesson will look at EBP as a means to improving patient care and influencing healthcare policy. EBP involves the use of the best available practices or evidence (what is known) to improve patient care and influence healthcare policy. Caveat: This evidence must be tempered by the clinical judgment of the healthcare professional actually providing the care. In other words, EBP is the clinical application of the best available evidence to the clinician's clinical judgment given the specific clinical situation, patient's circumstances, and preferences.

The ACE Star Model of knowledge transformation is a five-step systematic process for putting EBP into effect. Specifically, it helps one to make information from research findings more meaningful, so that the research can be used in direct patient care. The five points of the ACE Star Model include discovery, summary, translations, integration, and evaluation (Stevens, 2004).

Objectives

- Explain EBP and list the benefits of using EBP.
- List and describe the five points of the STAR model.
- Implement the STAR model with a real-world clinical problem framed using PICO.
- Conduct a literature review and synthesize the research findings into a single meaningful statement.
- Develop clinical practice guidelines.
- Formulate a plan to change individual and organizational practices through formal and informal channels.
- Evaluate the EBP based on patient health outcomes, provider and patient satisfaction, efficacy, efficiency, economic analysis, and health status impact.

EBP assists nurses in making clinical decisions using evidence from research. The ACE model provides a five-step systematic process for translating research findings into meaningful information to direct patient care.

Through the expertise of the clinicians, each patient in the actual practice setting is assessed where the patient exists with his or her own individuality, ideas, beliefs, values, intellectual capacity, and preferences. The clinician must weigh all of the situational variables as well as available evidence or best practices when making clinical decisions concerning individual patients. Therefore, EBP is the clinical application of the best available evidence to the clinician's clinical judgment given the specific clinical situation, patient's circumstances, and preferences.

Barriers to EBP exist. The main barrier is the translation of research or the know–do gap. There is a gap between those who know (researchers) and those who do (clinicians). We must focus on the translational needs of practicing nurses while making sure that the research is informed through practice as well.

The learner must apply EBP to actual clinical problems. Therefore, the learner is presented with a clinical problem and must follow each step of the ACE model to come up with an EBP solution.

Clinical Problem: Infection is a common problem in oncology patients. How can we prevent it?

This example provides the learners with a problem statement and introduces them to the model and how they should apply it to a clinical problem.

ACE Star Model

Step 1. Discovery: Ask the clinical question based on your identified problem.

State the problem as a question. Use PICO (patient population, intervention, comparison intervention, and outcome) to frame your question. For example: In adults (P), is music therapy (I) or massage therapy (C) more effective in reducing postoperative pain (O)? Complete a literature search to find three to four studies, and cite and include their references using APA style.

Step 2. Evidence summary: Synthesize the research into a single meaningful statement of the state of the science on this issue.

Synthesize all of the statements into one meaningful statement of the state of the science on this issue.

Step 3. Translation: State how you would translate this evidence into practice recommendations (clinical practice guidelines).

Step 4. Integration: State how you would change both individual and organizational practices through formal and informal channels.

Make sure that you address factors that affect the individual and organizational rate of adoption of the innovation as well as factors that affect integration of change into sustainable systems.

Step 5. Evaluation: Address how you would evaluate the EBP based on patient health outcomes, provider and patient satisfaction, efficacy, efficiency, economic analysis, and health status impact (quality improvement of health care).

For this EBP assignment, you must apply the STAR model to a clinical problem with your team. Therefore, you must reflect on your clinical practice areas and identify problems that need to be remedied. To complete the assignment, you must do the following:

- As a team, reach a consensus on the clinical issue or problem for which you will use EBP to affect a solution. Post your problem to the discussion forum. Clearly state your issue by giving it a title and thoroughly describing it.
- Apply the STAR model to your issue (Stevens, 2004). Collaborate on this project using your team's discussion forum and Google Docs.
- Prepare a final word document that clearly describes your problem and includes all five points of the ACE model. Each member of the team should use the rubric to ensure the group project contains all of the necessary elements (this rubric will be used by the instructor to grade your assignment).
- Finally, upload the final team document.

Reflect on how using the ACE model could impact you in your current position. Address the following questions. How will the model:

- Enhance your ability to make clinical decisions?
- Help you translate research results into evidence-based practice?
- Help you generate and disseminate knowledge?
- Facilitate your recognition and use of best practices?
- Enhance your nursing practice?

Finally, the learners must read all of the EBP projects submitted by the other teams and review their rationale as well as their supporting evidence. The learners must then critique their application of the model in relation to the problem.

Activity 2: Long-Term Evidence-Based Practice Assignment (Contributed by Nedra Farcas)

Weaving EBP throughout the curriculum is not an easy task. Some of the barriers include the different expectations from instructors of various courses, and changing student populations in multiple course sections. A blended accelerated 12-month RN to BS program with a cohort of students at Penn State University presents an opportunity to engage a group of students and a collaborative group of faculty in each step of the EBP process from the initial Nursing Transition course until the final capstone course in the curriculum. We will illustrate how the use of collaborative technology tools facilitates the implementation of this long-term assignment across a number of courses.

In the accelerated RN to BS curriculum, all courses are designed to include weekly onsite and online class sessions. Students who are unable to attend the onsite sessions have the option to participate live via Adobe Connect or to review the archived class session by logging onto a course-specific Web site. The onsite class sessions are also audio-recorded and available on iTunes as a downloadable podcast. The online sessions typically involve structured asynchronous class activities to be completed in the course management system or another Web-based application. This year-long, EBP assignment focuses on course objectives from six required nursing courses in the RN to BS curriculum that emphasize research, theory, practice, and technology. These objectives and related courses include:

- Applying critical thinking strategies in the analysis of issues that influence nursing today and the identification of future issues (Nursing Transition course).
- Identifying the relationships of nursing theory and research to professional nursing practice (Nursing Transition course).
- Identifying computer applications in the nursing profession (Nursing Informatics course).

- Demonstrating effective interaction in utilizing the computer for nursing applications in selected areas of nursing practice (Nursing Informatics course).
- Using coherent, comprehensive, and culturally sensitive communication techniques in oral and written form (Community and Family Health course).
- Analyzing biostatistic/epidemiologic data and nursing research findings to improve or enhance the delivery of nursing care to diverse populations in the community (Community and Family Health course).
- Identifying criteria for the evaluation of research for applicability to clinical practice (Nursing Research course).
- Identifying the process by which a researchable problem is formulated (Nursing Research course).
- Conducting a written review of the research literature on a given topic (Nursing Research course).
- Collaborating with colleagues in the design, implementation, and evaluation of nursing interventions (Adult Health course).
- Demonstrating interpersonal skills to support and guide clients, families, or significant others in the selection of appropriate health patterns (Adult Health course).
- Applying research and clinical guidelines promoting EBP in the nursing care of adults with complex health problems (Adult Health course).
- Demonstrating management of nursing care through appropriate use of leadership, change, systems, and group process concepts with families, population members, colleagues, and the multidisciplinary team (Capstone course).
- Acting to facilitate needed change in areas affecting the provision of nursing care to individuals, families, and aggregate populations (Capstone course).

Regardless of the model selected, EBP usually involves the common activities of identifying the problem; assessing internal data against established benchmarks; synthesizing the research; interviewing stakeholders; identifying an intervention; and developing, implementing, and evaluating a practice change. These activities are taught in each sequential course in the accelerated RN to BS curriculum as students develop, implement, and evaluate a collaborative EBP change.

During the required Nursing Informatics course, students learn the various technologies that may be useful in practice and in education. These include the principles and practices of developing a collaborative word document and PowerPoint presentation using Google presentation; the development of an e-Portfolio; the use of threaded discussions using chats, blogs, and discussion forums located in social networks; video conferencing using Adobe Connect, Skype, and iChat; social bookmarking using Web-based sites for storing, format-ting, and sharing Web and literature references; and development of educational materials using Web-based applications as well as Mac and PC software.

Identifying Problems of Interest

The Nursing Transition course focuses on concepts related to professional nursing, including the relationship among theory, research, and practice. Assign-ments in this course related to the EBP project include identifying problems in practice; examining nursing theories that may be helpful in examining the problems, and gathering resources for background information to describe and define the problems.

Students gather and brainstorm about problems in clinical practice that are common to all, and that require examination. Students record these brain-storming sessions in an online discussion forum located in the course manage-ment system and come to a consensus on one or more problems to address. Student teams form according to interests in a specific problem. The number of teams will vary, depending on the number of students in the class and the number of students interested in a specific problem. The class may agree to form one team to investigate one problem or form multiple teams to investigate different problems. Following the use of this initial text-based discussion forum, student teams have the option of continuing to use a text-based discussion format, or recorded voice boards or video conferencing for ongoing recorded discussions. If students meet for face-to-face discussions they record the meeting with a digital recorder and post as a podcast in a course-specific iTunes site.

Following a lesson on using an electronic library, student teams search for background information regarding the selected problem. They examine various perspectives of the problem, including their own viewpoints about the problem, as well as other supporting and contradictory viewpoints in the literature; vari-ables contributing to the problem, and alternative resolutions for the problem.

From this information, each team comes to a consensus about the problem statement and a position on the selected EBP problem. The students use Google Docs to write their introduction of the problem, the problem statement, the examination of the position, and the alternative viewpoints. The student group finalizes the document with a clear and concise statement of the problem to be examined.

Google Docs is an appropriate application to be used when developing a collaborative paper. It is a free Internet service and allows students to post their documents, share and edit the document in one place accessible by all members of the group. The instructor has the added advantage of viewing the history of revisions and knowing which students participated in developing and revising the document. The document is formatted in Word and can be saved, printed, or posted as a Web page.

During the Nursing Transition course, students are also introduced to nursing theories and related research in the development and verification of nursing theory. Students are assigned to examine a mid-range or practice theory that can be applied to the EBP problem. The students are encouraged to communicate with the theorist electronically about questions related to the theory or its usefulness in examining and defining the EBP problem. Communication tools vary and may include any of the following: e-mail, blog, Facebook, Twitter, discussion forum, Skype, or iChat (depending on the theorists' availability and willingness to communicate via one of these media formats). Phone conversations and regular mail are also options if these are the theorist's preferred methods of communication.

Finally, during the Nursing Transition course students search for and examine various EBP models and select a model to be used for their own EBP project. They develop a final proposal in Google Docs which includes the introduction of the problem, an organizing framework to use when looking at the problem, background information related to the problem, and a description of and rationale for the EBP model selected.

Student teams also select a social bookmarking site to share their Web references and comment on the Web sites they have identified that relate to their proposal development. The students will build information on this social bookmarking site throughout the accelerated RN to BS program. Students are also introduced to BibMe, an Internet site that helps them search, save, and format their reference citations for use in the paper.

Comparing Internal Data Against Benchmarks

The Community and Family Health course is a clinical course that focuses on the application of community and family health concepts. During this course students learn principles of family structure and process, group process, and patient and community education, as well as interviewing strategies and epidemiologic principles. Each of these learning activities provides an opportunity for the students to expand and enhance the ongoing EBP project. Students develop a collaborative relationship with an acute or community healthcare agency to complete the project. They identify benchmarks for comparing internal data, stakeholders to be interviewed (including patients and families), and establish stakeholder interview guides. They also examine various electronic educational activities formats that may be incorporated into an educational program related to the EBP project and presented to the collaborating agency. Finally, they identify internal data from the agency related to the EBP problem and compare the internal data with benchmarks they have identified through a Web search. This information is added to the evolving EBP proposal.

Appraising and Critiquing Research

The nursing research course focuses on research utilization as a component of the EBP project. Students expand the EBP proposal initiated in the Nursing Transition course as an integrative research review (IRR) proposal. The document is developed with the design, sampling, data collection, and analysis methods included. Students learn to conduct a search for research studies and critique the studies for utilization in practice. Students collaboratively develop a database entry form in Zoho (http://www.zoho.com) and enter their research study appraisals. A report is generated at the completion of the research course and students synthesize the results of their IRR.

Also during the Nursing Research course, students revise the stakeholder interview guides as necessary to include any additional questions based on evidence obtained from the research. They also participate as a team to develop and submit an application to request an expedited Institutional Review Board (IRB) determination of appropriate protection of human subjects for use in the next course in the curriculum when the stakeholder interviews are conducted.

Assessing Stakeholders

During the Adult Health course, students conduct interviews related to the EBP proposal using the interview guides developed in the community and family course. When conducting the interviews, students use a digital recorder and a digital pen to capture the information discussed during the interview. Students work in pairs for this activity as one conducts the interview and the other operates the electronic equipment. The information collected during the interviews is transcribed and reviewed by the members of the EBP team. The students have an opportunity to analyze quantitative data using Minitab and qualitative data using Invivo. During this course, students examine and analyze all information and identify a practice change recommendation. The final evidence is synthesized and presented to members of the collaborating agency. The presentation may be in the form of a PowerPoint or video presentation, which is shared with the collaborating agency during a scheduled meeting. During this meeting, the participants discuss the recommended practice change.

Developing, Implementing, and Evaluating a Practice Change

During the final Capstone course, students have the opportunity to develop, pilot, and evaluate an intervention with the collaborating agency. They develop a final report that is converted to a video file using the Mac application, iVideo; present it to the agency; and post the final report in their own e-Portfolios.

In summary, the courses in a baccalaureate nursing curriculum may afford students the opportunity to learn the process of developing, implementing, and evaluating an EBP project, while also developing technologic, collaborative, and project management skills.

References

Stevens, K. R. (2004). *ACE Star Model of EBP: Knowledge Transformation*. Available at: http://www.acestar.uthscsa.edu/Learn_model.htm. Accessed July 2, 2009.

A Case-Based Collaboration to Develop Ethics Expertise

The regulations related to the management of private healthcare information mandated by the Health Insurance Portability and Accountability Act (HIPAA) of 1996 provide a unique opportunity for nursing students to learn about and apply ethical principles. In this exemplar, we describe a course developed to help students gain expertise in ethical decision making related to managing health information. Using a constructivist approach to learning, we designed learning activities that encourage the learner to interpret and construct meaning from the information made available to them. The learning activities are designed to engage students actively in the content and require them to interpret, reflect, and apply the knowledge they have constructed in their individual analysis of a case as well as compare their case analysis to that of an ethics expert. A course development grant provided stipends for the ethics experts who contributed overviews of their ethics approaches, definitions of key ethics terms, answers to a frequently asked questions (FAQ) Web page, and analyses of the cases demonstrating the application of their particular ethics approach. After the students complete their analysis of a case, they are given the universal resource locator (URL) of a Web site that contains the expert's analysis of the case, hence, the designation of the course, Ethical Challenges of Healthcare Informatics as a case-based collaboration. Funding limitations dictate that the experts' contributions are static; however, we are exploring ways to incorporate live blogging with an expert into the course, which could be much more powerful for the students as they engaged with an expert to discuss a case. We are also considering ways to promote a cross-cultural or global exchange related to these cases among nursing students from other countries who have different privacy laws.

Since there may not always be clear-cut answers to these information management dilemmas experienced in health care, students benefit from practicing the systematic analysis required by the course. Comparing their analysis to that of an ethics expert helps them rethink their ideas and gain confidence in their abilities to arrive at an acceptable conclusion.

Once students have completed the course, they are expected to contribute at least one new ethical dilemma with an analysis to their e-Portfolio for each subsequent clinical rotation block, thus providing for an ethics curricular thread. The e-Portfolio contribution does not have to be limited to an information management issue, but can reflect one of the myriad ethics challenges a nurse might experience in practice. This ongoing requirement helps to ensure that students will grow and develop in their ethics expertise and remain cognizant of ethics dilemmas experienced in practice.

Objectives

- Explore models for ethics decision making and professional codes of conduct including advocacy and confidentiality.
- Identify and evaluate professional responsibilities for ethical use of healthcare informatics technology.
- Demonstrate critical thinking and intellectual responsibility.
- Examine the ethical implications of global healthcare informatics.
- Recognize ethical issues in healthcare informatics.
- Apply the concepts and theories of ethical analysis to ethical dilemmas in healthcare informatics.
- Synthesize an ethical framework for dealing with selected healthcare informatics dilemmas.
- Analyze practical ways of managing ethical problems in healthcare informatics.
- Work responsibly and effectively with teams and individuals.
- Demonstrate the ability to analyze problems, propose solutions, and make responsible decisions by the means of critical thinking and moral reasoning.

Activities

Lessons 1 and 2

Students begin the course by reading the articles posted in the electronic reserves in the course management system, and the content provided in the overview section on the course Web site that introduces the topics to be covered and provides summaries of the ethical principles and background information necessary for case analyses. Students also read the definitions section and the FAQ responses provided by the consulting experts. For Lesson 2, students explore the health information privacy regulations overview provided on the US Department of Health and Human Services Web site (http://www.hhs.gov/ocr/privacy/index.html) as part of this background information. In order to ensure that the students grasped the ethics overview and HIPAA content, they are required to answer a series of essay questions and submit these to the instructor for evaluation. Grasping the information contained in the overview section, the HIPAA review, and the related readings was critical to student success in the later case analyses. For this reason, if a student did not understand the concepts, the instructor would make specific suggestions for further reading and study and invite the student to rethink and resubmit the answers.

Lesson 3

Armed with the background information provided by the overview and HIPAA assignments, students were directed to study McGonigle's model for ethical decision making. The model breaks the process down into a series of steps for analysis. For a complete description of the model and its use, see McGonigle (2000). A brief overview of the model is presented here.

Examine the ethical dilemma.
Thoroughly comprehend the possible alternatives available.
Hypothesize ethical arguments.
Investigate, compare, and evaluate the arguments for each alternative.
Choose the alternative you would recommend.
Act on your chosen alternative.
Look at the ethical dilemma and examine outcomes while reflecting on the ethical decision.

Students were provided with a sample case and a complete case analysis to help them understand what was expected in the assignment. The sample case provided on the course Web site also had a completed evaluation rubric so that students would know how the analysis would be scored. The sample case analysis had a deliberate omission in the presentation so that the actual benefit of the scoring rubric would be evident to the student. After completing the preparatory activities, students chose one of the six case studies to analyze using the model provided. In the "T" step, students were asked to suggest three different alternative actions for each of the cases. For each of the alternatives, they were asked to identify good and bad consequences, whether or not any established rules would nullify the alternative action, the expected outcome of the alternative action, and the potential benefit or harm inherent in the proposed alternative action. The alternative action analysis requirement forced the students to consider that there may not be a completely right action, but that each identified alternative might have both positive and negative aspects. The alternative action analysis also prevented students from immediately latching on to a perspective without considering other ways of viewing the same dilemma. The case analysis was scored by the instructor using a scoring rubric, which, along with instructor comments, were directed back to the individual student. For an example of case analyses, please refer to Farcas, McGonigle, and Mastrian (2001a, 2001b).

Lesson 4

For this lesson, the instructor directs the student to the URL of the Web site that contains the ethical expert's analysis of the same case. Students review the expert's analysis and then submit a written compare and contrast analysis of their response to that of the expert's analysis of the case. Here is an example of a student's response comparing her analysis of a case to that of the expert's analysis. The case used in this assignment was:

> Dora N. is a utilization review coordinator for a busy metropolitan hospital. Part of her job entails finding community resources to help impaired patients manage more effectively in their homes. Transportation for impaired patients is one of the most difficult services for Dora to find in the local community.
>
> Dora's sister, Janice, recently opened a private escort service designed to provide transportation for impaired elders to doctor's offices and clinics. The business is growing very slowly and Janice confides her frustration to Dora.

Dora realizes that she can help her sister and solve her patient discharge problems by identifying potential clients from the hospital's database. In the next few weeks, Dora gives her sister the names and phone numbers of 10 recently discharged patients. Janice contacts the patients and solicits three of them for her escort service.

As you undertake your analysis, consider the following:

1. Identify the ethical issue involved.
2. Consider the case from Dora's perspective. What was she trying to accomplish for her clients?
3. If you were Dora's supervisor, what additional information would you gather?
4. Should disciplinary action be taken? Why or why not?
5. Is there an ethical way for Dora to connect her patients with her sister's escort service?

Compare and Contrast Assignment by Sherry Davis (used with permission.)

1. The expert discusses Dora's use of the patients' information without their permission. She also talks about the patients being a vulnerable population for her sister's business. I feel that I went into more detail or context regarding Dora using the patient's information such as the fact that it violates the HIPPA law, how it would benefit both herself in her position at work and how it would benefit her sister's business, and the possible negative effects of her actions on both her job position and her sister's business. I do agree with the expert with the statement that ethical decision making cannot be accomplished if we deal with issues because issues are without a context.
2. I agree with the expert's opinion that Dora was trying to solve the patient's transportation problems when they were home. However, I also believe that by using her sister's business, which was readily at hand, she was making her job a little easier and at the same time, she could help her sister's business.
3. I agree with the expert's opinion. How did Janice solicit the patient's business? Did the patients feel violated because a company was contacting them instead of them contacting the company? I would wonder what information Janice told the patients, and as Dora's supervisor, how that would negatively affect the hospitals reputation.

4. The expert does not believe that Dora's actions require any discipline. I believe that she violated the HIPAA law and should face disciplinary action of mandatory three days off without pay. Violating the HIPAA law in any way is a serious matter. Personal medical information needs to be safeguarded and if medical personnel cannot work within the rules then they should not be working with such delicate information. I do agree with the expert that Dora should have a review of training on what constitutes ethical behavior, such as watching a video. It was a good suggestion that the supervisor sit down with Dora and review the ethical behavior role as she can document this in Dora's personnel file.

5. I agree with the expert that the names of the escort services should be given to the patients to use when they get home. I also agree that Dora could have approached the patients and asked them permission to give their names to the services. I never thought of that approach. But, I still think that Dora should set up a permanent solution with the hospital to use Janice's business as one of their recommended escort services.

6. Applying ethics theory: The utilitarian approach applies to this dilemma because it makes you think about the consequences of Dora's actions. If done in an ethical manner the situation can be a good situation for everyone involved. The patients' privacy can be kept confidential, Janice's business could increase and she could keep from having complaints from the business community. Dora would not be putting anyone at risk by following hospital protocol to add her sister's business to the hospital list of providers. The way in which Dora approaches this situation is unfair to everyone involved. The patients' privacy is violated, Dora puts her job at risk, and her sister could suffer negative consequences in the form of Better Business Bureau complaints or unprofessional word of mouth. The best way for Dora to handle this situation is to speak with the appropriate hospital personnel and have her sister's business put on the list of businesses the hospital uses. This way no one could be negatively affected. That is my view of the situation.

   However, I also agree with the expert's opinion of using Symphonology. I agree that Dora as a professional has a higher standard and assumes more responsibility.

Here are my opinions as opposed to the expert's opinions of the bio-ethical standards.

Fidelity: I agree with the expert's opinion that Dora did violate this standard.

Beneficence: I do not completely agree with the expert on this standard. I agree that she was trying to help her patients out and her sister's business. However, I believe that by using her sister's business she felt some relief with her job. Using her sister's business meant she did not have to search for transportation needs. This would have been OK had she set up a professional relationship between the hospital and Janice's business. Therefore, I feel that she violated this standard.

Self-assertion: I do not agree with the expert's opinion on this one. I believe that she violated the standard by violating their privacy. I do not think she was thinking about saving the patient's time. I think that she was only thinking of how she could make her job easier, and how she could help out her sister. That meant using her sister's business. I think that without thinking of the consequences, she gave her sister the names and numbers of the patients. Thus, making her job easier and helping out her sister's business.

Objectivity: I agree with the expert's opinion; Dora had the option of what to choose to do, the patients did not.

Freedom: I completely agree with the expert's opinion. Dora took away patients' right to choose.

Autonomy: I also must agree with the expert's opinion on this standard. Dora treated all the patients as a means to an end instead of the individuals that they are. Again, I state that she did not think about the patients at all, just how to make her job easier and how to help her sister's business. By doing this, she took away patient's autonomy.

This exercise helped the student to appreciate yet another perspective on the same case or validated the student's work. Students were particularly pleased when their work agreed with the expert's opinion. In addition, some students made convincing arguments in their comparison papers that disagreed with the expert's viewpoint. Either way, this was a powerful learning tool.

Lessons 5 and 6

Students are directed to select a different case for analysis from among the six provided, and then complete another compare and contrast analysis. Completion of the assignments in this sequential manner helps to insure that student's performance improves on the subsequent assignments.

References

Farcas, N., McGonigle, D., & Mastrian, K. (2001a). Expanding the comfort zone of ethical decision making in nursing practice: Applying the ethical model for ethical decision making. *Inside Case Management, 8*(8), 1, 3–4.

Farcas, N., McGonigle, D., & Mastrian, K. (2001b). Expanding the comfort zone of ethical decision making in nursing practice: Applying the ethical model for ethical decision making (Part 2). *Inside Case Management, 8*(9), 5–7.

McGonigle, D. (2000). The ethical model for ethical decision making. *Inside Case Management, 7*(8), 1–5.

EXEMPLAR
V
Legal Aspects of Nursing Practice

In this exemplar, students will access at least two nursing practice acts, one from their current state of residence and one from a different state. They will mine the practice acts for important information on the definition of safe and competent nursing practice, the elements of delegation under the law, the definition of and consequences of professional misconduct, and the requirements for continuing education, including what types of activities count toward continuing education hours for license renewal. This lesson is related to American Association of Colleges of Nursing's Essential V: Health Care Policy, Finance, and Regulatory Environments. We want our students to know how to access the Nurse Practice Act for their state of practice and how to read and understand the important aspects of the law. Since students may practice nursing in a state different from the one in which they were educated, it is important for them to know how to find a copy of the nursing practice act, and how each state defines and regulates nursing practice.

Objectives

As a result of this lesson, the learner will be able to:

- Compare and contrast critical elements of two state Nurse Practice Acts.
- Define safe nursing practice under the law for each state.
- Identify criteria for safe delegation under the law of each state, and give an example of such delegation.

- List examples of professional misconduct and the consequences of such misconduct.
- Explore the requirements and processes for license renewal under the laws of each state.
- Describe the scope of practice for advanced practice nurses for each state.

Activities

1. Divide into teams and search online for a copy of your current state of residence's Nurse Practice Act as well as the act from one other state. As a second state act is identified, the team will claim it and other teams will be obligated to choose another state. Place copies of each of the Nurse Practice Acts in the team files section of the course management system.

2. Every member of the team will read each of the two Nurse Practice Acts and list elements of similarities and differences between them. Pay particular attention to the following elements:

    - The definition of nursing or nursing practice,
    - Criteria for safe delegation under the law,
    - Definition(s) of professional misconduct and the consequences of such, and
    - Criteria and process for license renewal.

    Develop a two-page paper on your first glance observations and post your paper to the team discussion forum in the course management system.

3. Next, the members of the team will meet electronically (using Adobe Connect or Skype) to collate the practice act comparison observations into a single document. In addition, they will insert the following:

    - One example of appropriate delegation for each Nurse Practice Act,
    - One example of inappropriate delegation for each Nurse Practice Act,
    - An example of professional misconduct that might result in a license suspension,

- An example of professional misconduct that is likely to result in a license revocation,
- A description of the scope of practice for one type of advanced practice nurse under each of the laws, and
- A determination of whether or not a nurse licensed in one state can provide care via telehealth methodology to a client in another state, as outlined in each of the laws.

The team will share the finished document with the other members of the class via Google Docs.

EXEMPLAR
VI

Informatics Case Studies

This exemplar contains a series of case studies related to American Association of Colleges of Nursing's Essential IV: Information Management and Application of Patient Care Technology. The use of case study pedagogy also relates to many other aspects of the essentials since this pedagogy encourages critical thinking by the learners. The knowledge and skills of learners are challenged by the realistic scenarios and the assigned tasks. Learners will need to seek additional knowledge and apply this newly acquired knowledge to the case studies. Cases can be presented in creative ways, using the different technologies such as podcasts, video, or a Second Life virtual scenario.

Objectives

Each case scenario in this exemplar is designed to reflect a potential situation in nursing informatics. As with all case studies, we expect the learners to place themselves in the situation and begin to think about and reflect on the following:

- Important issues, policies, practices, or trends surrounding this case, for which they will need to find and use additional information.
- Their reactions, opinions, and philosophy of practice.
- The conclusions drawn within the case and a comparison with the conclusions they are drawing.
- How their conclusions are similar or different from those within the case.
- Whether there is a solution to this case or a best outcome. If so, how did they arrive at it?

The authors would like to gratefully acknowledge that the following case studies were developed in collaboration with Ms. Nedra Farcus.

Activities

Case Study I

Two nurses, John, age 23, and Ann, age 48, are working together on a general medical unit of a local hospital. The hospital has recently merged with a larger medical system and has initiated computer-based critical pathways as a first phase toward an expanded electronic communication system. All nurses on the medical unit have received a 2-week training session with the program, a critical pathway decision making and documentation system, and it is being piloted on the medical unit beginning today. All nurses carry smartphones to be used for charting.

John is excited about the change. He carries his own smartphone with him everywhere and immediately begins working with the new unit. Ann, who has never used a computer outside of work (which to date only involved order entries), goes about her daily routine and ignores the smartphone she carries with her. She feels increasingly anxious as the morning progresses and is having a difficult time concentrating on her work. She realizes she is getting behind in her documentation and will need to face this task before the morning is over.

During break, John is anxious to discuss the changes and the efficiency with which he can complete his patient care and his documentation. He does not have a chance to say anything, because Ann immediately begins complaining about her day. Ann is angry and complains bitterly about the lack of caring for patients by administration and the diverting of much-needed patient care funds to technology-focused purchases. She continues to complain about her lack of desire to learn all of this new technology.

At the end of the day, John goes home and tells his significant other that he may start looking for a new job outside of hospital nursing. The negativity in his work environment and the aversion to change is difficult to deal with on an ongoing basis.

Ann goes home late from work after finally completing her work and tells her significant other that she may get out of nursing. "Nursing is not what it used to be," she explains. "Nobody cares about the patient."

Read the article, *Nursing in a Digital Age*, retrieved on July 2, 2009 from http://findarticles.com/p/articles/mi_hb6366/is_5_13/ai_n28871543/ and provided in the electronic reserves of the course management system before you complete the Case Study Questions.

Case Study I: Questions

Now that you have read the article, *Nursing in a Digital Age* and the case study, you are ready to answer the following case study questions that require you to apply information you gained from the article to the case study:

1. How do John and Ann represent two different generations? Identify the generation that each represents, and discuss how this influences each nurse's reaction to the introduction of computers in patient care.
2. What are the implications for nursing practice in this setting, based on the reactions of both individuals and the article's discussion of implications for nursing practice?
3. Which of these nurses do you identify with? Explain why.
4. If you were in this situation as John or Ann, what recommendations would you have for the administrators in an attempt to retain, and increase your satisfaction in the current work setting?

If there are any items you are unsure about, contact your professor via e-mail or tune in to the live chat on the course management system during the scheduled hour for a detailed explanation.

Case Study II

Ann and John both see an opening in the Staff Development Department for a nurse educator. Ann sees this as an opportunity to get away from technology. John sees this as a way to move into more technology usage. They both apply for the position. Ironically, a second position opens in the department and they are both selected.

Just when Ann thinks she has moved away from technology, the Director of Staff Education gives her this assignment:

Evaluate state-of-the-art portable computers on the market and select one that will enable you to create multimedia presentations for staff education.

At the same time, John is given this assignment:

> Investigate the different types of bandwidth connections and recommend the best bandwidth for uploading, downloading, and viewing multimedia presentations on the Internet. Begin to identify LISTSERV sites for various specialties in nursing practice. Identify any ethical or legal issues we need to inform staff about when using the Internet for course work and seeking information regarding clinical decisions.

Ann becomes very anxious about her assignment and requests permission to work as a team with John in completing their assignments. This permission is granted. John begins by giving Ann advice when searching about different configurations for a laptop. Some of the advice included:

- Webopedia (http://www.webopedia.com) is a great resource for finding definitions and descriptions of technology terms you might not know.
- Choose a Pentium processor.
- Select the largest RAM possible, the largest hard drive memory possible, and the greatest speed available.
- Add additional storage devices that will store the largest amount of memory.
- Go to an onsite dealer such as Dell, Gateway, IBM, Hewlett-Packard, Sony, or any other computer manufacturer. These sites usually provide you with an opportunity to customize the laptop.

Ann begins her own investigation.

Case Study II: Case Study Reflection

Now that you have read the case study, we suggest that you review computer and Internet terms.

Address the following:

1. Search the Internet for notebook computers and select one notebook computer to evaluate.
   a. What processor does it have? Why is it important? How much speed does this processor have?
   b. How much and what type of RAM does it have? What is RAM? Why is it important to know this feature and the available options when choosing a notebook for multimedia purposes?

   c. What size is the hard drive? What is a hard drive? Why is it important to know this feature?

   d. What types of storage devices come with it? Suggest an additional storage device that will enable you to store the largest amount of memory. How much data can be stored on this device? How reliable is this device?

   e. Describe what bandwidth means and describe two of the different bandwidth options available? What bandwidth would you choose? Why did you select this one?

2. Describe what a LISTSERV is and select one for a nurse in a particular area of clinical practice. State the area of clinical practice. Identify the LISTSERV. Describe the topics of discussion on the LISTSERV.

3. Describe one ethical or legal issue you believe nurses should be aware of when using the Internet for education and clinical decision making. Provide one reference to support your description of this issue. This may be an article, book, or Web site reference.

If there are any items you are unsure about, contact your professor via e-mail or tune in to the live chat on the course management system during the scheduled hour for a detailed explanation.

Case Study III

Read about Benner's novice to expert scale, retrieved on July 2, 2009 from http://www.sonoma.edu/users/n/nolan/n312/benner.htm and provided in the electronic reserves of the course management system before you complete the Case Study Questions.

   Ann and John continue to work together on their assignments. They have been informed that the laptops they purchased are now going to be used for data entry and documentation. Now that they have selected the hardware, they must next select the software and look at some of the issues involving data collection and storage. They are asked to identify systems software and application software for their laptops.

1. Ann asks the following question: "What is the difference between system and application software?" If you were John, how would you answer this question?

John says, "Look at the software I found. This will really help us. Ann, refer to the list below and determine which ones are system software and which are application software."

Microsoft Access
Windows
Microsoft Word
HP Printer driver
Microsoft Excel
Utilities software
Microsoft PowerPoint

2. Identify and describe one system software from the list that they might choose for their laptop.
3. Identify and describe application software from the list they might select for their laptop.
4. Explore reasons for their choices of system and application software listed.

Ann and John are investigating offline and online data storage devices. Ann tells John that she does not like online storage and has focused on offline. She found some great storage packages. Ann provides the following list:

DVD
CD
USB flash drive
Keychain drive
Thumb drive
Jump drive

John reviews the list and tells Ann that there are four items that mean the same thing. Ann is puzzled and reviews her notes. Ann cannot find the repetition, can you?

5. Which device on Ann's list would you prefer? Why?
6. State an advantage and a disadvantage of online storage.
7. What is an issue involved with online storage?

Ann and John must now investigate issues that pose threats to their data.

8. Identify one threat to each of the following:
   a. Information quality; describe one way to reduce this threat.
   b. Information availability; describe one way to reduce this threat.
   c. Data integrity; describe one way to reduce this threat.
   d. Confidentiality; describe one way to reduce this threat.

   John tells Ann that she did a great job identifying threats to data and asks her to describe the difference between a computer virus and a worm.

9. How should Ann explain this to John?

   Ann and John must make sure they are Health Insurance Portability and Accountability Act (HIPAA) compliant with their electronic records. Ann says to John, "I don't understand what HIPAA is all about and why we have to be so concerned about HIPAA. We are not covered entities." John says, "How would you know if we are a covered entity?"

10. If you were John, how would you respond to the question, "What is HIPAA?"
11. If you were John, how would you respond to the question, "Why do we have to be so concerned about HIPAA? We are not covered entities."
12. If you were Ann, how would you respond to the question, "How would you know if we are a covered entity?"
13. How would you suggest that Ann and John insure that information is not identified?
14. Could you describe several ways that Ann and John could help other nurses understand HIPAA?

Since Ann and John are representative of staff in regards to education and experience, they are asked to evaluate and propose the adoption of a Clinical Decision Support System (CDSS) for the staff on the general medical-surgical units.

1. How would you define the CDSS for the administration?
2. How would you explain the need for this software purchase?
3. How would you describe Ann's education and experience using Benner's model of novice to expert?
4. How would you describe John's education and experience using Benner's model of novice to expert?
5. What characteristics of a clinical decision support system will benefit both nurses with their differing educational and experiential backgrounds?

Case Study III: Case Study Reflection

Since you have worked through this case study, make sure you were able to answer or address each item. If there are any items you are unsure about, contact your professor via e-mail or tune in to the live chat on the course management system during the scheduled hour for a detailed explanation.

Case Study IV

John and Ann have been asked to attend a conference featuring an international panel discussion on the electronic health record (EHR) and return with a report for their administrators.

At the conference, John takes the opportunity to network with nurse informaticists from various states and nations. He learns about degree programs and certification courses in nursing informatics, as well as professional organizations of interest to nurse informaticists. John returns to work excited about the prospect of the EHR and the possibility of making a career move into nursing informatics. Ann is less enthused about the conference. She thinks the EHR will never happen; and she definitely did not agree that the field of nursing informatics was nursing at all.

John and Ann meet with their administrators to present a summary of the meeting. They decide to take two different approaches based on their own perspectives about the EHR and about nursing informatics.

John presents the positive perspective about each, while Ann presents the negatives.

1. State five positive points John should emphasize when discussing the EHR.
2. State five negative points Ann should emphasize when discussing the EHR.
3. Help John argue the position that nursing informatics is a role for nurses. What important supportive statements should he make?
4. Help Ann argue the position that nursing informatics is not really nursing at all. What important supportive statements should she make?

After the presentation, John's supervisor approaches him and states that she is interested in hearing more about how John might become a nurse informaticist. She asks John to provide her with information describing the role of the nurse informaticist, degree and certification programs in nursing informatics, and professional organizations for nurse informaticists.

How should John:

1. Define nurse informaticist?
2. Describe the responsibilities of a nurse informaticist?
3. Identify and describe two roles a nurse informaticist assumes?
4. Describe one degree program in nursing informatics. Identify the specific degree offered. State whether the program is offered online or onsite (or both). Provide a URL describing the program.
5. Describe the certification for nursing informatics. Identify the certification agency. Identify the certification requirements.
6. Describe one professional nursing organization for nurse informaticists and provide a URL for the nursing organization.

After you read and research nursing informatics and informaticists, answer the questions and reflect on the case study. If there are any items you were unsure about, contact your professor via ANGEL chat for a detailed explanation.

EXEMPLAR VII

Safety Issues

Computing and technology use causes safety issues for educators and learners. We must all be aware of the repetitive stress injuries (RSI) that can occur when we interact with our technology. Two of the most familiar are carpal tunnel syndrome and cervical radiculopathy, or disk compression, in the neck. Carpal tunnel syndrome arises from keyboarding and gaming hand movements that cause swelling in the tunnel of the wrist. Symptoms include pain, tingling, numbness, and loss of function. Neck issues arise from cradling phones on our shoulders or slumping and dropping our head when we use a keyboard or play a game.

Our goal, of course, is primary prevention. We must prevent these injuries before they happen, or find effective ways to treat them after they occur. In order to reach the goal of primary prevention, it is important that we understand ergonomics. This exemplar relates to American Association of Colleges of Nursing's Essential VII: Clinical Prevention and Population Health.

In a community health course, we ask the students to treat their campus as a community. The students' goals are to educate themselves and then others on the principles of ergonomics.

Objectives

- Define ergonomics.
- Describe ergonomics issues for students using technology.
- Apply the levels of prevention to known ergonomic issues.

- Develop a video and poster educating students in the campus community about ergonomics.
- Assess the educational materials produced by the other teams.

Activities

1. The students are divided into teams and directed to the Usernomics Web site at http://www.usernomics.com/ergonomics-news-feed-tutorial.html (retrieved on June 30, 2009). The team is required to obtain an RSS feed for Usability and Ergonomics News at the Usernomics site.

2. Each team is instructed to develop a paper on ergonomics. In the paper, they must define and describe ergonomics, and explain the typical problems that arise from computing and technology use. Each problem identified is then expanded on by applying the generally accepted public health levels of prevention.

3. Next, the team is instructed to develop a plan using Google Docs to educate the other students in the campus community about these preventative strategies. Once the plan is approved by the professor, the teams are asked to create a wiki. This wiki facilitates the team's development of their educational materials including their video script. They are then directed to the studio where they can film their video.

4. There are four teams and each team is assigned to one of the four computer labs on campus. The goal is to create an ergonomics video that will be aired at half-hour intervals on the computer lab video screens. The students in the lab must choose to tune into the video screen and not their workstation in order to hear the audio while they watch the video. The team also creates a poster based on their video to be displayed in their assigned lab.

5. The last phase of the assignment entails the students viewing each team's video and critiquing them using the course's ergonomic blog site.

This is a great exercise for our learners to raise their awareness and learn the principles of ergonomics while sharing and applying knowledge to improve the health and safety of their campus community.

EXEMPLAR VIII

Population Health

This exemplar relates to the clinical prevention and population health essential. It is important that we prepare our students for the role of change agent in our profession and society. They are charged with improving health outcomes by being advocates for each patient, family, group, community, and population that they care for in the healthcare delivery system. This advocacy extends beyond the healthcare initiatives they set for their patients and reaches into the healthcare delivery mechanisms. As advocates, they must not only care for their patients, but also help to make the healthcare delivery system more responsive to their patients' needs. This responsibility for advocacy requires that they develop a shared vision for population health and work toward creating the interdisciplinary teams necessary to make this a reality in their setting. Nurses must lead the charge to improve patient outcomes across our diverse healthcare delivery system. Nurses are well suited to the task of integrating diverse perspectives while working with multidisciplinary teams. As technology continues to advance, nurses need to use information technologies to support communication, information, and knowledge management, and decision making to enhance patient care initiatives. Students will gain skill in using sharing and collaboration technologies including Google Docs, Twitter, and blogs in this lesson.

Objectives

- Assess public health or population health issues that currently exist or will emerge in the near future.
- Determine an issue that can be addressed in the scope of this assignment.
- Analyze the issue from a community, city, state, national, and international or global perspective.
- Synthesize the significance of the issue using population health assessment data, and direct the focus to the population affected.
- Apply the levels of prevention to this issue and develop at least four recommendations for each level to prevent, diagnose, or minimize the impact on the population.

Activities

1. Each team will determine the issue they will address during the semester.
2. Using Adobe Connect, the teams will discuss this issue in real time with experts in the field including interdisciplinary teams researching this topic or a similar issue.
3. They will access all of the online data and statistics available to support their stance that this is an issue needing to be addressed. They are encouraged to contact the Centers for Disease Control and Prevention (CDC). The information should be used to analyze and present the issue from the micro to the macro levels, from community to the global level.
4. Using all of the evidence gathered, the team will develop a paper on their issue. This paper will include the micro–macro perspectives, and the levels of prevention strategies. Once it is complete, it will be shared with everyone in the class through Google Docs.
5. The team will also develop a tweet (adhering to the 140-character limit) using Twitter to entice others to read their paper reflecting their perspective on the issue.
6. Each team will review all of the other teams' papers and search for common threads or shared perspectives, as well as differences among the issues. These observations will be shared with the entire class using the course blog site.

EXEMPLAR IX

Telehealth and Telenursing

In this exemplar, nursing students will be primarily applying principles on telehealth, Health Insurance Portability and Accountability Act (HIPAA) legislation, and network security presented in the course text. In addition, they will be considering population health principles and practicing leadership essentials related to the provision of high-quality care within a complex organization. They will be honing their critical thinking and collaboration skills as they work in teams to craft a team proposal. Finally, they will engage in reflective practice as they journal about the learning experience and their role in the development of the final team proposal.

Objectives

- Define telehealth and telehealth technology.
- Explore the appropriate use of telehealth technology in nursing practice.
- Apply telehealth principles to a specialized setting.

Activities

1. Read Chapters 18 and 19 in the course text, *Nursing Informatics and the Foundation of Knowledge* (McGonigle & Mastrian, 2009). Then, review the information on HIPAA and network security presented in Chapters 11 and 12.
2. Complete the terminologies and abbreviations flashcard practice for Chapters 18 and 19 on the companion Web site.

3. Imagine that you are a nurse in a state prison and that you want to convince the warden of the value of developing a telehealth program for diabetic prisoners (or for a different chronic illness likely to be prevalent in a prison population). Write a two-page overview of the program you are proposing, detailing the advantages and potential benefits of such a program. Try to anticipate areas of administrative resistance to your proposal by also identifying the potential issues associated with the program and providing proposed solutions. Be creative in your proposal development as you apply the information you learned in the chapters and in your nursing education to date.

4. Post your program proposal to the discussion forum for your team in the course management system.

5. As a team, review and discuss the individual proposals presented by team members and craft a final team version of the proposal incorporating the best ideas from the members of the team, and post the final team proposal to the discussion forum.

6. Reflect on the insights you have gained related to telehealth, HIPAA, network security, population health, collaboration, negotiation, and quality and safety of patient care by writing an entry in your e-Portfolio blog.

Teaming

Teaming

Organizations throughout the world are realizing the value of teamwork and are shifting to place increased emphasis on teaming within their infrastructures. The tasks that are demanded of organizations within competitive markets have become very complex for lone individuals to process. One of the driving forces behind the complexity is the ever increasing evolution of technology.

As authority, responsibility, and accountability move down the corporate ladder, it is easy to understand why organizations are seeking to harness the power of the team. Just as organizations are harnessing the power of the team to accomplish their goals, educators are also using teaming to enhance the educational experience while preparing students for work in the real world.

A team has been defined in many ways. For our purpose, we will use McGonigle's (1996) definition of a team.

A small number of students (4–6) dedicated to a common purpose with performance goals, and individual, and mutual accountability. The team must develop its own collective operational style. It is imperative that teams are interdependent cooperatives or collaboratories that are not dominated by any individual but allow the strengths of the individual members to be used collectively to meet the team's goal(s).

Team Member Responsibilities

1. Remember the team rules.
2. Understand the nature of teams and the process of teaming.
3. Be committed to your team.
4. Put the team first.
5. Communicate openly with each team member and within your team.
6. Listen to the other team members.
7. Everyone on your team has a right to her or his own opinion.
8. Silence does not mean agreement; you must verbally present your opinion.
9. Present your opinion with supporting rationale; do not argue your opinion.
10. Respect other team members' opinions.
11. Cultivate interdependence among team members.
12. Foster information diffusion by sharing information openly with your team.
13. Work together to meet your common goal(s).
14. Do not operate using hidden agendas.
15. Use win–win strategies.
16. Evaluate your own performance; ask yourself, "How am I doing?"
17. Evaluate team performance; ask yourself and other team members, "How is our team doing?"

Helpful Tips for Teams

1. Develop an operational style conducive to meeting your goal(s).
2. Clarify the purpose or goal(s) of your team.
3. Establish clear expectations.
4. Assign duties.
5. Assign timelines with team consensus and stick to them.
6. Everyone must meet the timelines.
7. Avoid the last minute panic or push.

For Written Assignments or Presentation Projects

1. Use line numbering on all teamwork assignments for ease of critique.
2. Establish a review process and timelines.

3. Do not forget to allocate ample time for design and programming.
4. Create bullet points first, then review for content.
5. Elaborate on bullet points.
6. Review for content again.
7. Establish clear page and time limitations.
8. Weigh importance by section, or as dictated by specifications of project.
9. Develop first draft of entire project.
10. Critique first draft.
11. Revise, develop, and critique additional drafts as necessary.
12. Develop final draft.
13. Critique final draft.
14. Revise and prepare the final version for submission or presentation.

Evaluation

Individual: As an individual team member, you will be evaluated by each member of your team using the Peers' Teamwork Assessment Form that follows.

Team: Your team will also be evaluated based on the criteria of the team project.

Peers' Teamwork Assessment

Complete one section of the form for each member of the team, including yourself.

NOTE: If you do not submit an assessment or omit any team member, you will not earn your points.

Reflect on each team member's performance, including your own. Determine your ratings for each individual member using the scoring method below for each criterion on the Peer Team Assessment form.

Scoring Method:
0 - does not demonstrate these characteristics at all
1 - occasionally demonstrates these characteristics
2 - usually demonstrates these characteristics
3 - always demonstrates these characteristics

Peers' Teamwork Assessment Form

Name _____ Team _____ Project _____

Peer Being Assessed	Ability with Rationale	Score	Total Score
	Leadership		
	Cooperative		
	Communicative		
_____	Work ethic		_____
	Quality of work		
	Overall comment(s)		

References

McGonigle, D. (1996). Team assessments. Retrieved September 4, 1999, from http://cac.psu .edu/~dxm12/team.htm

Abbreviations

3-D—Three dimensional

AACN—American Association of Colleges of Nursing

ACLS—Advanced cardiac life support

ADDIE—Analysis, design, development, implementation, and evaluation

ADT—Admission-discharge-transfer system

AI—Artificial intelligence

ANGEL—A New Global Environment for Learning

BCMA—Barcode Medication Administration

CAT—Computerized axial tomography

CCHIT—Certification Commission for Healthcare Information Technology

CD—Compact disc

CDSS—Clinical decision support system

CMS—Course management system

CoP—Community of practice

CPOE—Computerized physician order entry

CT—Computerized tomography

DRG—Diagnosis-related group

EBP—Evidence-based practice

ECG—Electrocardiogram

EHR—Electronic health record

EKG—Electrocardiogram

ERP—Enterprise resource planning

FAID—Flexibly adaptive instructional design

FTE—Full-time equivalent

GIF—Graphics interchange format

HIPAA—Health Insurance Portability and Accountability Act

ILO—Intended learning outcome

IOM—Institute of Medicine

IWB—Interactive whiteboard

JPEG—Joint photographic experts group

LEAP—Liberal Education and America's Promise

LMS—Learning management system

MEDLINE—Online database of medical journals

MITA—Multiple intelligences teaching approach model

MMORPG—Massive multiplayer online role-playing game

MOO—MUD object-oriented

MRI—Magnetic resonance imaging

MUD—Multiuser dungeon

MUSH—Multiuser shared hack, habitat, holodeck, or hallucination

NANDA-I—North American Nursing Diagnosis Association-International

NIC—Nursing interventions classification

NOC—Nursing outcomes classification

NPC—Nonplayer character

NLN—National League for Nursing

P.A.T.C.H. —Pretest for attitudes toward computers in healthcare

PDA—Personal digital assistant

PLE—Personalized learning environment

PNG—Portable network graphics

QSEN—Quality and safety education for nurses

RHIO—Regional health information organization

RFID—Radio frequency identification

TEACH—Technology, Education, and Copyright Harmonization Act

TeP—Teaching e-Portfolio

TIGER—Technology Informatics Guiding Education Reform

USB—Universal serial bus

WebCT—Web-based course tools

Glossary

Academy—A way of referring to a collection of colleges and universities

Accessibility—Ease or convenience of use

Accountability—Responsibility for an action

Accrediting agencies—Organizations that possesses the authority to endorse or certify the quality of an educational program or higher education institution

Active voice—Using sentences where the subject performs the action expressed in the verb; the subject acts

ADDIE—Acronym used to describe the five general steps included in all instructional design models (analysis, design, development, implementation, and evaluation)

Adobe Connect—Web conferencing software used to dialogue and exchange information and documents

Advanced organizer—Information that is presented prior to learning and that can be used by the learner to organize and interpret new information

Affordability—Ease of finding the money for education

Algo-heuristic theory—Instructional design theory where the training is broken down into a small step-by-step process or algorithm that novices can use to become proficient in a particular skill

Analogical graphics—Graphics that show one thing and, by analogy, imply something else

Analytics infrastructure—Tools that support the study or examination of the data and information in an organization

Anchored instruction—Instruction that is centered around a real-world problem

Animated GIF—A graphic format for the Web that presents a series of images in sequence

Animation—The rapid display of a sequence of images of 2-D or 3-D artwork or model positions in order to create the illusion of movement

Arbitrary graphics—Tables, charts, and cognitive maps that have no real-life counterpart that they are attempting to portray

Artificial intelligence (AI)—Computer programming designed to mimic human intelligence

Assessment—Collecting information about the quantity or quality of change in learners for the dual purpose of informing instructional decisions and to inspire learners to learn

Assessment-centered environment—A learning environment that uses frequent formative assessment and feedback

Asynchronous—Not occurring in real time

Authentic assessment—Accurately evaluates learning by presenting the learner with real-world challenges that require applying the appropriate skills and knowledge to meet the challenge; effectively measuring or examining a learner's collective aptitude and skills and not merely testing for a retained fact or isolated skill

Avatar—One's virtual representation in a simulation, virtual world, or game

Bandwidth—The measurable amount of data that can be sent or received at a given time over the Internet

Barcode Medication Administration (BCMA)—An electronic system using barcode and scanning technology to support medication administration

Behaviorism—A learning theory that emphasizes observable, measurable behavior

Benchmarking—Measuring an organization or program against a point of reference

Biosignals—Electronically measured biological indicators such as brainwaves or heart rhythm

Biosurveillance—An electronic network designed to detect and track communicable disease outbreaks and widespread clinical conditions

Blended learning—Term used to describe learning or training events or activities where e-learning is combined with more traditional forms of education such as face-to-face training; also called hybrid learning

Blended learning environment—A combination of online and face-to-face components, where the components are seamlessly integrated

Blog—An individual's Web site that he or she maintains, typically adding regular entries of professional or personal comments, descriptions of events, video or graphics

Bloom's taxonomy—A classification of the different cognitive (learning) objectives that educators set for students

Bodily-kinesthetic intelligence—One of Gardner's Multiple Intelligences; involves the ability to do hands-on or performance activities well

Body of knowledge—All that is known or understood about a topic

Bot—Short for robot; a program that operates for a user or simulates human activity

Brain plasticity—The brain's capacity to change its structure and function as a result of new experiences

Certification Commission for Healthcare Information Technology (CCHIT)—A commission created by the US Department of Health and Human Services to review and certify healthcare technology software, especially electronic health records and their networks, to ensure robust and interoperable functionality

Chunking—Breaking instructional content into pieces that have a similar focus or topic

Clickers—An electronic device used in a classroom as a student response system

Clinical blog—An electronic journal (Web log) typically related to a specific disease or health-related condition

Clinical Decision Support System (CDSS)—See decision support tools

Clinical guidelines (clinical practice guidelines)—Electronic warehouse of evidence-based plans for clinical intervention

Cloud computing—Use of remote servers to store and access data

Cochrane Collaboration—An international organization that collects and evaluates clinical research and develops evidence-based practice recommendations

Cognition—The process of perceiving, thinking, reasoning, and analyzing

Cognitivism—A theoretical approach to understanding the mind using scientific methods; describes mental functions as information processing models

Cohort—A group of students in a program of study that share experiences over time

Collaboration—Working together to accomplish a goal

Communities of practice (CoP)—A group of professionals that collaborate to share ideas and knowledge

Community-centered environment—A learning environment that emphasizes collaborative learning activities

Compact disc (CD)—A disk that usually contains a recording of sound or data

Computerized physician order entry (CPOE)—A computer-based system used to collect and process doctor's orders in a healthcare system

Computer literacy—Having knowledge and skills related to the operation of a computer

Conceptual elaboration sequence—Type of sequencing strategy identified in elaboration theory where concepts are first presented broadly and then in more detail

Constructional design—A term that refers to a shift in instructional design from behaviorist and constructivist principles to constructivist principles

Constructivism—An educational approach the emphasizes a student's need to build or assemble his/her knowledge base

Constructivist—An individual that believes that knowledge is self-generated and that people construct their own understanding of the world

Content expert—A member of the faculty who is an expert in both the course content and course objectives

Copyright—The legal right to reproduce or distribute materials, such as an artistic work

Course management system (CMS)—Online systems designed to support classroom or online learning

Critical analysis—Significant and decisive study or examination of a phenomenon

Critical thinking—Purposeful and reflective thinking about one's thinking; significant and decisive reasoning

Curricular framework—The structure of a set of courses designed to support specific learning

Curricular reforms—Changes that are made to a program of study

Database—An electronic file designed to record and catalog information

Data mining—The ability to pull specific information from a database and analyze it to uncover relationships within that information

Data warehouse—The electronic storage area for facts and information related to an organization

Debriefing—A student-centered discussion during which the participants and observers reflect on performance during the scenario and make recommendations for future practice

Decision support tools—Software programs linked to a database or knowledge repository that assist clinicians in managing complex health issues by providing recommendations for interventions

Diagnosis-related group—A way to categorize patients according to medical diagnosis to aid in billing for medical services

Digital divide—The separation that exists between those who are comfortable using technology and those who are not

Digital natives—Those of the population that have grown up with computers, who seamlessly use technology in their lives

Digital pen—A specialized pen equipped with a digital camera that records written strokes on specialized paper and converts them into images that can be captured and uploaded to a computer

Diverse cultures—Distinct influences related to ethnicity, nationality, or customs

Domain expertise—Having thorough knowledge in a subject matter area

Early adopters—Respected members of a system who accept being exposed to the problems, risks, and aggravations associated with trying innovative strategies or methods

Educator—A person who is a specialist in the theory and practice of education; one that educates, plans, and directs education or teaching and learning

Elaboration theory—Instructional design theory that provides guidelines for organizing instructional content in a sequential manner

Electrocardiogram (ECG or EKG)—A recording of the electrical activity of the heart

Electronic health record (EHR)—A digitized format of an individual's health record

Emoticon—A symbol that is used to convey emotion when communicating without audio and video

Environmental fidelity—The degree to which the simulator mimics a real environment

e-Portfolio—A Web-based or digital repository of artifacts, that demonstrate competence and reflect an individual's learning

Equipment fidelity—The degree to which the simulator mimics a real person or a real environment

Evaluation—A systematic assessment of the worth or merit of some object; includes both formative and summative components; answers whether the instructional goals and objectives have been met; provides feedback and motivation for continued improvement and ensures that significant needs are addressed and met

Everyday cognition—A process of situation modeling that examines how people think and solve problems in nonformal situations

Evidence-based practice (EBP)—Clinical practice based on methods substantiated by examining a collection of research studies

Expert system—A specialized from of artificial intelligence designed for a single, specific task

Expository teaching—A method of teaching that involves the learner being presented with a problem and teacher-prepared instructions; learner practices solving problems, initially with the teacher-prepared instructions and then without, until able to solve novel problems on own

Faculty facilitator—A faculty member who helps to prepare students for the simulation and who guides students during the simulation experience

Fair use—Materials that can be used without permission of owner under certain circumstances

Feedback—Response given to a learner after an overt action is made by the learner

Fidelity—How well a simulation, virtual world, or game visually recreates what it was designed after

Flexibly adaptive instructional design (FAID) theory—Instructional design theory that describes a flexible, learner-guided process that is based in situated cognition learning theory; a software shell, called STAR Legacy, is used to assist instructional designers and instructors utilize this theory effectively

Folksonomies—A list of key words and terms that are developed informally by a group over a period of time

Font—A complete character set of a single size and style of a particular typeface

Formative evaluation—A type of evaluation used to identify areas that need improvement or revision in a course

4C/ID model—An instructional design theory that breaks down complex tasks into four components that are used to assist in designing instruction (learning tasks, supportive information, procedural information, and part-task practice)

Gagne's Nine Events of Instruction—Instructional design theory that describes nine sequential instructional elements that must be included in instruction to promote effective learning

Game—A structured activity undertaken for enjoyment

Generation X—Generation born between 1965 and 1980

Generation Y—Generation born between 1981 and 1995; largest consumer group in the history of the United States; also known as the Net Generation, iGeneration, Google generation, Millennials, Millennium Generation, or Echo Boomers

Globalization—The process of responding to forces related to worldwide or international influences

Graphics interchange format (GIF)—A popular format for graphic images placed on the Web

Guided discovery—A method of teaching where the learner is presented with a problem and prompted to solve it on his/her own. After solving the problem, the learner creates a set of instructions to use while solving additional problems of a similar nature. The learner then repeatedly practices solving problems, initially with his/her own instructions and then without, until he/she is able to solve novel problems on his/her own.

Haptic device—A device that provides tactile realism in a simulation

Health information technology—Electronic tools developed to manage health information

Health Insurance Portability and Accountability Act (HIPAA)—An act of Congress passed in 1996 that established the rules for the protection of private health information and provisions for health insurance portability between employers

Higher education—Formal instruction that occurs in a college or university

Humanism—A school of thought that humans are unique in capability, and different from other animals, behaving out of intentionality and values

Human patient simulator—A simulator that reproduces the responses of a human patient

Hybrid—Refers to a course or learning episode that includes blended formats such as face-to-face and online components

Hybrid course—A course consisting of online and face-to-face components that are seamlessly integrated; also called blended course

Informatics—The science of information management that includes principles from computer science, information science, and cognitive science

Informatics competencies—Abilities and skills that are identified and agreed upon as proficiency in the management of information

Information infrastructure—Tools that support the transmission of factual data and knowledge in an organization

Information literacy—Having knowledge and skills related to finding and managing information

Innovation infrastructure—Tools that support the improvement or advancement of an organization

Innovators—Refers to the highest level of expertise in informatics competencies, those who can apply informatics theory to practice as well as design, develop, and implement new technologies in a clinical practice

Integrative learning—Incorporating knowledge and skills in new situations

Interoperability—The ability of electronic systems to interface with each other and exchange information

Interpersonal intelligence—One of Gardner's Multiple Intelligences; involves the ability to interact effectively with others

Intrapersonal intelligence—One of Gardner's Multiple Intelligences; involves the ability to be aware of and use one's own feelings

iPod—Apple's portable media player

Joanna Briggs Institute—An international not-for-profit research and development organization specializing in evidence-based resources for healthcare professionals

Joint photographic experts group (JPEG)—A commonly used method of compression for photographic images

Kinetic learning—A student-centered instructional strategy in which students learn through movement or interaction

Knowledge—That which is known or understood about a subject

Knowledge-centered environment—A learning environment that utilizes the principles of constructivist learning in that learners are encouraged to construct their own knowledge

Knowledge era—A point in time where knowledge and intellectual capital are valued skills and knowledge is used as a resource to do things in newer and better ways, and to create new knowledge through collaboration

Knowledge management—An approach to improving organizational performance by integrating people, processes, and technology in a collaborative environment to capture and share existing knowledge and to create new knowledge

Landamatics—Another name for Algo-heuristic theory

Learner-centered environment—A learning environment where scaffolding is used to bridge that gap between what learners currently know and what they are expected to know as a result of the instruction

Learning community—A group of people who share common values and beliefs and are committed to shared learning; a group of people actively engaged in learning together

Learning culture—A culture that adopts and accepts a set of attitudes, values, beliefs, and practices that support and encourage a continuous process of learning

Learning domain—Categorizations of content based on the type of learning required; the most commonly used learning domains are cognitive, psycho-motor, and affective

Learning Management System (LMS)—Integrated learning environments that are used to provide a holistic learning experience

Learning outcomes—Attitudes, knowledge, and skills gained by students as a result of education

Learning taxonomy—A way of classifying different objectives according to increasing levels of difficulty within a learning domain

Logical/mathematical intelligence—One of Gardner's Multiple Intelligences; involves the ability to effectively use numbers and logic

Logico-mathematical graphics—Graphics used to illustrate a mathematical concept

Magnetic resonance imaging (MRI)—A diagnostic technique that produces images of internal body tissues

Mashup—Combining several forms of media into a new derivative work

Massive multiplayer online role-playing game (MMORPG)—A computer role-playing game in which large amounts of people interact with each other

Methods of action—A series of actions that lead to solving problems or performing tasks

Methods of prescription—Instructions or thought processes for solving problems or completing tasks

Microworld—The smallest subset of an environment that still allows one to interact with aspects of that environment

Millennials—Another name for the Net Generation; taken from the book *Generations: The History of America's Future, 1584–2069*, by William Straus and Neil Hower

Modifiers—People who possess an intermediate level of informatics competencies expertise and who use technology creatively in their clinical practice

MP3—Digital audio encoding format that is commonly used for consumer audio storage, transfer, and playback

MUD object-oriented (MOO)—Similar to a MUD, but with more advanced programming features

Multiple intelligences—Instructional design theory that identifies eight specific types of intelligences and how they are related to how people learn

Multiple Intelligences Teaching Approach (MITA) model—Teaching model based on Gardner's Multiple Intelligences theory; involves five phases based on constructivist learning theory

Multiuser dungeon (MUD)—A computer program, usually running over the Internet, that allows multiple users to participate in virtual role-playing games

Multiuser shared hack, habitat, holodeck, or hallucination (MUSH)—Like MUDs and MOOS, but with the ability of the user to extend the "world" by adding new rooms, objects, and features

Musical intelligence—One of Gardner's Multiple Intelligences; involves the ability to appreciate, understand, and create music

National Guidelines Clearinghouse—A searchable database of evidence-based clinical practice guidelines instituted by the Agency for Healthcare Research and Quality in the United States

Naturalistic intelligence—One of Gardner's Multiple Intelligences; involves the ability to be at one with nature

Navigationism—The ability to search through complex information and make sense of the information uncovered; proposed as a sophisticated type of information literacy

Neo-millennials—Generation born after 1995; named for the new millennia in which they will grow up

Net generation—Generation born between 1980 and 1995; also known as Millennials or Generation Y

Nonplayer character (NPC)—An individual in a simulation, virtual world, or game that is controlled by the program, not another person

Nonrecurrent skills—Skills needed to solve novel problems and are guided by existing knowledge.

North American Nursing Diagnosis Association-International (NANDA-I)— An international organization with the mission of developing evidence-based nursing diagnoses for use in practice

Nursing Interventions Classification (NIC)—A comprehensive, research-based, standardized classification of interventions that nurses perform

Nursing Outcomes Classification (NOC)—Comprehensive, standardized classification of patient/client outcomes developed to evaluate the effects of nursing interventions

Online—Utilizing a computer connected to the Internet

Open courseware—Course materials that are made available for educational use; materials typically can be used and modified freely if the original source is referenced

Open source—Software, lessons, or learning objects developed to be shared with all at little or no cost

Order entry management tools—Electronic tools that automate physician orders in a healthcare system

Outcomes accountability—Responsibility for results; in education, the responsibility for student learning as a product of education

Partial task trainer—A device designed to allow a student to practice a specific skill such as IV insertion, urinary catheterization, or intubation

Passive voice—Using sentences where the subject receives the action expressed in the verb; the subject is acted upon

Patient-centered care—Nursing care that is planned in partnership with patients and takes into account patient preferences, needs, and values

Pedagogic research—A study that examines or explores education-related topics

Personal digital assistant (PDA)—A handheld computer

Personalized Learning Environment (PLE) —An online environment designed by the individual to give access to information and lessons how, when, and where one wants them

Philosophy—Attitudes, values, and beliefs about a particular topic

Physical fidelity—The degree to which the physical aspects of the simulated scenario match the real environment, especially such aspects as equipment

Podcasts—Audio or video digital media files that are distributed over the Internet by syndicated download, Web feeds to personal computers as well as portable media players such as iPods

Population health—An accounting of the overall well-being of a group of people

Population registry—An online catalog that assists in tracking the incidence and prevalence of a specific disease

Portable network graphics (PNG)—A graphics file format for the Web

Pretest for attitudes toward computers in healthcare (P.A.T.C.H.)—A self-assessment tool designed by June Kaminski to help nurses explore their feelings about learning to use computers both in education and healthcare

Problem-based learning—A student-centered instructional strategy in which students collaboratively solve problems and reflect on their experiences

Problem solving—Developing an appropriate solution to a dilemma

Psychological fidelity—The degree to which the participant perceives that the simulated scenario is realistic

Public domain—Any property not protected by copyright laws that is allowed to be used by all

Quality—Degree of excellence, value, or worth

Quantitative literacy—Having knowledge and skills related to numerical measures and statistics

Radio frequency identification (RFID)—A system for identification and tracking using radio waves

Really simple syndication (RSS)—Web feed format used to publish works that are frequently updated such as blogs, podcasts, and news headlines

Recurrent skills—Skills needed for routine problems that are guided by a set of rules

Reflective commentary—Taking time to think through the learning process and write down the impact of one's experiences; attempting to make sense of one's thoughts, ideas, feelings, and reactions; enables one to recognize patterns, get to the bottom of uncertainties, and make decisions for managing similar or new situations that may arise

Reflective practice—Clinical practice that includes thoughtful, insightful, and reasoned action

Representational graphics—Graphics that closely resemble something in real life

Response—A reaction to a stimulus

Results management tools—Electronic tools that assist clinicians with the interpretation of laboratory and diagnostic testing outcomes

Scaffolding—Adding initial support for a task, then gradually removing this support over time

Schema—A mental structure that represents some aspect of the world

Science of education—A body of knowledge that informs teaching and learning practice

Semantic-aware applications—Applications that assist you in discovering connections between ideas

Serious game—A game designed for a purpose other than enjoyment

Simulation—An imitation of a real-life event or circumstance; in nursing education, the replication of a clinical scenario developed to provide an opportunity for practice in a mock situation

Simulation expert—A member of the faculty who possesses the technical expertise to develop and deliver case scenarios for simulations

Simulator—A mechanical or electronic device that provides an environment in which a simulation can occur

Situated cognition—Thinking, the contexts in which thinking occurs, and the resulting interactions that are inextricably linked

Smart objects—Objects that contain data about themselves and can share that data

Social bookmarking—A method for Internet users to share, organize, and search bookmarks of Web pages

Social networking—A group of individuals connected by a job or goal

Social presence—Computer mediated sharing and caring interactions between people who feel connected to or in an interpersonal relationship with the other(s)

Spiral sequencing—Sequencing content where topics are presented repeatedly in instruction, first a broad level and then with increasing detail at each mention in the instruction

STAR Legacy Software—Software template to assist instructional designers and instructors use of flexibly adaptive instructional design (FAID) theory

Stimulus—An outside force that acts upon an organism and causes a reaction or response

Strategic change—Deliberate and planned alteration or transformation

Stylus—A penlike device used to write on a Tablet PC screen

Summative evaluation—A type of evaluation used to determine if instruction is effective in meeting learning objectives and if it should be continued or terminated

Suspension of disbelief—A state that occurs when a simulated scenario is realistic enough to be believable

Synchronous—Occurring in real time

T3 connection—A very high-speed connection to the Internet

Task class—Grouping of tasks according to the level of complexity

Task expertise—Having thorough knowledge of how to perform a skill

Teaching e-Portfolio—An electronic or digital repository of a faculty member's teaching responsibilities, philosophy, goals, and accomplishments

Team—A group of people organized to accomplish a specific purpose or goal

Teamwork—Cooperation in a joint effort to achieve an outcome

Technology infrastructure—Underlying equipment and tools that support exchange of data and information in an organization

Telehealth—The delivery of health care over a distance

Theoretical elaboration sequence—Type of sequencing strategy identified in elaboration theory where principles are first presented broadly and then in more detail

3-C didactic model—A model for creating blended learning courses where the content is classified and analyzed according to three components: content, communication, and construction

3-D—Three dimensions

Topical sequencing—Teaching a topic or task thoroughly before moving on to the next topic or task

Transformative graphics—Graphics that facilitate or elicit cognitive processes

Translational knowledge—Converting or transforming research evidence into the knowledge base for clinical practice

Tweet—The verb used to describe entering a message into Twitter; must be 140 characters or less

Twitter—A Web 2.0 tool that allows individuals to send messages to their selected friends about what they are doing or thinking

Universal serial bus (USB)—A standardized interface socket that allows devices to be easily connected to a computer

Users—The lowest level of nursing informatics expertise as defined by June Kaminski; those who possess and can use basic informatics competencies

Verbal-linguistic intelligence—One of Gardner's Multiple Intelligences; involves the ability to effectively use verbal information and language

Virtual world—A computer-based simulated environment where users inhabit and interact with each other via avatars

Visual-spatial intelligence—One of Gardner's Multiple Intelligences; involves the ability to think visually and perceive spatial relationships

Web-based course tools (WebCT)—An online learning environment system used in colleges and universities

Web-enhanced course—A course that meets face-to-face but includes materials and assignments that are online

Web 2.0—Web-based tools that facilitate social interaction

Wiki—Web-based server software tool that permits editing, saving, and linking of content by multiple people; Wikipedia is the largest, free, multilingual encyclopedia created by wikis

Workflow—A measure of productivity that details the steps needed to accomplish a task

Workplace skills—Competencies necessary for successful job performance

Index

Note: Page numbers followed by "*t*" indicate tables.